Is not every doctrine of Holy Scripture as such a superfluous saying of 'Lord, Lord'?

K. Barth, *Church Dogmatics* I/2, 461.

Models for Scripture

• •

John Goldingay

WILLIAM B. EERDMANS PUBLISHING COMPANY
GRAND RAPIDS, MICHIGAN

THE PATERNOSTER PRESS
CARLISLE

© 1994 Wm. B. Eerdmans Publishing Co.
255 Jefferson Ave. S.E., Grand Rapids, Michigan 49503

Published jointly 1994 in the United States by
Wm. B. Eerdmans Publishing Co.
and in the U.K. by
The Paternoster Press
P.O. Box 300, Carlisle, Cumbria CA3 0QS

Printed in the United States of America

00 99 98 97 96 95 94   7 6 5 4 3 2 1

Library of Congress Cataloging-in-Publication Data

Goldingay, John.
Models for scripture / John Goldingay.
p.   cm.
Includes bibliographical references and index.
ISBN 0-8028-0146-3 (pbk.)
1. Bible—Inspiration. 2. Bible—Evidences, authority, etc. I. Title.
BS480.G59 1994

220.1—dc20   94-32319
                                                             CIP

British Library Cataloguing in Publication Data

A catalogue record for this book
is available from the British Library

ISBN 0-85364-638-4

*To the students and faculty of St John's College, Nottingham
(including for these purposes Peta Sherlock), with whom
I learned what is in this book, and to the students,
faculty, and scholars in ministry at Southwestern
Baptist Theological Seminary, Forth Worth,
with whom I discussed some of it in the
context of the Day-Higginbotham
lectures in February 1991.*

Contents

1. Introduction: Scripture's Varied Forms   1
Categories for a Doctrine of Scripture   1
Models for Scripture   7
Reconsidering Models for Scripture   12

PART I
SCRIPTURE AS WITNESSING TRADITION   19

2. Witness and Tradition   21
The Nature of Scriptural Faith and the Nature of Scripture   21
Biblical Narrative as Witness and Tradition   25

3. The Factuality Involved in Witness   29
As Witness Scripture Asks to Be Investigated Critically
    (Even If It Implies a Critique of Criticism)   30
Investigating the Witness of the Second Testament   34
Investigating the Witness of the First Testament   39
Living in Trust and Living with Ambiguity   42
As Witness Scripture Invites Us to Learn from the Events
    Themselves to Which It Points   46

4. The Interpretation Involved in Witness   49
The Gospels as Interpretative Witness   49
Witness and Tradition: Fact and Interpretation   52

The Theological Nature of the Witnessing Tradition's
   Interpretation   58

5. Witness in the Form of Story   61
   History and Story: How Stories Work   61
   The Place of "Fiction" in a Historical Story   67
   The Witness of "Pure" Fiction   71

6. Scripture as a Whole as Witnessing Tradition   77
   The Authoritative Canon as Witness   78
   The Inspired Word as Witness   78
   The Experienced Revelation as Witness   80

PART II
SCRIPTURE AS AUTHORITATIVE CANON   83

7. Authority in Scripture   85
   Worshipping by Scripture and Living by Scripture: Psalm 119   87
   Worshipping by Scripture and Living by Scripture:
      The Example of Jesus (Matthew 4:1-11)   89
   The Bible's Approach to Biblical Authority   93

8. Scripture as a Whole as Authoritative Canon:
   Narrative and Prophecy   99
   "It Is Written"   99
   Scripture and Canon   102
   Biblical Narrative as Authoritative Canon   108
   The Inspired Word as Authoritative Canon   115

9. Scripture as a Whole as Authoritative Canon:
   Norms for Christian Doctrine   117
   The Crisis of Authority   117
   Authority and Scripture   121
   The Experienced Revelation as Authoritative Canon   125
   The First Testament as Authoritative Canon for Jesus
      and the Second Testament Writers   131

10. The Development of a Canon of Jewish Scriptures   138
     From the Beginnings to the Persian Period   138
     Jewish Canons in the Greek and Roman Periods   142
     Developments during the Christian Era   145

11. The Development of a Second Testament   151
     The First Two Christian Centuries   151
     The Crises of the Late Second Century   155
     The Catholic Church's Response   158
     A Canon of Second Testament Scriptures   164

12. The Bounds of the Canon   168
     Which Books Belong in the First Testament?   168
     Criteria for Inclusion: Canon, Prophets, and Apostles   171
     The Determination and the Openness of the Canon   177

13. Scripture as Resource and Norm   183
     Tradition   183
     Reason and Secular Thought   187
     Human Experience   189
     Our Commitments   194
     Scripture as Resource and Norm   196

PART III
SCRIPTURE AS INSPIRED WORD   199

14. The Words of God in Human Words   201
     The Word of God at the Critical Moment: Jeremiah 36   201
     Prophecy as the Inspired Word of God   204

15. An Effective and Meaningful Word   209
     The Word of God: Certain to Come About   209
     The Inspired Word: Significant beyond Its Original Context   215
     The Inspired Speaker of God's Word   219

16. Forms of Inspiration   222
     Inspiration as God Using an Instrument   223

Inspiration as God Dictating to a Messenger 227

Inspiration as God Standing behind a Prophet's Own Words 231

17. Understanding the Inspiration of a Text 237

The Inspiration of Scripture in the Light of the Incarnation 238

The Inspiration of Scripture in the Light of the Spirit's Involvement in the Church 241

The Inspiration of Scripture in the Light of Creative Inspiration 244

The Inspiration of Scripture in the Light of the Nature of the Sacraments 246

The Inspiration of Scripture in the Light of God's Acts in History 248

18. Scripture as a Whole as Inspired Word 252

Extending the Model of Inspired Word of God: Its Application to Narrative 252

Authoritative Canon and Experienced Revelation as Inspired Word of God 257

19. Inspiration and Inerrancy 261

Attitudes to Factual Accuracy over the Centuries 261

The Nineteenth-Century Elaboration 266

Difficulties with Inerrancy and Approaches to Solving Them 268

Difficulties in Principle and Disadvantages in Practice 273

The God-Givenness of a Broadly Accurate Text 279

PART IV

SCRIPTURE AS EXPERIENCED REVELATION 285

20. Revelation in Theology and in Scripture 287

Revelation as a Theological Theme and as a Scriptural Theme 288

Revelation in the Apocalypses 292

21. Revelation: Personal, Propositional, Historical, and Reasonable 299

Personal Revelation? 299

Propositional Revelation? 302
Revelation in History? 304
Revelation and Reason 311

22. The Truth of Revelation 314
The Place of Imagery in Scripture 314
The Logic of Scripture's Language about God 319
The Truth of Daniel 10–12 322
The Symbolism of Patriarchy 326

23. Scripture as as a Whole as Divine Revelation 329
Revelation Elsewhere in Scripture 329
Diversity and Unity in the Scriptural Revelation 332
Theological Inerrancy 338
Progressive Revelation and Divine Condescension 341
The Clarity of the Scriptural Revelation 345

24. Human Experience and Theological Reflection
in the Two Testaments 348
Human Experience in Scripture 348
The Experience of Israel and Christian Experience 351
Theological Reflection and the Christ Event 355

25. Scripture as a Manual of Theological Reflection 360
The Reflective Nature of Scripture as a Whole 360
Modes of Theological Reflection in Scripture 364

Abbreviations 372

Bibliography 374

Index of Authors 404

Index of Scriptural and Other Ancient Jewish
and Christian Writings 412

• 1 •

Introduction:
Scripture's Varied Forms

I am concerned in this book with how we think about scripture, with the way we conceive of it doctrinally. The categories in terms of which this question has long been discussed are now subject to wide-ranging critique, a critique that puts us on the track of some important issues and that hints at ways in which our doctrine of scripture could be expressed more biblically than has classically been the case.

Categories for a Doctrine of Scripture

In order to think doctrinally about scripture, theologians have commonly used terms such as authority, revelation, inspiration, word of God, canon, infallibility, and inerrancy. At present discussion of the doctrine of scripture by means of these categories is in some disarray. James Barr and Edward Farley, for instance, have examined the notion of authority as applied to scripture, and questioned whether it is appropriate.[1] Gerald Downing made the same point with regard to the idea of revelation.[2] R. P. C. Hanson declared that the idea of scriptural inspiration was meaningless and should be abandoned, and W. J. Abraham suggested that this expressed a conviction implicit in other theologians' silence on the subject.[3] Writers such as

1. E.g., Barr, *The Bible in the Modern World;* Farley, *Ecclesial Reflection.*
2. See Downing, *Has Christianity a Revelation?*
3. Hanson, "The Authority of the Bible" 21; *The Attractiveness of God* 21; cf. Abraham, *Divine Inspiration of Holy Scripture* 6, 48.

1

John Barton[4] have critiqued treatment of the category of canon as a key to understanding scripture's significance. Conservative evangelical discussion that assumes that the traditional categories are still entirely serviceable has focused on the debate concerning infallibility/inerrancy, but even a writer such as Moisés Silva, who is committed to asserting the inerrancy of scripture, has noted that this assertion solves nothing if we do not know how to interpret scripture.[5]

Admittedly "claims about the collapse of biblical authority arise precisely at a time when membership in more evangelically and even more fundamentalistically oriented churches is increasing and when the membership in liberal and less biblically centered churches is decreasing"; simultaneously Latin American grassroots communities are finding scripture a resource for critique of the social and political order even as North Atlantic theologians proclaim the demise of scriptural authority.[6] It is tempting for Christians who want to reaffirm a commitment to scripture to suspect that much of the discussion just referred to is merely a restatement of the old liberalism, and recent conservative treatments of the doctrine of scripture generally confine themselves to reaffirming it in its traditional form. They do not assume that any new questions are being raised by books such as the ones we have noted. A key question those books press, however, is whether a doctrine of scripture formulated in the terms we have listed is itself scriptural.

Conservative Christians have utilized a set of deductive and inductive arguments — arguments, that is, starting from philosophical considerations or from within scripture — to support the case for the commitment to scripture that they themselves make and that they believe is demanded of the Christian church generally. The deductive approach begins by portraying humanity as dependent on God to reveal truth if we are to have sure knowledge of it and bound to submit to God's authority, in whatever form it is exercised. The complementary inductive approach argues from Jesus' attitude to the Jewish scriptures and from the attitude of writers such as Paul to their own work and concludes that the two Testaments[7] that

---

4. *Reading the OT;* cf. also Barr, *Holy Scripture.*

5. See *Has the Church Misread the Bible?* 2-4.

6. F. S. Fiorenza, "The Crisis of Scriptural Authority" 354.

7. I shall refer to the First and Second Testaments (cf. J. A. Sanders, "First Testament and Second" 47-48). The expressions "Old Testament" and "New Testament" tend to downgrade the Hebrew scriptures in a way that would have been repugnant to the early Christians. The term "Tanak," an acronym for Torah, Prophets ($n^e bi'im$) and Writings

comprise the Christian Bible should be regarded as the locus of God's revelation, as the instrument of God's authority, and as God's inspired and therefore inerrant word.

It may be asked regarding the inductive approach whether Jesus' attitude to the Hebrew Bible (the limits of which in his time are a matter of controversy) is a natural starting point for an understanding of the Christian Bible. And it may be asked whether material within the Second Testament or outside it offers any grounds for establishing what should be included in it.

Most telling for an approach that wants to be scriptural is the fact that virtually none of those familiar terms we have listed appears within scripture to describe scripture — for instance, when the Second Testament refers to the First. The Second Testament alludes to Jesus speaking with authority, to apostolic authority, to the authority of the state, and to authority in the army. But when it refers to the Hebrew scriptures or to letters that in due course came to be part of the Second Testament, and to the importance, status, and value attached to them, it does not do so with the term "authority." The scriptures refer to particular revelations given to Daniel and John and to revelatory experiences on the part of other people in scripture, but they do not use the concept of revelation to designate individual books within scripture, apart from *the* Revelation to John, or to designate scripture as a whole. The word "canon" appears in the canon (e.g., Gal 6:16), but not with reference to the canon. With regard to "inspiration" there is the single occurrence of the Greek word *theopneustos*, "given by inspiration of God" (KJV) in 2 Timothy 3:16; even there, it may be questioned whether the translation is appropriate, given that the term means more literally "God-breathed" (cf. NIV). The expression "word of God" refers to particular divine promises, commands, or messages, oral or written, and in the Second Testament characteristically to the gospel message itself, but it is not a scriptural term for scripture itself. The Greek equivalent of "infallibility" or "inerrancy"[8] comes once in the Bible (Luke 1:4), but is not predicated of the Bible.

The one strictly scriptural term for the scriptures as a whole is "scriptures" — or simply "books" or "writings," to use less religious-sounding words that as such compare better with the Greek words.[9] C. F. Evans has

---

(*k^etubim*), as "the proper designation of the Jewish Bible within Judaism" (Fackenheim, *The Jewish Bible after the Holocaust* 107), is also value-laden.

8. *Asphaleia* (NIV "certainty"). The word appears elsewhere with other meanings.

9. *Biblia, graphai, grammata.*

asked whether the idea of a holy book is compatible with the Christian gospel, which "abolished the category of the holy except as applied to God himself."[10] The Second Testament has no equivalent to other religions' holy places, holy time, priestly caste, and sacred rites (apart from a kiss!). But early Christian documents do occasionally refer to the "holy scriptures" or "sacred writings" (Rom 1:2; 2 Tim 3:15; cf. Rom 7:12). They imply that holy writings still had a place in Christian thinking when holy places, caste, time, and rites did not. In this respect Christianity indeed followed Judaism. There too "the Bible was not so much a revelation of the divine will, as a revelation of the divine Being." "One of the great contributions of Judaism to the history of religions is its assertion that the divine reality makes itself humanly comprehensible through the structures of language."[11] Sacredness lies here rather than in a special priesthood, time, place, or rite; for reasons we will consider further, it is through a written text rather than through one of those other means that God is known.

Admittedly terms such as "authority" and "canon," though they are not used of scripture in scripture, can with some degree of appropriateness be extended to apply to scripture as a whole. For example, in the Gospels Jesus is capable of responding to suggestions regarding his conduct with a resounding "it is written" (e.g., Matt 4:4, 7, 10), and the scriptures are functioning there for him as a rule whereby he measures someone's counsel. It is functioning, that is, as canon. Yet neither that expression nor the others we have mentioned is actually used, and pointers toward use of them can have set against them pointers in the opposite direction. Paul, at least, can give the impression of denying that he speaks infallibly or inerrantly (1 Cor 1:17) or speaks the word of the Lord (1 Cor 7:25) and of wishing to avoid talking in terms of either revelation (2 Cor 12) or authority (2 Cor 13:10).

The use of scriptural terminology does not guarantee that one's thinking is in accordance with scripture, as the Arians famously showed. Conversely, doctrinal thinking does not have to confine itself to scriptural terms in order to be scriptural — otherwise there would be no orthodox doctrine of the "Trinity." Sometimes we need terms from outside scripture if we are to pursue the task of reflective theological analysis of scripture's actual statements. In the present case it might cause less comment if the standard terms for discussing the doctrine of scripture derived from extrabiblical language, like those that aided the development of the doctrine of the

---

10. *Is "Holy Scripture" Christian?* 34-35.
11. Fishbane, *The Garments of Torah* 124.

Trinity from the second century onward, or were modern terms or concepts with which people writing in scriptural times could not have been familiar. But this is not so. All or nearly all are theological terms used in scripture itself, but not in connection with scripture. Some are used to describe parts of what eventually became scripture; thus prophecies are "the word of the Lord." But even those terms are not used to describe scripture as a whole or whole books within scripture. Scripture's failure to use terms such as "authority," "revelation," and "canon" in connection with scripture, despite its familiarity with them in other connections, alerts us to the question whether they imply categories that do not correspond very well to scripture's nature and function — whether these key technical terms fail to emerge for this purpose in scripture itself because they impose alien categories on scripture; whether the *formal* gap between the way scripture speaks of itself and the way theology has traditionally spoken of scripture is an outward sign of a *real* gap between the two.

Theology uses the category "authority," which most commonly suggests someone laying the law down or making final decisions that are binding on others. And scripture does sometimes lay the law down and make final decisions that are binding on the people of God. But that is not a dominant feature of scripture, and this is reflected in the fact that it does not talk in these terms about itself. Theology uses the category "revelation," which suggests a situation in which there are matters that are veiled and would remain hidden were it not for someone removing the veil. And scripture sometimes is a revelation of things that would otherwise be secret, as is the case in the Book of Revelation. But it does not generally have that form. Theology uses the category "inspiration," which suggests that scripture is "God-breathed," issuing from God's creative and speaking breath, and stresses the directly divine origin of scripture. And the prophets, in particular, do stress the directly divine origin of their words, while 2 Timothy 3:16 predicates this term of the Hebrew scriptures as a whole. But most of the scriptural writings do not make claims of this kind; indeed, some rather stress their human origin (see especially Luke 1:1-4).

To speak in terms of the authority of scripture, of scripture as God's revelation, or of scriptural inspiration is not so much untrue as a not especially plausible way to go about crystallizing a scriptural way of understanding scripture. Even the term "holy writings," the category that scripture does use for the whole of scripture, could beguile us into imposing inappropriate expectations on it: Robert Detweiler's interesting analysis of "sacred text" suffers from the attempt to make statements about this whole (e.g., that it is revelatory or provides the foundation for ritual) that apply only to parts.[12]

It was because of subsequent events in the history of the church and of secular thought that expressions that came into being for other reasons were applied to scripture and came to be used to express the significance of scripture as a whole. When the church began to function more fundamentally as an institution, the thinking that undergirded Roman law and government came to influence it and the technical term "authority" was used not only to describe one hitherto unlabeled function inherent in one specific part of the scriptures but to describe the function of scripture as a whole.[13] Then because authority was a problem in Western theology,[14] authority became a key category in this connection. Inspiration became a helpful category for the Reformed churches when they needed to formulate and defend the status they gave to scripture in the midst of controversy with the Roman Church on one side and the radical reformation on the other; then as a consequence of nineteenth-century debates over biblical criticism, inspiration had its connotations stretched so that it suggested a guarantee of the factual accuracy of scripture.[15] Meanwhile in the eighteenth century revelation had become a central issue in theology and thus also a central category for understanding the significance of scripture.[16]

So concepts that arose in connection with features inherent in particular types of scriptural material or in quite other connections came to be applied to scripture as a whole and came to have their significance stretched as a consequence. Then as the doctrine of scripture developed in response to historical factors, new implications came to be drawn from the use of these concepts in this new connection and utilized in order to help theologians formulate answers to new questions. It then became customary in seeking to formulate a doctrine of scripture to take these different concepts as all equally applicable (or inapplicable!) to the whole of scripture — and

12. See *Reader Response Approaches to Biblical and Sacred Texts* 215-23.

13. Cf. D. Brown, "Struggle Till Daybreak" 20-22, taking up the work of H. Arendt, "What Was Authority?", in *Authority* (ed. C. J. Friedrich; Cambridge, MA: Harvard, 1958) 81-112. Cf. Barr, *The Bible in the Modern World* 28.

14. So, e.g., Zizioulas, "Four Preliminary Considerations on the Concept of Authority" 166, quoted by Barr, *The Bible in the Modern World* 28. See also Lindbeck, *The Nature of Doctrine* 102-3.

15. E.g., Warfield, *The Inspiration and Authority of the Bible*.

16. See, e.g., H. D. McDonald, *Ideas of Revelation;* cf. Downing, *Has Christianity a Revelation?* and Downing's interesting review of Dulles's *Models of Revelation;* J. Barr, *Old and New in Interpretation.*

as all applicable to the whole of scripture in the same sort of way. But the variety of ways in which scripture itself speaks suggests that even where such categories do apply, they do so at different points and in different ways.

Models for Scripture

In the course of this development it has often been forgotten that the concepts we have been considering are *models* that the church used to help it crystallize its doctrinal understanding of scripture. Forgetting that has contributed significantly to the disarray in which the doctrine of scripture finds itself. "A *picture* held us captive. And we could not get outside it."[17]

Doctrinal thinking commonly involves the use of models. The task of doctrine is to aid our understanding of key realities of Christian faith such as God, salvation, the church, and the Bible. Many of these realities are by their very nature formidably deep or complex. A model is an image or construct that helps us grasp aspects of these realities by providing us with something we can understand that has points of comparison with the object we wish to understand, thus helping us get our mind round its nature.

In this sense a model is like a metaphor, for metaphors are also a way of extending our knowledge and understanding. But there are a number of ways of distinguishing between models and metaphors. A model is more likely to be a theoretical construct, an artificial thing that we *construct* rather than something that exists on its own in concrete form, as is normally the case with metaphors. If a model is suggested by something that does exist concretely, the comparison it facilitates may be one of a more analytic and systematic kind than is the case with a metaphor. It may also be characteristic of models to be more intellectual than affective, whereas metaphors are good at expressing "what ideas *feel* like."[18]

An illuminating book by Avery Dulles called *Models of the Church*

17. Wittgenstein, *Philosophical Investigations* 115; Thiselton (*The Two Horizons* 432) adds, "What misleads us is not simply the power of a model or metaphor as such, but the fact that all too often our way of seeing a particular problem is wholly dictated by a *single controlling* picture" which exercises a spell over us. (Emphasis original in both quotations.)

18. On the understanding of models see, e.g., Black, *Models and Metaphors;* Barbour, *Myths, Models and Paradigms;* McFague, *Metaphorical Theology;* Martin Soskice, *Metaphor and Religious Language* 97-117.

considers the church as institution, as mystical communion, as sacrament, as herald, and as servant. By applying the notion of models to the church Dulles is able to take account of two aspects of the church, that it is a concrete objective reality and that it is, nonetheless, one whose nature is complex and difficult to encapsulate. Some of the images emerging from the Bible and tradition that Dulles discusses might more naturally have been described as metaphors. Others are models in a stricter meaning of the word; the notion of an "institution" does not relate to something that in itself exists in the same sense as the church does, but as a construct it enables us to grasp aspects of the significance of the church conceptually.

Dulles later expanded part of *Models of the Church* into a further book called *Models of Revelation*. At that point difficulties arise, because speaking of "models of revelation" involves a change in the meaning of the word "model." There cannot be "models of revelation" in the sense in which there are "models of the church" because revelation is itself a metaphor or model. It is not an objectively existing entity like the church, or even God, but an image or construct capable of being applied in a more or less illuminating way to realities that do exist. Thus, as Dulles shows, people apply this model to the Bible, to world history or to a particular segment of history, to the person of Jesus Christ, to the church's teaching, or to the human experience of perceiving something meaningful in the world or of being confronted by God or hearing God speak. We may utilize models in order to grasp something of the significance and depth in concrete realities such as these, and revelation is one such model. But to speak of models of revelation itself is to use the term "models" in a different and looser sense from the one it has when applied to the church. Indeed, of late "model" has become a word of rather wide-ranging meaning. J. H. Elliott calls it "a current buzzword subject to such indiscriminate use that it often introduces more confusion than clarity."[19]

Clarity is not the only reason for questioning talk in terms of "models of revelation." Such talk begins from the reifying of a model (in the stricter sense) and then looks for the model's embodiments. Therefore the model itself, revelation, is treated as an indispensable theological category, and theologians find themselves drawn into arguments about whether its true embodiment is the Bible or the Christ event or tradition or history or experience and find themselves discussing odd claims such as the proposition that creation is a means of revelation — an odd claim not because it

---

19. *Social-Scientific Criticism of the NT and its Social World* 3.

is untrue but because talk in terms of revelation does not seem a very natural way of attempting to conceptualize the manner in which we discover truth from creation. Because revelation has become a mandatory theological concept, we have to attach it to the object we wish to commend as a source of Christian insight, but we may not thereby do justice to the nature of the object we wish to understand. This seems to be the case with scripture. To describe scripture as revelation is not so much untrue as not especially illuminating or natural. If Muslims are puzzled by the Christian scriptures because they do not resemble what they themselves see as divine revelation,[20] they may be onto something.

What is true of "revelation" is also true of "authority." In another recent book on the theological significance of scripture, *The Shape of Scriptural Authority*, D. L. Bartlett speaks of models for understanding scripture's authority, apparently referring to the way authority is embodied in the First Testament by narrative, law, wisdom, and prophecy.[21] In parallel, R. C. Leonard has distinguished four main views of canon: as inspired word, as the history of God's acts, as law, and as a cultic phenomenon, rooted in worship; here, too, a concept related to authority is being taken as key to scripture in its diversity.[22] Different genres such as narrative, law, wisdom, and prophecy indeed suggest different models for understanding scripture, an insight that I will want to take up shortly, but authority is one of those models, not the object being modeled. Like revelation, it is a model frequently applied to scripture, though not because scripture as a whole points toward it as natural for scripture. "It may be quite possible to live as Christians without the word 'authority' at all."[23] "Strange in a way that feminists have not yet seen that 'authority' is a concept from the male world of power-relations";[24] language of gift, encouragement, and influence would at least as well characterize scripture's way of speaking.[25]

20. Glaser, "Towards a Mutual Understanding of Christian and Islamic Concepts of Revelation" 22.

21. In his *The Authority of the Bible* Dodd similarly discusses the authority of individual inspiration in prophecy, that of corporate experience reflected in law and the poetic books, that of the incarnation, and that of history.

22. See Leonard, *The Origin of Canonicity in the Old Testament* (dissertation, Boston, 1972), as quoted by Beckwith, *The OT Canon* 63.

23. Buttrick, *Homiletic* 248.

24. Clines, *What Does Eve Do to Help?* 48.

25. Feminists have of course discussed the reworking of the notion of authority (see, e.g., Russell, *Feminist Interpretation of the Bible* 137-46). I believe that Buttrick's and Clines's point here is more radical.

In a parallel way L. Alonso Schökel applies the model of inspired word to the different parts of scripture. He distinguishes between objective, personal, and dynamic forms of inspiration, which appear respectively in narrative, psalmody, and prophecy.[26] As ways of expressing what we might mean when we speak of the inspiration of different types of material the scheme is helpful, but it begs the question of how well the model of inspiration illuminates the nature of the different parts of scripture.

The point can be illustrated from the liturgy. One morning in our college chapel we read Isaiah 5:1-7 and Mark 14:1-12, and after each the reader declared, as usual, "This is the word of the Lord." The problem with this affirmation regarding the second passage is not that the story fails to be an authentic, illuminating, and edifying reading that deserves our acquiescence and for which we are grateful to God. Our problem is that "word of the Lord" suggests a category mistake. A more appropriate response to it is some statement such as "This is part of God's story." Similarly, the appropriate response to some excerpt from the agonizing of Job or the questioning of Ecclesiastes is something along the lines of "Isn't it amazing the things you can say to God?" To either of these statements the standard congregational rejoinder, "Thanks be to God," would be entirely appropriate. That is more than can be said regarding the other common situation when these phrases bring a wry smile to one's lips, when they follow a reading such as Isaiah 5:1-7. After prophetic oracles (or dominical sayings) such as that, which are indeed the word of the Lord but which bring exceedingly bad news to their hearers, only listeners on autopilot can respond gratefully "Thanks be to God." Some other response is surely required, perhaps "God help us."

In scripture itself, then, models such as authority, inspiration, and revelation are little used to describe scripture, much less scripture as a whole. After the era of the Bible various models were applied to particular parts of scripture to express what hearers may expect to gain from them or what attitudes to them may be fruitful. Then these models were stretched so as to apply to scripture as a whole. Then this range of separate models for understanding scripture came to be treated as a set of theological concepts. This in turn generated a further difficulty as scholars sought the interrelationships between these concepts.

The different models of the church cannot be related to each other as

---

26. See *The Inspired Word* 134-50; he is taking up the work of K. Bühler in his *Sprachtheorie* (Jena: Fischer, 1934).

models. It is as difficult to find the relationship between the church as mystical communion and the church as servant as it is to combine elements of a painting of a cornfield by Van Gogh with elements of one by Constable. Each is offering an account of the whole from a particular perspective. They are not parts of a jigsaw. The models for scripture to which I have referred have commonly been treated as a series of interdependent concepts that are therefore capable of being brought into relationship with each other. One might speak, for instance, of a revelatory event that could be written about under divine inspiration in words that could thus be identified as the words of God and that would then have authority in the believing community. In one way or another revelation, inspiration, and authority could be interrelated, but only at the cost of ignoring the fact that they are separate models. They do not offer interrelated partial accounts of the significance or function of scripture as a whole but independent total accounts of part of it.

Theology long sought to conceptualize the significance of scripture by means of a standard paradigm based on models such as authority, revelation, and inspiration. These not only shaped conceptual thinking about scripture; because of their resonances they also encouraged attitudes such as an expectance that God would speak through scripture and submission to what God was believed to say through scripture. But theology has now gotten into severe difficulties over these models, difficulties that constitute a crisis of paradigm in this area of theological study. When theological concepts such as revelation and authority became dubious instead of mandatory and when there seemed to be overwhelming empirical evidence that scripture was not a set of wholly factual documents, the result was to discredit the stretched notions of authority, revelation, and inspiration, and thus to discredit those notions in principle. Worse, it was in turn to discredit the scriptures to which they had been applied. Scripture was the victim of that "principal danger in the use of models . . . , the loss of tension between model and modeled. When that distance is collapsed, we become imprisoned by dogmatic, absolutistic, literalistic patterns of thought." We perceive models not as models but as the way things actually are. "The characteristics of metaphorical thinking are lost — its flexibility, relativity, and tension."[27]

27. McFague, *Metaphorical Theology* 74.

Reconsidering Models for Scripture

A crisis of paradigm is a not a negative moment in the development of theology but a positive one. Indeed, "the real 'movement' of the sciences takes place when their basic concepts undergo a more or less radical revision that is transparent to itself. The level that a science has reached is determined by how far it is *capable* of a crisis in basic concepts."[28]

The radical way out of the difficulty we have been analyzing is to abandon the traditional models for scripture in order to attempt a revolutionary shift of paradigm. Thus Barr looks for how the Bible functions today, while Edward Farley's *Ecclesial Reflection* subjects the whole notion of authority in theology to a sustained fundamental critique. But escape from the models turns out to be more difficult than it looks. "Function" is rather vague, and while Farley demolishes "the house of authority" in the first part of his book, the second part is so concerned with "norms" that he may seem to be rebuilding a not wholly dissimilar new dwelling.

Overtly more radical explorations thus easily coalesce with overtly more conservative ones such as those of W. J. Abraham and K. R. Trembath on inspiration. Abraham's *The Divine Inspiration of Holy Scripture* keeps inspiration as a concept applied to the whole of scripture by developing an illuminating but quite novel starting point for the meaning of inspiration, the human experience of being inspired by someone to do something.[29] Building on Abraham's work, Trembath takes biblical inspiration to refer to "the enhancement of one's understanding of God brought about instrumentally through the Bible" rather than to the Bible itself.[30] Scholars such as P. J. Achtemeier redefine inspiration in a quite different direction, as the process whereby traditions were formulated, reshaped, and transmitted within the believing communities (of which inspired individuals were but part).[31] In turn, the notion of revelation is redefined by R. F. Thiemann as a way of affirming the prevenience of grace.[32]

But another move is logically prior to the abandonment or redefinition

28. Heidegger, *Being and Time* 29, his emphasis; "sciences" *(Wissenschaften)* include the humanities, such as theology. Cf. Moran, "What Is Revelation?" 217.

29. One might compare D. Brown's appeal to the etymological link between authority and authorship as he redefines the former in terms of the latter; see his "Struggle Till Daybreak."

30. See *Evangelical Theories of Biblical Inspiration* 103.

31. See Achtemeier, *The Inspiration of Scripture* 117.

32. See his *Revelation and Theology.*

of such terms for scripture. The old models are in difficulty partly because they were stretched to provide answers to different and broader questions than the ones they originally addressed. As a result they seemed to be discredited when we no longer liked the answers they provided to those questions (and indeed, no longer liked the questions). The least we can do before either discarding the old models or redefining them is to see if we can clean them of their encrustation by going back to the specific meaning intrinsic to each of them, which gets lost when they are stretched in order to handle other questions. For instance, the notion of authority is at home when someone is laying down the law about something; the notion of revelation is at home when something that would otherwise have remained secret or puzzling is unveiled publicly or clearly; the notion of inspiration is at home when we are confronted with a text or an artifact or an experience that seems so deep or significant or extraordinary or far-reaching that a merely human account of its origin is unsatisfying.

W. C. Kaiser has commented that it is strange to multiply discussion of topics such as inspiration and revelation without reconsidering the biblical material that relates to these concepts, as if Gaussen and Warfield had said it all.[33] It is ingenuous of Trembath to rule out any attempt to determine the nature of inspiration by consideration of a biblical passage such as 2 Timothy 3:16;[34] more "liberal" and more "conservative" scholarship is actually in a fair measure of agreement regarding the understanding of inspiration in the Second Testament period. But we are concerned not merely with the intrinsic meaning of such words but with the characteristics of the different parts of scripture that attracted such descriptions to it. "The analysis of religious discourse ought not to begin with the level of theological assertions," says Paul Ricoeur — assertions of a general, propositional kind. "A hermeneutic of revelation must give priority to those modalities of discourse that are most originary within the language of a community of faith," which "are caught up in forms of discourse as diverse as narration, prophecy, legislative texts, wisdom saying, hymns, supplications, and thanksgiving," forms that directly modulate various distinctive expressions of faith that cannot be abstracted from these forms.[35] Ricoeur, too, begins from what I have called a reifying of the idea of revelation, but his insistence

33. "A Neglected Text" 301.
34. See *Evangelical Theories of Biblical Inspiration* 6.
35. "Toward a Hermeneutic of the Idea of Revelation," *Essays on Biblical Interpretation* 90-91.

on considering the distinctive ways in which different biblical genres work offers an important insight as we consider how models for scripture function.

We have noted that one fundamental difficulty about applying familiar models such as authority, inspiration, and revelation to scripture as a whole is that scripture is not characteristically laying the law down or claiming to be of more than human origin or revealing things that have been veiled. But *parts* of scripture are doing these various things, and all these models can still be illuminating with regard to some of scripture as they bring into focus the nature or function of specific sections of it. The model of scripture as the inspired word of God of course fits prophecy in particular; the oracles of the prophets explicitly claim a divine origin. Laying down the law is what the Torah is characteristically doing, so that Jesus' deference to its commands corresponds to its own nature; it is the law that presents itself as an authoritative canon. The apocalypses of Daniel and Revelation purport to reveal what is otherwise veiled; it is the Book of Revelation that is the book of revelation.

Admittedly the biblical books themselves tend to be more complex than Ricoeur's dictum might suggest. The command material of the Torah or the Sermon on the Mount is contextualized in narrative; the "prophetic" books contain much apart from direct prophecy; apocalypses characteristically appear in combination with other literary forms (stories in Daniel, letters in Revelation); Paul's letters fit no one category very easily. Nevertheless it is heuristically useful to consider how the models function individually. It will then be illuminating to stretch them so that they apply to scripture as a whole, as has happened over the centuries. But we will do that more fruitfully and more circumspectly if we have begun from their earlier narrower application in specific contexts and from the intrinsic meaning that attracted Bible and tradition to them in the first place, and if we keep that intrinsic meaning in mind as we stretch the model, rather than allowing a model's meaning to emerge from its broader application and thus from extrinsic considerations. Some of the problems the models have come to raise will be avoided if in this way we distinguish between primary and secondary applications of them.

In addition to matching the old models more specifically to the material they suit, we will need to utilize some new models. These also need to be devised in relation to *specific* points, in particular points where the old models fail to serve. For instance, the poetic books in the First Testament and the epistles in the Second are genres that seem ill-served by the received models. Here some explicitly modern models that see scripture as issuing from human experience, theological reflection, preaching, or some combination of these may correspond well with the books' own account of themselves, given the way they overtly build on experience, reflection, and preaching.

Most importantly, none of the models naturally fits the narrative books that dominate both Testaments. It is not that these lack authority rather than possessing it, that they are uninspired rather than inspired, or that they purport to be God's revelation but do not actually transmit it. It is that such models are not as illuminating when applied to narrative forms of literature. Narratives do not lay down the law, even if they implicitly take an authoritative stance in requiring an audience to look at a story from a particular perspective; insofar as narratives refer to their origin, it is their human authorship they allude to, and that only rarely; and they tell of things that were visible to anyone who was there (though it is true that narrative is a genre for concealing as much as for revealing).

The notions of authority, inspiration, and revelation can be stretched to accommodate narrative works. The stretching is already taking place in the Second Testament in that one passage where translations commonly use the word "inspiration," which describes the whole Jewish scriptures in such terms (2 Tim 3:16). The Hebrew Canon's identification of Joshua-Judges-Samuel-Kings as the former *prophets* and the understanding of the Hebrew scriptures as a whole as Torah illustrate the same process. One of my concerns, however, is to draw attention to the fact that a stretching is required when we apply the model of authority or inspiration or revelation to a narrative text. We have grown so familiar with this stretching that we no longer notice that it takes place.

Two terms from scripture itself seem worth exploring as suggesting alternative primary models for narrative in particular. One is the idea of "witness," applied to scripture as a whole by Karl Barth[36] among others. The other is "tradition," which has come to be used illuminatingly of scripture in some recent discussion, partly arising out of ecumenical dialogue.[37] The narrative books are a witnessing tradition. As Farley puts it, as *kerygma* they preserve a record of the events in which the church's origin

---

36. *Church Dogmatics* I/2 §19; see Runia, *Karl Barth's Doctrine of Holy Scripture* 25-33. Cf. also Ricoeur, "The Hermeneutics of Testimony" and his "Toward a Hermeneutic of the Idea of Revelation," in *Essays on Biblical Interpretation* 110-17.

37. See *The Fourth World Conference on Faith and Order* (ed. Rodger and Vischer) 50-54 = Flesseman-van Leer, *The Bible* 19-23.

lay, written for faith, which makes available for each generation the origi-
native dimension of *tradition*.[38]

Both "witness" and "tradition" can help bind together two features
central to the theological significance of scriptural narrative, features that
easily fly apart and need very much to be kept in close association. The first
is a historical concern and reference. As witness, the narratives testify to events
that have happened that constitute the good news their message brings. As
tradition they pass on an account of events that have happened and that are
important for people who have not personally experienced them (for tradition's particular concern with passing on an account of events, see Luke 1:1-4;
1 Cor 11:23; 15:3). The second feature is that the witness is given by people
from their individual perspectives, while the tradition reflects the concerns of
those who pass it on and of its recipients. The witnessing tradition is not
merely factual chronicle. Thus both a historical concern and a literary concern
are appropriate to the interpretation of the witnessing tradition.

It is an important feature of the use of models in theology that a
multiplicity of models is commonly required to do justice to its subjects.
"An endless number of metaphors and models . . . is no 'death by a thousand qualifications'. . . . Rather, it is life by a thousand enrichments."[39]
Varied models offer independent, though not necessarily rival, accounts of
their subject. It is less appropriate to seek to interweave them or argue for
one rather than another, more appropriate to consider questions such as
what aspects of the object they represent well, what aspects of the model
need to be ignored because nothing corresponds to them in the object, what
characteristics of the object can only be brought out by other models, and
how the varied models act as mutual qualifiers that mark points at which
any one model ceases to apply. In the process the priority of some models
over others may indeed emerge, and in the case of models for scripture this
process may explain something of the way in which certain parts of the
scriptures are in practice more prominent than others.

It may not be wise to look for one model for scripture that takes
precedence over the others or holds all the models together. The quest for
such an overarching model threatens to compromise the important principle of diversity of models, which in the case of models for scripture
corresponds to the diversity of scriptural forms. If one model *can* overarch

38. See *Ecclesial Reflection* 276-78 (emphasis added).
39. I. T. Ramsay, *Models and Mystery* (London/New York: Oxford UP, 1964) 60, as
quoted by McFague, *Metaphorical Theology* 106.

the whole, it will not be one of the traditional ones (authority, revelation, inspiration, canon, word of God). Each makes its particular point in a sharp way, but precisely that makes each too narrow to form a satisfactory over-arching model or paradigm, and the fact that the models bring with them so much baggage from the history of secular and theological thought also presents difficulties.

An influential strand of contemporary study maintains that *the* pri-mary biblical genre is the one that dominates both Testaments, narrative,[40] corresponding as it does to the nature of the gospel itself. Indeed, it has been argued that narrative is *the* most elemental or primary cultural form.[41] It would be in keeping with this view to conclude that if there is one overarching model for scripture, it is the witnessing tradition. At least one might affirm that the scriptures are more fundamentally a witnessing tradi-tion that brings gospel to their hearers than they are an authoritative canon, which tells those hearers what to do, or a collection of oracles inspired by God, or a revelation of things otherwise hidden.

Yet it will be wiser to resist the temptation to give exclusive value-status to narrative. After all, many people have no story.[42] Theology is not to be reduced to story: It is "raw material for theology" rather than theology itself,[43] as is suggested by the move from narrative to reflection within scripture itself (especially Paul). Our example is rather Luther, who "did not adopt the Enlightenment's tendency to disregard narrative while re-taining the 'points' to be made from it, nor did he share Romanticism's embrace of story (or myth) as the unique vehicle of truth. He moved between the extremes."[44] There is at least a danger that " 'Narrative' has driven itself onto the same rocks that have shipwrecked most discussions of Scripture: the temptation to think that the hermeneutical deadlock has a single part — that, if we could discover the handle or the lock or the key, we could open the hermeneutical door."[45] It is fundamental to my attempt to think through the significance of scripture to resist this temptation.

40. So, e.g., Lindbeck, *The Nature of Doctrine* 120-21; but see M. Wiles's critique of such views in "Scriptural Authority and Theological Construction," in *Scriptural Authority and Narrative Interpretation* (ed. Green) 42-58.

41. Cf. Kort, *Story, Text, and Scripture* 8-13; among his references Crites's "The Narrative Quality of Experience" has been especially significant.

42. Lischer, "The Limits of Story" 31.

43. So Ritschl; see Ritschl and Jones, *"Story" als Rohmaterial der Theologie*.

44. Lischer, "Luther and Contemporary Preaching" 494.

45. Buckley, "The Hermeneutical Deadlock" 335.

I am concerned, then, to think through the doctrinal significance of scripture by considering the significance in scripture itself of various models for understanding scripture, to see how they illuminate the particular parts of scripture to which they initially apply, and then in the light of that to consider how they work when applied to other parts of scripture.

I have divided the models into four. We will consider scripture as a *witnessing tradition,* the special characteristic of the narrative books with their concern to pass on testimony to the events of Israel's history and the history of Jesus. We will consider scripture as an *authoritative canon,* the special characteristic of the instruction material in the Pentateuch and elsewhere. We will consider scripture as an *inspired word,* both human and divine, the special characteristic of prophecy. Fourthly, we will consider scripture as an *experienced revelation,* looking under this heading at experiential-reflective material such as appears in the poetic books and in the epistles, as well as the strictly revelatory material in the apocalypses. This last category is less coherent than the other three, though it is more coherent, as we will see, than might appear at first sight. These categories correspond broadly to the structuring of the scriptures themselves, at least as they appear in Christian Bibles: witnessing tradition and authoritative canon in Genesis to Esther and in the Gospels and Acts, inspired word in the prophets, and experienced revelation in the poetic books and in Romans to Revelation.

To emphasize diversity in this way is not to deny a unity to scripture but to recognize that scripture is characterized by the richness of a living reality, almost like a person who needs to be understood from different angles and in different roles if that person is to be understood at all. The person remains one person, and the "scriptures" are also "scripture." It is for this reason that scripture itself points us to this variety of models for the one reality.

I believe that a diversity in approaches to the interpretation of scripture appropriately corresponds to this diversity in approaches to a doctrine of scripture. I attempt to consider how this is so in a companion volume to this one called *Models for Interpretation of Scripture.*

• PART I •

SCRIPTURE AS
WITNESSING TRADITION

2

Witness and Tradition

"When asked what argument he would use to persuade a Buddhist or a Muslim of the truth of Christianity," Archbishop John Habgood "simply replies that he would tell them to read the Gospels."[1] Christians read the Gospels in the conviction that there they discover Christ. They are able to do that because over the centuries their spiritual forebears have done the same. Those forebears could do that because the church of the first few centuries had found itself compelled to preserve particular Gospels. It could preserve them because individuals and churches of the first century or two had felt constrained to write and to receive certain Gospels. And they had done so because they had recognized in Jesus the climax of a story that began in the First Testament, which it was natural to continue in narrative form. The narrative books in the two Testaments pass on indispensable witness to what God did in Israel in the story that comes to its climax in Jesus.

The Nature of Scriptural Faith
and the Nature of Scripture

Recalling the story of God's dealings with them in the past was always of key significance for Israel's ongoing life with God in the present. Three successive long Psalms illustrate the way in which (as we might now put it) scripture proclaims the history or story that puts our history and story in a broader framework. In Psalm 105, recalling Israel's history or story is

1. *The Independent* (London), 18 April 1987.

the secret to praise and commitment. The psalm recalls the story beginning with God's promise to Israel's ancestors up to their entry into the land, the story told at length in the opening six books of the First Testament. At the beginning of the psalm this story is the basis for thanksgiving and testimony, and at the end it is the basis for obedience and worship. By implication, if Israel has difficulty in opening its mouth or in directing its feet in any aspect of these activities, recalling its story is the means to putting the matter right.

In Psalm 106 Israel's story is the secret to assurance of forgiveness. From its very beginning in Egypt the story had related their neglect of God — their failure to recall and live by Yahweh's amazing commitment to them. But their neglect of God was never the end of the story. God might chastise them, but never abandon them, never let them down at a moment of crisis. The very nature or name of God made that impossible. On that basis, whenever the people of God realize that they are in trouble because of their neglect of God, they recall that God is one who does not hold such failure against them. They have to see themselves as sinners and not just as in need, but they can afford to do that because they are also invited again to put the scriptural story alongside their own. When they do so they find that it is often a story of the sin of believers — but then a story of God's forgiveness of those believers.

In Psalm 107 Israel's story is the key to hope. When people are in the wilderness, in the dark, in sin, or in deep water, Israel's story provides them with a counter-story that they are invited to treat as the ultimate story, thus setting their limited current story in perspective. Wisdom then lies in re-calling and living by the way in which God's commitment has been worked out in Israel's experience (v. 43). The Book of Daniel reflects the way in which the community under pressure in the second century recalls and lives in the light of its forebears' experience of deliverance from the pit, the fire, and other tests and of seeing the downfall of tyrants. The moment when that sort of experience seems not to be happening in the present is the moment when stories about that sort of experience are especially im-portant. When ordinary "realistic" readings of current historical reality are tempting, that is the moment when the involvement of God in those nor-mative originary historical experiences needs to be reaffirmed.[2]

The bulk of scripture takes the form of narrative. It opens in Genesis to Kings with an epic account of the story of Israel from the people's beginnings (traced back into world origins), through the peaks of their

2. Brueggemann, *Abiding Astonishment* 34.

history in the time of Moses and of David and Solomon, to the end of their independent history when they returned to that Babylon from which their forefather Abraham had once been called. It follows this in Chronicles to Nehemiah with an abbreviated retelling of that same story, taking it on into the period of the reestablishment of national life in Jerusalem after the exile. It also includes other shorter narratives, though the stories of Daniel and his friends are joined to a series of visions and Jonah is placed among the Twelve Prophets, while the English Bible orders the books so that Ruth can be read in conjunction with Genesis to Kings and Esther as a continuation of Chronicles to Nehemiah. The Second Testament is in turn dominated by four versions of a new kind of story, an account of a messiah who is unsuccessfully crucified. One of these four continues with an account of aspects of the early years of the church, persecuted equally unsuccessfully as the gospel of Jesus is carried as far as Rome.

Theologically speaking these longer and shorter narrative works are implicitly part of a more extensive overarching story that stretches from the creation of humanity and its turning away from God, through God's implementation of a purpose to restore the lost blessing of creation in and by means of the Israelite people, to a climax in the Christ event, with a coda (longer than the Second Testament at first sight suggests it will be) in the story of the church awaiting the final revealing of Christ and the new creation. This overarching drama invites its readers not only to find themselves in the way God deals with the world, the people of God, and the individual within that people, but also to see themselves as part of a humanity that was once created in a relationship with God and with the possibility of serving God, was then once-for-all redeemed so that the relationship might be restored and the possibility actualized, and now enjoys a life lived in the tension between the redemption achieved by Christ but not finally experienced by us until the End.

It is not by chance that the bulk of scripture is narrative. This characteristic corresponds to the nature of Christian faith. The fundamental Christian message is not an ethic, such as the challenge to humanity to live by the law of love, a challenge Christianity shares with some other religions. Nor is it a theology, a collection of abstract statements such as "God is love" — statements that it also shares with some other religions. It is a gospel, an account of something God has done, a concrete, narrative statement: "God so loved the world that he gave his only Son. . . ." Christian faith affirms the ethic and the theology just described, which it is glad to share with other religions, but it believes that the grounds for the former and the evidence of the latter is the gospel.

Of course such an account of the fundamental nature of Christian faith can be disputed. Many Christians might define the Christian faith along the lines we have just rejected or along other lines, and such understandings will then lead to other understandings of the Bible or to varying attitudes regarding the dispensability of the Bible. In discussing "In what sense is Christianity a 'historical' religion?" for instance, Maurice Wiles describes Christian faith as involving the convictions that there is a God of love who is the world's source and in whose hands is its destiny, and that men and women can respond to God and by God's grace overcome the evil of their own devising and that which the world metes out to them.[3] These convictions are based on their embodiment in Israel and in Jesus, but they are not essentially dependent on that embodiment. They could be true without it.

In contrast, Gerald O'Collins speaks of our experience of God being tied to and derived from certain historical events and persons, so that preaching and worship recite these in the belief that this past needs to become contemporary.[4] Paul van Buren defines the scriptures as "the story of the beginning of God's Way with His beloved creation into which we have been called to walk. It is therefore the story of the beginning of our Way," and therefore a story indispensable to us who now join that Way.[5] In traditional theological categories, Christian faith concerns redemption and not merely revelation. The gospel declares that God has acted in Christ to open the way for us into the presence of God. It was in Christ that God was reconciling the world. There is something once-for-all about what God did in the story that came to a climax in Jesus.

The heartwarming story of Pinocchio, the boy made of wood who was eventually turned into a real human being, suggests an attractive perspective on human existence, that the possibility of being turned from woodenness to real existence lies before us all. But it is only a wistful, naive idea; no such transformation has ever actually taken place, and there is no knowing whether it might happen for me. Some old religions spoke of a dying and rising god, but this is but another nice idea; there is no knowing whether a God really has died and risen (or dies and rises) for me. In contrast with the hopes of archetypal myth and fairytale, the perspective on human existence offered by the two Testaments invites a commitment in response

---

3. *Explorations in Theology* 4:61.
4. *Fundamental Theology* 101-2.
5. *A Theology of the Jewish-Christian Reality* 1:130.

to evidence. It offers to stand or fall by the factuality of events such as the exodus, exile, and restoration of Israel and the ministry, death, and resurrection of Jesus, events that demonstrate that Yahweh is God and that Jesus is Lord.

There is a coherence between an understanding of the Christian faith as fundamentally a gospel and a Bible that is dominated by narrative. Precisely by being narrative, the Bible reflects the nature of Christian faith; conversely, the narrative nature of the gospel itself points to the naturalness of the church's generating, preserving, and attributing special value to some narrative accounts of the gospel. There was no intrinsic necessity about the church preserving *four* Gospels,[6] nor can we prove that the church was right to preserve these particular four Gospels. On the other hand, if the Christian message concerns particular events that have taken place in world history, it would have been odd if the Christian church had not instinctively preserved some accounts of those events: That does seem intrinsic to Christian faith. The place of narrative scripture emerges from the fact that Christianity is a story. The specialness of scripture emerges from the specialness of the gospel. "The uniqueness and at the same time general relevance of [the Word] becoming flesh necessarily involved its becoming Scripture."[7]

Biblical Narrative as Witness and Tradition

I suggested in chapter 1 that two concepts from scripture itself are particularly suggestive for an understanding of scripture's nature as narrative: those of "witness" that has been given and of "tradition" that has been handed on. Luke's Gospel opens with the most technical self-description of any narrative in scripture. It designates itself as an orderly written form of what had been *handed down* by *eyewitnesses* who were themselves ministers of the word, so that the readers may be assured of the certainty of what they have been taught (Luke 1:1-4).

Luke thus designates itself as the embodiment of a witnessing tradition. Such a description would apply to most biblical narrative, though apart from Luke only the Fourth Gospel makes this explicit, in parallel though different terms: It is the written record of some of Jesus' signs, intended

---

6. Despite what Irenaeus writes in *Against Heresies* III.11.8 (on the basis of the four corners of the world, the four main winds, etc.).

7. Barth, *Church Dogmatics* I/2:500.

to draw readers to believe that Jesus is the Messiah and to find life in his name (John 20:30-31). John's Gospel is the witness that John bore, the reliable testimony that he offers (19:35). Indeed, A. E. Harvey has argued that John's Gospel as a whole is "a presentation of the claims of Jesus in the form of an extended 'trial'" that thus emphasizes the witness role of John the baptizer, of the disciples as those who see and hear Jesus, and of Jesus himself.[8] N. A. Dahl, in the context of studying the emphasis on memory and commemoration in early Christianity, calls John's Gospel "a witness and thereby an inspired 'commemoration' of the life and work of Jesus."[9]

Paul speaks of his own ministry among the Corinthians in a similar way. He exercised that ministry of the word of which Luke speaks, the preaching of the good news about Jesus. He regards himself as in some sense an eyewitness — one who has personally seen the risen Christ, albeit as one abnormally born. Like Luke, he has thus "passed on" what he himself "received": He specifically refers to the events of the Last Supper and of Jesus' death and resurrection (1 Cor 11:23; 15:1-3; cf. also 1 Thess 2:13). According to Luke, again, "witness" is the nature of the preaching of the Twelve concerning Jesus (e.g., Luke 24:48; Acts 1:8, 22; 2:32; 3:15): On the basis of what they have seen, they testify. Reference to the testimony of eyewitnesses is not all-pervasive in the Second Testament,[10] but it is evidently important in different connections to its major writers.

The imagery of witness and of passing on a tradition also appears in illuminating passages in the First Testament. The Israelites are to pass on to their children what they have seen and heard; they are to explain to them the basis for their obedience to God's commands, which lies in Yahweh's rescue of them from Egypt; and they are to teach them the significance of the stones placed in the Jordan, which are there to recall the Israelites passing through the river dryshod (e.g., Deut 4:9; 6:20-23; Josh 4). The exiles are to be witnesses to what Yahweh has said and done in their history, which establishes that Yahweh is God (Isa 43:9-10; 44:8). The central affirmation of Israel's faith is that Yahweh alone is God. But the fundamental assertion on which that faith is based is the assertion that Yahweh brought his people out of Egypt and will bring them out of exile. These are the events by means of which they "know that Yahweh is God" (e.g., Exod 6:7; Ezek 37:13).

---

8. *Jesus on Trial* 76; cf. Warner, *The Bible as Rhetoric* 163.
9. "Anamnesis" 28.
10. Nineham, *Explorations in Theology* 1:49-50.

In late Second Temple times interest in the narrative of the First Testament focused especially on its relevance as that which offers direct guidance for human behavior. Early Christianity retained Judaism's stress on scriptural narrative but treated it as witness to what God had done with Israel rather than as material primarily designed to shape what human beings should do. In this respect it could claim to be returning to the material's own inherent concern, though ironically in due course the church turned not only Israel's narrative but also its own new narratives, the Gospels and Acts, back into law.

Religious "tradition" can take forms other than narrative, and some Second Testament allusions to passing on tradition can be read as references to moral teaching parallel to that of Jewish halakah.[11] They can thus refer to the passing on of customs by Moses or by the scribes (Mark 7:1-13; Acts 6:14; Gal 1:14) or to the passing on of basic Christian beliefs and practices (Rom 6:17; 1 Cor 11:2; 2 Thess 2:15; 3:6; 2 Pet 2:21; Jude 3) — or to mere human tradition (Col 2:8). Yet narrative is the key form that tradition takes in both Testaments. Israel's "core tradition" witnesses to the facts of Yahweh's dealings with Israel; events in history are the great generators of tradition and its main focus.[12]

Scriptural narrative is thus *the* witness to the gospel. The idea of scripture as witness has been used to qualify scripture's authority: Scripture, it is said, is not itself revelation but only witness to revelation — fallible, human witness to real divine revelation. This is one side, though only one, to Karl Barth's use of the idea: "The men whom we hear as witnesses speak as fallible, erring men like ourselves. What they say, and what we read as their word, can of itself lay claim to be the Word of God, but never sustain that claim."[13] So N. L. Geisler attacks the view that scripture is "merely" a record and witness to God's revelation.[14]

There are no qualifications arising from the sense in which the Second Testament speaks of witness or from the sense in which I use the term here. To describe scripture as witness to the gospel is not to qualify scripture's

11. So, e.g., Bruce, *Tradition Old and New* 36-38; cf. Cullmann, *The Early Church* 64.

12. W. Harrelson, "Life, Faith, and the Emergence of Tradition," in *Tradition and Theology in the OT* (ed. Knight) 18-24; cf. Knight's own talking in terms of the witness of tradition (e.g., "Revelation through Tradition" 153, 161, 163); Achtemeier, *The Inspiration of Scripture* 124-26.

13. *Church Dogmatics* I/2:507. For the positive side, see, e.g., 463.

14. *Biblical Errancy* 232.

significance but to define and to emphasize it.[15] Scripture is *the* indispensable resource for a knowledge of the gospel. If we are to use authority and revelation and word of God language about scripture, then the authority of scriptural narrative lies in the fact that there alone can we discover that word of God that consists in the gospel message. If we lacked scripture, that gospel would be concealed and lost. Thus the fundamental reason for acknowledging the authority of the scriptures as the expression of divine revelation and the inspired word of God is the witness they bear.[16] Believing that the Bible is the Word of God means assenting to its witness concerning Christ. One cannot "be compelled to accept the revelation of Scripture on the basis of its God-breathed quality before being gripped by the message to which its words testify."[17] The first thing scripture seeks from us is an acknowledgment that its *witness* is true.

15. Cf. Runia, "The authority of scripture" 174.

16. A. T. Hanson and R. P. C. Hanson, *The Bible Without Illusions* 123; earlier R. P. C. Hanson, "The Authority of the Bible" 22-25; cf. Barton's chapter "The Bible as Evidence" in *People of the Book?* 36-47.

17. So rightly Berkouwer, *Holy Scripture* 166-67.

3

The Factuality Involved in Witness

We noted in chapter 1 that the idea of scripture as a witnessing tradition has two aspects. It designates scriptural narrative as concerned with historical events, and it suggests the presence in scriptural narrative of interpretation as well as "bare history." Both are consistent features of the narratives of both Testaments. They point us toward a twofold interest in the biblical story: We are concerned to discover the actual events of that history, the historical Israel and the historical Jesus. The instinct that has made generations of students feel that their library is incomplete without a copy of a book such as John Bright's *History of Israel* reflects a right awareness that the facts matter. And we are also concerned to discover the way that history has been shaped as narrative, for we recognize that we are reading not mere chronicle or annal but a story whose message is expressed in the way it is told. Therefore books on the interpretation of biblical narrative also belong on our shelves.

It is easy to let one interest exclude the other. Real historical events can seem so important that the literary creativity that features in biblical narratives can be ignored, or we can become so aware of this creativity that we cease to recognize the fact and/or the importance of the fundamental historicity of the biblical story. Within critical scholarship itself there is now a divide between people who still pursue a historical-critical approach to the text and people who take a literary approach. The notion of a witnessing tradition, and the biblical text itself to which we may apply that image, implies the importance of both.

The narratives of the First Testament form the deposit and the basis of Israel's witnessing tradition. We have used the term "epic" of Israel's account of its history, but that may be a misleading expression if it suggests a grand poetic work composed for cultic recital. Israel's story is narrated in prose and is a story about real human beings living in a real world.[1] The Gospels in turn tell the gospel story, a story about events that happened. The tradition that Paul passes on is that "Christ died for our sins. . . ." The Christian message declares that whereas people were or would have been cut off from God, now they have access to God as a result of a particular significant event. The testimony that the witnesses offer is to the fact that Jesus is risen from the dead: They have seen him. As the deposit of this process of tradition and this act of witness, the biblical narrative has a fundamentally historical concern. The phrase "a witnessing tradition" designates scriptural narrative as concerned with facts. How do we investigate this concern?

As Witness Scripture Asks to Be Investigated Critically (Even If It Implies a Critique of Criticism)

Biblical narrative's factual concern implies that it invites critical investigation in order to establish how factual it is.

Some forms of Christian faith put a question mark by the attempt to distinguish between what is historical and what is unhistorical in scripture. People who believe in scriptural inerrancy, for instance, will assume that this inerrancy rules out the presence of unhistorical elements in biblical "histories."[2] Although they seek in this way to safeguard the complete reliability of scripture's witness to historical events, their strategy for doing so may actually imperil that witness.

> Think of a body of testimony collected by the prosecution in a criminal trial. If the prosecutor claimed that his evidence was guaranteed to be inerrant before he set it before the jury, nobody would believe him. Testimony depends upon its own inherent power of conviction, not on a claim to infallibility.[3]

For quite other reasons, Rudolf Bultmann also protests at investigation of the "historical Jesus" so as to show faith's basis in historical events and thus

---

1. Talmon, "The 'Comparative Method' in Biblical Interpretation" 354; cf. Alter, *The Art of Biblical Narrative* 25.
2. So, e.g., Lindsell, *The Battle for the Bible.*
3. A. T. Hanson and R. P. C. Hanson, *The Bible without Illusions* 123.

to provide reason for faith. In a comparison that is itself open to question, he sees this as an epistemological form of the attempt to attain justification by works.[4]

Again, it is a principle of Karl Barth's approach to Christian faith that faith is based on the witness to Christ that the scriptures themselves offer, not on any historical reconstruction that we can devise in an attempt to get behind that witness to the "real" facts. Barth assumes that it does indeed matter that Christ died for us in the space-time history in which all humanity lives.[5] Jesus' resurrection, too, is an objective space-time event within the world (here he argues against Bultmann) even though it is different in not being the kind of event that can be handled by the ordinary methods of historians, because it breaks the rules they set for what can count as a historical event (here he agrees with Bultmann).[6]

Because he refuses to make the resurrection conform to what the modern historian counts as an event, Barth can be misunderstood as saying that the resurrection did not happen.[7] He is concerned to insist that the resurrection supremely belongs not merely to *Historie* or historical events in their this-worldly significance and as they can be investigated by the secular historian, but to *Geschichte* or space-time historical events in their context in the purpose of God, which gives them their truest meaning.[8] As such an event, one of a uniquely supernatural kind, its story is told not in the (relatively) more straightforward historiographic form of the crucifixion story but in the form of *Sage* or *Legende*. By that Barth means an intuitive or poetic, non-historiographic way of telling what is nevertheless a historical story, in the sense of a story about actual once-for-all space-time events.[9] Historiography, that is, corresponds to *Historie,* while *Sage/Legende* correspond to *Geschichte.*

Behind Bultmann and Barth (and also Paul Tillich, who remarks that we must "make the certainty of faith independent of the unavoidable in-

4. "Bultmann Replies to His Critics," *Kerygma and Myth* (ed. Bartsch) 1:210-11, with Mitchell's comments, *The Justification of Religious Belief,* on pp. 141-42. There is a different application of the argument in Ebeling, *Word and Faith* 55-57.

5. E.g., *Church Dogmatics* IV/1:223-24, 247-48.

6. E.g., *Church Dogmatics* III/2:446; IV/1:227, 333-41; IV/2:142-50.

7. So, e.g., Klooster, "Karl Barth's Doctrine of the Resurrection."

8. E.g., *Church Dogmatics* III/1:76-83.

9. E.g., *Church Dogmatics* III/1:81; III/2:452; IV/1:334-36. *Sagen* focus more on events ("stories" is a less misleading English equivalent than "sagas"), *Legenden* more on individual persons.

certitudes of historical research"[10]) is the figure of Martin Kähler. He declared that "the real Christ, that is, the Christ who has exercised an influence in history . . . *is the Christ who is preached,*" that is, "the Christ of faith." He also affirmed that "the reality of Christ himself has left its ineffaceable impress" on the Gospels' portrait of Jesus, a fact that underlies both the unending scholarly fascination with this portrait of his enigmatic figure and his continuous reality to countless believers.[11] But because of the nature, interests, and presuppositions of modern historical study, *"the historical Jesus of modern authors conceals from us the living Christ."* Whereas modern historical method takes similarity between the present and the past as a criterion for judging the past, what distinctively interests us as Christians about Jesus is his *uniqueness* as revealer and redeemer.[12]

Barth, in turn, emphasized that precisely because the essential nature of the resurrection as a real historical event hinges on its relationship with the purpose and activity of God, the scriptural account of it is not amenable to investigation by the ordinary methods of historical research. "There is no proof, and there obviously cannot and ought not to be any proof, for the fact that this history did take place *(proof, that is, according to the terminology of modern historical scholarship).*"[13] And in this respect, in the fact that its meaning hinges on its relationship with God's purpose and activity, the resurrection is actually paradigmatic for scriptural events in general. We cannot get behind the scriptural witness to these events in order to reach "actual" events. As the events they truly are, they are inaccessible to the historical method. "As critical-historical research spreads its net around the raised Christ to capture and 'have' him, he, passing through the midst of it all, will 'go his way.' The transcendence of the Raised One is not amenable to such man-handling."[14]

With Barth's argument regarding the Christ event may be compared Walter Brueggemann's questioning of the standard critical approach to Israel's history. This approach methodologically excludes that which elicited the sense of wonder with which Israelites told their history.[15] Also com-

---

10. Foreword to C. E. Braaten's ET of Kähler's *The So-called Historical Jesus* x. On Kähler in relation to Bultmann and Barth, see Pannenberg, *Basic Questions in Theology* 1:81-86.

11. *The So-called Historical Jesus* 66, 79 (emphasis original); cf. Moule's review of C. F. Evans's *Is 'Holy Scripture' Christian?* 420.

12. *The So-called Historical Jesus* 43, 58-61, emphasis original.

13. *Church Dogmatics* IV/1:335 (emphasis added); cf. more broadly III/1:76-83.

14. Carnley, *The Structure of Resurrection Belief* 24.

15. *Abiding Astonishment* 37-38.

parable is Donald Evans's observation that academic study is pervaded by an epistemological perspective that excludes the possibility of direct awareness of spiritual reality and thus of any possibility of taking as a real event an event such as the Transfiguration.[16]

Barth's stance draws attention to the fact that historical research cannot establish the truth of the gospel. But he recognizes that ordinary historical facts are of importance to this gospel, and logically he ought surely to grant the possibility that "historical study of Jesus, though provisionally abstracting from the totality of his existence, serves to illumine more fully the meaning and significance of the biblical testimony to him," and also that "a failure on the part of historical-critical method to attain some historically reliable conclusions about the person of Jesus would seriously prejudice the Christian claim that God was decisively present in the person of Jesus Christ."[17]

One's longing for certainty may make one wish that the truth of the gospel was guaranteed by some evidence immune from criticism, but we cannot have the virtues of history without its risks. Nor ought we to fear the risks if "the really destructive atheism is fear of facts," the fear that questions whether all facts are God's.[18] If the gospel asserts that God acted in history and that history is the setting for the demonstration of God's power at work, historical events demand to be investigated. The witness of scripture itself points in this direction. Much recent study of biblical narrative urges us to take seriously the final, canonical form of the biblical text, and we will have reason in due course to note the strengths of this emphasis, but there are limitations to it. "There is no question that Jesus 'canonically' rose from the dead, but it is the extrinsic resurrection that matters for faith."[19] The Word did not become narrative, nor did the Word become proclamation: The Word became *flesh*.[20] Wolfhart Pannenberg has thus especially emphasized over against Barth that it matters that the scriptures'

16. "Academic Scepticism, Spiritual Reality and Transfiguration," in *The Glory of Christ* (ed. Hurst and Wright) 175-86.

17. Ogletree, *Christian Faith and History* 211, 213; cf. Carnley's comments in *The Structure of Resurrection Belief* 130.

18. A. Miller, *The Renewal of Man* (Garden City: Doubleday, 1956) 137, quoted in connection with theologians such as Barth in Harvey, *The Historian and the Believer* 137.

19. J. Barr, "Childs' Introduction to the Old Testament as Scripture" 21; cf. Barton, *People of the Book?* 49; Barr, *The Bible in the Modern World* 74.

20. Bartlett, *The Shape of Scriptural Authority* 51-52.

witness is factual and that the question of its factuality must be open to examination.[21] Bultmann's disavowal of historical facts entirely fits with his existentialist version of the gospel, but if the gospel is a message about what God has done for us in Christ, some historical facts are needed to provide part of its justification. The resurrection must be approached both as a historical event and as an event of suprahistorical significance: Each of these models takes us some way toward understanding it.[22]

How, then, do historians discover what historical witness the scriptures provide? What kind of investigation they undertake and even more what kind of discoveries it leads to vary with the material they are studying. We can illustrate the point by considering the Second Testament's witness to Christ and the First Testament's witness to three key events, the creation, the occupation of Palestine, and the fall of Jerusalem.

Investigating the Witness of the Second Testament

The Second Testament offers four accounts of the story of Jesus, and further testimony to his significance appears especially in Paul's letters. In considering this witness, one begins by asking how near the events the authors were, which involves being critical, if necessary, about received understandings of the authorship and date of biblical material. We are accustomed to connecting the Gospels with Matthew, Mark, Luke, and John, but the Gospels themselves do not make these connections directly. These views of their authorship may as easily be imposed on the texts as derived from factual information. Phenomena within a work such as incidental references to circumstances and events of the author's day, which may be later than the period with which the work is directly concerned, provide pointers to its origin and date that are less intentional and perhaps more reliable than later traditions. On this basis the Gospels of Matthew and Luke are now commonly reckoned to have been written in the light of the fall of Jerusalem in AD 70 (compare Matt 24 and Luke 21 to Mark 13). Mark is usually considered the earliest of the Gospels, though not as early as many of the letters of Paul (and Matthew and Luke also include much material not from Mark that goes back at least as far as much of Mark).

It is not clear that any of the Gospels was written by someone who had

21. See, e.g., "Redemptive Event and History," *Basic Questions in Theology* 1:56.
22. Cf. Carnley, *The Structure of Resurrection Belief* 143-44 (Carnley has "eschatological" for "suprahistorical").

personally witnessed Jesus's life, ministry, death, and resurrection, though that does not preclude that they passed on eyewitness material that they had received. Behind the earliest Gospels lies a generation of Christian witness, reflection, and teaching. On what grounds can we determine how far they witness to the actual Jesus? Recent decades have seen intensive study of the processes whereby stories about Jesus and accounts of his teaching developed from the 20s or 30s to the 60s and 70s of the first century and whereby the Evangelists themselves went about writing their Gospels. Some of that study has taken the view that this process involved a wholesale recasting of the tradition in order that the material might speak to the needs of the church. Clearly if this is so, we may not be able to extract from this material any testimony to the Jesus who could have been seen and heard in the 20s or 30s.

So can we trust the witnesses? The very notion of witness suggests that those who speak have something to say and deserve to be treated as fundamentally trustworthy. Admittedly the critical approach to history requires us to avoid the kind of unquestioning acceptance that might once have been accorded to testimony regarding what someone claims to have seen and to tradition merely because it was tradition. It obliges us to test or sift evidence, including that of eyewitnesses, especially when they claim to have witnessed the miraculous. We must take seriously the possibility that they might be fraudulent. In the medieval period historians' implicit trust in their sources had become an encouragement to deliberate fraud on behalf of what were believed to be justifiable causes. We cannot treat people who claim to be witnesses as having unquestionable authority simply because they make their claim.

But to take the view that the authentic historian's attitude is necessarily skepticism is to leap to another extreme.[23] We should be wary of assuming, for instance, that people were invariably more gullible in earlier ages. The inhabitants of the Greek and Roman worlds were not unaware of the difference between fact and fiction and of the necessity in some contexts — such as those in which eyewitness testimony is important — to establish whether things did or did not happen.[24] They knew that dead people do not rise, as they knew that people born blind do not come to see (John 9:32). As David Hume notes, the Romans were well aware of the difference between likely and unlikely testimony, even when it came from unimpeach-

23. Gunton, *Enlightenment and Alienation* 124, commenting on the work of V. A. Harvey.
24. Cf. R. Trigg, " 'Tales Artfully Spun,' " *The Bible as Rhetoric* (ed. Warner) 130.

able authorities: "I should not believe such a story were it told me by Cato," ran a proverbial saying.[25] In the ancient world awareness of the link between causes and effects coexisted with a yearning for and an openness to the miraculous, as it does today.[26] Perhaps we should not even attribute to that world too "naive and literalistic" an understanding of stories about, for example, floating axheads and inexhaustible cruses.

Although for the most part the Second Testament is not directly the work of eyewitnesses, the view that the tradition about Jesus was radically changed between his day and that of the work of the Evangelists presupposes that those who passed it on were either unconcerned or unable to pass on historical testimony to Jesus, and this seems implausible. The tradition may not have preserved material out of a concern with mere facts and may have preserved only what seemed relevant to it, but this does not mean that it preserved nothing or that it invented material from scratch. We have noted that at least the earliest Evangelists lived within thirty or forty years of the events they relate, and that the gospel by which they and their churches lived (and in some cases died) implied a concern with historical facts. The churches had reason to preserve factual witness to Jesus, and the Evangelists were in a position to relate it. Such considerations are not grounds for abandoning investigation of each story they tell, as if we thereby had guaranteed for us the inerrancy of their witness. We must allow for the possibility that some witnesses do embellish their evidence. But these considerations do suggest that — perhaps contrary to the scholarly consensus — there are good grounds for an attitude of fundamental trust in their testimony to the life and character of Jesus.[27] The Second Testament witnesses deserve to be treated more like friends we should be able to trust than potential deceivers whom we need to suspect and torture.

When they testify to events that cannot be satisfactorily explained in terms of normal natural or human causation as we experience it, examining their witness becomes more complicated. As we have hinted already, we need not assume that every story involving a floating axhead is to be taken as witnessing to a literal historical event. But stories such as those of Jesus' resurrection and his miracles are a different matter from stories of a be-

---

25. *An Enquiry Concerning Human Understanding* (London: Cadell, 1777; reprinted Oxford: Clarendon/New York: OUP, [2]1902) X/89; cf. Stout, *The Flight from Authority* 120. The saying is quoted from Plutarch's *Life of Cato*.

26. Abraham, *Divine Revelation* 129 and n. 44.

27. So, e.g., Stanton, *Jesus of Nazareth,* esp. 117-36; cf. Goetz and Blomberg for a systematic discussion of the "burden of proof" in connection with the historicity of the Gospels.

headed saint walking to a cathedral carrying his head under his arm and there singing the *Te Deum,* not least because of their place in the context of the wider story of God's action.[28] They are a different matter regarding their significance for our lives. S. M. Ogden comments that the resuscitation of a man's corpse "would be just as relevant to my salvation as an existing self or person as that the carpenter next door just drove a nail in a two-by-four."[29] But we are not speaking of the mere resuscitation of an ordinary corpse. They are also a different matter regarding the grounds for believing them. As we have noted Barth rightly affirming, the very nature of the stories about Jesus means that they are not amenable to decisive arguments based on the usual principles of historical causality. The witnesses testify not to the resuscitation of an ordinary corpse but to the bringing back to renewed life by God of the Messiah, who is also the unique Son of God. The event they report by its very nature does not conform to the rules for assessing more ordinary events.

It might turn them on their head. If we are talking about such a person, arguably his death is actually more difficult to believe than his resurrection. At least a resurrection of that kind of significance is no harder to accept than a death with the significance that these witnesses also speak of, a death of decisive importance for the whole of history. The death and the resurrection are equally part of the ultimacy of the Christ event and are equally believable or unbelievable. Anyone who can believe that Christ's *death* was of once-for-all significance should be able to believe that it could appropriately be followed by a resurrection of once-for-all significance. And if his resurrection be granted, we can hardly declare *a priori* that (for instance) the story of Jesus walking on water must be nonfactual simply on the basis of the fact that we know that no one can walk on water.[30]

A converse might also be suggested. If we follow the story of Jesus through his ministry and to his death, his resurrection may seem the only possible conclusion. Testimony to the resurrection of a person with a quite different life story might carry less conviction. It is in this sense that one might grant that at certain points we may accept testimony regarding Jesus that would be inconclusive regarding someone else. And once we come to faith in Christ, we may rightly accept further testimony regarding him — for in-

28. Abraham, *Divine Revelation* 132-34, 152-54, referring to Harvey, *The Historian and the Believer* 116.

29. *Christ without Myth* 136.

30. Against C. Hartlich, "Is Historical Criticism Out of Date?" in *Conflicting Ways of Interpreting the Bible* (ed. Küng and Moltmann) 5.

stance, regarding his virgin birth — which would be inconclusive regarding someone else, as we might believe things from a friend that we would not believe from a stranger.[31] This way of thinking also lies behind the observation that in the context of Christian belief "'resurrection' is part of what 'incarnation' means."[32] To confess the incarnation contains and entails the conviction that Jesus is risen from the dead. How could it be otherwise? And both presuppose the reality of God and are inconceivable without it.

Ernst Troeltsch himself noted that such considerations illustrate how the question whether the witnesses can be trusted in this connection involves setting the approach of "empirical historiography" — using ordinary historical method — in the broader context of one's "philosophy of history."[33] Indeed, one's historical method inevitably works within the context of a philosophy of history that opens up possibilities or sets boundaries for the hypotheses that historians necessarily formulate in order to do their thinking. If one accepts, for instance, that "the concept of God . . . should really be indispensable for the historian,"[34] that makes a fundamental difference in this connection.

Christians do not consider the purported resurrection of Jesus as a happening in isolation but as an event that makes sense in the light of other beliefs and as one that helps to make sense of those other beliefs. This does not prove that it happened, but it does alter the way in which we come to a judgment on whether it happened.

> If there were, as in principle there might be, evidence to justify an entirely straightforward naturalistic explanation of what occurred, the scientific historian must, of course, accept it; but if there is not, he is under no obligation to adopt the most plausible naturalistic explanation on offer in order to leave no gaps in the "closed web of cause and effect."[35]

31. A. M. Farrer, "An English Appreciation," in *Kerygma and Myth* (ed. Bartsch) 1:220-21. In *The Structure of Resurrection Belief* Carnley argues systematically that the church's experience of the risen Christ helps both to illumine and to establish the nature of the Easter event.

32. Lash, *Theology on the Way to Emmaus* 171.

33. "Historiography" 721, quoted by Abraham, *Divine Revelation* 113-14.

34. Pannenberg, "Redemptive Event and History," *Basic Questions in Theology* 1:76; see also 70-71, and 38-50 on the God-excluding anthropocentrism of the historical critical method.

35. Mitchell, *The Justification of Religious Belief* 152, quoted by Abraham in his critique of the views of Troeltsch and Harvey, *Divine Revelation* 113 — and see further 133-34, 153-54.

And when we come to our judgment, in principle it justifies a real personal commitment of ourselves.

The fact that we want and need the witnesses' testimony to be true means that it would be easy for us unintentionally to fudge the evidence during this process. We will therefore pay grateful attention to the work of historians and critics who do not share our faith and who may dare to interrogate the witnesses more sharply. On the other hand, we will not feel under obligation to accept their results just because of our predilection to believe the witnesses. Working from a position of faith has its disadvantages but also its advantages, and working from outside a position of faith has the opposite advantages and disadvantages.

Investigating the Witness of the First Testament

In the First Testament the creation, the Israelites' entry into their promised land, and the fall of Jerusalem all feature in that epic work with which the Bible as a whole opens. Older Bibles refer to the first five books of the Bible as the Books of Moses, but the books themselves do not make that claim. Genesis through Kings is a continuous work, not a collection of separate works, and in the form we have it must date from after the fall of Jerusalem and the exile of many Judeans to Babylon, the last events to which it refers. That setting makes good sense for it; Genesis through Kings functions at this point as an account of how Israel reached such a tragic point in its history.

The account of the fall of Jerusalem in 2 Kings 25 closes this work. It has the nature of material that sits close to the event itself, which is chronicled in a series of painful moments and lists. There is no overt interpretation of the event. Whereas the end of the previous chapter sets 2 Kings 25 in the context of a statement about the expression of God's anger in this event, in ch. 25 there is no reference to its purported theological significance to take the account from the realm of *Historie* or historical events in their this-worldly significance to that of *Geschichte* or these same events in their context in God's purpose. That chapter is thus closer to historiography than to *Sage* or *Legende* — perhaps as close as the Bible ever gets. It conveys an atmosphere of numbed grief, and only an ambiguous hint of a hopeful future in its last paragraph. It contains nothing inherently implausible and can be related to material that appears in other Middle Eastern documents of the time such as the account of the period in the Babylonian Chronicle.

There is thus every reason to take this as a close-to-the-event narration of actual events.

Matters are quite different with the story of creation that opens this epic. It tells of events that took place millennia before the completion of the work in which we read of them. It might in principle be the case that the content of Genesis 1 was much older than the exile and was incorporated into this later work, as has been widely believed with regard to the Adam and Eve story in Genesis 2. As with the Gospels, historical study thus looks for indications within the work that the material it contains is of earlier origin. Here, however, such study suggests that the chapter indeed comes from the exile. It reflects concerns of the exile such as the status of the sun, moon, and stars and the sabbath; it shows signs, that is, of being written to controvert the understanding of creation expressed in the Babylonian creation story. Furthermore, most of the events it narrates are in any case events of which there could have been no human witness.

So did the narrator receive a revelation from God as to the process of creation? Unlike revelatory material elsewhere in the Bible such as the Revelation to John, the narrative makes no such claim. When the authors of the biblical histories tell us about the process whereby they wrote (notably in Luke 1:1-4) they suggest that their work was undertaken in the same way as any other historical writing. God's involvement with them in the execution of their God-given task did not bring with it the gift of additional hard facts. They tell us that their facts came from the same sources as anyone else's. The natural inference with regard to Genesis 1 is that the chapter came into existence by the same process as the rest of Genesis through Kings, by the narrator working from traditional material, empirical evidence (working backwards from the nature of the known world), and theological conviction. Genesis 1 parallels 2 Kings 25 in that it is talking about real events, but the nature of its witness to them is quite different, and more imaginative. As Derek Kidner comments with regard to Genesis 3, the chapter deals with an actual historical event, but it is "an open question whether the account transcribes the facts or translates them: *i.e.*, whether it is a narrative comparable to such a passage as 2 Samuel 11 (which is the straight story of David's sin) or to 2 Samuel 12:1-6 (which presents the same event translated into quite other terms that interpret it)."[36]

Matters are different again with the story of the Israelite occupation of

36. *Genesis* 66.

Palestine. The fall of Jericho and the fall of Hazor (Josh 6; 11) were events that like the fall of Jerusalem would have had human witnesses whose testimony could have been included in the tradition incorporated in the First Testament. But they were events that took place over 600 years before the books from Joshua to Kings reached their final form. Once again, then, we look for evidence that these books are preserving much older material. The usual scholarly view is that they do: The Book of Joshua brings together material of varied nature and background, much of it considerably older than the exile. A quite mainstream view has been that within the accounts of Israelite victories included in Joshua 11, for instance, is material relating to actual events of the thirteenth century BC — though other traditions of scholarship are more questioning about what happened.

The story of the fall of Jericho in particular involves a supranatural involvement of God, a "miracle," and when witnesses talk of miracles, as we have noted already, examining them becomes more complicated. If someone tells us that God has done something miraculous for them, our first reaction will be to assume that they are speaking figuratively. If we discover that they mean something that "defies the laws of nature," we will expect more spectacular evidence than we do for ordinary events. So it is with a story such as Joshua 6. A natural instinct is to infer that it, too, speaks figuratively and offers a dramatization of the truth that Yahweh gave Israel their land. That instinct then notes that as a story Joshua 6 reads more novelistically than some more straightforward narratives concerning the occupation of Palestine in Joshua and Judges — though the latter, too, are combined with statements regarding the total nature of Joshua's victories that ask to be taken figuratively, because they are belied by other statements in the context that make clear that Joshua's victories were far from complete (Josh 13:1; also Judg 1).

Theological considerations also give us less reason to think in terms of trumpets literally causing walls to fall than they give us for thinking in terms of Jesus being literally dead but then alive. For all its importance, the fall of Jericho is not an event like the vindication and restoration of the crucified Messiah who is also the unique Son of God. In the case of stories of floating axheads and inexhaustible cruses, too, both theological considerations and literary considerations concerning the form of the stories point all the more strongly away from a literal understanding of their meaning.

The novelistic or parabolic understanding of Joshua 6 is subsequently confirmed by archaeological investigation of the site of Jericho (in contrast to that of Hazor, for instance). Archaeologists have found not only no evidence of an act of destruction such as Joshua 6 describes but also no evidence that the city was even in existence in Joshua's time. By the nature of the case historical study cannot prove that the story told in Joshua 6 never took place: The suggestion has been made that the evidence for the city's occupation disappeared during the period the city was abandoned, or that the event took place earlier, when the city was occupied. But the evidence we do have suggests that the story makes a theological-historical statement about God's gift of the land to Israel, by means of a theological-novelistic narrative.

Living in Trust and Living with Ambiguity

A critical examination of the biblical tradition's witness to historical events thus leads to varied results. There is tradition that comes from very close to events and that seems of clear historical value (e.g., 2 Kgs 25). There is tradition separated by a generation or two's reflection, but deserving our fundamental trust (e.g., the Synoptics). There is tradition separated by centuries from the events it relates, material about which on purely historical grounds we may have to be at best agnostic (e.g., Josh 6). And there is tradition that does not actually mediate historical evidence in the ordinary sense at all (e.g., Gen 1). In all these cases, to one degree or another the texts make theological claims that ordinary methods of historical study are not designed to handle.

The material that is most difficult to live with is the third, that which makes a historical claim that critical study seems not to vindicate. This is characteristic of the stories concerning the key events from Abraham to David. G. W. Ramsey, asking "If Jericho was not razed, is our faith in vain?" suggests that the validity of such a biblical story stems from its ability to make sense of our lives *rather than* its connection with historical events.[37] But the stories imply that their vision of reality, their world, is built on supposed historical events that they relate. These events are part of the evidence for their vision.

To put it another way, narrative characteristically portrays reality in patterned, plotted form, with a beginning, a shape, and an ending and with

---

37. *The Quest for the Historical Israel* 124; Ramsey follows Harvey's discussion in *The Historian and the Believer.*

less of the untidiness and open-endedness that it has in our experience, and the biblical narratives imply the conviction that some of the justification for such an emplotted view of reality lies in their connection with actual historical events in which the plot can be perceived. The story, in leading to an ending, presupposes *the* End. To put the matter again in the context of the witness of the whole scriptural story, it is the fact of the Christ event that justifies hope for and faith in that End, which the Christ event anticipates.[38]

The fundamental historicity of the story told by the First Testament seems necessary to its theological message, yet that historicity cannot always be established by the use of critical methods. The reason for this is not generally that historical method has difficulty in handling the extraordinary nature of the historical events on which the story from Abraham to David centers, as is the case with Christ's resurrection. Its difficulty is with the nature of the historical sources for these events. The sources date from centuries after the events, they take a nonhistoriographic form that tends to submerge historical concerns beneath religious concerns in a way that makes it difficult for us to gain access to them,[39] and they are difficult to correlate with other Middle Eastern source material for the period. These difficulties by no means rule out the possibility that the events are historical, but they mean that we cannot make out a normal historical case for that view. At best the sources only justify agnosticism on the question. Ramsey suggests that the assertion of history's essential significance may seem to die the death of a thousand qualifications when we consider what we can actually affirm *on purely historical grounds* about an event such as the fall of Jericho.

This is how I live with this situation: The story of the Israelites' occupation of Palestine is an early stage in the story that reaches its denouement with the Christ event. Jesus comes as the high point toward which the story of Israel has been working. That conviction is expressed vividly, though strangely to us, in the genealogy with which Matthew begins the story of Jesus, a genealogy in which Rahab the prostitute of Jericho appears. Jesus comes as the climax to a story that includes the fall of Jericho, and he himself treats the story related by the First Testament as one that can and should shape his own self-understanding and that of other people. In this sense we receive the First Testament from Jesus (as we shall note further

38. So Pannenberg, e.g., *Revelation as History* 144.
39. Clements, "History and Theology in Biblical Narrative."

in Part II below). It was this story that made Jesus the person he was. A different story would have produced a different Jesus.

The fact that Jesus was who he was implies that the story that shaped him had whatever historical content it had to have. Jesus' relation with the history that leads up to him and his affirmation of the story emerging from that history offers a form of reassurance to us that the actual historical events must have been what could justify people believing that Yahweh was indeed God. Often we cannot establish what events took place; but then we are like a man who "can be confident that a jury will find his friend innocent of a crime — since he 'knows' independently that this friend is innocent, although he must wait for the judgment of the jury." V. A. Harvey[40] uses this analogy to describe a particular stance that can be taken to the Second Testament documents.

In that context Harvey questions this stance, and rightly. We have noted that it is both necessary and possible to question the Second Testament witnesses for ourselves and to get answers that we can live with. It is desirable to question the First Testament witness to events before the time of David in the same way, but their nature is such that in practice such questioning will not reach agreed results. Different people who question these witnesses emerge from that process with different convictions regarding their answers. The nature of the materials means that on purely historical grounds we cannot have the same confidence in the adequacy of their testimony. Thus it is possible to claim that we can trust the witnesses whose testimony is included in the opening books of the First Testament, but it would be difficult to base one's life on that testimony. In contrast, however, the nature of the Second Testament documents is such that they give us grounds for basing our life on their testimony to Jesus; and Jesus then gives us grounds for trusting the documents in the First Testament even when we cannot directly justify that trust on critical grounds.[41] The attempt to get behind the narratives to "real events" is not to be ruled out as a matter of principle, as Barth argued, but when we discover that we cannot get behind them in practice, on the basis just suggested we can live with that situation and learn from the narratives even though we cannot directly verify them.

One clear significance that attaches to investigation of the historical

---

40. *The Historian and the Believer* 196.
41. I have discussed this issue further in " 'That You May Know that Yahweh is God.' "

events to which the biblical tradition witnesses is thus that it has the potential to provide a necessary if not sufficient ground for accepting the message that the tradition builds on those events. That Yahweh brought the Israelites out of Egypt does not prove that Yahweh is God of all gods, any more than their being taken off to Babylon proves the opposite. But if the exodus did not take place, the ground on which Yahweh chose to base a case for the claim to be God of all gods disappears. That Jesus came back from the dead does not prove that he is the firstfruits of a final resurrection; after all, the Bible itself tells of other people coming back from the dead. But if he did not come back from the dead, a major ground for believing that he is the firstfruits of a final resurrection disappears. Otherwise "the question that remains is whether a creative word alone can set the captives free."[42]

There are satisfactory critical grounds for believing that the Second Testament is fundamentally historical and consequently for putting one's trust in Christ, and thus adequate religious grounds for trusting that the First Testament is also fundamentally historical. I know no formula for enabling us to move from such general statements to an answer to the question *how much* historicity the Bible has to have and does have. Each passage has to be looked at on its merits in terms of critical and theological warrants.

In order to play their part in drawing us to trust in Christ, the scriptures must give adequate testimony to the facts about him. To affirm that the Bible offers us adequate testimony is not to affirm that its narratives are inerrant. In a court of law and in other contexts where testimony matters, we are dependent on the general reliability of witnesses, and in the absence of general reliability we are at sea. But we are not dependent on witnesses making no mistakes, nor are we troubled when they contradict each other over certain matters. The concept of witness carries within it the notion of general reliability, but not that of inerrancy. Belief that scripture is entirely adequate witness neither necessitates nor justifies belief in its factual inerrancy.

I will argue in Part III below that belief in the God-breathed inspiration of scripture also neither justifies nor necessitates belief in scripture's factual inerrancy. Indeed, we have no theological grounds for believing that scrip-

---

42. Vanhoozer, *Biblical Narrative in the Philosophy of Paul Ricoeur* 239; he implies (e.g., 171) that Ricoeur answers this question affirmatively and contrasts him with Hans Frei (on whom see further ch. 5 below).

ture's witnessing tradition is wholly free from error. (Nor do we have theological grounds for believing that it is not.)

But we do have important and precious theological grounds for believing that the scriptures provide us with fully adequate witness to the events they narrate. The message declared by the narrative of scripture requires that this narrative contain a solid basis in fact, and the grounds for believing that it does so lie in God's own character. The God who acted for the world's salvation in Israel and in Christ would hardly have left the world without adequate witness to those acts. The theological foundation for our conviction that the scriptures give us adequate witness lies in the saving nature of God. The theological foundation for our understanding how the scriptures give us adequate witness lies in the providence of God, which could ensure that the right people transmitted the right information. We may trust that the love and the power of the God and Father of our Lord Jesus Christ will have ensured that we have not been left without an adequate witness to what God has done for us. But the nature of the gospel message does not give us grounds for believing that scriptural narrative needed to be historically inerrant witness. What we know of God and of God's providence, however, can give us confidence that scripture contains sufficient historical information for its accounts of God's acts to be adequate witnesses to the gospel. Thus the statement of faith we may rejoice to make is, "On the basis of the nature of God and of what I can discover empirically I believe this is an entirely adequate human witness; and as part of inspired scripture I believe it can do its work and speak today."

As Witness Scripture Invites Us to Learn from the Events Themselves to Which It Points

Suppose we grant that the biblical tradition is a reliable guide to the events it relates, and to their significance. That is not to imply that it offers an exhaustive account of them. John's Gospel closes by observing that it cannot tell us everything that Jesus did (John 21:25), and we cannot infer that it offers an exhaustive account of the events it does relate — hence the multiplicity of new versions of stories within scripture itself. We discover more about the significance of what God was doing in Israel and in Jesus by investigating the actual events that lie behind the scriptural witness. The investigation is warranted by the very fact that this witness points away from itself to these events and claims no validity independent of them.

Scripture witnesses to the actual history of God's acts in Israel that came to a climax in Christ. It thus invites us to learn from the actual events to which as witness it points.

"Historical enquiry can thus *shape* faith." It cannot in itself generate faith or prove faith, but it can "inform us about what it might *mean* to confess Christ." So Paul Fiddes,[43] who gives as examples three strands of recent investigation into the historical Jesus: investigation into his conflict with religious institutions of his day that emphasized Torah observance, into his political significance as a disturbance that both religious and secular authorities needed to deal with, and into the sense of sonship out of which he prayed "Abba, Father." All three have implications for a theological understanding of Jesus' death, and all three emerge from historical study that seeks out the facts behind the witness of the Second Testament. Our doctrine of the atonement can thus be enriched by study of the historical Jesus. History shapes faith. Feminist study of the historical Jesus' relationships with women and of the role of women in the early decades of Christianity provides another instance where study of the historical realities that lie behind the direct witness of the Gospels and other Second Testament documents may suggest theological insights that reflect only in part the awarenesses of the witnesses themselves, or even subvert them.[44]

In a parallel way the actual history of Israel is, like the story that the First Testament tells, a potential source for theological insight and the shaping of faith. John Bright's *Early Israel in Recent History Writing,* for instance, is a polemical work, but is also one that sees its aim as furthering the writing of a straightforward, objective guide to events covered by the First Testament. By its very title N. K. Gottwald's *The Tribes of Yahweh: A Sociology of the Religion of Liberated Israel 1250-1050* B.C.E., which covers the same period, indicates that it has different assumptions, tone, and aim, as well as different conclusions. It presupposes the view that history writing, whether its authors recognize it or not, both reflects political commitments on the part of its authors and encourages political commitments on the part of its readers. The "sociology" of which Gottwald speaks is a perspective on society that he is aware of bringing to the biblical text as a source for Israelite history, that he finds illuminating in analysis of how Israelite society actually operated, and that he believes is then fruitful for allowing Israelite history to suggest insights on the problems of society in the modern

---

43. *Past Event and Present Salvation* 38, 39 (emphasis original).
44. So E. Schüssler Fiorenza; see esp. *In Memory of Her.*

world. Faith and life are shaped by considering the historical reconstruction of the the contrast between the functioning of Israelite society in the pre-Davidic and monarchic periods, a reconstruction made possible by looking beneath the biblical text to the events to which its witness points.[45]

The actual history of Israel is also the background to the Christ event. We would make an assumption of this kind with regard to any historical event or person. Understanding someone requires some awareness of their background, history, and experiences, which are what have made them what they are. To understand the Christ event we must see it as the climax to a story that reaches centuries back into pre-Christian times, the story of the relationship between the God and Father of our Lord Jesus Christ and the Israelite people, whom that God chose as a means of fulfilling a purpose for the world as a whole. One reason that the story of Israel has an importance for Christianity that Indian or Chinese or Greek history does not is that that story is the one that in a special sense Jesus brings to a climax. A Christian is committed to gaining as clear as possible a grasp of Israel's story because understanding it is an indispensable key to understanding the Christ event, which is its climax.

Earlier in this chapter we viewed the gap between the literal sense of the scriptures and the historical facts to which they are referring as a difficulty. Pannenberg describes that gap as one of the two causes of "the crisis of the scripture principle" that has developed since Luther.[46] Yet there is a sense in which that distinction between the witness and the history is enriching. The resources available to us include both the witness of the scriptures themselves and the discoveries we make through looking where they point.

---

45. Cf. also the work of Mendenhall, e.g., "Covenant Forms in Israelite Tradition"; *The Tenth Generation;* "The Monarchy."
46. *Basic Questions in Theology* 1:6.

• 4 •

The Interpretation
Involved in Witness

We have considered one aspect of the idea of scripture as a witnessing tradition, the way it draws attention to the factuality of the gospel and of scripture. There is now a complementary point to be made, for the image of a witnessing tradition suggests and reflects the presence of interpretation as well as facts within scripture itself.

The Gospels as Interpretative Witness

Although their functioning as a witnessing tradition causes the Gospels to be concerned with historical events, it does not cause them to aim at "pure" history. Luke begins by affirming his desire to put the gospel into orderly written form, but he does not attempt to tell a wholly chronological story. A comparison of his Gospel with Matthew's and Mark's reveals, for instance, that he tells us of Jesus' rejection at Nazareth before other events that preceded it. There is good reason for this: It helps us to see where the story is going and to understand it as it subsequently unfolds. Luke assumes that the reordering or rewriting that turns "story" into "discourse"[1] may make the significance of the story clearer than a merely chronological account would. It means he is not attempting pure history. Nor can his prologue therefore be treated as a decisive argument that he could not have included traditions whose historical value he could not control, any more than is the case with other biblical writers.

1. Chatman, *Story and Discourse.*

49

The same is true of Matthew itself. To the eyes of most modern readers, Matthew has a most unpromising beginning, an unexciting list of bare names. Our attention soon moves on to the more inviting stories in 1:18–2:23. But the Jewish reader who came to faith in Jesus through reading the earlier material responded to it in a way Matthew would have appreciated: This reader would have seen that it embodies a particular assertion about Jesus. By relating his genealogy, it affirms that Jesus was a Jew whose ancestry went back to Abraham — and a Jew with a genealogy of a particular kind, a member of the tribe of Judah and the family of David; he thus had the formal qualifications to be regarded as the Davidic Messiah. The unusual inclusion of several women in the genealogy (including Rahab whom we noted in chapter 2), drawing attention to the contribution that some questionable unions made to that genealogy even before and during David's own time, hints that the apparently questionable circumstances of Jesus' own birth (1:19) hardly imperil his claim to be David's successor.

But Matthew's presentation of the history that led up to Jesus involves a patterning of that history. He tells us that there were fourteen generations between Abraham and David, fourteen between David and the exile, and fourteen between the exile and the Christ. Historically there were not those precise numbers of generations, as a look at the First Testament itself soon reveals. Matthew's presentation creates something more artistic and easier to remember than it might otherwise be, and something that expresses and reflects the conviction that the Christ event comes about by a providence of God that has been at work throughout the history of the Jewish people but now comes to its climax. This presentation involves schematizing earlier history in a way that does not confine itself to offering a historical account.

Another aspect of the interpretation that can be involved in witness emerges from a comparison of accounts of the same events in different Gospels. In the story of the storm on the lake in Mark 4:35-41, for instance, the disciples shout "Teacher, don't you care if we drown" and Jesus rebukes them for having "no faith." In the version in Matthew 8:18-27 they shout "Lord, save us" and are rebuked as people "of little faith." The plausible explanation of such phenomena in the Gospels is that Matthew is adapting the tradition of what the disciples and Jesus said so that it applies more explicitly to the church to which he writes. As Christians discover that faith takes them into storms, they cry out "Lord" (the characteristic title for Jesus within the church, after the resurrection) and "save us" (the characteristic gospel verb) and are addressed as "of little faith" (because as Christians they cannot be identified as having no faith).[2] This example makes clear that the process of reinterpretation was one that affected what Jesus said as well as details of things that happened. Another notable example of development of what he said is how "Why do you call me good?" (Mark 10:18), evidently capable of being misinterpreted, becomes "Why do you ask me about what is good?" (Matt 19:17).

In John's Gospel there appears a Jesus who speaks quite differently from the one in the first three Gospels, the "Synoptic" Gospels. It might be that the sayings and parables of the first three and the discourses and "I am" sayings of the fourth Gospel equally come from the historical Jesus. It is more commonly assumed that John puts onto the lips of Jesus many statements that in his lifetime he never made. Assertions such as "I am the bread of life" are then the fruit of meditation on the significance of things Jesus actually said, did, and was in the light of John's and the church's ongoing experience of Jesus. Either way Jesus has been interpreted — by selection from what he said or by development of what he said.

The former has often felt a more comfortable view, in that it saves John's fundamental historicity, though that feeling may be deceptive. Such is the difference between the Synoptics' and John's portrayals of Jesus that it implies that no Gospel gives us a fair account of Jesus' actual self-understanding and teaching. It has been suggested, for instance, that six times, not just three, Peter denied knowing Jesus. The suggestion makes it possible to hypothesize that each Evangelist mentioned three of these denials and to fit all the details into a composite picture derived from the four Gospels.[3] But the implication of the theory is that none of the Gospels can be relied on when it portrays Peter as denying Jesus *three* times. In parallel with that difficulty, the suggestion that both the Synoptics and John are reliable in the words they attribute to Jesus implies that none of them is reliable in its general account of him.

Conservative readers have often been concerned about the suggestion that scripture offers anything other than factual history, though they themselves find it difficult totally to evade this characteristic of scripture. Thus R. K. Harrison takes some of the statistics in Numbers and Chronicles as having symbolic significance. What we know from other sources indicates, for instance, that two million people could not have been involved in the exodus, so the narrative must be interpreted symbolically.[4] A thoroughly

2. See further Bornkamm in *Tradition and Interpretation in Matthew* 52-57.
3. So Lindsell, *The Battle for the Bible* 174-76.
4. See Harrison, *Introduction to the OT* 633, 1163-65.

literalist approach to narrative material is qualified because there seems to be no alternative. The principle of such interpretation seems to be "take the text as a description of literal history except where you are compelled to do otherwise and where the traditional view simply cannot be maintained."[5] A more principled principle is required.

Witness and Tradition: Fact and Interpretation

Phenomena of biblical narrative such as those we have just noted are positive features of its nature as a witnessing tradition.

Witness is a personal matter, and witnesses usually vary in their accounts of an event. They may all bear true testimony but they do not bear identical testimony; they will have noticed some things and missed others because of their varying vantage points or perspectives. They will interpret what happened differently and thus include different elements in their account of an event. An inquiry that seeks to gain as rich an understanding as possible of an event will be glad if it can listen to the testimony of a number of witnesses and will be concerned to take account of all of them. Philosophers have long argued over the relation between facts and interpretation. It seems safe to assume that there are no such things as bare facts, only interpreted facts, but also that that does not mean that there are no such things as real facts, though they are known to us only in the context of some form of interpretation.

We might have expected the Bible to include one authoritative account of the Christ event; if the fact that it contains four were not so familiar, it might surprise us. Four witnesses are better than one, not merely because they may give more grounds for certainty about the factuality of events, but also because they offer more resources for understanding the significance of events.

Perhaps this connects with the further surprising fact about the Gospels as witness, that they are for the most part not directly eyewitness testimony. They do not claim to be, the early church did not think that they were, nor were they accepted into a Christian canon under the misapprehension that they were. Their testimony to events was able to reflect a generation's ongoing experience of Christ and preaching of the gospel;[6] whatever eye-

---

5. Cf Barr's comments in *Fundamentalism* 40-55.
6. Nineham, *Explorations in Theology* 1:58-59.

witness testimony underlies them, they offer mature, and sometimes polemical, interpretation of the events they relate.[7] In the narrow sense, this characteristic of the Gospels is peculiar to them, but it is also only a specific instance of a more general point, that narrative is frequently written in the light of the fact that the full significance of events only emerges as time unfolds and may be largely hidden from the people involved in the events.[8]

It is an exaggeration to infer that we understand "foundational events" to be such only in the light of their subsequent "historical effect."[9] If there is anything to the *story* of the exodus or the Christ event, something of its epoch-making significance surely pressed itself on people from the beginning. It was not that an ordinary event (or even an unusual one) happened, only to be interpreted later as an act of God. The event itself was experienced as a miracle. "The historical reality of Israel leaving Egypt cannot be grasped if the conception of the accompanying, preceding, guiding God is left out. . . . What happened was experienced, while it happened, as the act of God."[10]

It is the case, however, that an event's fuller significance emerges and proves itself over time. The significance of the exodus is in due course seen in the entry into the land, so that the story of the exodus comes to shape the way people tell the story of Israel's entering the land, and Israel's experience in the land also comes to influence how they tell the story of the exodus.[11] Looking behind the biblical narrative for its earliest testimony to events is important as we seek to establish exactly what these events *were*, but the implication is not that we discard the interpretation of the events that the narrative itself offers. It is this developing and developed interpretation that gives us our insights on what the events *meant*.[12] In an unending process later events such as the exile, the Christ event, and contemporary experience bring out the significance of a foundational event such as the exodus.[13] Nevertheless the instinct to freeze some versions of earlier witness to such events appropriately corresponds to our having an interest in fact (and proximity to the event is of value in a witness to fact)

7. Cullmann, *The Early Church* 39-54.
8. See Ricoeur, "The Hermeneutical Function of Distanciation."
9. As Croatto implies in *Exodus* 1.
10. Buber, *Moses* 76, 77; cf. Brueggemann, *Abiding Astonishment* 32.
11. Croatto, *Biblical Hermeneutics* 37-39.
12. Cf. Koch, *The Growth of the Biblical Tradition* 56.
13. Croatto, *Biblical Hermeneutics* 39.

as well as in interpretation (which benefits more from distance) and to the fact that the earlier stages of this process of interpretation are themselves part of the foundational events.

The notion of tradition parallels that of witness in also suggesting writings that attempt more than bare chronicle. The gospel tradition that Paul first received and then handed on concerned the fact that "Christ died."[14] That deceptively "bare statement" is already an interpreted fact. Talking about the importance of *Jesus'* death rather than those of other crucified Jews such as the two thieves presupposes an interpretation of the importance of that particular death, and calling the crucified man *Christ* points clearly toward an aspect of the specific interpretation presupposed. Indeed, as we noted in chapter 3, to suggest that *Christ* (of all people) *died* is to make a quite extraordinary statement in itself. Further, in his summary of the tradition Paul goes on more overtly to declare that it concerns not a mere event ("Christ died") but the purpose of that event ("for our sins"). The Easter proclamation does not come to us as a fusion of uncontentious historical fact and debatable theological evaluation, as theologians have often implied. The facts themselves are contentious, not least because if they are facts at all they are theologically freighted.[15]

By its nature, furthermore, tradition tends to be changing rather than static. Passing things on does not leave them unchanged — this not merely by default but by the positive dynamics built into the process. They are transmitted to other people and are adapted to bring out their significance for the people to whom they are given. It is widely assumed, for instance, that several versions of the exodus story are brought together within the Pentateuch. Formally these parallel the four Gospels, though there is an important difference: To some extent the Gospels offer independent witness to the historical events they relate, but there is little suggestion that the different sources of the Pentateuch do that. Rather they are successive *retellings* of the exodus events. The significance of the events is brought out in different ways as people who pass on the tradition apply it to different audiences in the light of the demands, questions, and needs that new situations bring to these audiences. In due course several understandings of what actually took place are interwoven, with the result not that we are

---

14. For the point that follows see Caird, *The Language and Imagery of the Bible* 211; I think I owe my original awareness of it to Caird's lectures on New Testament theology, which I heard as an undergraduate. On the relationship between tradition and interpretation in the Second Testament see Funk, *Parables and Presence* 159-64.

15. Cf. Carnley, *The Structure of Resurrection Belief* 31-32.

confronted by a misleading amalgam of true and untrue information, but that we are enriched through the combination of several portraits or imaginative reconstructions (or cartoons) of events.

The retelling of the story of pre-exilic Israel in 1 and 2 Chronicles provides a less hypothetical illustration of the process whereby an interest in real people and events from the past is combined with a concern for a presentation of them that makes explicit their significance for a later community's day. It is that interest that explains the substantial difference between Samuel-Kings' and Chronicles' presentation of the same story. The successive retellings of events were concerned with real history, but they select, order, and rewrite their material to make the message of history clear for their contemporaries.

The notions of witness and tradition thus draw attention to the humanity and historicality of the biblical writings, not as proclivity to deceive or to make mistakes but as writings by and for people with specific characteristics and concerns who belong in and speak to particular contexts. The witnessing of scripture parallels as well as generates the witnessing through which God does the miracle of bringing someone to faith in Christ. Both involve the use of ordinary words of human testimony; the "miracle of Scripture" is a miracle "of the human witness empowered by the Spirit" interpreting in specific ways the significance of Christ for the particular circumstances of their times.[16]

The biblical writings are exercises in interpretation before they are objects of interpretation. To put the point in another way, and a less individualistic one, the Israelite community as a whole keeps alive the memory of its exodus from Egypt long ago, but precisely in keeping it *alive* (life being dynamic and changing) also allows the memory of the event continually to reshape the story of the event, so that its significance for new stages in Israel's life can be apparent in its retelling. The community wants to provide not merely a window on the past but also a lens that allows some matters to come into focus and others to be ignored, and a mirror in which each generation sees itself. "Biblical traditions therefore remember the past for the sake of the present and the future."[17] They are concerned overtly with what Israel has been, but covertly with what Israel is, will be, and should be, with what could happen, not just with what has happened.

16. Berkouwer, *Holy Scripture* 167.
17. Achtemeier, *The Inspiration of Scripture* 125.

Even narratives such as ones in 2 Kings that are thoroughly historical and come nearest to straight historiography do not confine themselves to mere archive or chronicle. They, too, relate more than historical fact. They play a part in a nightmare review of Israel's relationship with God and thus acknowledge the justice of God's judgment.[18] They are thus designed to draw Israel into an act of confession and thereby to open up the merest possibility of their having a future with God once again. The truth of the story involves more than mere historical factuality. This is even more the case with the Bible's stories about Beginning and End. While making a claim about linear history, they also function like myths: Because they portray a time when things are as they should be, they "provide a paradigmatic or exemplary symbolic complex that is so raised above ordinary experience that it provides a norm and a shape for it."[19]

Biblical narrative throughout seems to combine factual, historical material and interpretative or traditional material in proportions that vary. The ratio of factual/historical to interpretative/traditional increases the nearer one reaches the writers' own day, because being close to the events gives writers more access to facts but less access to their long-term significance. One can illustrate this conveniently from Genesis through Kings as a whole. The factual is at its minimum in the opening chapters of Genesis. It is present, in that these chapters are the beginning of a narrative work that is as a whole concerned with historical events, and it is unlikely that at any point such a work lacked any historical interest at all; in some sense Genesis 1–2 refers to the chronological Beginning of history. But the proportion of "story" (Alter lists myth, lore, etiology, archetype, folktale, and fictional invention[20]) as opposed to "history" in Genesis through Kings is at its highest at the opening of the work. It is at its lowest at the end, where the events in focus had taken place not long before the work's writing. The story of Israel's exodus and their occupation of the land lies somewhere in between. Broadly, as the work unfolds the amount of interpretation thus increases and the amount of fact increases. Put diagrammatically:

18. So von Rad, e.g., *Old Testament Theology* 1:342-43.
19. Beardslee, "Narrative Form in the New Testament and Process Theology" 305.
20. *The Art of Biblical Narrative* 33.

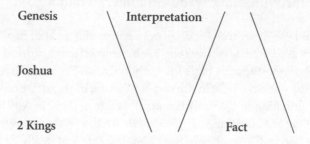

Genesis   Interpretation

Joshua

2 Kings   Fact

Much biblical story

> has a different effectiveness from that of historical writing, bridging the gap between the present and the past, and showing that what appears as past events contains a hidden relevance to the present. The narrator and his hearers identify themselves with the deeds and sufferings of their forebears. God's intervention in favour of their forebears is intervention in favour of themselves. . . . The later narrators' experiences of God and the world affect the stories of earlier periods.[21]

Far more sermons are preached and far more theology is based on narrative with a high interpretation content than on narrative that is pure history. Facts are an important basis for faith, but on their own they are not very articulate regarding the nature of the faith. It is not the demystified, rationalized account of Israel's history that has a life-giving and revolutionary effect in Israel's life and in the life of later communities, but the exodus *story*.[22] James Barr observes that the story of Jesus' birth "has its main effect" on people "before the question of historical events or external realities is answered"; further, "even when this latter question has been answered, it has not added to the effectiveness of the story." He notes that in liturgical and devotional usage of the Bible, too, its historical reference may not be close to the surface; "the more one hears of the exodus of Israel from Egypt as part of the liturgy for the baptism of infants in water, the less one is concerned to ask whether any Israelites ever came out of Egypt and, if they did, how they got out."[23]

21. Koch, *The Growth of the Biblical Tradition* 156. Koch describes such narrative as *Sage:* see chapter 3 above. The English translation "saga" is misleading.
22. Brueggemann, *Abiding Astonishment* 60.
23. *The Bible in the Modern World* 57-58, 59.

The Theological Nature
of the Witnessing Tradition's Interpretation

There is a more explicitly theological component to this second aspect to scripture's nature as a witnessing tradition. We have noted that historical facts are a necessary but not sufficient basis for faith in Christ. Faith in Christ is a response to the story about Christ in the respects in which it is not susceptible to historical confirmation or disconfirmation as well as in those in which it is so susceptible. What actually brings people to faith in Christ is the message that "Christ died for our sins" — not bare facts about his life and death, or even about his being restored to life, but a reading of those facts in the context of a broader perspective on the reality, purpose, and hand of God at work in the world. The Hebrew Bible, too, tells its story in this way, omitting the apparently more purely factual royal annals in favor of documents such as Kings that are less straightforwardly factual but have a theological vision.[24] The latter's account of King Omri provides a vivid illustration. By normal standards of historical importance he was one of Israel's greatest kings, but the biblical narrative is uninterested in such criteria and famously dismisses his reign in six verses (1 Kgs 16:23-28). Conversely the question of truth regarding the Israelites' crossing of the Red Sea is not merely whether the parting of the seas really happened but whether the scriptural narrative of this event "adequately renders to the imagination God's act in saving the people of Israel."[25]

The Gospels' reading of the facts about Jesus has its starting point in his resurrection even when they are telling the story of his life and death. They seek to transmit not a knowledge of Christ "according to the flesh" (2 Cor 5:16) but a knowledge of him as one on whom the Holy Spirit's verdict has been passed in bringing him to the life of the age to come. Even their earlier parts are thought out in the light of this sequel, and the story of the crucified one is told as the story of one they know as risen.[26] "The gospels certainly recount the life-history of 'Jesus of Galilee.' . . . But they tell the story of his life in the light of his resurrection" in the conviction that "the raising did not merely happen *synchronically* to the dead Jesus; it also happened *diachronically* to the whole Jesus in all the moments and aspects of his life and proclamation . . . from birth onwards."[27]

---

24. As Alter notes in *The Art of Biblical Narrative* 35.
25. Green, *Imagining God* 139.
26. Barth, *Church Dogmatics* IV/1:320; IV/2:132.
27. Moltmann, *The Way of Jesus Christ* 75, 76.

The Second Testament tells of other miracle workers than Jesus, other crucified criminals, and other people restored to life, but sees the facts about Jesus as having a significance that does not attach to those others. Indeed, the resurrected Christ is not only the true subject of the Gospel story. He is also in a sense the teller of the tale. "He speaks for Himself whenever He is spoken of and His story is told and heard."[28] The living Christ speaking to us of himself, of the living Christ, is what brings people to faith in the living Christ. Indeed, the telling of the biblical story has a more comprehensive horizon. There is a further theological reason for the difference between events and the story told about them. The story is larger than life because it is told in the light of that complete perspective on reality that will only be visible at the End, when we have all the pieces of the puzzle and not just the fragmentary elements available to us now. The story about the past was written in the light of hope for the future. Even someone like Pannenberg who argues historically only does so by placing the evidence for the resurrection in the broader context of faith and dogma.[29] Neat history is not the ground for faith.

All four Gospels in different ways reflect the fact that they were written after Easter and after Pentecost. They were written in the light of the fact that the one who walked and spoke in Galilee and Jerusalem was raised by God to a new form of human life and continues to walk and speak in the midst of his church. This affects the way his earlier story is told — not by neglect or by accident but by design because later events bring out aspects of the true significance of earlier events and thus make possible a more accurate telling of Jesus' earlier walking and speaking. D. L. Bartlett offers an example from the story of the crucifixion in Mark 15. This story would not have its power if it were relating an event that did not happen, if it did not have its place in the context of a long antecedent tradition about God's purpose at work in Israel, or if it had not fictionalized its story by its handling of the response of the centurion and the tearing of the veil, which are suggestive anticipations of the future. The narrative, that is, witnesses to one event by setting it in the context of events that preceded it and events that will follow it.[30] "The presumed equation of the Word of God with a 'historical' record is an inadmissible postulate that does not itself originate in the Bible at all but in the unfortunate habit of Western thought

---

28. Barth, *Church Dogmatics* IV/1:227.
29. See Carnley, *The Structure of Resurrection Belief* 94.
30. *The Shape of Scriptural Authority* 52-59.

that assumes that the reality of a history stands or falls by whether it is "history." "[31] Actually, the fact that the Gospels were written for the post-resurrection church makes it easier for us as members of post-resurrection churches to interpret them.[32]

John the baptizer warns his audience that facts by themselves are not enough; merely having the right history does nothing for us. He urges his hearers not to say to themselves "We have Abraham as our father" (Matt 3:9). Having the right history places us in a position of special privilege, but it requires that we respond to the God who has been active in that history if we are actually to enjoy this privilege. The story is quite capable of turning into a tragedy if we allow it to do so: "The ax is at the root of the trees . . ." (Matt 3:10). That God has been working out a purpose in history is of crucial significance for Christian faith, but it accomplishes nothing until it leads us into personal trust and obedience in relation to God. Scriptural history is related in such a manner as to bring out the way the story applies to its hearers and the demand it makes on them. It is not a matter of mere facts. Here lies another ground for its willingness to forgo mere accuracy in order to be more true.

31. Barth, *Church Dogmatics* III/1:82. "History/historical" in the quotations represents *Historie,* history as that which can be investigated by the historical method; see the discussion in chapter 3 above.
32. Franklin, *How the Critics Can Help* 11-23.

5

Witness in the Form of Story

Tradition can take many forms, but witness characteristically takes the form of narrative. The witnessing tradition thus naturally appears in scripture as narrative or story. Story relates to history but also to fiction, and the overlap between these categories helps us to see further the positive features of the presence in scriptural narrative of fictional as well as historical features. Among them are the way stories work in creating a world before people's eyes and ears and drawing hearers into that world.

History and Story: How Stories Work

So the witnessing tradition incorporates an interpretation of the events to which it testifies. Facts do not speak for themselves; understanding them is itself a hermeneutical enterprise. Any writing of history involves making sense of facts by bringing to them some vision of meaning that is capable of turning them into a story with a beginning, a middle, and an end. Thus even when biblical narrative is fundamentally historical, it is literature, not merely archive or chronicle. Narratives are more than collections of data; they are the fruit of the imagination. The plots and configurations of history-writing are the same as those of literature — or vice versa.[1] They are the means by which we "re-configure our confused, unformed, and at the limit mute temporal experience."[2] On their own, events are unfollow-

---

1. So White; see his *Metahistory*, also "Interpretation in History," "The Historical Text as Literary Object," and Danto's *Analytical Philosophy of History*, e.g., 112-42.
2. Ricoeur, *Time and Narrative* 1:xi.

able; only by faith do we render them intelligible as narrative.[3] Further, biblical narrative is "full of the usual ingredients of literary narrative — adventure, mystery, brave and wise heroes, beautiful and courageous heroines, villains who get their comeuppance, rescues, guests, suspense, romantic love and pageantry," so that "most parts of the Bible resemble the world of imaginative literature . . . more closely than they resemble the daily newspaper or an ordinary history book."[4]

Theological books generally offer their teaching about God and about the relationship between God and humanity in the form of direct statement made as clearly as possible to the mind. A story communicates in a quite different way, less directly than is the case with a straight statement. It leaves the hearers to do more of the work, if they are to learn from it. Perhaps precisely because of that, it may communicate more powerfully than a direct statement will. Everybody responds to stories. Therefore television is dominated by them, and advertising and documentaries characteristically focus their attention on what the product does for a specific family or how government policies affect people on a particular street.

Stories, whether factual or fictional, and biblical stories in particular, create a world before people's eyes and ears.[5] They portray the world in which we live, but "arranged into a meaningful pattern, in contrast to the fragmented pieces that make up our moment-by-moment living." Calling us back to the essential, the enduring, the fundamental, the truly real, a story portrays "both a better world and a worse world than the one we usually live with, and demands that we keep looking steadily at them both."[6]

Biblical stories create a world before our eyes and ears. It is a world in which God promises blessing and shows a readiness to overcome all manner of obstruction, resistance, and delay in order to keep that word. It is one in which God hears the cry of an oppressed and demoralized people, rescues them from their affliction, and draws them into a new relationship of worship and obedience. It is one in which a woman's life falls apart but is remade through the extraordinary loyalty of a foreign girl and the extraordinary love of a kinsman. It is one in which a prophet runs the other way

---

3. Lash, *Theology on the Way to Emmaus* 72-73, comparing Kermode, *The Genesis of Secrecy* 117, 145.

4. Ryken, *Triumphs of the Imagination* 22, 94.

5. On the notion of a life-world, see Husserl, *The Crisis of European Sciences and Transcendental Phenomenonology* 103-89.

6. Ryken, *Triumphs of the Imagination* 85, quoting Frye, *The Educated Imagination* 97.

when God calls him, has to be redirected by means of some foreign sailors and a bizarre monster, succeeds against his will in drawing his audience to repentance, but never quite comes to accept the nature of God even though he understands it quite well. It is one in which an extraordinary Galilean teacher and healer loses his life but regains it and promises to be with his followers always. It is one in which Palestinian artisans and Greek intellectuals begin to turn the world upside down by preaching about this man.

The world into which these stories invite us both attracts us and makes us hesitate to be drawn into it. It makes us draw near and draw back equally by its realism and by its vision. It is ruthlessly true to the suffering and the sin that run through life and history: deprivation, animosity, fear, anxiety, hunger, guilt, injustice, immorality, loss, frustration, disappointment, grief, failure. That draws us because we want to be able to face these realities, to take account of them, to overcome them. It also makes us draw back lest these realities cannot be comprehended or overcome and lest to face them will thus bring a further pain that we can hardly bear or a cost that will be too high to pay.

Stories can both reassure and challenge, support and confront, reinforce and unsettle; they may offer identity or disturb it. Different stories may work more one way or the other; some that are a true comfort in one context would be false comfort in another (e.g., Chronicles if it had been written in the time of Amos), and some that are rightly disturbing in one context would be in another a kick to someone who is already down (e.g., Kings in the time of the Chronicler). The best stories hold together comfort and confrontation, as they reflect life itself in interweaving suffering and hope, cross and empty tomb, life in its gritty reality and death in which are the seeds of resurrection.

The Bible portrays a world in which the realities of sin and suffering can be faced, comprehended, and overcome, because active in it is also a God who blesses, who intervenes, whose providence works behind scenes, who refuses to give up when we insist on doing so, who in Christ walks earthly soil and in the Spirit walks in the midst of the people of God. God meets with us in the midst of these very realities. The Bible's story invites us to believe that what God did for other people might also be true for us. African American slave songs, for instance, had that as the basis of the hope they set before people.[7] The story's portrait draws us, because we would like to live in such a world. It also makes us draw back, because we wonder whether that world actually exists.

If we are to live in that world, we have to be drawn into it as a child is

---

7. Witvliet, *The Way of the Black Messiah* 77-78.

drawn into a story, with its characteristically open-ended, imaginative, and experiential nature inviting a response without appeal to other forms of "proof."[8] Indeed, a full understanding of a story depends upon allowing oneself to be drawn into it, entering the common world of each participant, their individual worlds, and the world of God embodied in the story. The Gospel story is designed to make something happen to people when they are drawn into its everyday but extraordinary world. It addresses not merely the intellect but the whole being, in the power of that reality that it portrays and that created it. It grasps us and draws us into face-to-face involvement with the God of Israel and with Jesus the Messiah active in our world, and changes us as we come to link our story onto the one related in the Gospel narrative. A "language-event" takes place.[9] The story has the power to draw us into it almost against our will.

Two famous tales concerning Israel ben Eliezer, the Baal Shem Tov, founder of Hasidism, illustrate the point. According to one, a disciple of his who was disabled was asked to tell a story about his teacher. He related how the Baal Shem used to hop and dance when he prayed. He rose as he spoke, and was so swept away by his story that he himself began to hop and dance to show how the master had done so. From that moment he was cured of his disability. "That's the way to tell a story!"[10]

The other tale relates that

> when the Baal Shem had a difficult task before him, he would go to a certain place in the woods, light a fire and meditate in prayer — and what he had set out to perform was done. When a generation later the "Maggid" of Meseritz was faced with the same task he would go to the same place in the woods and say: We can no longer light the fire, but we can still speak the prayers — and what he wanted done became reality. Again a generation later Rabbi Moshe Leib of Sassov had to perform this task. And he too went into the woods and said: We can no longer light a fire, nor do we know the secret meditations belonging to the prayer, but we do know the place in the woods to which it all belongs — and that must be sufficient; and sufficient it was. But when another generation had passed and Rabbi Israel of Rishin was called upon to perform the task, he sat down on his golden chair in his castle and said: We cannot light the fire, we cannot

---

8. Brueggemann, *The Creative Word* 23-27.

9. So Fuchs, e.g., *Studies of the Historical Jesus* 191-228. Cf. Thiselton, "The Parables as Language-Event"; Funk, *Language, Hermeneutic, and Word of God* 20-71.

10. See Buber, *Tales of the Hasidim: The Early Masters* v-vi.

speak the prayers, we do not know the place, but we can tell the story of how it was done. And, the story-teller adds, . . . the story which he told had the same effect as the actions of the other three.[11]

Stories are designed to work, to do something. They are "speech-acts,"[12] not just statements with propositional content but utterances with "illocutionary force," intended to effect something. They are not pure literature (but then neither is literature!). The narratives in scripture speak in the past tense and refer to things that actually happened in the past, but they covertly relate to the future. By portraying a past or imaginary or other world they issue a promise, a challenge, or an invitation that opens up a future or a possible world.[13] They portray a world that should be, once was, and therefore can be again. What they relate remains unfinished insofar as "these stories span our lives and wait our answer."[14] They invite people to live in their world as the real world, even if it contrasts with the world of their hearers' current experience. They invite us to make their story our story. Biblical interpretation involves not the attempt to translate scripture into our categories but the redescription of our experience in the light of the scriptural story.[15]

This way of expressing the matter goes back to Hans Frei's book *The Eclipse of Biblical Narrative*, which has played an important role in the development of interest in the Bible as story. Frei argued that we are the heirs or victims of a change in ways of reading scripture that began to come about in the eighteenth century. Before then, as the writings of the Fathers and the Reformers reveal, people assumed that the narrative they were reading corresponded to events that we would have been able to witness if we had been present and that the history that we ourselves are living is one with that history. Beginning two hundred years ago, however, scholars began to look for the *actual* events behind the narrated events, saw our world as essentially discontinuous with that world, and began to judge the narrative's presentation of its world by ours rather than the other way round. Frei's study pointed interpreters once more toward the actual text

11. Scholem, *Major Trends in Jewish Mysticism* 349-50.

12. For introduction, see White (ed.), *Speech Act Theory and Biblical Criticism* (esp. the article on Gen 2–3 by Lanser); also Thiselton and Walhout in *The Responsibility of Hermeneutics.*

13. Barr, *The Scope and Authority of the Bible* 36, 126-27; cf. Beardslee, *Literary Criticism of the New Testament* 21.

14. Wilder, *Early Christian Rhetoric* 68.

15. Bartlett, *The Shape of Scriptural Authority* 118.

of scripture, the story Israel told, as the proper subject for interpretation, rather than the events that lay behind the story being that subject for interpretation. It is the story that is life-giving. "A report about ourselves is included in that report about God"; it relates an "inclusive" history.[16] Thus "the question of a hermeneutical gap between the Gospels and today is a technical or methodological issue that is solved theologically."[17]

The Bible came into existence because people wanted others to share its world. Books such as the Prophets and the Epistles make quite explicit their practical aim: to draw people to faith and obedience. The narrative texts of scripture may presuppose the same beliefs and seek the same commitment as those other books, even though they do not normally make this overt. They achieve their aim by more subversive means. They flesh out the explicit information and challenge of Prophets and Epistles, which might be unintelligible without the stories that they presuppose.[18] Occasionally they actually express their didactic point, but in contrast with the Prophets and the Epistles, they generally avoid doing so too explicitly (a passage such as John 20:31 that does so is exceptional). A story whose didactic is too overt may become contrived and may thus cease to work as story. It has to work indirectly or subliminally if it is to work at all.

With direct instruction such as that in Paul's letters, form and content are distinguishable. The contents of the doctrinal or behavioral teaching can be summarized, commented on, or reexpressed without necessarily losing anything. The ideas expressed in the words are what counts. A story, however, cannot be summarized or turned into an abstract statement without losing something. The content comes through the story form and only through this form. The medium *is* the message. "A literary work *is* its own meaning, and its meaning cannot be univocally abstracted from it."[19] Admittedly, "narrative . . . is *translatable* without fundamental damage" in a way that poetry, for instance, is not; stories cross cultural boundaries easier than many other forms.[20] But a story cannot be turned into straight

16. Barth, *Church Dogmatics* IV/1:7, 16.

17. Ford, *Barth and God's Story* 34. Note that the two gaps referred to here are those that constitute "the crisis of the scripture principle" of which Pannenberg writes (*Basic Questions in Theology* 1:1-14).

18. So Tracy, "Metaphor and Religion" 102; cf. Ebeling, *Theology and Proclamation* 174.

19. R. M. Frye, *Perspective on Man* (Philadelphia: Westminster, 1961) 43, as quoted by Barr, *The Bible in the Modern World* 70.

20. So R. Barthes. See White, "The Value of Narrativity" 5-6.

didactic. The crucifixion story does things to the hearer that an exposition of the doctrine of the atonement does not. The doctrine of the atonement can help me appreciate the story of the crucifixion more fully, but it does not replace the story, that is, the gospel. The legitimacy of the doctrine of the Trinity "rests on its claim to articulate the implicit grammar of scripture," but it is the "crude" scriptural narrative itself, not developed theological precision, that captures the religious imagination of believers.[21]

The Place of "Fiction" in a Historical Story

We implied in chapter 4 that the story nature of the biblical witness involves more than merely the turning of pure fact into emplotted narrative. Not everything in biblical stories is factual. They are augmented in the light of the events to which they led and of the situation of their expected hearers, with the aid of the storytellers' imagination and experiences.

In everyday life we recognize how a story that is not historical in the literal sense can make a genuinely historical point. The film *Chariots of Fire* includes a scene where Harold Abrahams wins a race round a particular Cambridge quadrangle. The scene is fictional: There was no such race. But it is a reliable, though legendary, portrayal of the significance of the man. As fact can be used to convey untruth, fiction can be the best way to represent historical truth about the past.[22]

It may, in fact, be the only way. It is difficult to convey a vivid character by means acceptable to historians. David Ford, speaking of Solzhenitsyn, suggests that *fictional* method may be the only way to a *historical* presentation, a way of pointing to the actual identity of a person.[23] The general ancient approach to the portrayal of character is very different from the modern one. It has less concern with chronological precision, historical background, personal appearance, and the development of character than we are used to in biographical and quasi-biographical works; it suggests people's attitudes by

21. Green, *Imagining God* 68.
22. Cf. Green, *Scriptural Authority and Narrative Interpretation* 79-96; cf. *Imagining God;* Oeming, "Bedeutung und Funktionen von 'Fiktionen' "; Hunsinger, "Beyond Literalism and Expressivism."
23. *Barth and God's Story* 68-69. Lundin (*The Responsibility of Hermeneutics* 60) notes how Faulkner's novels made a historical statement about the burden of guilt hanging over the southern United States because of the facts of slavery and segregation. Cf. Lowenthal, *The Past Is a Foreign Country* 224-31 on the historical nature of fiction.

the words and actions it attributes to them more than by the feelings it attributes to them.[24] Thus if there is "unhistorical" detail in the Gospels' portrait of Jesus, this does not mean that we cannot press the detail in order to learn from it in devotional and other ways; it can still be true.[25]

In scripture this is so with Jesus and other figures in the Gospels, though the story of Abraham's offering of Isaac in Genesis 22 also offers an instructive example. We are told nothing of anyone's feelings as this horrific narrative unfolds, but hints of their feelings are suggested by words and actions: the pathos of the word order in God's description of Isaac (v. 2), indicating that God knows the horror of what Abraham is being asked; Abraham's getting up early in the morning to do what he has to do, indicating his commitment to it, yet his leaving the hewing of the wood till last, perhaps suggesting his reluctance to do it;[26] and the extraordinary, yet not unambiguous, words he utters to the servants and to Isaac. As the divine aide declares, it is the deeds that reveal the man (v. 12).

Scripture's realistic but not wholly factual presentation of character is its way of portraying the real, historical person. Among biblical stories often reckoned to be based on a good range of firm historical facts, David's story provides an example. Even this is "not, strictly speaking, historiography, but rather the imaginative reenactment of history by a gifted writer who organizes his materials along certain thematic biases and according to his own remarkable intuition of the psychology of the characters" — devising their interior monologue and private dialogue and thus authoritatively declaring what were their inner personal feelings, intentions, and motives.[27] If a biblical narrator "does not do it as one who knows, he does it as one who dreams. If his eye fails, his imagination steps in and fills the gaps."[28] We are not "to read all Scripture narratives as if they were eye-witness reports in a modern newspaper, and to ignore the poetic and imaginative form in which they are sometimes couched."[29] Dale Patrick[30] finds the Hebrew Bible's fictional-but-true approach to narrative presentation also shaping

24. So Stanton, *Jesus of Nazareth in New Testament Preaching* 117-36.
25. Here the Nineham of *Explorations in Theology* 1:90-91 seems more reliable than the one of 1:51-52!
26. So G. J. Wenham, *Genesis 16-50* (Dallas/Milton Keynes: Word, forthcoming).
27. Alter, *The Art of Biblical Narrative* 35.
28. Schlatter, *Die christliche Dogma* 411 (²377), as quoted by Barth, *Church Dogmatics* III/1:83.
29. Packer, *"Fundamentalism" and the Word of God* 104.
30. *The Rendering of God in the Old Testament.*

its portrayal of God. It envisages God as a character taking a part in the scriptural drama and presents so compellingly the reality of that God and of the events in which God is involved that we are irresistibly drawn into believing in them. It is precisely the serious theological concern of scripture that makes it find that midrash, legend, and saga serve its purpose alongside the more prosaic form of historiography.[31]

We have noted that there are passages in the Hebrew Bible that seem to offer straightforward historical accounts of events on the basis of eye-witness testimony. The story of the fall of Jerusalem in the closing chapter of 2 Kings, richer in its detailed account of events than in theological interpretation of them, thus contrasts with the narratives in Daniel, which begin with the same events. These are stories that are carefully plotted and offer coherent theological interpretations of the events. Here, as elsewhere in Kings itself, a historical framework is filled out with legendary material that helps to bring out the *historical* significance of Israel's story.

Many Second Testament scholars believe that this is the purpose of the Gospel stories of Jesus' conception by a virgin and his bodily resurrection. Such scholars do not necessarily imply that incarnation is a hyperbole imposed on Jesus and resurrection a metaphor for a change that took place within the disciples. In Jesus God truly became human and after his death he was truly restored to life. Talk in terms of conception by a virgin and empty tomb offers vivid pictures of those truths. Thus W. Marxsen, for instance, describes the hypothetical process whereby Christians first saw Jesus alive, then reflected that he must have been brought back from the dead and could be represented as resurrected, then inferred that his grave must therefore have been empty and also began to tell stories along those lines.[32]

In my view the stories are closer to historical factuality than that, and there seems to be something incoherent about the view that Jesus came back to life while his body remained dead in the tomb.[33] But this is not to imply that in principle scripture cannot contain stories that are "fictional" yet true in the sense that they give us accurate insight into the actual Jesus. Hans Frei described the gospel narrative as "at once intensely serious and historical in intent and fictional in form,"[34] and in principle it could be an open question how far the Gospels count as midrashim, as fictions that

31. Against Pinnock, *A Defense of Biblical Infallibility* 28.
32. *The New Testament as the Church's Book* 110-28.
33. But see Carnley, *The Structure of Resurrection Belief* 53.
34. *The Identity of Jesus Christ* 145.

give imaginative concrete expression to truths such as Jesus' incarnation and resurrection. Whether individual narratives are of this kind would need to be decided by examining them individually.

In his study of the birth narratives R. E. Brown concluded that they included some midrashic elements, including the story of the wise men, though not that of the virgin birth itself.[35] Dennis Nineham notes that even the more conservative critical scholars doubt whether Matthew 1:1-17 contains entirely factual genealogical information on Jesus' family background; it, too, is midrashic.[36] Yet such scholars also note that this does not mean that these narratives are not designed to provide what is in their own terms a true historical account of the significance of Jesus: "Given that Jesus was in fact the Davidic saviour, then this is how things must have fallen out in the past."[37] As Nineham notes, if Matthew begins that way, it may later include other stories in which history is imagined in the light of theological conviction.[38] But this is not to imply that much of Matthew's Gospel might well therefore be fiction.

It is most obviously true that the opening chapters of the Bible should not be regarded as history in the sense we normally give to that word. Genesis 1 and 2 offer two story accounts of creation that cannot be naturally harmonized as if both had direct historical reference. Yet both accounts tell a true story about creation, and they need to be read in their own right for the information they give us on God's creative work. Something parallel might be said about the accounts of Judas's death in Matthew and Acts. Attempts to harmonize these two stories seem forced; designating one as more historical, the other as midrashic, may correctly explain something of their background, but it does not resolve questions of their interpretation. Barth asks instead what each signifies as a story and contributes to the wider story of Judas in the Second Testament. He also notes that they agree on "the utter absence of any future ascribed to Judas himself" and that both stories enrich our understanding of Judas and of the Israel he represents because of their different scriptural resonances.[39]

It should not surprise us if biblical narrative "spirals back and forward

35. See *The Birth of the Messiah* 188-96.
36. *Explorations in Theology* 1:173-76, comparing Johnson, *The Purpose of the Biblical Genealogies* 254.
37. Nineham, *Explorations in Theology* 1:178.
38. *Explorations in Theology* 1:179.
39. *Church Dogmatics* II/2:465-71, quotation from 467 (cf. Ford, *Barth and God's Story* 88).

across history, sometimes coming closer to it, sometimes going farther away from it."[40] We are familiar with writings that have real but quite varied relationships with historical facts, such as history and biography, historical and biographical novels, docudramas, fiction with a close accurate background in facts (such as spy stories), science fiction, and history on the grand scale (such as Gibbon's *Decline and Fall*).[41] Even autobiography may be "literally true half the time" while "psychologically true the whole of the time."[42] Such characteristics of human writings are hardly in themselves weaknesses, and it is a strange phenomenon that we are troubled when scripture shares them. My own working assumption is thus that nearly all biblical narrative belongs somewhere on the continuum between historiography and imaginative writing, as perhaps does most nonbiblical narrative — including much of what we watch on television — so that we ought to feel more at home with biblical narrative located between the poles of fact and fiction than we often seem to be.

The task of investigating how much historical material scriptural narratives contain has been a focus of their interpretation for two centuries, and the fact that they are designed to function as witness justifies that. But this concern often assumes that material that is judged unhistorical should then be discarded and thus does not take account of fiction's capacity for rendering fact.

The Witness of "Pure" Fiction

Biblical narrative includes some stories that are fictional not in the sense that they offer imaginative nonfactual presentations of historical realities but in the sense that their narrative does not directly refer to historical events at all. The least controversial examples are the parables of Jesus. The story of the man mugged on the way to Jericho or that of the bridesmaids whose oil supply ran out implies no claim about the factual historicity of these events.

The parables thus provide clear scriptural indication that the question whether a story is true cannot be reduced without remainder to the question

40. Barr, *The Scope and Authority of the Bible* 8.
41. S. Sutherland, "History, Truth, and Narrative," *The Bible as Rhetoric* (ed. Warner) 108-12.
42. So the novelist J. G. Ballard regarding his own autobiography, as quoted in *The Sunday Review* 2 in *The Independent* (London), 15 September 1991.

whether it is historically factual. It would not do if the whole Bible were fiction, because it could hardly then be a message about what God has done for us. But some of the Bible does give imaginative expression to the way God deals with people — not to the way people merely imagine that God deals with them, but to the way God actually does deal with them. It may be deeply appropriate, theologically speaking, if God "offers himself to the imagination of his creatures by means of a 'fictional' narrative — that is, one whose truth cannot be independently ascertained. In this way God 'captures the imagination' of the faithful, the only kind of conquest that leaves them free."[43] Fiction shares the implausible but winning weakness of a cross.

In everyday speech fiction commonly belongs in the same semantic field as error, fantasy, and deceit and stands opposed to fact, truth, and reality. But in some specialized forms of speech fact and fiction can be close relatives rather than opposites. "Fiction" can have positive connotations. Aristotle noted that fiction, being not limited to what has been, can describe what could be; legal fictions avoid application of laws where they should not be applied; mathematics and physics deal in fictions such as the atom and negative numbers; and philosophy affirms the value of heuristic fictions.[44] Greek writers drew an ambiguous antithesis between *logos* and *mythos* similar to the one we draw between fact and fiction. In some contexts the distinction gives value to *logos* as truth over against falsehood, as witness that would hold up in court over against tales that would not, but elsewhere the distinction gives a positive evaluation to both *logos* and *mythos* as signifying historical and poetic truth, or even implies the greater value of the latter.[45]

In literature fact and fiction are more closely related than the antithesis implies. We have noted that the reporting of factual events characteristically issues in what we call historical narrative, expressed as a story that can be followed, one with a plot involving human action, thought, intention, and feeling and with a beginning, a middle, and an end. Such a story is a whole that is coherent without being predictable, partly because it is expressive of the historian's vision rather than necessarily required by events themselves.

43. Green, *Imagining God* 147.

44. Oeming, "Bedeutung und Funktionen von 'Fiktionen' " 259-60; see more generally Vaihinger, *The Philosophy of "As If."* For Aristotle's point cf. Scholes and Kellogg, *The Nature of Narrative* 120-21; Frye, *The Secular Scripture* 19; Tracy, "Metaphor and Religion" 100.

45. R. Trigg, " 'Tales Artfully Spun,' " *The Bible as Rhetoric* (ed. Warner) 126-32.

"History is a species of the genus Story."[46] "The *plot* is the structural factor that grounds a certain family resemblance between historical and fictional narratives."[47]

This unity of sense is accompanied by a unity of reference. Fact over against fiction suggests true over against false, real over against imaginary. But history itself requires imaginative reconstruction and the turning of a mere list of facts into a story with a plot in the light of the historian's vision, which makes historiography literary creation as well as representation of reality.[48] The same applies to fiction. It is concerned to redescribe reality, to generate a new reality; it, too, thus refers to a world outside its own bounds and reflects human historical experience. It is based on factual human experience and without this would neither exist nor be intelligible or interesting to us.[49] But precisely by not being limited to the contingent it may capture the essence of the actual human world of action. To reexpress Aristotle's point, "could we not say that by opening us up to the different, history opens us to the possible, while fiction, by opening us up to the unreal, brings us back to the essential?"[50] Fictional worlds "function as models whereby we explore the possibilities of understanding and living in the world."[51]

It may be unlikely that there is any pure fiction in scripture; the human instinct has usually been to base imaginative literature on a factual starting point. Even Jonah existed as the nationalist prophet his book portrays him to be (see 2 Kgs 14:25), and Daniel, Job, and Esther were more likely real people than wholly fictional creations. But those real people become the vehicles for fictional creations that probably go far beyond anything that the people themselves were, and the mere fact that they existed is hardly germane to the interpretation of the stories about them. J. J. Collins has observed in connection with Daniel that "fiction and truth are not mutually exclusive,"[52] though if the stories completely lack historical reference to events in the Second Temple period I am not sure that their hearers in the

46. Gallie, *Philosophy and Historical Understanding* 66; cf. Ricoeur, "The Narrative Function" 182.

47. Ricoeur, "The Narrative Function" 186, emphasis original.

48. So White, e.g., his *Metahistory* (but I think the phrase "imaginative reconstruction" is R. G. Collingwood's).

49. Lundin, *The Responsibility of Hermeneutics* 60.

50. Ricoeur, "The Narrative Function" 191, 198.

51. Lundin, *The Responsibility of Hermeneutics* 59.

52. "Inspiration or Illusion" 36.

second century would have felt that their theological and parenetic point was still compelling or that as pure fictions they could generate the kind of life commitments that they sought. As "metaphor for exilic experience" they attracted people because they were indeed "too good to be true."[53] But I suspect that they needed to be within reach of actual experience, not wholly discontinuous with it. My own working assumption is that the Daniel stories, too, belong somewhere on that continuum between historiography and imaginative writing.

Robert Alter suggests that all the narrative in the Hebrew Bible is in some sense presented as history, with only two exceptions: "Job, which in its very stylization seems manifestly a philosophic fable (hence the rabbinic dictum, 'There was no such creature as Job; he is a parable') and Jonah, which, with its satiric and fantastic exaggerations, looks like a parabolic illustration of the prophetic calling and of God's universality."[54] In form Job is close to being a play, it is nearly all in verse, and it parallels other ancient fictional treatments of its theme. It is an inspired fictional portrayal of a man's life that brings out a number of issues concerning God's ways with us. That it is fiction in no way lessens its capacity to speak the truth about God and humanity. It may even do so more effectively by not being limited to the historical facts of one person's experience.

Danna Nolan Fewell is clear that the stories in Daniel are fiction, while Shemaryahu Talmon declares that they "are obviously intended to be read as historical reports," though fictitious ones![55] Distinguishing between narrative intended to be taken as fact and narrative intended to be taken as fiction may be one of the most difficult critical enterprises. This is so not merely in the sense that it is difficult to tell when an author is trying to be factual but makes a historical mistake, though that may also be the case. There is a deeper difficulty involved in telling whether an author is trying to be factual, and Frank Kermode asks whether it is ever possible to make that distinction.[56] Fiction authors are often concerned to make their fiction as fact-like as possible, not to deceive but to make their stories lifelike; by definition, therefore, the aim is to hinder our telling the difference between the two. When Alter declares that generally Hebrew narrative is presented

53. Nolan Fewell, *Circle of Sovereignty* 84.

54. *The Art of Biblical Narrative* 33.

55. See Nolan Fewell, *Circle of Sovereignty* 12; Talmon, "Daniel," in *The Literary Guide to the Bible* (ed. Alter and Kermode) 344.

56. *The Genesis of Secrecy* 116.

as history, he means only that, with the two exceptions of Job and Jonah, it is history-like, not that it is historiography in the sense that it aims to convey only historical fact. None of it involves "the sense of being bound to documentable facts that characterizes history in its modern acceptation."[57] Paradoxically, it might even seem that "the more realistic and detailed the account, the higher the illusory effect of the text, the more fictive the text, and the closer the approximation of a universal truth."[58] "Whether or not a work is literature is for the readers to decide, whether or not it is fiction is for the author to decide"; what makes it fiction or fact is the stance of the author toward it, the author's intention.[59]

In scripture, the division between fact and fiction may be other than we first assume. Often the accounts of extermination in the past in Joshua and in the future in Revelation are taken as actual and rather repelling descriptions of what has happened or will happen, but they may not be that. Joshua and Judges make it clear that Israel did not actually slaughter the Canaanites as one might infer from some passages in Joshua, and critical and archaeological study points away from Joshua being a straightforwardly historical work. Amos Wilder describes such narratives and visions as imaginative fictional expressions of the human sense of threatening chaos.[60] They are not merely accounts of events but also expressions of or invitations to present faith, hope, and commitment in the context of such threat.

To see narratives in general, and parables in particular, as living portraits of an alternative world thus helps us align them with the future concern of the apocalypses. The apocalypses take the symbolism of revelation and the linear portrayal of narrative and project them onto the future. They arise out of contexts where the implicit promise of past narrative is insufficient, and they portray a future that contrasts with the unhappy present, a world that should be, will be, and perhaps therefore can be.[61] The apocalypses also illustrate how the portrayal of an alternative world may use conventions that are highly "unrealistic," like those of C. S. Lewis's fantasy stories, without implying that the story is remote from reality. It may convey more truth than documents that are completely factual but quite shallow or insignificant.

57. *The Art of Biblical Narrative* 24.
58. Lategan, *Text and Reality* 88.
59. Searle, "The Logical Status of Fictional Discourse" in *Expression and Meaning* 59, 65, 66; cf. Wolterstorff, *Works and Worlds of Art* 231-34; Thiselton, *New Horizons in Hermeneutics* 362-63, 474.
60. *The New Voice* 59.
61. Beardslee, "Narrative Form in the New Testament and Process Theology" 305.

Whether or not scripture contains both fact and error, it contains both fact and fiction. The awareness that this is so is a liberating one. It invites us into the imaginative approaches to interacting with scripture that we would use with other literature of the imagination, and into the possibility of avoiding becoming bogged down in a study of scriptural narrative that makes it as boring as old-fashioned school history.

6

Scripture as a Whole
as Witnessing Tradition

It is scriptural *narrative* that is the witnessing tradition par excellence. But the Torah and the Prophets in their entirety — suggesting in this context the whole First Testament — witness to the righteousness of God manifested in Christ (Rom 3:21). In turn the Second Testament as a whole witnesses to the story begun in the First that comes to its climax in Jesus Christ. Its doctrinal statements and its directives about behavior, in the Epistles and in the Gospels, may be seen as not so much eternal truths or timeless ethical norms as proclamations of Christ himself. "In its entirety and in all its parts it is nothing but this witness of Christ, his life, his death and his resurrection."[1]

Under the category of witness we can thus unite virtually all the Bible's contents.[2] "The witness of our Bible" to Jesus the Christ emerges from every part of the scriptures, First and Second Testament.[3] The model of witness reminds us that the text itself is not what finally matters. What matters is the one that the text points to. Its concern throughout is simply to point to that one. It thereby also reminds us that the first and fundamental concern of scripture as a whole, as witnessing tradition, is to testify to the grace and activity of God rather than, for example, to urge human commitment. The whole of scripture is witness to the gospel. It passes on good news about God.

1. Bonhoeffer, *No Rusty Swords* 317 (Fontana ed., 312).
2. Hanson and Hanson, *The Bible Without Illusions* 123.
3. Kähler, *The So-called Historical Jesus and the Historic, Biblical Christ* 86.

The Authoritative Canon as Witness

Paul thus values the Torah and the Prophets primarily as witness rather than command, and his own letters, even when issuing imperatives, may be seen as more fundamentally reflective witness to Christ than a body of commands. Viewing the command material in the Torah and the Epistles as part of scripture's witnessing tradition enables us to give some account of the fact that the contents of such parts of scripture do not always seem permanently valid or relevant in the way one might expect. This material witnesses to what God was doing in the life of Israel and of the early church as they sought to reshape their lives in the light of God's involvement with them. The Torah and the Epistles record the solutions that early Christian groups reached to the questions facing them, and we understand those solutions in relation to their specific problems as part of their witness. We do not have to assume that these solutions are always universalizable and directly binding on us.[4] They are part of the witnessing tradition.

A parallel point might be made about the Psalms. In principle they are in scripture as a normative resource to shape our prayer and praise. But some (e.g., Ps 137) puzzle us in this connection and it may be that they are there more because they are part of Israel's story than because we are expected to pray the way they pray.

The Inspired Word as Witness

One role the Second Testament attributes to the First Testament in general and to the prophets in particular is that of giving anticipatory witness to Christ and anticipatory confirmation of the apostles' witness (see, e.g., John 5:39; Acts 10:42-43; Heb 2:6). As part of the witnessing tradition, prophecy builds on the story of God's work with Israel and in Christ, in retrospect and in prospect.

The function as witness of prophecy links with the question of the canonical status of the prophetic words that appear in scripture. I will suggest in Part III that the process whereby inspired scripture came into existence was not unique; when God speaks a prophetic word through someone today, the process is similar to that which obtained in the case of a scriptural prophet. Nor did the utterances of the scriptural prophets at

---

4. Houlden, *Connections* 158.

every point reach a higher level or depth than any prophecy outside scripture. The reason for the canonical status of these prophecies is that they are words that God gave in connection with the achieving of that purpose in Israel that came to a climax in Jesus. They witness to the achieving of that purpose by anticipation, as scriptural narrative witnesses to it retrospectively.

The prophets themselves bear witness to events of past, present, and future. Their work takes further existing witness to past events such as the exodus and future expectation regarding events such as the day of Yahweh. Often their calling is to offer a form of negative witness, which may involve denying that certain events took place in the past (famously Amos 5:25) or drawing attention to ambiguous elements in Israel's tradition of its past, such as the telling portrayal of the ancestor from whom they received both their name and their nature as a competitive grasper, ever inclined to resist God (Hos 12:3). More characteristically they deny the popular interpretation put on past events, with their "prophetic 'No' to Israel's traditions."[5] Israel's exodus from Egypt and conquest of Palestine indeed happened, but in themselves they give no grounds for confidence about a relationship with Yahweh in the present and have no more special significance than the movements of other Middle Eastern peoples (Amos 2:9-11; 3:2; 9:7). Jehu's revolution indeed took place, but it was an unholy bloodbath (Hos 1:4). Israel's history as a whole is the history of a vine that has failed to fruit (Isa 5:1-7), of a people given to idolatry and disobedience (Ezek 20), of a whore (Ezek 16; 23).

The prophets' word also speaks about the future, announcing Yahweh's imminent act and putting Yahweh's purpose into effect. There words precede events rather than merely following them.[6] Indeed, the prophets effect a more radical denial of standard interpretations of Israel's past history by removing the focus of any witness from events in the past to events in the future. The exodus from Egypt happened, but it will be reversed (Hos 8:13). Gerhard von Rad prefaces his treatment of the prophets with the command in Isaiah 43 to forget what Yahweh *has* done and look to what Yahweh is about to do.[7] The center of gravity in history, as the prophets see it, lies in the future, not in the past. The prophets still pass

5. W. Zimmerli, "Prophetic Proclamation and Reinterpretation," *Tradition and Theology in the Old Testament* (ed. Knight) 69, taking up R. Smend, "Das Nein des Amos," *Evangelische Theologie* 23 (1963) 404-23.
6. Against Croatto, *Exodus* 2.
7. *Old Testament Theology* 2:1.

on a received tradition concerning the acts of God, but the tradition they transmit concerns events still to come.[8] They still witness to events in history and declare the significance of those events, but their witness and the witness that they promise that Israel will offer (Isa 43:8-13; 44:6-8) concern events to come, not events that have already happened. In reaction to a view of the prophets as prognosticators of events in the far future that lack clear relevance for their contemporaries, it has been maintained that the prophets were "forthtellers" of the demand of God in the present rather than "foretellers" of God's future intention. They indeed address the people of God where they are, but they speak to them about the future because of its relevance to where they are now, in particular about the immediate future that hangs over them.

Like witnesses in court, the prophets are concerned with proving something, namely, that Yahweh is God, but the evidence to which they point lies in what people are about to see, not in what can have already been seen. These events may be discomforting (e.g., Ezek 7:4, 27) or comforting (e.g., Ezek 37:6, 13), but either way they belong to the future, not to the past, and contradict the view of the future that Israel itself holds. It was not that the tradition Israel inherited lacked witness to the future. On the basis of the witness it gave to victories won and blessings bestowed by Yahweh in the past, it spoke of a coming day when such past victories and blessings would become complete. But here, too, the prophets declare their "No," testifying to the nature of that victory as won *over* the people of God rather than *for* them (Amos 5:18-20), over Jerusalem rather than for Jerusalem. The real Abrahamic increase, exodus from the house of bondage, making of a lasting covenant, occupation of the land, and Davidic triumphs lie in the future, not in the past (e.g., Isa 51:1-3; 52:11-12; 54:1-3; 55:3-5; Jer 31:31-34). Yet those promises reflect something true from the beginning of the prophetic witness, that the prophetic "No" has speaking in dialectic with it Yahweh's "Yes," which is committed to fulfilling a purpose through Israel.

The Experienced Revelation as Witness

Paul's ministry was that of a witness (see, e.g., Acts 20:24; 23:11; cf. 1 John 1:2; 4:14; Rev 1:9). It involved the public portrayal of Christ as crucified

8. W. Zimmerli, "Prophetic Proclamation and Reinterpretation" 72.

(Gal 3:1). Paul's theology regularly takes the form of witness to the past acts of God in cross and resurrection. Much of the theological reflection that the Epistles do is a matter of reflective analysis of the significance of such past events. One of the two central theological enigmas with which Paul wrestles is the question of the status within Christian faith of the body of God's commands incorporated within the Torah. That becomes a problem precisely because Christian faith involves a renewed witness to the acts of God as the primary determinant of faith, though it is also this latter conviction that points the way toward a resolution of the enigma as even the command material becomes part of the story to which faith witnesses.

Paul's spoken testimony evidently included a witness to future events (see 1 Thess 1:10), and so does that of the Epistles. The second of Paul's theological enigmas is the strange fact of Israel's failure to recognize their Messiah. For Paul the Jews' salvation must be certain but it must also be related to Jesus. He can see a purpose in their temporary rejection of Jesus, which leads to the concentration on offering the gospel to other peoples, but he witnesses to a faithfulness of God that will show itself in the future when Israel is grafted back into its own olive tree and finds salvation (Rom 11).

At the end of Romans 11 anticipatory witness gives way to worship. In the Psalms, worship is also a form of testimony. The rejoicing of Israel's hymns is often a rejoicing at God's acts in bringing Israel out of Egypt and in caring for them in their subsequent journey — their literal journey to Canaan and the metaphorical journey they continued to make in their life there (especially Pss 106 and 107). Their worship is thus their witness. It is witness sometimes offered in spite of empirical facts. The Psalms declare that Yahweh is king (e.g., Ps 97) and affirm the ideology attaching to Yahweh's anointed (e.g., Ps 2) despite the paucity of empirical evidence for their declarations. Like Paul's theological reflection in Romans 11, they illustrate how faith is a matter of sure conviction regarding realities that are real but not present, or real but not visible (Heb 11:1).

The cry of Israel's laments derives from the lack of anything in experience to witness to. The tradition of Yahweh's great deeds was belied by experience. Job and Qohelet (Ecclesiastes) are the end term of this sense of there being no activity of God to witness to. Von Rad locates Qohelet at the very frontier of Yahwism, having strayed so far from the confession of the acts of God.[9] Qohelet's problem is that God has not been acting in such

---

9. *Old Testament Theology* 1:458; *Wisdom in Israel* 315.

a way that the testimony to God's acts that one might long to give can actually be given.

The praise of Israel's thanksgivings responds to God's having acted again. The great acts of God have been reduplicated in some way in a later generation's experience. Similarly Paul complements his exposition of the significance of the cross in Romans with a testimony to Christ's appearing to him, in 1 Corinthians 15 and in Philippians. That witness to which he had been commissioned when the Lord appeared to him was one that would involve testifying to what God had done in his own life as well as to what God had done in the Christ event itself (see Acts 22:15; 26:16). "Primitive Christianity never perceived any fundamental difference between the eye-witness testimonies of the life of Jesus and the encounter with the resur-rected Lord."[10]

There is another sense in which letters such as 1 Corinthians belong within the witnessing tradition. The allusions to events in the lives of the churches that appear in them are indications that these letters are historical in the sense that they are part of the church's story, in which later readers such as we are now invited to join. To do so involves being drawn into them in the way one is drawn into a story, as is suggested by the way narrative approaches to interpretation can be applied to them.[11]

So the experienced revelation of the poetic books and the Epistles is also a witnessing tradition, as is the authoritative canon of the command material and the inspired word of prophecy. But it is not only that, and not all its aspects can be looked at in this way. Often it looks at the present through the lens of the relationship between the world and its creator rather than that of the historical acts of God; as we shall note in considering the experienced revelation in its own right, those historical acts are not the whole of biblical faith. That is the converse of the fact that there is a narrow sense in which the narrative material in scripture represents its witnessing tradition as well as a broader sense in which the whole of scripture can be considered in the light of this model.

10. Ricoeur, "The Hermeneutics of Testimony," *Essays on Biblical Interpretation* 135; cf. Bartlett, *The Shape of Scriptural Authority* 113-30. Compare Barth's emphasis (noted in chapter 4 above) on the Gospels' portrayal of Christ's ministry having being written in the light of the presence of the risen Christ in the church.

11. Cf. Hollenweger, "Intercultural theology" 5-12.

• PART II •

SCRIPTURE AS AUTHORITATIVE CANON

7

Authority in Scripture

The notions of authority and canon have been particularly prominent in discussion of the theological significance of scripture over the past century. In themselves these models apply most naturally to situations in which decisions are being made, instructions being given, or actions being evaluated, and these are the senses they have in scripture itself. It speaks of the authority possessed by Joshua with a view to people obeying him (Num 27:20), by Shebna, but destined to be given to another (Isa 22:21), by Esther and Mordecai in enjoining the observance of Purim (Esth 9:29), and by no one with regard to postponing the day of their death (Eccl 8:8).[1] The Gospels refer to the authority that Jesus exercises, for instance in teaching on human behavior in the Sermon on the Mount (Matt 7:29), in expelling spirits (Mark 1:27), and in forgiving sins (Mark 2:10), and also of the authority possessed by a centurion and by his superiors (Matt 8:9) and by other secular powers (Luke 20:20).[2]

Matthew 7:29 and 8:9 illustrate two different connotations that can attach to "authority":[3] It can denote a quality intrinsic in a person, something that other people acknowledge on the basis of their own recognition of the person and of his or her words, not because they are required to recognize it by some external or institutional constraint. Jesus taught as one who had this kind of authority (Matt 7:29). He said, "Follow me," and people often did.

1. The words are *hôḏ, memshālâ, tōqep,* and *šilṭôn.*
2. The word is *exousia* except in Luke 20:20, where it is *archē.*
3. See S. I. Benn's discussion in the *Encyclopedia of Philosophy* (ed. P. Edwards; New York: Macmillan, 1967) 1:215-16.

Authority can also denote something extrinsic to a person and deriving from his or her office. We bow to what is said on the basis of this form of authority even where we cannot see intrinsic good reason for what is said. In the Church of England it is necessary to seek official permission for changes to the fixed furniture of a church building. If that permission should be withheld, a minister who thinks the decision is unreasonable is expected nevertheless to abide by it rather than flout it, on the basis of acceptance of the institutional authority of the people who made the decision. A Roman centurion compares Jesus' intrinsic authority over illness with the extrinsic authority that the centurion himself possesses: He is "a man under authority" and expects his subordinates to obey him unquestioningly just as he obeys his superiors (Matt 8:9).

The English word "canon" transliterates a Greek word that appears in Galatians 6:16, referring there to the cross as the rule or measure of Christian discipleship. The word was widely used elsewhere during the early Christian period for a standard, exemplar, model, or pattern in art, architecture, or grammar, something to follow or something to measure by.[4] In the Hebrew Bible equivalent terms for rule or measure are used both to determine something prospectively, notably the dimensions and form of the new Jerusalem (Jer 31:39; Ezek 40:3-8; Zech 1:16), and to evaluate it retrospectively, notably the life of the old Jerusalem (2 Kgs 21:13; Isa 28:17).[5] The word "canon" later becomes a standard term to describe ecclesiastical decrees and laws.[6]

"Canon" is not used about scripture within scripture,[7] but what it would suggest when applied to scripture is that scripture both prospectively lays down the nature of Christian discipleship and retrospectively tests whether that is being lived up to. As a canon it is a lamp to the feet and light to the path of the believing community and the individual (Ps 119:105). Terms for authority, too, are not used of scripture within scripture, though clearly scripture does show a concern for authoritatively declaring what God's authority requires of humanity.

---

4. McDonald, *The Formation of the Christian Biblical Canon* 40-42.

5. Ezekiel speaks of a measuring rod (*qāneh*, the term cognate with Greek *kanōn*), the others of a measuring line (*qāw*). Perhaps cf. also the "plummet" of Amos 7:7-8 (*ᵃnāk*), though its meaning is uncertain. On the word "canon," see Metzger, *The Canon of the New Testament* 289-93.

6. See Funk, *Parables and Presence* 151-53.

Worshipping by Scripture and Living by Scripture: Psalm 119

Psalm 119 is the passage within scripture that expresses most systematically a set of attitudes to those words of God that take the form of authoritative canons for behavior — laws, precepts, statutes, decrees, commands, judgments, and the like (see, e.g., vv. 1-8).

The psalm responds to parts of scripture that teach us about priorities and standards. The issuing of instructions regarding behavior is not a feature of scripture with which the modern world is comfortable, and Christians have sometimes felt that Psalm 119 looks suspiciously like legalism.[8] Jewish thinking has found it easier to recognize the nature of God's command as gift. The Bible sees humanity as finding its fullest humanity, in part, in being addressed by God's word of command. And humanity loses its fullest humanity by asserting its freedom from that word. "I am commanded, therefore I am."[9] The proclamation over Israel of the Torah, embodying Yahweh's will, is an act of binding but not an act of bondage; it is the means by which Israel's election is put into effect.[10] By using human words to speak of such divine words, Psalm 119 draws attention to the way the metaphysical gap between God and humanity is crossed from both sides, by the word of command confronting people with God's will and the word of prayer reaching out in response.[11]

In theory and in principle the original foundation of Israel's life with God was the promise by which God had taken hold of the people of Israel and the events in which God had acted with them in fulfillment of that promise. In the Second Temple period, however, they saw little of such acts of God in history. One way in which they responded to that experience was by putting the focus of their faith more on the Torah, in which God had also reached out to them, which they certainly possessed, and which could be the means of their reaching out to the God of the promise and the exodus — without this meaning that covenant-thinking and covenant-

---

7. Tertullian (*Prescription against Heretics* III.1) apparently takes Galatians 6:16 to refer to the "rule of the faith."

8. See Weiser, *The Psalms*, where he gives this longest of the Psalms very short shrift; also Noth's comments in *The Laws in the Pentateuch* 85-107.

9. A. Heschel, *Who Is Man?* (Stanford: Stanford UP, 1965) 97-98, 111-12, as quoted by Brueggemann (*Finally Comes the Poet* 82) with the gloss "I listen, therefore I am."

10. See von Rad, *OT Theology* 1:192-95; 2:390-95.

11. Fishbane, *The Garments of Torah* 53-54.

making ceased.[12] Psalm 119 is perhaps an instance of this response in that context.

While it could be used to express a legalistic attitude, the psalm's presence in scripture implies the conviction that when we have got clear that our foundation is God's reaching out to us, we can then focus on the appropriate response to God that we build on that foundation. Psalm 119 makes this point by relating our obedience not so much to what God long ago did in great acts of redemption such as the exodus, but to acts of grace that we ourselves have experienced and to further acts of grace that we expect in the future. "I recounted my ways and you answered me: Teach me your statutes" (v. 26; cf. vv. 88, 145-146). Being open to God's command is the result of seeing God's grace at work. The psalm assumes no tension between God as the one who blesses and as the one who commands. Indeed, the revelation of God's will is itself a gift of grace and a means of renewal (vv. 10, 29, 93). The psalm presupposes the openness of wisdom to traditional teaching and the openness of the mystic to God's speaking now as well as the openness of the Torah student to the Torah.[13]

Another form of so-called legalism is one that sees a life of obedience as involving a focus on individual unrelated commands. Once we have seen that our life is one whole, however, we can seek to get the detail right. For all its concern for a detailed obedience, Psalm 119 is not in itself legalistic in this sense any more than in the first sense we have considered. Nor is its spirituality concerned with merely outward acts, but also with worship, joy, wonder, and awe (vv. 7, 14, 18, 130). It involves love for God's command (vv. 47-48, 102-4) and leads into freedom, not bondage (v. 45). God's words of command are more desirable than gold or silver (vv. 72, 127) and sweet to the taste, sweeter than honey in the mouth (v. 103). This motif in Psalm 119 is taken up in Jewish spirituality: "Torah-life is joyful. . . . Torah-living is a joyful enterprise."[14] God's commands are not a burden to people: The more commands there are, the more joy! It is not the case that a relationship with the Torah replaces one with God. Rather, people relate to God by relating to the Torah. Terms for attentiveness, trust, homage, intimacy, and belief, which elsewhere express an attitude to God, express in this psalm an attitude to the Torah (see vv. 30, 31, 42, 48, 66).[15]

12. See J. Blenkinsopp, "Sectarian Tendencies," in *Jewish and Christian Self-Definition* (ed. Sanders) 2:20.

13. See Levenson, "The Sources of Torah."

14. Van Buren, *A Theology of the Jewish-Christian Reality* 2:219.

15. Fishbane, *The Garments of Torah* 70-71.

One basis upon which God's word can be loved is the conviction that it reflects how the world is and how God is. God's commands have reasons for them. There is a consistent structure about God's acts and about God's words; they reflect each other. This is the theological implication of the Jewish idea that the Torah is one of the three things by which the world is sustained, or was the instrument by which the world was created (e.g., Mishnah 'Abot 1:2; 3:15). The nature of reality and the declaration of God's will are in harmony. So our obedience can be joyful as well as awed and costly.

Yet God's commands often go against the way the world sees things. What the contemporary world says about justice or environmental issues may overlap with scripture, but this may seem to be less so with what it says about money, work, sexuality, drink, the importance of the nuclear family, or possessions. There is thus a difficulty involved in taking authoritative canons in scripture seriously. A church with a close relationship with society will find it particularly hard to take a different stance from the one accepted in that society. "No theologian before the age of Constantine (and the new-found relation of church and state that it implied) was ever anything but pacifist and anti-abortionist"; the post-Constantinian church changed its stance on both these issues to one that fitted that of the state.[16] It is to be expected that there will be points at which there is a tension between the assumptions of society and those of the church, and it is likely to be difficult to stand by the latter.

There may, therefore, be a personal cost involved in taking God's commands seriously. It may lead to unpopularity, attack, and even physical assault (Ps 119:87). That is no doubt one reason why the believing community is tempted to delude itself regarding the extent to which it is submitting to God's authoritative command and thus to be led astray in self-deception (see vv. 10, 29). It knows the possibility of straying from the right path but commits itself to keeping God's authoritative canons in mind (v. 176).

Worshipping by Scripture and Living by Scripture: The Example of Jesus (Matthew 4:1-11)

Immediately after his baptism Jesus is led off into the desert and offered three suggestions of greater or lesser plausibility that will establish whether

16. Gill, *Prophecy and Praxis* 16, 17.

he will put that same commitment into effect. Could he not satisfy his hunger by turning stones into bread? It is natural enough to use one's gifts to meet one's personal needs, which one must have met if one is to minister to others. Or why should he not throw himself from the top of the temple building, trusting in God to preserve him in a spectacular way? After all, Psalm 91 promises such protection to the one who is in special relationship with God. Or why should Jesus not secure sovereignty and honor in the world by submitting to the devil? That sovereignty and honor were in any case due to him in due course.

Jesus refuses all these possibilities. To each he responds "It is written . . ." and quotes Deuteronomy. Human beings are not dependent for life on mere physical food, but on God's word (8:3), and Jesus must rely on that rather than unilaterally utilizing powers available to him as the Son of God. He is not to test whether God will fulfill promises of protection (6:16) but to trust God to do so when the moment requires it. He is to worship and serve the Lord alone (6:13): It cannot be right to ignore this fundamental principle even to gain the worldwide authority and honor that do ultimately belong to him. "It is written" and that settles it. This formula occurs frequently in Hebrew narrative to indicate or urge compliance with regulations in the Torah, or to regret noncompliance with them (e.g., Josh 8:31; 1 Kings 2:3; 2 Chron 23:18; 30:5; Ezra 3:2, 4; Neh 8:15).

Jesus takes his standards from Deuteronomy 5–11, chapters that describe the basic attitudes God expects of Israel as it keeps its side of the covenant relationship. Jesus presupposes that his life should be shaped by these imperatives expressed in the authoritative canons given to Israel. Perhaps there is an implication that here in the wilderness the one true Israelite takes seriously that set of principles for life given in the wilderness to Israel but never properly observed by them. As a Jew Jesus will have been brought up to know the scriptures and to make them the measuring line by which to live his life. Evidently he has both profound and wide knowledge of the scriptures and insight in handling them that enable him to identify at each point a passage that goes to the root of the questionable attitude to God that the three suggestions involve.

He is also able to discern the difference between use and abuse of scripture. The devil, with his own "it is written," appeals to scripture in the same way as Jesus does, illustrating how mere formal acknowledgment of that authority does not necessarily indicate any substantial acknowledgment of it. Both feminist theology and South African black theology have to take as one of their starting points that the Bible has been used as a tool of oppression by people who claimed to accept its authority but were able to use it in their own favor. A common South African saying relates, "When the white man came to our country he had the Bible and we had the land. The white man said to us, 'Let us pray.' After the prayer, the white man had the land and we had the Bible."[17] The appeal to scripture can be self-serving and demonic.

It is a devastating criticism of people who emphasize the authority of scripture that they constitute a religious tradition that uses the form rather than the reality of biblical authority as a shield for their tradition — just what they attribute to Roman Catholicism — so that for them scripture is the supreme religious symbol but is not actually preached or read.[18] Scripture has an objective givenness over against us, and in theory thus has the capacity to protect us from ourselves. But it can only offer us the *possibility* of escape from the limitations of our present convictions; it cannot stop us from continuing in self-deception if we are set on it. Augustine laments the way people can argue about biblical interpretation, "not because they are godly and have seen in your servant's heart what they say, but rather they are proud and have not considered Moses' meaning but only love their own — not because it is true but because it is their own."[19]

The devil's interpretation of scripture is entirely Christ-centered, but this, too, does not prevent abuse of scripture. Perhaps his interpretation needed to be more God-centered since Jesus responds to him at this point as at every point by quoting a passage that expresses a pivotal feature of our relationship with *God*. We are to submit to God's word, to worship God's name, and to trust in God's promise rather than putting God to the test. Jesus sets the clear, direct demand of a fundamental passage in Deuteronomy against the devil's christological reapplication of another passage to a particular set of circumstances. One guideline for discerning the difference between the use and abuse of scripture, then, is to test possible applications of scripture by direct assertions of scripture elsewhere. The need for a broad knowledge of scripture is underlined by the devil's misuse of it.

It is also noteworthy that the devil was able to produce a relatively plausible misapplication of the text because he took it out of its context. Psalm 91 promises God's protection to the person "who dwells in the shelter

17. West, *Biblical Hermeneutics of Liberation* 35, quoting T. Mofekeng, "Black Christians, the Bible and Liberation," *The Journal of Black Theology* 2 (1988) 34-42 (see 34).

18. J. Barr, *Fundamentalism* 11, 36-38, 107.

19. *Confessions* XII.25; cf. M. Wiles, "The Uses of 'Holy Scripture,' " in *What About the New Testament?* (ed. Hooker and Hickling) 159-60.

of the Most High, who abides in the shadow of the Almighty." In origin it is likely a royal psalm, promising God's protection to the king in particular, and it is thus a passage that would be understood messianically in the Second Temple period. This would give special point to the devil's quotation of it. He is inviting Jesus to prove that what the psalm says about the (coming) king is indeed true about Jesus himself. But here the devil's interpretation goes wrong. The psalm promises God's protection whatever danger or attack comes; it says nothing to encourage the courting of danger or the taking of avoidable risks. The devil is able to abuse his text in applying it to Jesus because he has abused it exegetically, taking particular phrases and promises out of context. His misuse of scripture points toward the fact that acknowledging scripture's authority requires, as well as a knowledge of scripture as a whole, a care in interpretation that is able to handle individual passages in a way that is faithful to their particular assertions.

"The synoptic Jesus lived as a law-abiding Jew."[20] Like other Jews he saw love for God and for one's neighbor as epitomes of the Torah's own two chief concerns, he attended the synagogue, he avoided actual work on the sabbath, he accepted the sacrificial system as a means of atonement and purification, he insisted that religious observances should not substitute for the making of practical amends for wrongdoing, he paid the temple tax, and he sought to settle disputes by aggressive discussion of biblical interpretation (Mark 2:23-28; 10:2-9). His controversial stance on matters such as the sabbath and divorce were within the parameters of first-century Judaism. He was prepared to be independent and creative in his interpretation of scripture, but he did not thrust the scriptures to one side. Rudolf Bultmann declared that "Jesus agreed always with the scribes of his time in accepting without question the *authority of the (Old Testament) Law*."[21] He expected new depths to be discerned in the Torah and built his own teaching on the foundation of the Hebrew Scriptures, assuming that they spoke with God's authority. They were not God's last word ("But I say to you . . ."), but they were God's first word. Jesus "puts himself under the authority of scripture and so under the authority of God."[22]

20. Sanders, *Jewish Law from Jesus to the Mishnah* 90.
21. *Jesus and the Word* 61 (emphasis original); cf. Schweizer's comments, *Jesus* 30.
22. Caird, *The Gospel of St Luke* 81.

The Bible's Approach to Biblical Authority

We have noted that the Bible is familiar enough with the notions of authority and canon, yet strikingly does not apply them directly to scripture itself. This may reflect the fact that the Bible does not tend to stand on its own authority. It does sometimes require certain actions without giving reasons for them, and we have noted that the formula "it is written" is used in this way to denote scripture as the binding command of God. But characteristically scripture provides reasons for the actions it expects. Gabriel Josipovici comments that when he read the Bible he was struck by how unauthoritarian it was. "It seemed much quirkier, funnier, quieter than I expected." He suggests we need to resist questions about whether and why the Bible has authority and instead "trust the book itself and see where it will take us."[23]

In the characteristics Josipovici notices, scripture reflects the characteristics of God, who "is to be found not in the centers of power — in canon, in hierarchy, in group ascendancy — but in powerlessness, not in self-assertion but in anonymity, not in grasping but in emptying" (see, e.g., Phil 2).[24] God is not interested so much in controlling people as in giving them freedom, and this aspect of God's authority, like others, is presumably shared by scripture.[25]

While there is little ground for reckoning that the Torah itself is inherently legalistic, when we conceptualize scripture as an authoritative canon we are but a step away from making it a written code which kills (2 Cor 3:6). According to Romans 7 "a body of instruction and commandment in written form which comes from God and is expressly 'holy and just and good', may nevertheless provide an opportunity and incitement for evil"; if that is true of the Torah, it is presumably true of scripture as authoritative canon as a whole.[26]

Jesus himself speaks and acts with an authority that he possesses despite his lack of rabbinic credentials (see Mark 11:27-33) and that he manifests when he is speaking on his own authority and not merely when he is expounding the significance of the already existent scriptures. His words

23. *The Book of God* x, 27.
24. Kort, *Story, Text, and Scripture* 127, summarizing M. C. Taylor, *Erring* (Chicago: U Chicago, 1984).
25. Wright, "How Can the Bible Be Authoritative?" 14-16.
26. J. Barr, *Beyond Fundamentalism* 119.

and actions manifest an originality, freshness, and freedom; there is also something compelling about them. It is an authority tied up with who he is as a person. He occasionally appeals to his authority (e.g., Matt 28:18), but the kind of authority he has is also reflected in the fact that he uses logic and appeals to reason in his teaching. He does not simply lay down the law.

Jesus' parables, the distinctive vehicle of his teaching, characteristically begin from what can be learned from the world that he and his audience share. Jesus manifests something of the wisdom tradition's confidence in learning from the world and from experience and looks for the response "Yes, that's true, isn't it? I hadn't seen it before but I see it now that he puts it that way." The controversy stories in Mark 2–3 illustrate the point. Jesus is prepared there to speak in terms of the authority of the Son of Man (2:10, 28; cf. vv. 17, 20) and of scripture (2:25-26), but in each of these stories he also urges people to think things out for themselves (see 2:9, 17, 19-22, 27; 3:4). In his teaching on behavior in the Sermon on the Mount he is concerned to appeal to reason like any other moral teacher, even while he is challenging the normal conventions and attitudes of social life with a radical claim regarding the "reasonableness" of quite another style of behavior.[27] L. Hodgson's characterization of the scholarly or critical way of undertaking theological argument, with its "This is how I see it. Cannot you see it too?" is not so far from Jesus' own method.[28]

Paul may stand on his authority more often than Jesus, especially when he is in a tight corner and no other strategy seems to be working (1 Cor 11; cf. 14:37). When he acknowledges that he has no command from the Lord — no word from the earthly Jesus and no direct revelation from the heavenly Jesus — he expects his own words to be treated as having authority, though he may expect them to carry less force (1 Cor 7:12, 25, 40).[29] The authority he claims comes not from who he is in himself but from his

27. Harvey, *Strenuous Commands* 157.

28. See, e.g., *On the Authority of the Bible* 10; cf. Nineham, e.g., *Explorations in Theology* 1:144.

29. So Bruce, *1 and 2 Corinthians* 66-78. Other writers assume that a command from the Lord and the judgments of a "trustworthy" person or one who has the Spirit of God all have the same level of authority. So Barrett, *A Commentary on the First Epistle to the Corinthians* 153-87; W. A. Grudem, "Scripture's Self-Attestation and the Problem of Formulating a Doctrine of Scripture," *Scripture and Truth* (ed. Carson and Woodbridge) 47. This seems less plausible. Richardson ("'I Say, Not the Lord'") concludes that the level of authority is the same but that even in referring to the Lord's word Paul is not laying down the law but leaving room for believers to come to their own decisions.

having been commissioned by Christ to preach the gospel (Gal 1:1), from his relationship with the churches to which he writes (1 Cor 4:14-15), and from his embodiment of the gospel of crucifixion and resurrection in his own life (2 Cor 4). The depth of Paul's talk about authority and the way he transforms its significance by relating it to the cross point away from too suspicious an attitude to Paul's talk of his authority.[30]

Through Christ's commission and the preaching of the gospel that comes forth from that commission, Paul becomes the "author" or creator or father of the churches that issue from his preaching. Because his authority has another basis than the merely historical, in that it stems from the gospel, which he also mediates to other churches and which he embodies in his own life, it is not limited to those churches. " 'Gospel' and 'apostle' are correlative terms."[31] The churches then share on equal terms with him in the gospel and in its authority, but on the same basis; he only continues to exercise authority over them when they fail to embody the gospel and to exercise its authority themselves, but that authority continues to be one that stems from his own relationship with the gospel rather than one inhering in him. Therefore, this authority need not have been confined to the early apostles. But it did come to be associated with them and to be transferred, appropriately enough, to writings through which they could continue to offer their indispensable witness to the gospel, share its authority with the churches, and exercise that authority over them when they do not exercise it themselves.[32]

Before Paul the prophets, too, assume an authority that they derive from their call. The Pentateuch offers scripture's most systematic working out of a concern with authoritative canons for behavior, and there scripture also comes closest to standing on its extrinsic or institutional authority. The prominence of authoritative canons for behavior in the Pentateuch suggested a model for understanding it as a whole as Torah, a model in turn extended to the Hebrew Bible as a whole. Torah, however, means teaching (literally "direction") in a general sense. It lacks the narrower connotations of "law." Its contents can be described by terms such as "statute" and "decree": Israel is expected to be prepared to obey the Torah's commands simply because they are its commands. Yet the conventional

---

30. See Young and Ford, *Meaning and Truth in 2 Corinthians* 217-20. Shaw's *The Cost of Authority* is thus a vastly overstated but important analysis of this feature in Paul.

31. Childs, *The New Testament as Canon* 253.

32. Cf., e.g., Schütz, *Paul and the Anatomy of Apostolic Authority* 204, 281-83.

understanding of its imperatives as "laws" easily suggests a legal cast to Israelite faith that no more characterizes it than it does Christian faith and that belongs no more to the Torah than it does to Psalm 119.

The non-legalistic nature of Israel's relationship with Yahweh is reflected in the very fact that these commands appear in the context of a narrative recalling God's relating to Israel's ancestors, delivering them from oppression in Egypt, preserving them through the wilderness, and giving them their own land. Israel recognized in worship that their obedience to Yahweh's commands in the land was the goal to which the history of Yahweh's working with them was designed to lead (see Ps 105). Living in the context of a relationship with Yahweh required them to live in obedience, but it was Yahweh's own initiative that actually established the relationship. Their obedience was not a precondition of the relationship any more than is the case with the relationship sealed through the death of Christ.

It is possible to make a broad distinction between two kinds of imperatives in the Torah. Some are categorical commands such as "You must not murder," "You must not steal." Others are more like case law, prescribing what is to be done when certain offenses are committed. At first sight the latter look stronger because they contain explicit warnings regarding the punishment that will follow ignoring them. But actually the categorical commands are the stronger and more authoritative kind of imperative. They indicate no punishment because they envisage no disobedience. They are the firmest possible demands and prohibitions.

It is then to be noted that even they are capable of argument and reasoning. Even the Torah seeks assent, not merely compliance. As we noted in considering Psalm 119, it is not merely law to be obeyed but an outworking of principles according to which the universe itself is structured. Thus obedience is not incompatible with freedom, except the freedom to behave in a way which ignores the nature of reality.[33]

When the legalistic connotations of Law and laws are removed from the authoritative canons of the Torah, it is easier to see the links between them and the authoritative canons for belief and behavior that appear in the teaching of Jesus and the teaching of Paul. The Gospels have a narrative form like that of the Torah: Jesus' teaching on behavior appears in a nar-

---

33. See Gunton, *Enlightenment and Alienation* 75-76, following I. Murdoch, *The Sovereignty of Good* (London: Routledge/New York: Schocken, 1970); Gunton later cites Jesus' handling of the tempter as an instance of the paradoxical freedom of obedience (see 92-94).

rative context relating what God has done for Israel and for the world. Theologically speaking, Paul's teaching on behavior also appears in this narrative context insofar as it is linked theologically with the gospel.

The notions of authority and canon apply most naturally to scripture's role in shaping the behavior that issues from faith in the creator and redeemer God, rather than to its role in shaping people's actual beliefs. An illuminating feature of Reventlow's study of *The Authority of the Bible and the Rise of the Modern World* is that it incidentally demonstrates how from the late medieval period to the eighteenth century references to biblical authority indeed related primarily to what should be done rather than to what should be believed. When Wyclif, for instance, insists on the principle "scripture alone," he presupposes that "the whole Bible is understood in a legalistic sense"; as the Law of Christ it is "the principal basis for the whole of life, including political life." Erasmus has a "christocentrically based scriptural theology," but of a moralistic kind. The Anabaptists' "theology of scripture culminates in an ethic of discipleship." The Puritans' concern with scriptural authority related to their "fight against ceremonies and the hierarchical ordering of the church"; "the Bible has to take the place of the canon law which hitherto has governed the outward form of the church." Richard Hooker saw that the question of the authority of scripture was central not only to liturgical ceremonies and vestments but to all areas of religion, politics, and social life.[34] Reventlow's study shows how the practical authority of scripture for moral, social, political, ecclesiastical, and personal life continues to be the focus of discussion of scripture's status into the eighteenth century.

It is similarly striking that the World Council of Churches symposium *Biblical Authority for Today* was specifically concerned with the Bible and ethics or "the biblical authority for the churches' social and political message."[35] Fundamentalist emphasis on the authority of scripture often has the same concern for scripture to be ethically normative. The very notion of authority is most at home in relation to questions about behavior. It is about doing what Jesus says and doing the Father's will, not merely about calling Jesus Lord (Luke 6:46; Matt 7:21).

The notion of authoritative canons may seem quite at home in a religion such as Judaism with its concern for behavior in accordance with rules. I do not make this point polemically in relation to Judaism, nor with

---

34. Reventlow, *The Authority of the Bible* 32, 35, 42, 54, 98, 110, 116.
35. *Biblical Authority* (ed. Richardson and Schweizer) 3.

the implication that Judaism is a legalistic religion any more than the religion of the Hebrew Bible is.[36] Judaism is simply more interested in orthopraxy than in orthodoxy. The idea of canonical documents such as the Torah and the Talmud thus fits the nature of Judaism. Such canons define the terms of the relationship between God and humanity.[37] If we understand Christianity as primarily about behavior, we would expect the category of authority to be central to it in a parallel way. In relation to the humanist and Anglo-Saxon tradition, however, Reventlow wishes to reaffirm Luther's discovery of the centrality of the gospel of God's grace. If we understand Christianity as primarily a gospel, it becomes a puzzle why the category of authoritative canons has been so important to it; the category is actually less at home here.[38] This may hint that the common Christian attribution of legalism to the Hebrew Bible and to Judaism, to which we have referred a number of times, is actually a projection onto Judaism of something that Christianity rightly finds it difficult to come to terms with in itself. When Muslims find the Christian scriptures puzzling because they do not seem to focus on providing detailed instruction on everyday living as well as not having the form of revelation, they may again be onto something.[39]

36. See Jackson, "Legalism."

37. J. Barr, *Holy Scripture* 61.

38. Cf. Farley, e.g., *Ecclesial Reflection* 147-49.

39. Cf. Glaser, "Towards a Mutual Understanding of Christian and Islamic Concepts of Revelation" 22; cf. p. 9 above. I discuss the interpretation of the command material in scripture in *Models for Interpretation of Scripture*, Part II.

• 8 •

Scripture as a Whole as Authoritative Canon: Narrative and Prophecy

Theology involves critical reflection on Christian praxis in the light of the Word.[1] Scripture is the church's measuring line when it reflects on its life and commitments. The whole of scripture facilitates this reflection, not only the parts that explicitly issue commands, because narrative, prophecy, and experienced revelation all have implications for behavior. Scripture as a whole in manifold ways normatively shapes the character of the human person and the human community.[2] Furthermore, narrative, prophecy, and experienced revelation shape and evaluate not only human behavior but also human faith.

"It Is Written"

The notion of authority belongs directly to material that offers us instructions, but already in scripture the notion of authority, though not the terminology, is extended to other material. "Is it not written in your Law, 'I have said you are gods'?" asks Jesus (John 10:34). He thus uses the phrase

---

1. Cf. Gutiérrez, *A Theology of Liberation* 13.
2. Daly characterizes the four modes in which Christian existence is expressed, in scripture and elsewhere, as narrative, imperative, experiential or parabolic, and mystical (*Christian Biblical Ethics* 58-61).

"it is written" to introduce a passage from *Psalm* 82:6, describes it as "in the Law," and treats it as authoritative teaching regarding a controversial theological point with implications for behavior. To clinch the point he adds that as law "scripture cannot be broken." All scripture has the kind of authority that the Torah has. In John 15:25 Jesus refers in a similar way to Psalm 35:19 as what "is written in their Law," treating it, nonetheless, as a prophecy. Paul makes a comparable reference to Isaiah 29:11-12 (1 Cor 14:21) and elsewhere alludes to passages from the Psalms and Isaiah and from Genesis 16 and 21 as "the Law" (Rom 3:19; Gal 4:21-22) to support theological points intrinsic to his gospel.[3]

Parallel with this phenomenon is the use of "it is written," with its connotations of authority, in connection with material other than commands. It can introduce allusions to annals or other records (e.g., Josh 10:13; 1 Kgs 11:41) or refer to narrative passages with implications for the present (e.g., John 6:31; 1 Cor 10:7; 15:45; 2 Cor 8:15; Gal 4:22). In the Gospels it most commonly introduces a prophecy and thus suggests what is bound to take place because of the power of this word. In Romans, 1 and 2 Corinthians, and Galatians it characteristically introduces a proof text in support of a theological point (e.g., Rom 1:17; 3:4, 10; 1 Cor 1:19; 2 Cor 9:9; Gal 3:10, 13). Such use of "it is written" and "the Law" implies that in an extended sense the ideas expressed by the terms "authority" and "canon" apply to narrative, prophecy, and theological statement.

We noted in chapter 1 that neither Hebrew nor Greek has a special word for "scripture"; in modern translations this term renders words that in secular contexts meant "writings" in general.[4] Integral to the notion of scripture is thus the idea of material put in writing. At various points scripture itself finds reason to refer to the writing of commands, oracles, poems, accounts of events, and other forms of teaching — to use our categories to structure our thinking about scripture. Within the two Testaments themselves what connotations attach to the notion of written documents?

Kings and Chronicles allude frequently to annals, annals of kings in Kings and of prophets in Chronicles. These annals include events and sayings or oracles (e.g., 1 Kgs 11:41; 1 Chr 29:29; 2 Chr 34:27; but see also Josh 10:13-14). Genealogies and other lists of people were also put into writing (e.g., Neh 7:5; 12:23). Records of wrong deeds were put in written

---

3. Cf. Warfield, *The Inspiration and Authority of the Bible* 138-40.
4. Greek *graphē* and *grammata*.

form as reminders to Yahweh to ensure that they were punished (Isa 65:6). The implied object of writing was, then, to ensure the preservation of records of past events that were not dependent on fallible memory, though it must be said that the connotation of writing with regard to such material is not made explicit.

Edicts and laws were put into writing to ensure that they would be taken seriously and could be referred to, and this significance carries over into the writing down of divine commands and of the terms of covenants between Yahweh and Israel (e.g., Exod 32:16; Deut 31:9-13, 24-26; Neh 9:38). Writing is a way of making a claim stick, in contrast to the prophetic word, which has to reassert its claim again on every occasion of its utterance.[5] This is the connotation of some Second Testament references to what is written (e.g., Matt 4:1-11; Gal 3:10). The object of writing is implementation and accountability.

Prophetic oracles were put into writing as an evidence that they were expected to come true — they would then be open to being checked — and as a means of putting them into effect, like a royal edict (e.g., Isa 8:1; 30:8; Jer 30:2; 36; 51:60-64; cf. also Exod 17:14; Deut 29:20-21). This is a common connotation when the Second Testament refers back to what is written or to the "writings," that is, "scriptures" (e.g., Luke 24:44, 46; Rom 15:26). The object of writing is fulfillment and verification.

More surprisingly, poems, songs, and other wisdom material were put into writing so that they could be taught, in parallel with the commands of the Torah (e.g., Deut 31:22; 2 Sam 1:18; 2 Chr 35:25; Prov 22:20). The object of writing was communication.

It may be in part because "scripture" strictly means simply "writing" that terms such as *sacred* writings or *holy* scripture come into use. In their significance they need to be distinguished from *canonical* scripture or *authoritative* writings, even though the two kinds of descriptions can refer to the same works. The Talmud prohibits placing a book of a lesser degree of sanctity on top of one with a greater degree — for example, Psalms on top of the Pentateuch. The Pentateuch also has greater sanctity than the Talmud. Yet the Talmud has greater authority than the Pentateuch, which it is understood to interpret, because it is the Talmud that is the direct object of obedience.[6] The sacredness of scripture and the authority of scripture are distinct ideas.

---

5. Blenkinsopp, *Prophecy and Canon* 38 (with reference to the words of Jeremiah); cf. Bruns, "Canon and Power in the Hebrew Scriptures" 475.

6. So "Ask the Rabbi," in the London *Jewish Chronicle,* 12 May 1978.

Scripture and Canon

What, then, is the relationship between "scripture" and "canon"? While the word "canon" first meant a rule, it came also to mean a list, as "something fixed and established, by which one can orient oneself." It was in this sense of "list" that the term was first applied to the scriptures by Athanasius. But these two senses of the term should hardly be opposed too sharply, especially as the word soon came to be used of scripture in the broader and more original sense, that of "rule."[7] "Scripture as canon" and "the canon of scripture" are thus related but distinct ideas, and scholars who emphasize one or the other meaning of "canon" are sometimes at cross purposes.[8]

"Scripture as canon" suggests a key function which can be fulfilled by unwritten traditions or by written scriptures at various stages of their development. One can speak, for instance, of the shaping of books so that they can function canonically, of the canonical status attaching to certain collections of "laws" that are now incorporated within the Pentateuch, or of the Four Gospels as canonical, in the sense of normative, in certain circles during the second century. We have noted already that canonical, regulative functions can also be fulfilled by written documents outside scripture, such as the Talmud or ecclesiastical canons.

In contrast, "the canon of scripture" suggests the existence of a formal list of books that by its very nature as a list draws attention not only to what is within but also to what is outside the canon. The works in the canon are circumscribed and set over against other writings or words. Their status is irrevocably determined and it will be natural if their text is now especially carefully preserved and not subject to further development. The existence of such lists belongs to a later stage of the development of the Bible, so that "canon" can be described as "a most inappropriate term to describe the Scriptures of Jews and Christians in the first few centuries of our era."[9]

The use of the word canon in this narrower connection can form part of a possible description of a clear three-stage developmental process. First, there are "traditions" or "writings," inspired and religiously significant but not mandatorily authoritative. Even people who acknowledge a set of scriptures may also value prophetic words or other words beyond those scriptures, as is evidenced by the Qumran writings, the Second Testament (e.g.,

7. Metzger, *The Canon of the New Testament* 291, 292, 293.
8. Barton, *Oracles of God* 32-33.
9. *Ibid.,* 44.

Jude's quotation from *1 Enoch* and Paul's appreciation of the Wisdom of Solomon), and the Fathers.[10] Second, there are "scriptures," with the idea of normativeness implied by that word. Writings such as the Prophets, at least, began life as prophetic traditions and only subsequently became scriptures. Third, a gradually increasing collection of scriptures may become a defined "canon," a definitively closed and exclusive list of normative writings that comes into being through an act of canonization. By this act what has already established preeminence as scripture and thus de facto recognition receives official ratification. The act of canonization does not *give* authority but does *restrict* authority.[11]

There are three advantages to this schematization of history. First, it draws attention to the fact that the drawing up of actual lists of authoritative writings characterizes a relatively late stage of the story of Israel and of the church, a stage when the community needed to define its identity over against pagan forces or groups that it saw as deviant or heretical.

Second, this understanding of the history of canonization allows for the fact that the canon of scripture was not designed to include every inspired utterance that has ever been uttered or every word of Jesus or letter of Paul. It was, instead, a collection of some of these that the communities had come to consider of particular longterm significance and normativity. The discovery of another letter of Paul or the identification of authentic sayings of Jesus in noncanonical gospels thus does not necessarily open up the question whether such material should be added to the canon. This view of the canon's history thus encourages us to utilize the spiritual resources represented by other Jewish and Christian religious writings, which are a resource without being an inescapable norm. In principle we are on the same level as such resources and can engage with them in a dialogue that may lead to some new insight in the growth of the tradition in which both text and reader stand.[12]

At the same time, third, this view of the history of canon draws attention to the way in which the scriptures become *scripture:* A closed canon comes to be seen as a complete and unchangeable revelation, given directly by God, of all that is to be believed and done in worship and everyday life.[13]

10. *Ibid.,* 62.

11. Keck, "Is the New Testament a Field of Study?" 33.

12. C. M. Wood, "Hermeneutics and the Authority of Scripture," *Scriptural Authority and Narrative Interpretation* (ed. Green) 6 — though Wood is describing a way of reading scripture itself.

13. See Farley, *Ecclesial Reflection* 58, 69 on this "scripture principle."

Its presupposition or consequence is that people know themselves to be in a postbiblical situation and do not produce scriptures themselves;[14] importance comes to be attached to exegesis and to the conviction that later stipulations only render explicit what was earlier implicit.[15]

But the difficulties of this historical scheme outweigh these strengths. First, it risks exaggerating the distinction between scripture and canon. The term scripture itself implies that the material so designated is normative for the beliefs and behavior of the people of God — for orthodoxy and orthopraxy. Scripture does not become canonical only when there is a formal canon. To reserve the notion of normativity for "canon" as opposed to "scripture" is to render the latter expression vacuous.[16] It is thus not surprising that Barton finds himself having to maintain both that the books that we call the Prophets and the Writings, along with the Torah, were "authoritative for religious practice and/or doctrine" in Jesus' day and also that they were *not* "a 'norm' or regulative standard" as the Torah was.[17] Nor is it the case that Israel or the church lacked norms before they possessed written documents: Preexilic Israel, for instance, had normative traditions to shape its self-understanding, Torah to shape its life, and prophetic words already identified as God's words, before pressures such as the destruction of the Temple led to these traditions being turned into scripture.[18] Nor is it the case that the canonical books are distinguished from other "scriptures" by being authorized for use in worship. In the ancient church, as in the modern church, books outside a canon can be read in church. Nor did canonical status in itself make a difference to the inviolability of a work's text form. "A primary character of canon is its *adaptability* as well as its *stability.*"[19] Again, "scripture" is itself a limiting and exclusive term, like "canon." To call some writings "scripture" is implicitly to give them a significance denied to other writings; to include is implicitly also to exclude.

Second, the scheme reserves the term "canon" for a stage in the ca-

14. Talmon, *Qumran and the History of the Biblical Text* 378-79.

15. J. Blenkinsopp, in *Jewish and Christian Self-Definition* (ed. E. P. Sanders) 2:6, 301.

16. See Kelsey, *The Uses of Scripture in Recent Theology* 89.

17. See *Oracles of God* 56, 63.

18. See Farley, *Ecclesial Reflection* 52-57.

19. J. A. Sanders, *Canon and Community* 22 (emphasis original), though Sanders misses the implication that the flexibility of the Psalter or the Torah at Qumran is thus no witness against their canonical status (see his "Cave 11 Surprises and the Question of Canon," in *New Directions in Biblical Archaeology* [ed. D. N. Freedman and J. C. Greenfield; Garden City: Doubleday, 1969] 101-16; *Canon and Community* 13-14).

nonical process that arguably not only had rather subordinate importance but also never actually took place. Even in the medieval period the canons of most communities still existed de facto and as a matter of custom rather than because they had been definitively and officially determined by some competent body. This is true of the Hebrew canon of Judaism and of both the First and Second Testament canons in the Eastern Church. We know of no moment when either the Jewish or the Christian canon was formally closed or when a de facto canon was formally ratified by Judaism or by an ecumenical council of the Christian church. Canonization, in this sense, is a dubious concept; de facto acknowledgment of certain groups of writings by different communities is all we have evidence of. For Jews the Hebrew canon, for instance, may have reached its final form in the Antiochene period, but whenever this took place, it has never been formally closed. Nor has any body definitively closed the Christian canon.[20]

All this reflects a fact about how works come to have authority, a fact often acknowledged in theory but not taken account of in practice. In general, "texts are made into literature by the community, not by their authors,"[21] nor by critics; George Steiner suggests that critics determine what they believe should be appreciated, but audiences determine canons, that is, what actually is appreciated.[22] In a parallel way "the books of the Bible were appreciated by their earliest audiences, i.e. became canonical before the critics placed them on the syllabus."[23] "During the period of the origin of the canon the authority of scripture is not in fact any juridical or formal authority," but derives from its content; juridical authority comes later as the church develops as an institution.[24] The canon emerged from below before it was imposed from above.

Third, the historical scheme that we have described unwittingly implies that the Jewish scriptures were never a canon, because those scriptures were never a closed and exclusive authority for either Jews or Christians. For Jews they were supplemented by the Mishnah and the Talmud, for Christians by Christian writings. It would also be impossible to speak of a canon of the Torah at an earlier stage, or a subsequent canon of the Torah and

20. See Barth, *Church Dogmatics* 1/2:473-81. See further chapters 10 and 11 below.
21. Ellis, *The Theory of Literary Criticism* 47.
22. " 'Critic'/'Reader' " 445-47. The point is stated differently in *Real Presences* 184.
23. Keegan, *Interpreting the Bible* 9. Keegan refers to the critics literally. I take them as a figure for canonizers.
24. Schillebeeckx, *Christ* 68-69.

the Prophets, because each was in due course to be supplemented. Nor does the attitude of a church theologian such as Luther give the impression that in his day he views the canon as irrevocably determined.[25]

Here, then, I will follow the usage that sees the key characteristic of the notion of canon as lying in the function of normativity, which applies, in this case, to written scriptures, whether or not they yet comprise an identifiable collection with de facto limits. There can be a canon even when it is an "open canon."[26]

The development of the canon, then, was a historical process whereby historically rooted writings were shaped, preserved, collected, and ordered so as to function as norms for faith and behavior in the ongoing life of believing communities. These documents did not wait until the end of these complex literary processes before they began to have religious authority. They went through the process partly because they had such authority and the community wanted them to be able to exercise it through changing circumstances, in new contexts, for new purposes. Neither was the community concerned only to transfer the message of these documents from one limited historical situation to another similar one, but to render them more generally applicable.[27]

The effect of some aspects of the canonical process is to obscure its historical nature in such a way as to make it easier for readers in other historical contexts to identify with the text. The canonical process took place, of course, in a particular historical and social context.[28] Indeed, bringing purported normative declarations from God, reapplying them to new circumstances, shaping them to function normatively in a less time-limited way, and including them in a canon, that is, in a collection of normative written material, no doubt all took place in the context of discussion, debate, disagreement, dispute, and struggle about the nature of the Jewish and Christian communities. The scriptures we have are the legacy passed on by the victors in this process. They reflect struggles for power; indeed, " 'canon' is not a literary category but a category of power."[29] The

25. See, e.g., Barth, *Church Dogmatics* I/2:476-78.

26. Ackroyd, *Studies in the Religious Tradition of the Old Testament* 209-24; cf. Bruns, "Canon and Power in the Hebrew Scriptures" 467.

27. So Childs, e.g., *The New Testament as Canon* 25.

28. Gottwald, "Social Matrix and Canonical Shape" 318-20.

29. Bruns, "Canon and Power in the Hebrew Scriptures" 478. Cf. Pui-Lan, "Discovering the Bible in the Non-Biblical World" 35-36, with her quotation from Detweiler, *Reader Response Approaches to Biblical and Secular Texts* 217.

same sociocritical questions thus apply to the canonical process as apply to the existence of scripture in general. Everything is affected by ideology, including the shaping of scripture into its final canonical form.[30]

The reworking of prophetic material such as that of Jeremiah can then be seen as a "priestly appropriation of prophetic authority by means of the superior forces of writing and textuality," which could signify the silencing of prophecy.[31] In the Second Temple community there may well have been groups who emphasized Yahweh's acts and presence in the community and groups who could see little in the present and focused on the future. The Torah and the prophetic books as we have them are the deposit of the interaction between such groups.[32] We can then see among the churches of the second century how the canon emerged from disputes over the true nature of the Christian faith and the bounds of the Christian community.

The canon did not fall from heaven. But neither does it merely reflect the views of the powerful or the views of one group. Different groups had grasped aspects of the truth and each of those aspects came to be part of the canon. This may itself reflect the need for consensual as well as conflict models of the social processes that generated the canon, as Bruns hints.[33] The monarchical episcopacy of the Fathers did not gain pseudonymous entry into the Second Testament, and the Second Testament's stress on submission is accompanied by a subversive recognition of other rights. Power was *a* factor in the canonical process, but not the sole factor, and awareness of it as an aspect of the process should not lead to a reductionist approach to that process. Nor can we assume that a process of consensus rather than struggle is more likely to have produced a canon of lasting significance.

Josipovici asks whether Shakespeare is the national poet of England "for some intrinsic reason related to the quality and nature of his work, or because those in power have, for their own ends, decided to make him so." Such factors of power may have generated myths that played a part in giving Shakespeare the position he has, and the same is true of the Bible. "But that does not automatically mean that Shakespeare and the Bible are nothing but the product of such myths."[34] Terry Eagleton's antithesis — either

---

30. Brett, *Biblical Criticism in Crisis?* 95-96, 150-52.

31. Bruns, "Canon and Power in the Hebrew Scriptures" 474.

32. See Blenkinsopp, in *Jewish and Christian Self-Definition* (ed. E. P. Sanders) 2:4-9.

33. "Canon and Power in the Hebrew Scriptures." Bruns himself, however, is committed to conflict models and does not draw the inference that I have drawn from his work.

34. *The Book of God* 26, 27.

Shakespeare was "great literature lying conveniently to hand, which the literary institution then happily discovered" or "he is great literature because the institution constitutes him as such"[35] — requires us to choose between unreal alternatives. They are not the only possibilities. R. Detweiler describes the canonization process as one of "arbitrary decision-making" in that it issues from struggles among the religious leadership of the community, whose victors then manage to persuade the community that *their* texts are sacred.[36] But it seems unlikely that even the "victors" can fool all the people all the time.

Biblical Narrative as Authoritative Canon

The canons that eventually emerged comprised not only directions for behavior but narrative, prophecy, and other theological, epistolary, revelatory, and religious works. What is the significance of regarding these differing types of material as authoritative canons?

Biblical narrative is not primarily designed to make moral points but to witness to what God has done. The witnessing tradition is fundamental to normative scripture precisely because it relates the gospel, which is the essence of the faith. The nature of Christian faith itself and the nature of scripture as witness to the gospel events suggest a theological rationale for the instinct which led to the development of a collection of scriptures or a canon of the kind that we have, with their narrative focus. This narrative form reflects the fundamental nature of Christian faith as a piece of news about what God has said and done in Israel and in Jesus. Christian faith is an indicative before it is an imperative.

The link between authority and canon on the one hand and commands on the other suggests that canon hardly provides *the* model for understanding the narrative material in scripture; nor does narrative provide *the* paradigm for understanding the nature of canon. The witnessing tradition is of essential importance to Israel's understanding of itself and its relationship with God, but to view a piece of history or story as having authority or functioning as a canon for a community has a certain logical oddness about it. Yet although the witnessing tradition does not directly offer instructions to people, it is of key significance for the Judeo-Christian idea

35. *Literary Theory* 202.
36. *Reader Response Approaches to Biblical and Secular Texts* 215.

of canon. Normative narrative has a distinctive place in the Judeo-Christian tradition because that tradition shaped its self-understanding and preserved its identity through its affirmation of what God had done for it in the events which, in Christian conviction, came to their climax in Jesus. That was why a canon came into being.[37]

To put it another way, the canon as such might seem to deconstruct itself, for a body of writings designated as having imperatival significance — a canon — turns out to be dominated by the indicative. But a contrary implication of calling a narrative a canon is that this narrative itself is designed to fulfill a normative function. The canonical nature of the biblical story thus points to a limitation to the popular and valuable literary approaches to narrative. Biblical narrative was written as a means to an end; if we ignore the fact that narrative is part of the canon, our interpretation of the canon falls short of the canon's nature.[38] The canon contains an implicit imperative. "Authority is author-ity, the authorship, authorization, of the Christian Story."[39] It is easy for us to give highest authority to a set of theological concepts derived from the gospel story, but the biblical story makes demands on theological reflection that are prior to those of these derived concepts. The biblical story exists independently of our stories, pulls us away from our subjectivity, and makes a claim of its own on our present existence.[40] It has authority. We do not read our stories into scripture, but make the scriptural story our story and tell our stories in the light of scripture. We do not translate scripture into our categories but redescribe our experience in its categories.[41]

The authority of scripture derives from the authority of the gospel. It is for this reason that scripture possesses an authority not possessed by the Qur'an or by church tradition. In this connection questions about the authority of scripture also arise from the study of the significance of scripture in liberation theology, both political and feminist. Both suggest contexts out of which scripture can be read afresh, so that interpreters perceive aspects of scripture that have been hidden from others who lacked the eyes

37. W. D. Davies, "Canon and Christology," in *The Glory of Christ* (ed. Hurst and Wright) 27-29.

38. Lischer, "The Limits of Story" 27.

39. Fackre, *Authority* 51.

40. Cone, *God of the Oppressed* 103-4; cf. Witvliet, *The Way of the Black Messiah* 258.

41. Lindbeck, *The Nature of Doctrine* 118. Thiselton (*New Horizons in Hermeneutics* 557) notes the significance of this for pastoral theology.

to see them. At other points scripture adopts a perspective that stands in tension with both liberation interpreters and other interpreters.

Underlying the question of the status of scripture is then a question about the location of the gospel. Liberation theologians emphasize God's current involvement in human history, and if our history reflects this involvement we will naturally expect to gain insight on God's purpose from a consideration of and a sharing in that involvement. They believe that a contemporary event, the history unfolding in Latin America or the emergence of feminism, is a key act of God in our age; our history as well as the history witnessed to in scripture reflect God's activity, and each throws light on the other. What, then, is the relation between these sets of events? Where does *the* gospel lie?

The question is one on which liberation theology has been equivocal. Raúl Vidales, for instance, has spoken of a "dialectical activity" that "obliges the theologian to re-read the Bible from the context of the other 'Bible' known as human history" in the conviction that "human history is the manifestation of the Christ-fact." The reference to a dialectic between contemporary experience and biblical witness suggests that the two have parallel significance. Later, however, Vidales speaks of theology's need to maintain its critical function over against both church and society by means of a constant reference back to scripture. One is then not sure what is the relationship between these two "Bibles."[42] Is praxis subjected to critique and reinterpretation in the light of the scriptural witness, or is the reverse movement also possible?

H. Assmann is less equivocal. "How can we talk candidly of the 'gospel' when there is so much truth in what one committed Christian once said to me: 'The Bible? It doesn't exist. The only Bible is the sociological bible of what I see happening here and now as a Christian.'" Liberation theology's "text" is our situation, and our situation is our primary and basic reference point — not any other resource such as scripture.[43] The Christ of faith is subject to critique as a dehistoricized, depoliticized version of the Jesus of history.[44]

A similar ambivalence appears within feminist theology; indeed, the question may surface more sharply here because it is harder to show that

42. See "Methodological Issues in Liberation Theology" 40, 47; for the same ambiguity see Cone, *God of the Oppressed* 113, 205.

43. Assmann, *Practical Theology of Liberation* 61, 104.

44. Kee, *The Scope of Political Theology* 18-20. Cf. Fierro, *The Militant Gospel* 215-16, with his quotation from Pannenberg.

the God of the Bible is committed to women than it is to show that this God is committed to the poor. Feminist interpretation can thus be driven to be more critical of the biblical text than other liberation interpretation, though the development of sociohistorical and materialist approaches takes interpretation of a liberationist type in the same direction.[45] Thus Elisabeth Schüssler Fiorenza notes that the biblical texts are "social constructions by men and for men" that nevertheless offer clues enabling us to look behind them for the different historical reality comprised by the egalitarian early Christian movement, which they hide.[46] She unequivocally affirms that "the revelatory canon" for theological evaluation of scripture with its inevitably androcentric nature "cannot be derived from the Bible itself but can only be formulated in and through women's struggle for liberation."[47]

The question of the relation of present and past thus arises in a particular form in feminist and liberation interpretation. But feminist theologian Pamela Dickey Young notes that it is neither confined to nor derived from such approaches: Any theology has to work with both these givens.[48] Leslie Houlden speaks of the present as well as the past as " 'given' to us."[49] Again, it is not surprising to discover that when Nineham queries the notion of scripture he also queries the notion of the Second Testament events being of once-for-all significance as acts of God.[50]

The canonical nature of the biblical story suggests a further sense in which authority attaches to scriptural narrative. Insofar as it is the scriptural narrative that gives us access to the gospel story, it has an authority analogous to that which belongs to any direct historical source. It is the scriptural narratives that give us access to Jesus. The Bible is an authoritative source for Christian faith because, although biblical faith was not a faith in the Bible but one centered more directly on Jesus,[51] subsequent Christian faith has to be biblical if it is to follow biblical faith in its centering on Jesus. When we see face to face (1 Cor 13:12), then, too, there will be no need of scripture, which is destined to "become a 'self-consuming artifact'; the

45. D. Jobling, "Writing the Wrongs of the World," in *Poststructural Criticism* (ed. Phillips) 95.

46. *Bread Not Stone* 112.

47. *In Memory of Her* 32; cf. *Bread Not Stone* xv, xvii, 138-39; Pui-Lan, "Discovering the Bible in the Non-Biblical World" 36-38.

48. *Feminist Theology* 58.

49. *Connections* 163.

50. *Explorations in Theology* 1:99-100.

51. See J. Barr, *Holy Scripture* 1-2.

power of the word will have subsumed itself into the life of the community, embodied itself without remainder," in accordance with Jeremiah 31:34.[52] In the meantime and to that end, however, the existence of a body of permanently normative writings, set apart from others that may in their way be inspired and illuminating, is a natural correlative to a central feature of Christianity, its focus on a particular line of historical events. In this sense the existence of a canon belongs to the nature of Christian faith. Scripture's connection with the gospel story does not explain why these precise books constitute the canon, but it does provide a theological rationale for the existence of *a* canon along the lines of the one we have.

There is a more human link between narrative and authority. The narrative form of a written Gospel enables its author to make the most authoritative possible statement regarding the gospel.[53] Jesus simply *is* God's Son; God simply *spoke* from heaven. No grounds for these assertions are offered except the implicit ones of the story as a whole. Another implicit imperative contained within this canonical narrative derives from the suggestion that some Hebrew narratives and perhaps all the parables are not verbatim accounts of what happened or of how the story was told but summaries that act as an *aide-mémoire* for the storyteller.[54] The biblical story exists to act as a control or canon for the oral story.

The normative nature of the events related by the canonical story again points to one reason for the need for such control. In every age there are mixed feelings about the relative importance of the oral and the written. In the early Christian centuries such mixed feelings mirrored feelings in the surrounding Greco-Roman world.[55] Indeed, all the major world religions seem to emphasize the oral for its lively power and originality.[56] Much later Luther contrasted "scripture" (the First Testament) with "proclamation" (the spoken message of the gospel, which is by its nature a living voice rather than a written document). He rather regretted the necessity to put

---

52. Hays, *Echoes of Scripture in the Letters of Paul* 129. The internal quotation takes up the title of Stanley Fish's *Self-Consuming Artifacts*.

53. Shaw, *The Cost of Authority* 199. Cf. Polzin's analogous comments on the Deuteronomist (e.g., *Moses and the Deuteronomist* 9-11, 27-28): The Deuteronomist implies the claim that only he knows Moses face to face.

54. A. F. Campbell, "The Reported Story," in *Narrative Research on the Hebrew Bible* (ed. Amihai, et al.) 77-85.

55. L. Alexander, "The Living Voice," in *The Bible in Three Dimensions* (ed. Clines, et al.) 221-47.

56. Coward, *Sacred Word and Sacred Text* 161-82.

the gospel into writing, given that by its own nature it was a living, preached message, but he recognized that it was a necessity, in order to safeguard the truth.[57] R. H. Lightfoot asked whether the production of the first Gospel was "the first serious failure of nerve on the part of the infant church" or a sign of the operation of original sin in the church.[58] If the gospel is essentially a living, preached message, it can only be killed by the attempt to capture it in written words. "Scripture represents the worldliness of the church and tradition points to its supernatural origin and basis," not the other way round.[59] The distinction between written scripture and oral tradition can be nuanced further by noting the further distinction between oral tradition and the fresh immediate direct oral word.[60] Perhaps the key point is that a reality is passed on *(traditio)*, not merely whether it is oral rather than written.[61]

We noted in the first section of this chapter that the scriptures seem to feel no unease about written documents. They feel no necessary tension between scripture and tradition and picture scripture and tradition as working together (Luke 24:27; John 2:22; Acts 5:30-32; 8:35; Rev 1:3).[62] On its own either may be dangerous: the one alive but too malleable, the other fixed but frozen. "The writings of early Christian authors were first cited as the earliest, most trustworthy deposit of tradition about Jesus of Nazareth and the origins of the church. Here 'Scripture' is functioning as a control of tradition running rampant." It "functions to control and measure the continuing traditioning event and proclaiming of that event to all nations."[63] The insistence on going back to the sources eventually encapsulated in the formula "scripture alone" formally parallels the principle of humanism, but its motivation is quite different: It relates to the nature of the gospel. It is another way of saying "Christ alone."[64] Without the Bible,

57. See, e.g., "A Brief Instruction on What to Look For and Expect in the Gospels," *LW* 35:123; cf. Bornkamm, *Luther and the Old Testament* 84; Althaus, *The Theology of Martin Luther* 72-73; Ebeling, *Word and Faith* 312-13, quoting *WA* 10/1/1:625-28.

58. See Nineham, *Explorations in Theology* 1:110; Evans, *Is "Holy Scripture" Christian?* 6-7.

59. Evans, *Is "Holy Scripture" Christian?* 7.

60. Funk, *Parables and Presence* 155.

61. Cf. Schillebeeckx, *Revelation and Theology* 17.

62. Berkouwer, *Holy Scripture* 334-35. Cf. F. F. Bruce, "Scripture in Relation to Tradition and Reason," in *Scripture, Tradition and Reason* (ed. Bauckham and Drewery) 37-42.

63. Farley, *Ecclesial Reflection* 78, 79; cf., e.g., 149, 278.

64. Ogden, "The Authority of Scripture for Theology" 253.

James Smart thus comments, "the remembered Christ becomes an imagined Christ."[65]

Scripture's connection with the gospel story also suggests a theological rationale for the closing of the canon or the instinct that failed to keep that collection growing as the centuries of church history unfolded. The canonical documents are ones in which the church found the best evidence for the nature of its faith as formulated during its classical period. No later Christian writings, however inspired, true, and edifying, could have the same status as scripture itself. They could not be part of a witnessing tradition in the same sense. It is also noteworthy that the clarification of the canon went on at the same time as the clarification of the gospel by the patristic church. There is an inner connection between these two. Even if Augustine, Calvin, or Barth illumine the nature of the gospel more clearly than some canonical works, they are not normative. They themselves emphasize that their commentary on the significance of Christ, at its most illuminating, is secondary to that of scripture at its least illuminating.

It was appropriate that material stopped being added to the scriptures because their story had reached its resolution. God did not stop acting at the end of the biblical period, and we may look for that activity now; Christians have often been slow to ask what God is doing in contemporary events. Nevertheless within the total activity of God in world history a special significance attaches to the events of the history of Israel, which came to a climax in Christ. Not that they are a series of salvation events that happened on some different plane from the rest of the history that we know and experience, nor that they are (generally) acts of God in a supranaturalist sense — as the critique of writers such as C. F. Evans seems to imply.[66] But they are particularly significant acts for the fulfillment of God's purpose, with particularly important consequences for human destiny. The fact that God is involved in all history should not obscure the particularity of God's work through certain specific events. The continuing history of Judaism and the history of the church do not have the inherent theological significance that attaches to the history related in scripture itself, if the gospel is gospel in the sense that Christianity believes it to be.[67]

65. *The Strange Silence of the Bible in the Church* 25; cf. Thiselton, *New Horizons in Hermeneutics* 188.

66. *Is "Holy Scripture" Christian?* 59, quoted in Barr, *The Bible in the Modern World* 79; cf. my discussion in *Approaches to Old Testament Interpretation* 66-96.

67. Cf. Barth's remarks in *Church Dogmatics* II/2:342.

This suggests that the canon is not irrevocably closed as a matter of principle. When a new salvation event occurred, the older scriptures were interpreted anew, a new literature emerged, and some of it became canonical: a Second Testament was added to the First. One cannot exclude the possibility that this might happen again. The canon remains open to the recognition of a new act of God.

The scriptural narrative links with the authoritative canons, which explicitly concern behavior, through the fact that in scripture these commands are commonly introduced by narrative statements. The narrative may, for instance, provide backing for the commands: "I am Yahweh your God who brought you out of the land of Egypt, out of the house of bondage. You are to have no other gods over against me . . ." (Exod 20:2-3). One framework for the institutional authority of the obligations in the Torah is thus their connection with the covenant. The covenant intrinsically involved stating obligations and accepting them; both story and obligations are put into writing. There is thus an important link between the notions of canon and covenant, and a link to the ascription of normative significance to the story told in Genesis to Joshua, which can be seen as an epic expansion of the historical preamble in a covenant document.[68]

The covenant narrative has a more intrinsic link with the covenant commands. A passage such as Jesus' appeal to Genesis 1–2 in Mark 10 draws attention to the fact that the significance of scripture for ethical questions does not emerge exclusively, perhaps not even primarily, from the content of its explicit commands. The authority of scripture for ethics is exercised also through the perspective on human life that appears in the story of creation with its portrayal of humanity made in God's image and in the story of redemption with its vision of humanity freed from bondage. The history of God's acts with Israel provided Israel with an authoritative, normative resource for understanding itself and its relationship with God as centuries unfolded. The gospel story then came to be determinative for what the church believes and does.

The Inspired Word as Authoritative Canon

The nature of scripture as God's inspired word also links with its being canonical: All scripture, being God-breathed, is of value for teaching, re-

---

68. Kline, *The Structure of Biblical Authority*.

proof, correction, and training in righteousness, so that everyone who belongs to God may be complete, equipped for every good work (2 Tim 3:16-17). It is normative and life-shaping. The prophets are commissioned as messengers of the heavenly monarch, and they speak with the authority of the one who sent them. They utter the authoritative decisions of God and put them into effect. The words of the prophets, like the narratives of scripture, have implications for ethical norms. They express ethical values such as justice, faithfulness, and compassion and set before us a vision of a renewed world and a renewed Israel, and that vision becomes the inspiration and goal of our action.

Nevertheless the prophetic oracle does not provide the best paradigm for understanding the nature of canon. Not every inspired word becomes canonical, and not every canonical rule comes into being by the direct act of God, as is suggested by the notion of inspiration, though it may be God-given in a broader sense. Further, the specific claim of 2 Timothy 3:16 that scripture is "profitable" in behavioral connections is quite mild compared with the doctrine that has been built on such passages.[69] The essence of canon is not inspired word; its roots do not lie in prophecy.[70]

69. J. Barr, *Escaping from Fundamentalism* 3.
70. Against Beckwith, *The Old Testament Canon* 63-64.

9

Scripture as a Whole
as Authoritative Canon:
Norms for Christian Doctrine

Modern discussion of the authority of scripture relates to questions of doctrine as often as to questions of behavior. Here, then, we consider how the model of the authoritative canon applies to doctrinal thinking, looking at the theological reflection of the Second Testament itself and the way it utilizes the First Testament as a theological resource and norm.

The Crisis of Authority

"Scripture's authority . . . for the church's common life consists in its being used in certain rulish and normative ways so that it helps to nurture and reform the community's self-identity and the personal identities of her members."[1] The expressions "nurture" and "reform" suggest that the church attends to the exposition of the scriptures so that they can, first, provide the framework for its theologizing. Then in reflecting on its own living, thinking, listening, and talking, it attends again to the scriptures as the measure of whether it is getting this theologizing right. To affirm the authority of scripture as canon is thus to declare that scripture has a foundational and a final role within Christian faith. It may not exactly

---

1. Kelsey, *The Uses of Scripture in Recent Theology* 208 — though I am drawing a contrary inference from Kelsey's own.

117

determine our worldview; its own worldview may be simply that of the Middle East or the Mediterranean world in its own period. It does inform our worldview, in causing us to take a different attitude in many areas of life, an attitude shaped by the reality and creativeness of God and the fact of Christ's incarnation, death, and resurrection. Calvin's image is that scripture is like a pair of spectacles that corrects our visual astigmatism, a lens that refocuses what we see into an intelligible pattern, rather as a scientific theory provides us with a lens that makes sense of miscellaneous data.[2] The process is illustrated by Peter's Pentecost sermon, which gives people no new facts on their history but repatterns that history in the light of the story of Jesus. Scripture "enables its hearers to imagine God."[3]

If scripture as authoritative canon functions both prospectively and retrospectively, there is a case for locating discussion of the doctrine of scripture near the beginning of a theological system as part of a consideration of the sources of the faith. But there is also a case for locating it nearer the end in recognition that all the faith and life that have been described are subject to reconsideration in the light of this measuring line. In the Church of England's Thirty-Nine Articles of Religion, matters concerning scripture appear only after five articles outlining the church's trinitarian faith, thus implying that scripture is the church's retrospective measuring line. The heart of Anglican worship as the Prayer Book prescribes it, however, is systematic reading of scripture — not selective preaching of scripture — which is assumed to be capable of speaking for itself.[4] The Church of England thus suggests that scripture authoritatively shapes Christian thinking as well as authoritatively assessing it, as the Westminster Confession makes clear that scripture is to be the source of the church's doctrine by placing matters concerning scripture at its beginning.

We have noted a distinction between two main ideas of authority, an authority intrinsic in what someone says and an authority extrinsic to a person or his or her words that is given because of his or her position in some authority structure. For many centuries theology was assumed to work on the basis of the second kind of authority. The Bible or the church or some other entity has an unquestionable authority to tell people what they must believe. Whether or not its statements make sense, they are to

2. *Institutes* I/6, 1; cf. Green, *Imagining God* 107, also quoting M. Polanyi and M. Prosch, *Meaning* (Chicago: U Chicago, 1975) 37.

3. Green, *Imagining God* 124, 119.

4. O'Donovan, *On the Thirty Nine Articles* 50.

be accepted: "If the Bible told me Jonah swallowed the whale, I would believe it." Dennis Nineham asks, "Am I then committed, as a Christian, to the view that biblical writers can never have been simply wrong for their own times and/or irrelevant for ours?"[5] Recognition of scripture as canon has some such implication.

But in Western society, at least since the Enlightenment, people are less inclined to accept things unquestioningly on the "say-so" of a person such as a parent or teacher or minister, or of a community and its tradition. In theology, appeal to what "the Bible says" or "the church says," or even "Jesus says," does not carry the weight it once did. Theological statements have to stand for themselves on the basis of evidence and inquiry. "The house of authority" has collapsed.[6] Agreement that God has authority in the church and in the world does not carry with it clarity on the means by which God exercises authority or the means whereby we avoid human opinion being the arbiter of truth and falsehood, good and evil.

Since Descartes's "I think, therefore I am" philosophers have been looking for a way of providing a linear chain of reasons to justify such beliefs. They have not discovered one. One can declare that scripture, for instance, is the foundation of everything but not explain what is the foundation for that commitment. It seems that any "foundationalism" must now be allowed to die (or be recognized to have been stillborn). In coming to our faith commitments or testing them, in practice we take account of a number of factors rather than just one.[7] Consciously or unconsciously we ask how far the belief in question corresponds to accepted empirical facts and to current human experience, has internal coherence, provides a satisfying total picture and one we can live with, generates a view of the world and of life that makes sense, rings bells with us or is existentially meaningful, contributes practically to personal and social change, and enables people to worship and to endure suffering.

One must be wary of *a priori* arguments regarding authority. The fact

5. *Explorations in Theology* 1:96.

6. See, e.g., Farley, *Ecclesial Reflection* 165-68; cf. D. A. Pailin, "Reason in Relation to Scripture and Tradition," in *Scripture, Tradition and Reason* (ed. Bauckham and Drewery) 207-38; also Harvey, *The Historian and the Believer* 39-42 on the autonomy of the historian.

7. See the survey in Tracy, *Analogical Imagination* 62-63; also D. A. Pailin, "Authenticity in the Interpretation of Christianity," in *The Cardinal Meaning* (ed. Pye and Morgan) 127-59; Dulles, *Models of Revelation* 16-17; Lash, *Theology on the Way to Emmaus* 114-17; cf. Brett, *Biblical Criticism in Crisis?* 159.

that modernity has difficulty with the notion does not in itself establish whether it is theologically appropriate. Theology has to be prepared to "relativize the relativizers."[8] But *a priori* arguments are equally hazardous when used to support the idea of scriptural authority. It has often been posited that there must (logically? psychologically? morally? theologically? philosophically?) be a locus of final authority somewhere, the sole question being where it lies. B. B. Warfield declared that "without such an 'external authority' as a thoroughly trustworthy Bible, the soul is left without sure ground . . . for its faith and hope."[9] J. I. Packer describes the problem of authority as "the most fundamental problem that the Christian Church ever faces. . . . The Christian's most pressing need in every age is to have a reliable principle by which he may test the conflicting voices that claim to speak for Christianity and so make out amid their discordant clamour what he ought to believe and do."[10] But "the natural human desire for an infallible authority is no argument at all that God has seen fit to provide one."[11] If the problem of authority is "the central issue of theology,"[12] it is certainly odd that Scripture fails to speak of itself in terms of authority.

We noted in chapter 1 that, as Orthodox theologians have noted, preoccupation with authority is a Western Christian peculiarity. The early church did not have this concern, and it only arose when churches began to disagree with each other and had to try to prove which one was right by appealing to the authority that they all accepted. Before Augustine's day scripture was simply the gracious gift of the love of God.

There is an element of exaggeration here. Paul's "it is written" commonly introduces a proof-text to buttress some theological point, often in the context of controversy with unbelieving Jews or recalcitrant Corinthians or Judaizing Galatians with whom he has the authoritative scriptures in common. In the second century, Irenaeus's and Tertullian's stress on the "canon of the faith" is an indication of a concern with authority, even if the term is not yet used of scripture. "Tertullian understands the authority of Scripture as law."[13] This understanding and the associated understanding of Jesus as the law-giver may have been particularly good news in the

---

8. Berger, *A Rumour of Angels* (Penguin ed.), e.g., 57-59.
9. *The Inspiration and Authority of the Bible* 124; cf. Boone, *The Bible Tells Them So* 65.
10. *"Fundamentalism" and the Word of God* 42-44.
11. Hanson, in Hanson and Fuller, *The Church of Rome* 156.
12. Henry, *God, Revelation and Authority* 4:15.
13. Jansen, "Tertullian and the New Testament" 198.

context of the second-century Roman Empire, where moral canons lacked a coherent theological base.[14] It is in the third century that the actual phrase "the authority of the scriptures" first appears, in Novatian (ca. 250), in the context of controversy among Christians over the Trinity.[15] It does seem to be the case that questions about authority came to be more important after the Reformation and that both the assertion that such questions are important and the questioning of that importance are relatively modern preoccupations.[16]

At the same time, a writer such as Paul insists on reasoned argument in his theological work at least rigorously as do the Torah or the Gospels in their authoritative teaching on behavior. We can take that as a warning against dismissing Farley's thesis, described in chapter 1 above, as a typically modern, secular, antichristian stance. Scripture as a whole is more inclined to seek to persuade us of the truth of things than to expect us to "believe seven impossible things before breakfast." It is no more fond of laying down the law, without argument, about doctrine than it is about behavior. Further, for an audience that is suspicious of authority — or neurotically seeking it — in commending the Christian faith the phrase "the authority of scripture" may sound or be unbiblically authoritarian. Conversely, abandoning an authoritarian stance may lead to recognition of the inherent truth of scriptural insights: Sometimes "when a fearsome dogma has been overpowered and shorn of its authority, we take to it more kindly and are attracted by its defencelessness, begin to find it charming, and even fall to wondering whether there was not perhaps some quality in it that might account for its having become a dogma in the first place."[17]

Authority and Scripture

We noted in chapter 4 that the scriptural documents that we seek to interpret are themselves exercises in understanding. Their authors had seen or heard something, which they then expressed in writing. Their writings are expressions of their authors' understanding before they are the object of our understanding. In this respect the scriptures resemble other human documents. Now when we seek to enter into the way other documents look

14. Bray, *Holiness and the Will of God* 95-98.
15. *The Trinity* XXX (*auctoritatem scripturarum*).
16. Cf. Josipovici, *The Book of God* 26; Stout, *The Flight from Authority*.
17. Clines, *What Does Eve Do to Help?* 123.

at reality, there is a sense in which we do so on equal terms with them, and we feel free to evaluate them on the basis of our own understanding of reality. They may confirm it, complement it, modify it, or be judged by it. If the Bible, too, is an exercise in hermeneutics before it is an object of hermeneutics, are we also ultimately on equal terms with a writer such as Paul when we seek to understand his attempts to interpret the Christ event and the realities of which he speaks?

Leslie Houlden describes the reflections of the Second Testament writers as either judgments that are on the same footing as ours, that is, the judgments of our peers, or as a weighty and ever-increasing legacy burdening our shoulders and dictating our judgments.[18] This seems a false antithesis. People who affirm the authority of scripture do not generally understand or experience scripture as exercising its authority in an authoritarian way. Packer's chapter on "Faith" in his *"Fundamentalism" and the Word of God* makes it clear that commitment to scripture is a response to what faith sees, not to what it cannot see but acknowledges under pressure. He himself elsewhere caricatures the authoritarian attitude: "God is in heaven, and you can't catch him — now open your mouth and swallow the creed."[19] If asked why they take the Bible so seriously, people who affirm the authority of scripture are likely to see their attitude as a willing response to its compelling insights, to the dynamic of its message, and to its daily proving of its ability to speak to them, rather than implying that scripture has a quasilegal hold over them as unwilling subjects. Scripture's correspondence to reality is in part evidenced by the reality it generates. The test whether the spectacles enable us to see clearly is a public and practical test, not merely an individual and private test.[20]

If the scriptures are to be seen as the church's key theological resource and final norm, it will be so on the basis of their meeting the cumulative test described in the first section of this chapter. Acknowledging scripture as canon involves a step of faith, but it is not fideism. It is a rational step of faith, if this acknowledgment, even if not problem-free, is the most plausible commitment among alternatives. With Pascal we have to accept that we make decisions and commit ourselves, or refrain from committing ourselves, on the basis of plausibility or probability rather than of logical certainty.[21] With any doctrine or with a scientific theory the question is not

18. *Connections* 162.
19. *Keep Yourselves from Idols* 10.
20. Green, *Imagining God* 108-9.
21. Stout, *The Flight from Authority* 5-7, 25-61.

whether the commitment in question lacks loose ends or anomalies.[22] The question is whether it is the best available account of the matter: "A paradigm is refuted only by appeal to a more persuasive paradigm."[23] Even if we cannot provide a chain of linear logic to justify openness to scripture as authoritative canon, the insight that drew us to scripture in the first place may make it a better bet or a smaller risk than absolutizing our present position with its inevitable ideological features.

In practice, when people hold to the conviction that the Bible is the crucial resource and norm for belief and behavior, this commonly has a background in a personal history of involvement with the Bible. If they come to have a theory as to how and why the Bible has such authority, this theory takes shape some time after they have known the Bible speaking to them, encouraging them, giving them a perspective on life, and challenging them. Biblical authority is a living reality before such people begin to theologize about it, try to explain it, or seek to defend it.

It is thus not surprising that arguments for the special status of the scriptures tend to be convincing only to people who are already prejudiced in their favor (as I believe James Barr has put it somewhere). This may be a common characteristic of theological arguments: They are faith seeking understanding. J. I. Packer, the foremost twentieth-century intellectual expositor of a conservative attitude to scripture, describes how he came to his convictions at a student meeting: "I went in, not at all sure that the Bible was the Word of God, and came out absolutely certain that it was, though all that had happened was the one visionary chapter of the Book of Revelation had been reverently expounded." Only later did he discover that what had taken place was that the Holy Spirit had given him the certainty that the Bible is indeed God's word.[24]

We move from uncertainty to conviction with the aid of the "internal testimony of the Spirit." But we accept scripture "not *because of* but *through* the Spirit's testimony."[25] The process parallels the process by which we become convinced regarding the truth of the gospel and come to believe in Christ. Indeed, it is another version of that process. The mere preaching

---

22. Cf. J. Skorupski, *Symbol and Theory* (Cambridge: CUP, 1976) 218, noted by Stout, *The Flight from Authority* 105.

23. Green, *Imagining God* 142.

24. "Inerrancy and the Divinity and Humanity of the Bible," in *The Proceedings of the Conference on Biblical Inerrancy 1987* (Nashville: Broadman, 1987) 135.

25. H. Bavinck, *Gereformeerde Dogmatiek* (Kampen: Kok, [4]1928) 1:568, as quoted in Berkouwer, *Holy Scripture* 52. See further pp. 179-80 below.

of the message does not draw a person to a confession of faith. That objective requires God to open a person's eyes, but God opens the person's eyes to the truth of this message and through the preaching of this message. "An otherwise unconvincing message cannot attain the power to convince simply by appealing to the Holy Spirit."[26] So "Christian faith is not faith in a closed Bible, but in an open Bible. . . . Faith in the Scriptures does not precede the message that they proclaim, but is produced by the latter. I do not believe in Jesus Christ because an Apostle tells me He is the Son of God . . . but . . . because God Himself has convinced me that He is the Christ, just as He has convinced the Apostle." I believe through the apostle's witness, not on the apostle's authority, but because the Holy Spirit permits the apostle's witness to dawn on me as a declaration of God's truth.[27]

Achtemeier makes the point by noting that the Bible's authority stems from "the life-transforming power that those words have demonstrated in the life of the community of faith."[28] That comment makes clear that the experience with scripture to which we have referred is not purely individualistic. Even personal reading of the scriptures, by which people prove the scriptures' capacity to function as a norm for faith and life, generally takes place through the encouragement of the community to which they belong, which itself testifies to the scriptures' power and right to function in this way and encourages an expectant and open attitude to them on the part of the reader. Such experience with scripture that authenticates scripture is not a matter of mere religion or piety. The Bible's claim rests on "how it is acted out in the Christian community" — and is most severely threatened by that question.[29]

In having a living relationship of such a kind with the Bible, contemporary Christians repeat an experience that Christians have had over the centuries. It goes back to the response that various churches had to some of the earliest Christian documents, which led to churches collecting such documents and in due course giving them canonical status. The Second Testament reached us and was able to speak authoritatively to us only because these churches preserved certain documents and saw special significance in them.

The logic of their doing so can be inferred from the nature of the

26. Pannenberg, *Basic Questions in Theology* 2:34; cf. Thiselton, *The Two Horizons* 90.

27. Brunner, *Revelation and Reason* 169.

28. *The Inspiration of Scripture* 159.

29. Pui-Lan, "Discovering the Bible in the Non-Biblical World" 29.

documents themselves. The argument for acknowledging the authority of the Bible emerges from the content of the Bible. If one was to explain to someone who Jesus is, describing his life and teaching, his death and resurrection, and if the hearer were then to ask why he or she should believe in Jesus, we would feel this to be an odd question. It would imply that they had not really understood our exposition. We would have difficulty in imagining what we could add to it if they were not convinced by it. In the same way the central argument for acknowledging the Bible as the church's resource and norm is the content of the Bible. If someone is not convinced by the Bible's account of the gospel they will hardly be convinced by extrinsic arguments for the Bible's status.

The Experienced Revelation as Authoritative Canon

If we are to consider how we may think of scripture as a body of material that is authoritative for belief, we may most naturally do so in connection with the Epistles and the other material that we will consider more directly under the heading of the "experienced revelation" in Part IV. While the theological reflections of the wisdom tradition or of Paul have implications for ethical norms and work out a vision for areas of life such as marriage and sex, politics and land, work and pleasure, and family and community, their normativity does not relate first to behavioral matters.

"In Judaism the functional genre of Scripture is that of Torah"; that is, scripture's primary function is to regulate individual and community life. "But the Christian two-testament Scripture modifies the functional genre from Torah to doctrine." The key question becomes what people believe. This two-testament scripture comes into being in the course of second-century controversies over which account of the gospel is true, and in that context "its function is not to provide authority for regulating the life of the community but authority for right teaching, belief and confession."[30] In this respect it relates closely to the outline "canon of the faith" or "rule of the faith" as it functioned in relation to doctrinal disputes within the church. The Epistles, in particular, are *the* repository of scriptural thinking regarding the nature of that faith.

The Bible is the church's authoritative source and norm because of its nature in relation to the nature of Christian faith. We have noted in

30. Farley, *Ecclesial Reflection* 76, 77.

chapter 8 that the place in the canon of narratives about Israel and about Jesus stems from the nature of the Christian faith as a gospel about God's work in Israel and in Jesus: These narratives are our sources for a knowledge of that gospel. The rest of the scriptures are also part of the story of God's working in Israel, in Jesus, and in the church, but they belong there for a further reason, too, because they are more directly an exposition of the implications of that story as it goes along. The Epistles, in particular, work out the implications of God's acts with Israel and of the life and achievement of Jesus in terms of what they mean for theology and for attitudes to the future as well as what they mean for how we behave or how we pray. Such matters are implicit in the narratives but explicit in much of the rest of the scriptures. It is such documents that shaped the life of the church, proving themselves to be embodiments of the gospel and establishing why they have a significance not possessed by profound and influential works such as Augustine's *City of God* that are not in the same sense foundation documents of the church. These scriptural documents, those that work out the implications of the gospel narrative, thus define historically what the Christian faith essentially is. Their use as norms for the church's beliefs is not so far from the intentions of their writers or of the individuals or communities who reworked them into the form they now take. There are thus theological reasons for treating Paul's writings as more than those of a peer.

The idea of scripture as canon has been questioned from a number of perspectives. Why should one particular collection of books be given this status, and why this particular collection? Were any of these writings designed to be treated as a means of making quasi-juridical decisions on doctrine? Why should the norm for what it means to be Christian (or Jewish) lie in interpretations of the faith made over one particular millennium rather than in interpretations people come to today? Why is it that the answer to questions about the Christian position on anything always has to be answered by reference to the past? Dennis Nineham suggests — against Barth — that in fact the church ascertains the truth by being "engaged in a dialogue with herself" in the present; "the community is the revelation — or at least the locus or source of revelation."[31]

---

31. *Explorations in Theology* 1:92, 109, 107; see Barth, *Church Dogmatics* I/1:118 (2nd ed., 105). Cf. further Nineham, *The Use and Abuse of the Bible*; Evans, *Is "Holy Scripture" Christian?* also the report by the Doctrine Commission of the Church of England, *Christian Believing*.

James Barr's response is that actually "the status of the Bible is something implied in the structure of Christian (and of Jewish) faith" in that

> Christian faith is faith structured upon a certain basic model of the understanding of God. The fundamental model was "first worked out and appropriated" in the Old Testament. That model was reaffirmed, restated and reintegrated in Jesus. Christian faith is faith that relates itself to this classic model. The God in whom Christians believe is the God who was known in the Bible; the Jesus in whom they believe is the Jesus of the New Testament.

Even if there is no sharp distinction in type or date between canonical and noncanonical works, the demarcation of certain books makes sense because these give classic expression to what the faith is: "Christian faith is not whatever a modern Christian may happen to believe . . . but faith related to Jesus and to the God of Israel. The centrality of the Bible is the recognition of the classic sources for the expression of Jesus and of God."[32] In itself, Barr hastens to add, this does not imply that the biblical documents are especially inspired or inerrant. They are a human response to human experiences of God and of Jesus, not a divine revelation — not so much Word of God as "Word of Israel, Word of some leading early Christians"[33] — but they are the logically necessary guide to the nature of this faith.

In the sentences above Barr himself quotes Gordon Kaufman, who notes that personal beings are not known mainly by being described in terms of general characteristics but through "a positive and concrete history in which the singularity of the individual under consideration comes through" in the individual's acts and words. This will also be true of God as a personal being. And the Bible "contains the principal documentary remains from the history in and through which men's understanding of what we call God developed," insofar as the life of Israel and the life of Jesus actually were definitively — though not exclusively — where God has acted and spoken. Indeed, that was why the biblical documents were written, edited, preserved, and collected. Without reference to the Bible we will not know the meaning of the word God, which is a proper noun, not a common noun. Its meaning was gradually established in Israel, but "the importance of the New Testament lies in the fact that it reports the further history in

32. *The Bible in the Modern World* 115, 118. For similar comments see Bright, *The Authority of the Old Testament* 30; Thiselton, *The Two Horizons* 437-38.
33. *The Bible in the Modern World* 120.

which this fuzzy and ambiguous revelation of God comes into sharp focus" in Jesus, in the image, activity, and destiny of one man.[34]

The point is taken further by Edward Farley. To be Christian is to believe that there is something normative about what the Christ event brought about, as was discerned by those who first experienced it. This normativity is not merely a matter of the event itself but also of the way it was interpreted, for "discernment does not occur without language. And the significant achievement of the so-called apostolic period was the clothing of the normative event in a language," its linguistic sedimentation in the gospel, which is thus also normative.[35] R. L. Hart makes the point in another way by commenting on the significance of the Second Testament's imaginative language as standing in closest proximity to the paradigmatic events themselves.[36] While the Gospels are normative because they relate the gospel and do so with an authority that as witnessing tradition only they can have, the Epistles are normative because they represent the first exploration of the gospel's significance and do so with an authority that belongs to them as the original experienced revelation.[37]

There could be more than one sense attaching to the Epistles' normativity. A World Council of Churches consultation raised the following possibility: Scripture reflects a conversation between God and people. Might it be that this conversation is relevant for us not because of its particular content but because the fact of it promises that we can be involved in our own conversation with God?[38]

Some feminist interpreters take up analogous possibilities. E. Schüssler Fiorenza sees scripture not as a root model for Christian thinking and thus not as an archetype, "an ideal form that establishes an unchanging timeless pattern," but as a historical prototype, a model "critically open to the possibility of its own transformation."[39] She contrasts her view with that of other feminist scholars such as R. R. Ruether and L. Russell, who still seek for a "normative biblical tradition" and adhere to the archetypal paradigm.[40] Sallie McFague, too, sees scripture as normative in the manner of

34. "What Shall We Do with the Bible" 99, 100, 107.
35. *Ecclesial Reflection* 224; cf. 249.
36. *Unfinished Man and the Imagination* 290.
37. Of course I schematize for clarity. We have noted already that the Gospels also explore the gospel's significance and that the Epistles witness to the gospel events.
38. Cf. Barr, et al., "The Authority of the Bible," 147-48.
39. *In Memory of Her* 33; cf. *Bread Not Stone* 61.
40. *Bread Not Stone* 13, 86-87; cf. Ruether, "Feminism and Patriarchal Religion"; Russell, "Feminist Critique," in "The Effects of Women's Studies on Biblical Studies" (ed. Trible) 54-66, 68-69.

a series of case studies or as a prime Christian classic. It provides sample models for our theological thinking and indicates the way Christian theology is done rather than the content of that theology, which will vary from age to age.[41] David Tracy also sees the Bible as the Christian classic, though in a different sense, based on a view of the classics as expressions of the human spirit that "so disclose a compelling truth about our lives that we cannot deny them some kind of normative status."[42]

Barr's way of seeing this matter implies that the scriptures were designed to be not merely a set of sample models but a definitive set, normative in their content as well as illustrations of a method. They are not merely *a* Christian classic but *the* Christian classic.[43] The experiential nature of Tracy's definition is its weakness. Classics shape rather than merely reflect experience; the Bible embodies "the classic paradigm of the Christian imagination," for the reasons that Barr describes.[44] The notion of the scriptures as the Christian classics is not a theory of reception.[45] The Christian faith was not worked out in apostolic times merely as a case study. It is a normative paradigm. F. S. Fiorenza pictures scripture as the church's constitution rather than its classic: It has this position because it is the primary source for understanding the church's confession that Jesus is the Christ and the indispensable foundation on which all else is built.[46]

Schubert Ogden suggests that while the assertions of a first-century theologian such as Paul cannot (logically) determine what is actually true, it can determine what counts as Christian.[47] Pamela Dickey Young takes up his point and regrets the tendency in Christian feminist theology to speak as if all that is credible to the feminist is by that very fact Christian. Feminist theologians claim the description "Christian" for whatever liberates women. But how is their appropriation of the term "Christian" to be justified when it is disputed or the term is claimed by someone else? Feminists need to be able to claim a distinctive continuity with the Christian tradition if they are to claim to be Christian and not simply to be right.[48]

---

41. See *Metaphorical Theology* 59-65; *Models of God* 43. Liberation theologians make a similar point: cf. Segundo, *Liberation of Theology* 33-34, 110-22; Cone, *God of the Oppressed* 197-200; Miguez Bonino, *Revolutionary Theology Comes of Age* 103.

42. *The Analogical Imagination* 108.

43. Cf. Kähler, *The So-Called Historical Jesus and the Historic, Biblical Christ* 139.

44. Green, *Imagining God* 119-22.

45. Jeanrond, *Text and Interpretation* 141-42.

46. "The Crisis of Scriptural Authority" 363-65.

47. See "The Authority of Scripture for Theology" 242-45.

48. *Feminist Theology* 73-75.

W. Marxsen has described the Second Testament as a series of sermons preached on a text that consists in the person of Jesus himself or the earliest apostolic tradition about him. This implies that, strictly speaking, not scripture but Jesus himself or this earliest tradition is the canon, because he was the text of those sermons.[49] But our preaching has access to this "text" only through the canonical sermons themselves. They provide normative guidelines for our understanding of the God of Israel, who is also the God and Father of our Lord Jesus Christ. When Marxsen asks why the first-century sermons are normative in a way that twentieth-century sermons are not,[50] the answer is that the earliest years of the church and of its formulation of its understanding of the gospel story are themselves part of the gospel story; the presence of Acts in the narrative part of the Second Testament is a parable of this point. If the Second Testament is a series of sermons, then these sermons are normative in content and not merely examples of one way in which the gospel could be preached in one context.[51]

This is not to preempt hermeneutical questions or imply that we can preach Christ only in terms used in scripture. It does mean that we have to take seriously both foci of the question: If that is how the truth was expressed by people in that day who thought within that framework, how must it be expressed in ours?[52] In one sense the meaning of the Christian faith has to be worked out afresh by every generation in the light of the ways of thinking and the questions of its day. In another sense its meaning has been worked out once and for all in scripture. Scripture's account of it is the paradigm or norm for ours.

In the process of engaging in a dialogue with itself, then, the church decided it needed to establish norms for its ongoing internal dialogue, norms to help it stay in touch with the apostolic tradition in a way that ongoing oral tradition could not. Tradition, after all, was the church's means of continuing its important ongoing dialogue with itself, of allowing the gospel to be appropriately new in new circumstances. That itself means that it needs to be tested by its source. Otherwise what was designed to make the gospel contemporary ends up replacing it. Belief in a "self-evident continuity" between the Second Testament and the church in any subse-

---

49. *The New Testament as the Church's Book* 44-49, 61. Cf. Ogden, "The Authority of Scripture for Theology"; Dickey Young, *Feminist Theology* 80-87.

50. *The New Testament as the Church's Book* 55.

51. So Childs, e.g., *The New Testament as Canon* 24.

52. Hodgson, *For Faith and Freedom* 2:15-16; "God and the Bible," in *On the Authority of the Bible* 15. Cf. Nineham, e.g., *Explorations in Theology* 1:66.

quent age has to be "placed on the touchstone of the gospel."[53] An evidence of the wisdom of the church's decision to establish its norm may be that Fathers of the late second century such as Irenaeus and Tertullian, who possessed the bulk of what became the Second Testament, have a surer grasp of the gospel than most of the Apostolic Fathers, who lived nearer to the apostolic period but did not have as much of the Second Testament.[54]

The First Testament as Authoritative Canon for Jesus and the Second Testament Writers

The *Shorter Oxford English Dictionary* defines "Christian" as "believing in, professing, or belonging to, the religion of Christ." "Christ," whatever else he is, is a figure of the past, and "the religion of Christ" is one constituted and formulated through events of the past. If we refer to Jesus and the Second Testament writers in order to discover what counts as Christian, one discovery we make concerns their attitude to scripture as an authoritative canon.

Christian faith is "faith related to Jesus and the God of Israel."[55] That phrase thus draws our attention to a further reason why it was natural for the churches to collect story and teaching into a Second Testament. They already possessed collections of stories and teaching associated with God's activity before Jesus' coming. The Christians were not the first believers to find themselves in possession of a body of writings that came from the past but seemed to have a continuing authority. The Jews had such a collection, larger than the Second Testament would turn out to be, yet similarly balanced: just over half mostly narrative of God's dealings with Israel, the rest mostly occasional documents offering direct challenge and exhortation about topics such as what to believe, how to behave, and how to pray. If Christians were not to abandon the Hebrew Bible, it would have been surprising if the churches had not eventually added some new covenant scriptures to those of the first covenant. Theologically, we might indeed reckon that it would almost have required indications to the contrary if the pattern that obtained during earlier stages of Israel's story were not to continue with God's climactic act in Christ,[56] even if historically it was

---

53. Berkouwer, *Holy Scripture* 307; cf. 305-6.
54. Cullmann, *The Early Church* 96.
55. Barr, *The Bible in the Modern World* 118.
56. Packer, *"Fundamentalism" and the Word of God* 66-67.

some centuries before the inevitability of a Second Testament to follow the First seemed self-evident.

Jesus and the early Christians were brought up in the context of weekly synagogue worship, at the heart of which lay reading of the scriptures with people's response in prayer and praise; their thinking gained its framework from this study of scripture. Christian worship was modeled on this pattern, and the early Christian writings that became scripture gained that status by a natural process that included accompanying the reading of the ancient words of God with reading of some of the writings that had arisen from God's new act.[57] Matthew carries on naturally from Malachi — or from Chronicles, in the order usual in the Hebrew Bible. The foundation documents of the new covenant such as Paul's Epistles supplement the foundation documents of the first covenant such as the Torah. The Second Testament was parasitic on the First; because there were already Jewish scriptures there came also to be Christian scriptures — even though theologically the status of the Hebrew Bible within Christian faith comes in part retrospectively from the fact that in his person Jesus brings its story to its climax.

The Second Testament writers followed Jesus in accepting the canonical principle, that it was appropriate for the believing community to have generated and utilized accounts of what God had done, records of authoritative teaching, and other such material. They also followed him in assuming that the scriptures they inherited were not merely human witness to the nature of the faith, but spoke with God's authority.[58] Jesus saw himself as the climax of Israel's story and the fulfillment of its hopes; the gospel story begins as the story of Israel. Jesus appears in the Gospels as a charismatic healer and prophet rather than as a teacher of Torah or an expository preacher with a Bible in his hand, yet in declaring the nature of the righteousness that God requires he affirms the authority of the scriptures as a starting point and does not decline to discuss the interpretation of Torah. In questions of theology and spirituality, too, his life and teaching indicate the formative influence of the Jewish scriptures. At his baptism the voice from heaven describes his calling in terms from the Psalms and Isaiah (Mark 1:11). Challenged by John the baptizer regarding his status, he offers a collection of Isaianic phrases as criteria for establishing whether he is the Coming One (Matt 11:2-6). Looking

---

57. Cf. Westermann, *The Old Testament and Jesus Christ* 76.
58. See, e.g., Hanson, *The New Testament Interpretation of Scripture* 3; cf., e.g., von Campenhausen, *The Formation of the Christian Bible* chapters 1-3.

forward, he finds the pattern for his calling, including the cross, in the scriptures (Mark 8:31; 9:30-31).

In discussing questions of behavior Jesus' handling of scripture combines prophetic creativity with standing in the scriptural tradition. That combination reappears in his theological use of scripture. His own ministry is to be understood in terms of "the son of God," "the servant," and "the son of man." These are titles or roles that emerged in connection with particular historical situations in Israel: the Davidic monarchy, the Babylonian exile, and the Antiochene persecution. They influence Jesus, but they are also then influenced by him, because his person causes them to be brought into a new creative juxtaposition. Disparate elements in a diverse biblical typology of leadership or of redeemer figures are brought together and become part of a whole that was not perceived before because it was not there before. The First Testament interprets and is interpreted by the Christ event. The canon provides normative symbols for understanding Jesus, but his person has a retroactive effect on them. The church began with the same scriptures as Judaism, yet they are not the same scriptures because they are read in the light of Jesus. The scriptures provide the means of understanding Jesus and determine what Jesus meant. And Jesus provided the means of understanding them and determined what they meant.

Jesus' more personal use of the scriptures further illustrates how they provide a key for the interpretation of his experience, and he provides a key for interpreting them. To express his suffering on the cross (Mark 15:34) he utilizes the expression of tortured loneliness and the sense of abandonment with which Psalm 22 opens. Another of the sayings from the cross, "into your hands I commit my spirit" (Luke 23:46), apparently comes from Psalm 31. Jesus expresses his deep troubling in Gethsemane (Mark 14:34) in terms that recall Psalm 42. To be able to express affliction in words from scripture is to find a context of meaning. Jesus gains a form of deliverance from his isolation by taking up the cry of isolation that another has uttered before. In scripture he finds a situation with which he can identify and where he can thus find meaning. The scriptures once again illuminate and interpret the event of Christ. The point would be unaffected if the quotations were put on Jesus' lips by the Evangelists. It may be that here, too, the Christ event also interprets the scriptures. On Jesus' lips there are none of the Psalms' pleas for vengeance on one's enemies, but rather a plea for their forgiveness (Luke 23:34), a plea that matches the description of the servant who keeps his mouth shut under oppression and affliction and who makes intercession for the transgressors (Isa 53:7, 12).

The scriptures provide a context within which Jesus needed to be interpreted. Anyone has to be interpreted against the background of the general theological and cultural context in which they live and within the particular theological tradition that nurtured them. Whether by positive influence or by provoking a reaction, these forces shape the questions that come to be addressed. In this sense the theology and culture of his day are the context for interpreting Jesus. As well as those scriptures themselves that context integrally includes the tradition of interpretation prevalent within the Judaism of his day, in the light of which he will have read the scriptures, just as it includes material outside the Hebrew canon as well as material inside it. The scriptures Jesus and his contemporaries read and related to were read in the context of an interpretative tradition, though hardly more so than is the case with readers of scripture or other documents in any context.

Jesus' own use of the scriptures indicates that they are also the context for understanding him in another sense: They indicate questions that he must address as a matter of principle, and not merely because of the historical context in which he lives, and they indicate some right approaches to addressing these questions. They offer a range of insights into the purpose of God that provide a normative framework for understanding how God's purpose is fulfilled in Jesus.

The diversity of these insights reflects both the range of contexts in which they arose and the complexity of reality itself. Various pictures of a redeemer figure are needed to do justice to Jesus; both Ruth and Ezra are needed if justice is to be done to God's openness to people of all races and also to God's concern for Israel's particular role; both Chronicles and Daniel are needed if justice is to be done to God's concern for the here-and-now of worship and also for the historical consummation of the divine purpose. This necessary diversity of the scriptures also complicates how they can function as canon, and requires that Jesus interpret them as well as being interpreted by them. He provides the key for their understanding. In this sense the First Testament cannot finally be understood in isolation from the Second, any more than the Second can be understood in isolation from the First, on which it consciously builds.

Jesus and the Second Testament writers do not show the kind of exegetical interest in the scriptures that appears in some of the Qumran writings.[59] The Second Testament does not include biblical commentaries. Its exegetical

59. Lindars, "The Place of the Old Testament in the Formation of New Testament Theology" 62-64.

work is occasional and related to christological, ethical, or ecclesiological questions that arise for their own sake and not through direct study of the scriptural text for its own sake. In this particular sense scripture does not set the agenda. Nevertheless the influence of the scriptures that we have just been describing is not confined to a reactive measuring of whether some already existent view or practice is correct. For Jesus scripture fulfills both the prospective and the retrospective function of a measuring line. It is both a resource and a means of evaluation. In line with that, for the church scripture provides a context for understanding the events that we experience and a collection of earlier responses to the acts and the inactivity of God, with which we can compare our responses to such acts and inactivity.

The Second Testament documents themselves vary in their relationship with the Hebrew scriptures. There are letters such as Romans and Hebrews that could not exist without their scriptural quotations. There is a work such as the Revelation to John that includes not one biblical quotation but utilizes scriptural imagery and phraseology in every paragraph. There are letters such as Philippians or 1 John that lack either quotation or allusion, even if their understanding of God is still ultimately shaped by the scriptures. The first kind of document makes clear how natural is explicit reference back to the scriptures, the last how dispensable such explicit reference can be, given the reality of God speaking now.

It remains a general truth that "in the Christian faith from the very first both elements, Jesus and the Scripture, were mutually and inseparably related"; even outside a Jewish context "there could be little hope of 'teaching' the new salvation in Christ, and making it comprehensible to the heathen without making use of the 'Scripture.' "[60] Even the documents that do not explicitly refer to the scriptures presuppose their understanding of God and humanity. Paul's letters to the churches have the authority of the apostle, but they also claim the authority of the scriptures. It is striking that "when he is offering them revelations of a wide-ranging theosophical and speculative kind — concerning, for instance, the special character of the resurrection body or the destiny of the Jews — he supports his case either explicitly or implicitly with Old Testament texts. . . . It would be quite impossible for anyone to be a greater believer in Scripture than he"[61] — even if there is the occasional passage where "in Paul's hands scripture becomes a ventriloquist's dummy."[62]

60. Von Campenhausen, *The Formation of the Christian Bible* 21, 22.
61. *Ibid.*, 27.
62. Shaw, *The Cost of Authority* 44.

Thus C. F. Evans, who asks whether "holy scripture" is Christian, him-self notes that "Christianity is unique among the great religions in being born with a Bible in its cradle."[63] It is from the First Testament that the Second gains its concepts, presuppositions, and symbols, and the questions to which it believes the gospel is the answer.[64] "Apart from the Old Testa-ment account of God's activity in history," including its testimony to the promises of God still to be realized, "Jesus Christ cannot be understood."[65] The gospel expressed an understanding of Jesus couched in a specific frame-work, one that looked back to the Hebrew scriptures. A variety of factors could have led the church to abandon the Hebrew scriptures (Jesus' "But I say to you," the trend to desacralizing noted by Evans, Paul's emphasis on the annulment of the Torah, the immediate experience of the Spirit em-phasized especially at Corinth), but did not do so.[66]

Jesus' attitude to the Hebrew Bible has long been a cornerstone of the argument for an acceptance of the authority of scripture.[67] This argument needs to be nuanced or qualified. It may not be a good starting point for a statement of a doctrine of scripture; scripture's status derives more in-trinsically from its own nature than from Jesus' endorsement of it, so that the latter is its buttress rather than its foundation. We have to take account of the difficulty of knowing exactly what counted as scripture in Jesus' day. Jesus' words can only affirm the status of the First Testament, not that of the Second. Further, Jesus is capable of dismissing aspects of the First Testament's practical demands on people. Nevertheless he does seem to have shared the view of Jews of his day that there were scriptures that had special authority, they seem to have been the same scriptures that these Jews in general accepted, and the books we know as the Hebrew Bible remain as near as we can get to establishing which books they were.

The strength of this argument for Christian acceptance of scriptural authority is presupposed by the manner in which people who do not wish to accept it seek to avoid its thrust. They do not dispute that Jesus took this attitude, but question whether this binds us. His sharing the views of Jews of his day on this matter may be seen as a minor consequence of the

63. Is "Holy Scripture" Christian? 2.
64. Cf. Ogden, "The Authority of Scripture for Theology" 260; also Ebeling, The Study of Theology 36; M. Hooker, "In His Own Image?" in What about the New Testa-ment? (ed. Hooker and Hickling) 41.
65. Mildenberger, "The Unity, Truth, and Validity of the Bible" 403.
66. Thiselton, The Two Horizons 435.
67. See, e.g., Wenham, Christ and the Bible.

self-emptying involved in incarnation and can be ignored without compromising our commitment to following Jesus. This point is often made in
the form of the "absent-minded professor" argument:[68] "If . . . an absent-
minded professor tells me that the train for Penzance leaves Waterloo at
noon and I find that in fact it leaves Paddington half an hour before, I do
not conclude that . . . his reputation as a scholar rests on a fraud." Barr uses
this argument only to reduce the force of Jesus' apparent ignorance regarding the real authorship of some of the biblical books,[69] but Huxtable
explicitly appeals to it also in connection with Jesus' attitude to the authority
of the First Testament.[70] The importance in principle and in practice of the
question whether the scriptures are a normative religious resource, however,
suggests that for Jesus to be misleading in his attitude to the First Testament
is more like the professor of physics being wrong about the atom. It seems
that for Christians christological questions do, in fact, arise out of declining
to share Jesus' attitude to the Jewish scriptures.

68. Huxtable, *The Bible Says* 70.
69. *Fundamentalism* 74. Cf. the discussion in McDonald, *Theories of Revelation* 137-60.
70. In response to Packer's comments in *"Fundamentalism" and the Word of God* 59.

10

The Development of a Canon
of Jewish Scriptures

If there are narratives, imperatives, words from God, and experiences that have normative authority within the believing community, it is important to know what they are. There is a sense in which the existence of such normative material goes back to the earliest origins of the community, before this material was actually put into writing, but in due course the canonical process issued in recognized groups of Jewish scriptures. Rabbinic Judaism accepted the Torah, the Prophets, and the Writings, the Samaritans simply the Torah, while many Christian churches came to accept longer canons including books such as Maccabees and Wisdom. But we have little hard information on how any of this came about.

From the Beginnings to the Persian Period

Biblical and postbiblical sources point to a number of moments when circumstances led to the recognition of particular documents as canonical or to considered reflection on the extent of the canonical collection. As modern readers we have to keep reminding ourselves that until well into the Christian era the canonical scriptures were never one volume, still less a volume of which ordinary people might possess a copy. There is thus no difficulty about the canon of scripture being periodically augmented.

The biblical narratives themselves record several occasions when the Israelite community came to acknowledge specific written materials as having regulative authority within its covenant relationship with Yahweh, in the time of Moses, Joshua, Samuel, Josiah, and Ezra (Exod 24:1-8; Josh 24:25-26; 1 Sam 10:25; 2 Kgs 23:1-3; Neh 8–10). It is historically plausible to see some of these occasions, or other occasions like them, as moments when the Covenant Code in Exodus 20–24, the Deuteronomic Code, and the Pentateuchal Code as a whole came to be publicly acknowledged, though in none of the cases is this by any means certain.[1] Deuteronomy 31 requires that the covenant document in Deuteronomy be kept in the shrine; the expectation that the priests provide the king with a copy of it (Deut 17:18-19) and the fact that it was discovered there in due course (2 Kgs 22:8) presuppose this happening. M. G. Kline especially emphasizes the link between a covenant-making ceremony such as that at Sinai and the accepting of a canon.[2]

Insofar as the notion of canon applies primarily to command material, and particularly to the regulations in the Pentateuch, that is the end of the story. In the form in which we have it, however, the Pentateuchal commands are embedded in narrative. Furthermore, this narrative is one that does not come to an end with the end of the Pentateuch itself but continues into Joshua-Kings. It surely always included some version of the story of Israel's occupation of the promised land that forms the conclusion to its fundamental story line. It seems inherently more likely that it was this whole narrative (in whatever recension existed at the time) that gained acceptance, including its account of the occupation of the land, than that a truncated form of it should have become canonical independently of the narrative that continues it.[3] If this is right, there was never a time when the Pentateuch alone constituted Israel's canon. But we lack evidence on the process whereby the Pentateuch itself, the succeeding narratives, the Prophets, and the Writings came to have formal canonical status, and widely variant theories on the subject abound.

G. Östborn saw a close link between canon and worship:[4] The canonical scriptures are writings that emerge from use in worship and that are authorized for use in worship. Both aspects of this understanding may be questioned. First, "the public reading of the Old Testament books in wor-

---

1. J. Blenkinsopp, for example, questions whether even all the pentateuchal *law* was in force in Ezra's time: See "Interpretation and the Tendency to Sectarianism," in *Jewish and Christian Self-Definition* (ed. Sanders and others) 2:6.

2. See *The Structure of Biblical Authority* 27-38. Cf. chapter 8 above.

3. Cf. D. N. Freedman, "The Law and the Prophets," *Canon and Masorah* (ed. Leiman) 6.

4. See his *Cult and Canon*.

ship seems to have been a result, not a cause, of their canonicity."[5] In the course of Israel's history material is read in worship because it is acknowledged to have divine authority, not vice versa (e.g., Exod 24:3-8; 2 Kgs 23:1-3), while the Writings, at least, became part of the canon without most of them having been used in worship. Second, as far as we know only certain parts of the books that became canonical were ever used in worship. The whole Torah was read over a period, sections from the Prophets provided second lessons, the Psalms were used in the Temple in connection with various sacrifices, services, and festivals, and Esther, for example, was read at Purim, but as far as we know most of the Prophets and Writings were never used in worship itself.

There is a link between the temple and the canon. To judge from the way matters worked with the Torah, what counted as canonical was whatever books were in the temple archive in Jerusalem. Admittedly "archive" is too secular sounding. The scriptures were "holy"; that will have been both a cause and a consequence of their being kept and used in the holy shrine. While allusions in the First Testament to the depositing of scriptures in the temple refer explicitly only to the Torah, references in later Jewish sources indicate that other scriptures were also kept there.[6] The many references in the narrative books to existent narratives or annals presuppose that such official records of events were preserved, and the archive of the temple, the national shrine, is the plausible location for them. Whether Israel's major narrative works, Genesis-Kings and Chronicles-Ezra-Nehemiah, were written to provide official accounts of Israel's story or were adopted to constitute that, as official accounts they would find a place in the temple archive.

The words of the prophets tended not to be immediately accepted by the community and were perhaps initially preserved only among the prophets' followers. They were not designed to be canonical documents in the way that the codes of the Torah were, nor did they immediately become so. Here at least there is truth in Morton Smith's dictum that the material in the First Testament was in origin preserved by different groups and parties in Israel and only subsequently became one tradition.[7] In due course — perhaps as their words were believed to have come true — the work of

---

5. Beckwith, *The Old Testament Canon* 64; see further 63-64, 146-49 for what follows.

6. Cf. *ibid.,* 80-86.

7. *Palestinian Parties and Politics that Shaped the Old Testament.*

particular prophets did come to be recognized beyond the immediate circle of their followers. This process is hinted at by the development of Deuteronomic editing and shaping of their words, which may suggest that the Deuteronomists played a key role in the development of a canon of both narrative and commands along with prophecy.[8] The corpus of the (Latter) Prophets was then designed to supplement that of Genesis-Kings.[9]

Works such as Psalms, Proverbs, and Lamentations are more official in their nature than the Latter Prophets and may have been publicly acknowledged from the beginning. Song of Songs and Ecclesiastes may have gained attribution to Solomon as either a cause or a consequence of official acceptance, but the "may have" should be emphasized because we lack evidence (just as we lack evidence for the often stated conviction that the Song of Songs only gained official acceptance when it had been interpreted allegorically).

For the Samaritan community, only the Pentateuch was canonical. This has been taken to imply that that was so for all Jews when the separation between the Samaritans and the Jerusalem community took place, perhaps not long after the time of Ezra and Nehemiah. But we have seen reason to question whether canonical status would have been ascribed to the Pentateuch as such, with its truncated narrative framework, in isolation from its narrative continuance in Joshua. More likely the Samaritan canon resulted from a shortening of a longer collection that was too Jerusalem-focused for the Samaritans.

Hippolytus, Origen, and later Fathers, followed by many modern writers, believed that the Sadducees also acknowledged only the Pentateuch and not the Prophets or the Writings.[10] But when Jewish sources list differences between the Sadducees and the Pharisees and Essenes (such as attitudes to the afterlife, to oral tradition, and to the calendar), they do not include this among them. The Fathers presuppose an association between the Sadducees and the Samaritans, and as a result they may be conflating the two groups' differing views on the canon. No doubt an argument from the Pentateuch would carry more weight with the Sadducees than one from the Prophets or the Writings, but that might be true for any Jew; it perhaps further encouraged the Samaritans in confining their canon to the Pentateuch.

8. See Clements, *Prophecy and Tradition* 54-55.

9. D. N. Freedman, "The Law and the Prophets," *Canon and Masorah* (ed. Leiman) 259.

10. Hippolytus, *Refutation of all Heresies* IX.24; Origen, *Against Celsus*, I.49. Cf. Beckwith, *The Old Testament Canon* 87-91.

Jesus' appeal to Moses in an argument with the Sadducees over the resurrection follows from their own initial allusion to Moses (Mark 12:18-27) and need not imply that he is implicitly working within the terms of their "canon within the canon."

Jewish Canons in the Greek and Roman Periods

The covenant-making in the time of Moses that is portrayed in Exodus constituted the initial ordering of the Israelite community. The covenant-making in the time of Josiah and then in the time of Ezra signified the community's reordering in times of crisis. Jewish sources refer to two other events with comparable significance that may have involved action or reflection over the canon of scripture: the Second Temple's desecration in the second century BC and its destruction in AD 70.

According to 2 Maccabees 2:14-15, in 164 BC Judah the Maccabee "gathered together for us all the books that had been scattered" during the Antiochene crisis. A list of such books would be useful to us now! Beckwith sees this as the moment when the Hebrew canon of the Torah, the Prophets, and the Writings was finalized in the form that we have it — not necessarily through the addition of any works, but through the affirmation of its contents and the structuring of the collection into this threefold form.[11] The evidence is compatible with such a view and no other view is as compelling, though the argument falls short of proof. The revised Schürer suggests that "the main evidence for a complete canon by c. 150 BC is provided by the fact that Daniel, dating to c. 160 BC, is the last work to enter the Hebrew Bible."[12]

The first specific references to a threefold Hebrew canon have commonly been reckoned to come in the prologue to Ecclesiasticus (Sirach), written by the author's grandson in about 130 BC. He refers to "the Torah and the Prophets and the others who followed in their steps," to "the Torah and the Prophets and the other books of our ancestors," and to "the Torah itself and the Prophecies and the rest of the books." These expressions suggest three collections with known contents[13] more naturally than they

---

11. *The Old Testament Canon;* cf. Beecher, "The Alleged Triple Canon," for the conviction that the canon came into being by a gradual process of aggregation rather than a three-stage process.

12. In E. Schürer's *The History of the Jewish People in the Age of Jesus Christ* 2:317, n. 10; cf. Ellis's comments in *The Old Testament in Early Christianity* 36.

13. So Ellis, *The Old Testament in Early Christianity* 39-40.

do, for example, two collections of fixed content and one whose bounds were vague.[14] The writer of the prologue seems to see Ecclesiasticus itself as a wisdom book of great value but one subordinate to these scriptures and not a "candidate for admission" to a canon; its purpose was to help people to live as the Torah itself directs.

References in sources such as the Second Testament provide evidence that the Torah and the Prophets were canonical by the Roman period, and among the Writings there is less controversy over the status of Psalms, Job, Proverbs, and Daniel than over the other books. The sources may refer to Ecclesiastes, Lamentations, Ezra-Nehemiah, and Chronicles, but contain no clear references to Ruth, Song of Songs, or Esther. The view that the Hebrew canon was established by this period receives some support from the fact that at the end of the first century AD, 2 Esdras 14:45 is able simply to take for granted a canon of twenty-four books and Josephus one of twenty-two books.[15] The difference apparently indicates two ways of dividing up a common list rather than any variation in the components of the list; Josephus assimilates the number to the number of letters in the Hebrew alphabet. R. H. Charles believed that Jubilees 2:23, dating from the second or first century BC, already referred to a collection of twenty-two books.[16] The bounds of the Hebrew canon are presupposed early in the second century AD by the Greek translation of Aquila.[17]

There is some slight evidence that the Qumran community had a distinctive canon. We should not read too much into their valuing a number of apocalypses, rules, and other works outside the Hebrew Bible (e.g., Ecclesiasticus and Tobit). In itself this need not suggest that these books were part of the community's scriptural canon. The apocalypses may have been among their religious resources without being canonical or normative for faith and behavior, while their rules may have been canonical or normative for faith and behavior without being among their scriptures — like the Book of Common Prayer for the Church of England. Nor can one draw inferences from their variant text(s) of the Psalter: When a work becomes canonical it does not thereby become immune to further reworking and expansion.

14. Barton (*Oracles of God* 47) takes "the Torah and the Prophets" to denote scripture, the "others" to be other writings in general.

15. *Against Apion* I.8.

16. There is a textual problem in regard to the crucial verse, and the point depends on Charles's reconstruction of the text; Beckwith believes the phrase was at least in the Greek text in the first century BC (*The Old Testament Canon* 235-40).

17. Beckwith, *The Old Testament Canon* 277.

Similarly the fact that they continued to generate writings in scripture-like forms and would not have seen themselves as living in the postbiblical period, like "nascent rabbinic Judaism," carries no implication that they would not recognize the concept of a canon.[18] Chronicles recognizes the canonicity of the Torah and refers to it in the new scripture-like narrative that it generates, and the first Christians acknowledged the concept of a canon yet also generated prophecy, instruction, and apocalypse. On the other hand, the absence of Esther from discoveries at Qumran — in contrast to its popularity elsewhere — does hint that the Essenes did not accept that book. Perhaps its acceptance among other Jews postdated the formation of the Essenes as a distinct group.[19] Furthermore, we cannot necessarily be sure that books such as Daniel that appear in the Hebrew canon had a different status at Qumran from other apocalypses that do not.

As far as we can tell Jesus accepted the same body of scriptures as most other Jews of his day, the collection we know as the Hebrew Bible. He refers to "the Torah and the Prophets" (Matt 7:12; 11:12) and frequently quotes from various parts of these divisions of the Hebrew scriptures. He also refers frequently to the Psalms, and to Daniel and Chronicles, though not to Job, Proverbs, the Five Scrolls (Ruth, Song of Songs, Ecclesiastes, Lamentations, and Esther), or Ezra-Nehemiah. His reference to the martyrs from Abel to Zechariah (Matt 23:35 = Luke 11:51) might be an allusion to the first and last martyrs of the Hebrew Bible in canonical order, in Genesis 4 and 2 Chronicles 24:20-21, or perhaps the first and last historically, since neither he nor his hearers would have had a set of scriptures in a particular literary order and might not have been acquainted with any existent list that put them in a particular order. In Luke 24:44 he refers to the Torah, the Prophets, and the Psalms; "Psalms" may have been a title for the Writings as a whole, taken from the largest by far of the works among them.[20] But he normally refers simply to the Torah and the Prophets, which points if anything to a canon with two divisions.[21] He never alludes approvingly to any other known Jewish writings, including those later included in the Apocrypha.

Nor do any Second Testament authors quote from the latter, though they

18. Against Talmon, *Qumran and the History of the Biblical Text* (ed. Cross and Talmon) 378-79.

19. See Beckwith, *The Old Testament Canon* 291-94, 312-13. Similar considerations may underlie the distinctiveness of the Qumran Psalter: see Sanders, "Cave 11 Surprises and the Question of Canon," *Canon and Masorah* (ed. Leiman) 47-48.

20. So Beckwith: see *The Old Testament Canon* 111-12.

21. Barton, *Oracles of God* 35.

do include a number of quotations from other works that evidently had some form of religious status. The best known is Jude's quotation of 1 Enoch 1:9, but it is introduced by the phrase "Enoch prophesied . . ." rather than by a phrase that would necessarily indicate belief that the work counted as scripture. The other such quotations apparently come from works that cannot now be identified. The clearest example is James 4:5, which quotes a "scripture" that appears in no writing known to us. Earle Ellis sees such sayings as oracles from Christian prophets, which would then be evidence that not every inspired word from God had to be incorporated into the canon.[22] Like other Jews of their time, Second Testament writers reflect the influence of Jewish books such as Wisdom and Ecclesiasticus as well as books within the Hebrew canon, though the influence of a book is also no indication that it was viewed as scripture.[23]

Barton suggests that first-century Jews would have been likely to accept the scriptural status of the books we have in the Hebrew canon — and also that of other works beyond these.[24] With regard to Jesus and the early Christians, at least, there are few pointers in that direction. The extent of the canon does not seem to have been a controversial issue between Jewish and Gentile Christians or between Jewish Christians and other Jews.[25]

Developments during the Christian Era

Since the work of H. Graetz the finalization of the Hebrew canon has commonly been seen as part of the aftermath of the temple's destruction in AD 70, even if the contents had been informally established during the second century BC.[26] The temple's destruction necessitated a fundamental rethinking of what it meant to be Jewish, and during subsequent decades the most formative efforts at redefinition took place in a Pharisaic theological community established at Yavneh (Jamnia), between Jaffa and Ashdod. The Pharisees were, after all, people who especially stressed the Jewish calling to work out a detailed obedience to the scriptures in one's everyday life, and after the destruction of the temple this was what being a Jew would

---

22. *The Old Testament in Early Christianity* 4-5.

23. Sundberg gives a list of Second Testament allusions to extracanonical books (see *The Old Testament of the Early Church* 54-55).

24. *Oracles of God* 91.

25. Ellis, *The Old Testament in Early Christianity* 6.

26. See Ryle, *The Canon of the Old Testament* 189-90, on the significance of Graetz's *Kohelet* (Leipzig: Winters, 1871).

most obviously mean. Among the subjects discussed at Yavneh was that of the status of some of the books in the Hebrew Bible.

Yet we must be wary of building too much on thin evidence concerning what happened at Yavneh.[27] Our knowledge of discussions there derives from a mere handful of references in the Talmud, which are scattered and allusive. To describe Yavneh as a "synod" gives a misleading impression, suggesting that rabbis gathered there as a formal decision-making body. They did discuss the status of Ezekiel, Ecclesiastes, and the Song of Songs, but hardly in such a way as to justify calling their action "the formation of a normative canon of sacred scriptures" that were now "formally declared binding."[28] Yavneh was not a decree-making council like Nicea or Chalcedon. Rabbinic discussions regarding whether books such as those just mentioned should be "withdrawn" likely envisaged withdrawing them from public use[29] or from liturgical use in particular[30] because of difficulties they could cause for people, rather than withdrawing them from the canon or refusing them a place in it.

Discussion of whether such books "defiled the hands" likewise is unlikely to have signified discussion of their canonical status. S. Z. Leiman[31] suggests that the use of this phrase, too, presupposes that the books under discussion were already canonical. The rabbis' comments concerned whether they were also inspired. A book could be canonical in the sense of normative for thinking and practice without having been produced by prophetic inspiration; this was so in due course with the Talmud. But if it was produced by prophetic inspiration, it required a particular form of reverence, and the question that concerned the rabbis was which books indeed required this.[32] Leiman's suggestion coheres with our underlying emphasis on distinguishing among models such as canon and inspiration.

There is no evidence that Yavneh discussed the status of Ecclesiasticus or of any other book that eventually found a place in one of the longer canons. Rabbis and others did debate the status of specific books before and long after Yavneh; such debates carry no implication regarding whether

27. Cf. Lewis, "What Do We Mean by Jabneh?"
28. Eissfeldt, *The Old Testament: An Introduction* 568.
29. Moore, *Judaism* 1:247.
30. Barton, *Oracles of God* 66-72.
31. *The Canonization of Hebrew Scripture* 102-20.
32. Barton (*Oracles of God* 66-72) also connects the question with aspects of their use in the liturgy.

these books already officially have canonical status. The very fact that discussion at Yavneh involved Ezekiel, a long-established member of the Prophets, argues against the view that the rabbis were attempting to delineate the canon's boundaries for the first time. They were asking a question in the context of an already existing established canon. If that is the significance of their discussions with regard to Ezekiel, it is likely that this was also the case at other points. It may have been a totally theoretical debate, parallel to Luther's later division of the Second Testament into two parts and his well-known critique of James, which were no indication that the Second Testament canon was not established in his day. It may have been connected with the fact that the new situation for Judaism after AD 70 was going to give the (existing) canon new significance. The practical result was in due course the Masoretic interest in the finalizing of the correct *text* of the Hebrew Bible. It is this rather than the finalizing of the canon that is ultimately the fruit of the destruction of the Second Temple. Although the Hebrew canon has quite firm edges to it and no "apocrypha" or "deutero-canonical writings," we know of no occasion when a body made a decision to establish this canon. The absence of evidence suggests that there was no such occasion; the canon simply stopped growing.

It has been a common view that in the first Christian century the Torah and the Prophets were established but no bounds had yet been fixed to a third body of writings. The evidence that Barton collects may suggest that the official collection of scriptures, which coincided at least approximately with the Hebrew canon, had two divisions that could be referred to as "the Torah and the Prophets" or as "the Torah and the Tradition." The later division between the Prophets and the Writings merely made a distinction between books that were used in the regular lectionary and ones that were only "written" not "read" books.[33] Although all the books we know as the Hebrew Bible were thus recognized as scripture at the beginning of the Christian era, Barton emphasizes that this does not make these a canon in the sense of an exclusive list. Indeed, he infers that only the Torah was strictly canonical, though this makes it difficult to see how and when the Hebrew canon did come into being. It was the need to fill this gap that led to Yavneh having this role ascribed to it, but we have seen that Yavneh is unable to fill the gap. More likely in Jewish circles the Hebrew canon had frozen in the form we have it well before Yavneh, and later variation among Christians reflected their intentional or unintentional deviation from Jewish practice.

33. See Barton, *Oracles of God* 35-95.

Discussions at Yavneh were by no means the end of the story of the canon of Jewish scriptures. We have noted that sources such as the Qumran documents and the Second Testament indicate the use, if not the scriptural status, of a number of other Jewish works in addition to books that appear in the Hebrew canon. Most other first- and second-century writers confine themselves to works in the Hebrew canon, though *Barnabas*, for instance, quotes at least from 2 Esdras 4–5 (as "another of the prophets") and from 1 Enoch 89 (as "scripture") in chapters 12 and 16 and includes other quotations from "scripture" that do not appear in the Hebrew Bible or other extant Jewish writings. Irenaeus's allusion to Susanna, however, may only prove the rule, if it is an accidental result of reading Daniel in Greek.[34] Melito's list, compiled about 170, corresponds to the Hebrew canon except that it lacks Esther,[35] which does, however, appear in another slightly later list.[36] Origen's list (about 230) includes 1 Esdras (unless by 1 and 2 Esdras he means Ezra and Nehemiah) and the Letter of Jeremiah (perhaps a reference to Baruch as an appendix to Jeremiah); it lacks the Twelve Prophets, apparently by accident, and explicitly omits Maccabees.[37]

In Alexandria, *the* center of learning in the early Christian centuries, Christians came to treat some other Jewish works on a level with writings within the Hebrew canon, all of which they read in Greek. By the fourth century this was the usual Christian view. It is assumed by Augustine and by the Synods of Hippo (393) and Carthage (397), though Augustine recognizes that books such as Maccabees are canonical only for Christians and not for Jews.[38]

In contrast, in his *Easter Letter* of 367 Bishop Athanasius of Alexandria lists as the Christian collection the Hebrew canon as we know it, except that he associates Baruch and the Letter of Jeremiah with the Book of Jeremiah and lists Esther with Wisdom, Ecclesiasticus, Judith, Tobit, and Hermas as not canonical but read for edification. His attitude to Baruch and the Letter of Jeremiah, paralleled elsewhere in the period, may have a

34. Irenaeus, *Against Heresies* IV.26.3; cf. Ignatius's references to Daniel 13 in Magnesians 3.

35. See Audet, "A Hebrew-Aramaic List." Both this and Melito's list omit Lamentations, perhaps seeing it as part of Jeremiah.

36. See Eusebius, *Church History* IV.26.

37. Eusebius, *Church History* VI.25. Aland takes Origen's comment "apart from these are Maccabees" to indicate that Maccabees is within the canon (*The Problem of the New Testament Canon* 7).

38. *City of God* XVIII.36.

similar background to Irenaeus's use of the longer text of Daniel. Bruce attributes Athanasius's omission of Esther to his use of a deviant Jewish source.[39] Paralleled as it is elsewhere, however, it may reflect the unease with Esther that reappears in Luther and in the modern period.

Jerome's position is similar to that of Athanasius. He distinguishes between the Hebrew canon and the books he knew only in Greek, introduces the designation "apocryphal" for the latter, and declares that the church "does not admit them among the canonical scriptures" but "reads them for the edification of the people, not to give authority to doctrines of the church."[40]

It was long assumed that the Christians of Alexandria inherited their longer canon from the Greek-speaking Jews of Alexandria.[41] The usual current view is that the Christians themselves became interested in a wider range of Jewish books than those in the Hebrew canon and in due course came to view books such as Wisdom as canonical in a way that Jews did not. The longer canons were, therefore, Christian expansions of the Jewish scriptures.[42] The great fourth- and fifth-century Christian manuscripts of the scriptures such as the Sinai Codex include the books that appear in one of the longer canons, and a number of longer Christian canons are preserved in various Catholic and Orthodox churches. The evidence of Athanasius, among others, indicates that there was no universal Christian understanding regarding the extent of either the Jewish or the Christian canon of Jewish scriptures,[43] though it also indicates that there was not a universal commitment even in Alexandria to a longer canon.

There were no formal declarations regarding the First Testament canon until Christian churches started making such declarations in the context of the Reformation. Catholic appeal to 2 Maccabees 12:43-45 as scriptural evidence for belief in purgatory led Luther to declare that Jewish books outside the Hebrew canon could not be used to establish doctrinal points.[44]

---

39. *The Canon of Scripture* 80.

40. *Preface to Proverbs, Ecclesiastes, and Song of Songs.*

41. So still D. Barthélemy, "L'état de la Bible juive depuis le début de notre ère jusqu'à la deuxième révolte contre Rome (131-135)," in Kaestli and Wermelinger (ed.), *Le canon de l'Ancien Testament* 9-45.

42. Sundberg, *The Old Testament of the Early Church.*

43. Aland, *The Problem of the New Testament Canon* 4-8.

44. "Defense and Explanation of All the Articles," on the thirty-seventh article from Luther's disputation with Johann Eck in 1519; ET, *LW* 32:96. Luther was notoriously rude about whether Esther should be in the canon, but he did not formally attempt to remove it (see Bornkamm, *Luther and the Old Testament* 188-90).

In response the Council of Trent in 1546 made the first dogmatic decision regarding the canon of which we know, declaring that all the books that appear in the Latin Vulgate translation were uniformly canonical. The Church of England Articles followed Luther and thus Jerome,[45] despite the oddity of thus committing oneself to the belief that a book such as Judith is of value for morals but a book such as Wisdom (with its influence on Paul) is of no value for doctrine. In turn the Orthodox Church in 1642 and 1672 affirmed the Greek Canon (including 1 and 2 Esdras and the Prayer of Manasseh, which appear in an appendix in the Vulgate). The Westminster Confession, in contrast, declared that the apocryphal books were not of divine inspiration, not canonical, of no authority in the church, and of no greater significance than other human writings. For someone outside one of these confessions, comments F. F. Bruce diffidently, the limits of the canon are simply a matter of tradition.[46]

---

45. Cf. R. Hooker, *Treatise on the Laws of Ecclesiastical Polity* V (1597) 20, 7.
46. *Tradition Old and New* 129-30.

11

The Development
of a Second Testament

It was over several centuries that the Christian church developed a canon of new scriptures to set alongside the First Testament; even then this process came to a conclusion less tidy than is often realized. The first stage in the process took most of the opening two centuries of the Christian era, during which the foundational Christian writings came into being and began to come together in informally recognized groups. The second stage was precipitated by a series of crises over the nature of true Christian belief in the late second century, which hastened the clarifying of which were the key normative Christian documents. The third comprised a further longer period during which generally informal agreements were reached about the bounds of the Second Testament canon.

The First Two Christian Centuries

A church asked in AD 50 whether it had a Bible would have given an affirmative reply and would have pointed to Jewish scriptures. It would have copies of at least some books of that canon, though perhaps not all, and it might well be uncertain about the precise limits of the total collection. If one had gone on to ask whether these writings alone shaped its faith and life, its members would of course have answered that the life and words of Jesus were of key significance in that connection, but that these were known to them not through any writings but through people who had known Jesus during his earthly lifetime, through the preaching and the conversation of others who had themselves known such people, and through his own present speaking as the church's exalted Lord. In this sense the faith of the early Christians was not founded or focused on scripture but on the person of Jesus. The importance of Jesus to them meant that they also read the Hebrew scriptures in the light of Jesus' life and words. For them the *Hebrew* scriptures were the *Christian* Bible, the "book of Christ."[1]

Over subsequent decades there came into being writings such as the letters of Paul and other figures that expounded something of the significance of Jesus' life and teaching in the context of questions arising from the life of the church. Such pastoral letters were not written or received as canonical scripture; they were essentially occasional documents. They were not designed to tell people of Jesus' life and teaching; they assume the dissemination of the story of Jesus through preaching and testimony in the way just referred to and presupposed by allusions in passages such as 1 Corinthians 11 and 15. They sometimes refer to specific things that the Lord said (see 1 Cor 7:10; 9:14; 11:23; 1 Thess 4:15; cf. also Acts 20:35), presumably during his earthly lifetime, though some of these passages have been taken as referring to later sayings of Jesus through the Holy Spirit. If the Lord had spoken, the implication was, that settled the matter. Elsewhere these letters reflect the teaching of Jesus without making it specific that this is what they are doing (e.g., Rom 12–15).

The copying and dissemination of Paul's letters, encouraged by Paul himself (cf. Col 4:16), reflects a recognition among the churches of the authority that he claimed, though this does not mean that his letters were canonical scripture, and it is paralleled by the attitude expected of and taken to the letters of some of the Apostolic Fathers. Historically it was pure accident that Paul had to write the way he did to the Romans or the Corinthians. He saw himself as addressing needs of particular churches, not writing documents to make up a Bible. But this was not felt to prevent his writings from being providentially intended gifts for the whole church.

After Paul's activity in mission and writing reached its height, a number of writers came to produce narrative accounts of Jesus' life and words and of their central significance for the church. That in due course would open up the possibility of setting some such documents alongside the Hebrew scriptures. Indeed, the more that Jesus' climactic significance was asserted and the more Judaism and Christianity moved apart from each other, the more it might become an open question whether the church should continue to acknowledge the Hebrew scriptures. But when these accounts of the gospel

1. Von Campenhausen, *The Formation of the Christian Bible* 328.

story were being written, as far as we know they neither sought nor received universal, exclusive, or final authority as *the* account of Jesus. They, too, were neither written nor received as scripture. Each was one person's or one church's perspective; each came to be treasured in particular circles.

A church asked in AD 100 the question we have imagined asking in AD 50 might, then, have given a more complicated answer. It would have begun with the Hebrew scriptures and gone on to oral accounts of Jesus' words and life that had been passed on to the churches, but in response to a further supplementary question a church might have been able to mention possessing a memoir about Jesus and copies of a number of letters by apostolic and postapostolic figures, which had a form of authority for them without counting as part of a canon.

Written memoir and living testimony now existed alongside each other, but were appealed to in different contexts. An overtly second-generation Christian writing such as *1 Clement* still quotes from "the words of the Lord Jesus" (in chs. 13 and 46) not as they appear in a written document (even though such existed by Clement's day) but apparently as they were passed on in the church. Ignatius in *Philadelphians* 8 provides a parable of the uncertainty regarding the relationship between living testimony and written account in his allusive report of a disagreement with Christians who insist on limiting themselves to what can be proved from the Hebrew scriptures. In the absence of evidence from these scriptures, they say, they will not accept something as part of the gospel — or do they mean they will not accept it merely because it appears in the Gospel? Is Ignatius affirming the importance of the written Gospel over the living testimony or that of the gospel itself over the pre-Christian scriptures? He makes the latter point elsewhere,[2] while Polycarp also asserts that the command of Christ mediated by the preaching of the apostles stands theologically prior to the proclamation of the prophets.[3] In chapter 8 we noted the ambiguous attitude to oral and written that regularly appears in religious traditions, and noted how Christian faith can hardly do without the written.

In the early second century it is doubtful whether the term "gospel" yet applies to a genre of writing; hence our avoiding it so far in this chapter. Justin uses the older term "memoir," adding "so-called gospels," for works that have more the authority of written historical records than that of holy scripture. It seems to have been Marcion who first unequivocally applied

---

2. E.g., *Magnesians* 9; cf. the emphasis in the next chapter of *Philadelphians*.
3. *Philippians* 6; cf. Metzger, *The Canon of the New Testament* 60.

the term "gospel" to a document, having misunderstood Romans 2:16.[4] Papias in his *Exposition of the Sayings of the Lord* confesses his own preference for the "living voice" of people who had themselves known Jesus' disciples, but it is also he who gives us the first tantalizing external hints about the origin of Matthew and Mark.[5]

Beyond the Hebrew scriptures and oral and written accounts of Jesus, Paul's letters, Hebrews, 1 Peter, 1 John, Judith, Tobit, the Wisdom of Solomon, and traditions from postapostolic times (c.g., concerning the deaths of Paul and Peter) are also reflected in the letters of Clement, Ignatius, and Polycarp. That all this is included there means that we cannot assume that every quotation from some document indicates that the document counts as scripture or that listing who an author quotes thereby establishes the contents of that author's canon. Among the documents that these three Fathers do quote, Paul's letters are preeminent: "Paul is 'the Apostle' *par excellence* — that is how he is referred to throughout the second century."[6] But the term "scripture" is used only for the Hebrew Bible, which is quoted more often than either Jesus or Paul, and for one or two unidentifiable sayings of the kind that also appear in the Second Testament.[7]

Some letters of Paul do count as scripture for one of the writings that itself also came to be included in the Second Testament, 2 Peter (see 3:15-16). Its date is a matter of controversy, but whether or not it was actually written by Peter, the work of the Apostolic Fathers contrasts with it in being overtly of second generation, postapostolic origin. If 2 Peter is actually itself a postapostolic work, it too bears witness to the cruciality and uniqueness of the first generation by presenting itself as coming from this period and seeking to restate the apostolic faith in a new context. Insofar as this is what it does, it is apostolic in content even if not literally apostolic in authorship.[8] That it speaks of Paul's letters as "scripture" is significant, but we must set alongside that the fact, just noted, that documents within the Second Testament and outside it use the term "scripture" of various other materials that did not come to be part of the scriptural canon. "Scripture" seems to have been a broader term than it is for us.[9]

---

4. See Koester, *Ancient Christian Gospels* 35-41.
5. Eusebius, *Church History* III.39.
6. Von Campenhausen, *The Formation of the Christian Bible* 143.
7. E.g., James 4:5-6, noted earlier; cf. *1 Clement* 8; 46.
8. Farmer, "Some Critical Reflections on Second Peter" 40-42; cf. Farkasfalvy, "The Ecclesial Setting of Pseudepigraphy in Second Peter" 25-29.
9. See Hanson, *Tradition in the Early Church* 205-8.

So far, then, extant early Christian writers assume that the Hebrew Bible has a specific position as holy scripture, that the words of Jesus as transmitted in preaching or in writing have natural importance, and that special significance attaches to some first-century letters and other documents. But the church had not formulated a way of thinking about the status of such writings or determined whether there were particular writings to which such special status should attach.

About 150 Justin Martyr describes Christian worship as including reading from the memoirs of the apostles or from the writings of the prophets (*First Apology* 67). He himself makes frequent use of Matthew and Luke, presumably knew Mark, perhaps uses John, and also occasionally quotes from other traditions about Jesus, some of which appear in Gospels such as *Peter* and *Thomas*.[10] His disciple Tatian treated Matthew, Mark, Luke, and John as of special significance, but he both indicated and compromised that recognition by not leaving them separate but weaving them into a harmony, the *Diatessaron*, which also incorporated a few sayings known to us from other Gospels.[11] Tatian's harmony was effectively the canonical Gospel text in Eastern Syria for three centuries.

Justin's remark about the apostles and the prophets implies that some Gospels had a status at least analogous to that of the Hebrew scriptures, and perhaps prior to them. That reflects the passing of a century during which the preaching of the message about Christ has been notably fruitful among Gentiles and relatively unfruitful among Jews. Synagogue and church are clearly distinguished from each other, and the latter is a predominantly Gentile institution. While Justin's affirmation of the significance of the Gospels marks a new stage in Christian thinking, "he is one of the last representatives of that era in Christian history . . . when there was no other 'scripture' to which men could appeal in their preaching of Christ except the traditional Old Testament."[12] He is a bridge figure.

The Crises of the Late Second Century

We do not know the historical reasons that the particular documents we have in the Second Testament (these Gospels, these letters . . .) came to

10. Koester, *Ancient Christian Gospels* 360-402.

11. W. L. Peterson, "Tatian's Diatessaron," in Koester, *Ancient Christian Gospels* 403-30.

12. Von Campenhausen, *The Formation of the Christian Bible* 102.

have a distinctive status in the church. William Farmer has suggested that the pressures of persecution and the possibility of martyrdom generated a canon that emphasized the death and resurrection of Jesus and the challenge to be faithful to him even to death.[13] It is more usual to emphasize the need for the church to clarify its mind at certain key points on the nature of right Christian belief in the context of the critical period through which it was passing in Justin's day. As we now see it the story concerns how orthodox, catholic Christianity vindicated itself against the pressures of heretical views. Historically the "orthodox" view was, indeed, in the center of the stream; it is this that Celsus attacks, not Marcion or the gnostics.[14] Alongside it, however, stood a number of older and newer Christian traditions that would also claim to represent the true faith.

First, a significant section of the church believed that it could combine gnostic beliefs and faith in Christ. Gnosticism had various forms, but among its basic characteristics were the belief that the world was created not by the supreme God but by a subordinate deity, the God of the Hebrew Bible, who revealed the Law in its inadequacy. Christian gnostics were thus disinclined to believe in the incarnation, crucifixion, or resurrection of the Son of God. Their special *gnōsis* (knowledge) supplied the real truth about this world and the world(s) above and the key to escaping to the latter and thus to finding salvation. The documents that eventually found a place in the Second Testament, like those in the First, have a very different understanding of God, the world, Jesus, and salvation, and some oppose views of a gnostic type (e.g., Col 2:8, 18). At the same time there are elements in these earlier Christian documents (e.g., John 1 and Colossians itself) that could be read in a gnostic way, in the light of the system that is expounded in the gnostic writings. The latter include Gospels said by gnostic Christians to convey secret revelations that Jesus gave the disciples, and these Gospels may include sayings that go back to Jesus himself and independent versions of sayings that appear in the four Gospels.

The gnostic Christians' attitude to the status of the Hebrew scriptures, to the tradition about Jesus, and to documents such as the written Gospels and Paul's letters, and also the degree to which they used these documents, was in one sense quite within the range of regular Christian attitudes and practice during the second century. Valentinus's disciple Heracleon, indeed,

---

13. *The Formation of the New Testament Canon* 7-95.
14. Wilken, "Diversity and Unity in Early Christianity" 107. Farmer also allows for the significance of this need for the church to clarify its mind.

wrote a commentary on John, the oldest surviving commentary on any of the works in the Second Testament. What made the difference was setting the Hebrew scriptures and the early Christian documents in the context of a broader range of writings that generated a quite different theological system, in the light of which these earlier writings were interpreted.[15]

A second form of Christianity that drove catholic Christianity to clarify its thinking was that of Marcion, a layman from Turkey who went to live in Rome and joined the church there. He formulated views that overlapped with those of the gnostics but went beyond them in his attitude to the Hebrew scriptures. He, too, distinguished between the true God and the subordinate God who created the world and gave Israel the Law, and he also did not believe in the incarnation. He saw Christian faith as a radically new revelation and rejected the Hebrew scriptures and the understanding of the Christian faith expressed in the catholic church's preaching, which it believed went back to the apostles and which was inextricably linked with the Hebrew scriptures, throughout which it found itself prophesied. He based his own beliefs instead on the safer foundation of written documents, a combination of "Gospel" and "Apostle." As far as we know "Marcion was the first Christian teacher to present a closed canon."[16] As his Gospel he chose Luke, for reasons he does not tell us, though clearly this provided a securer link with true original Christianity than either catholic or gnostic tradition or new revelation. The "Apostle" meant ten of Paul's letters, those later included in the Second Testament minus the Pastorals. Despite their occasional nature, which makes them not obviously suitable as normative documents, these letters were a logical choice because they expressed the nature of the gospel as Marcion believed it. It was a choice embarrassing to the catholics because for them, too, Paul was "'the Apostle' *par excellence*," though they hardly comprehended him; hence the quip in Harnack's *History of Dogma* that Marcion alone understood Paul, and even he misunderstood him,[17] as is reflected in his need to purge Paul as well as Luke of considerable "Judaizing interpolations."

A diametrically opposite view of Christian faith was embodied in the

---

15. See Irenaeus, *Against Heresies* I.9.2; cf. Thiselton, *New Horizons in Hermeneutics* 156.

16. Farkasfalvy, *The Formation of the New Testament Canon* 140.

17. A. Harnack, *History of Dogma* (ET London: Willams and Norgate, 1894; [2]1897/Boston: Little, 1899) 1:89; the remark is said to have originated with Franz Overbeck. See Metzger, *The Canon of the New Testament* 93; Thiselton, *New Horizons in Hermeneutics* 155.

more Jewish Christianity expressed in Matthew's Gospel and maintained by later Jewish Christians, who saw faith in Christ as a way of being Jewish. It coexisted with adherence to the Torah, though it found that it could not do so consistently, and determined — to judge from the *Homilies* mistakenly attributed to Clement — that the Torah's sacrificial system and the morally offensive aspects of the lives of its heroes such as Abraham and Moses must reflect corruption of the original revelation.[18]

Contemporary with the spread of Marcion's views in the second half of the second century was the spread of the movement begun by Montanus, who also came from Turkey. This movement stressed the present activity of the Spirit in speaking through prophets, the imminence of the End, and — in due course — the importance of strict penitential discipine. Prophecies were written down, collected, and treated as sacred writings that might seem to have a status like that of the Hebrew scriptures, the sayings of the earthly Jesus, or the Epistles. One result of this was to threaten to bring discredit on documents utilized by these pentecostal Christians or comparable to theirs, notably the Gospel of John with its promise of the outpouring of the Spirit, which Montanus stressed, Hebrews with its stress on discipline, and Revelation with its prophetic claim and its promise of the New Jerusalem.

The battle for the identity of Christian faith encouraged a substantial crystallization of the catholic Christian view, in which the work of Irenaeus and Tertullian played a key part. Like Marcion and Montanus, Irenaeus came from Turkey, but about 180 he became bishop of Lyons in France, and thus bridged the Christianity of the eastern and western Mediterranean. In his treatise *Against Heresies* he can claim the capacity to pronounce on the faith of the worldwide church; the catholic faith was not a mere local phenomenon like that of the "heretics." Tertullian in Carthage, about twenty years, later took similar views on the nature of the faith and on the contents of the scriptures; even though he himself became a Montanist he came to accept a consensus that Hermas should not be accepted as scripture.

The Catholic Church's Response

There were three key aspects to the developments encouraged by these conflicts within the church as a whole. First, they led the catholic church

---

18. *Pseudo-Clementine Homilies* II.50-52; III.47.

to clarify how it saw the relationship between the faith of Israel and the faith of the church. A number of views were held on the matter. The Jewish Christians emphasized continuity between Jewish and Christian faith, while the gnostics and Marcion so emphasized the newness of the gospel that they wished to have nothing to do with the Hebrew scriptures or the Hebrew God. The gnostics formally accepted the Hebrew scriptures but interpreted them in the light of a framework from elsewhere, which transformed their meaning. Marcion and his followers took the Hebrew scriptures literally and saw that they were incompatible with faith in Christ: Arguably Marcion alone understood the Hebrew Bible, and even he misunderstood it, but his understanding and rejecting it encouraged catholic Christians to misunderstand it in order to accept it. The regular Gentile Christian use of the Hebrew scriptures linked the faith of the church with the faith of Israel; but it did this by reading the scriptures through Christian spectacles in such a way that their meaning was transformed and they were turned into vehicles of specifically Christian teaching. This hermeneutic was similar to that of gnosticism, but it operated by means of a different alien framework.

Over against Marcion the catholic church was clear that it acknowledged the Hebrew scriptures. Irenaeus provided it with a way of sailing between the Scylla of Jewish Christianity and the Charybdis of Marcion or the gnostics in its approach to the relation between these scriptures and faith in Christ. His orientation point was an insight he took over from Justin:[19] God, creation, and the Hebrew Bible on the one hand and Christ, redemption, and Christian writings such as the Gospels and Paul on the other both belong to one salvation story. It is one story, but with earlier and later stages, which allows for and accounts for both continuity and discontinuity between Israel and the church, the Hebrew scriptures and the church's faith.

Irenaeus's understanding of biblical faith as focusing around a story that has earlier and later stages with elements of continuity and discontinuity betweeen them opened up the way to a more literal interpretation of the Hebrew scriptures like those of Jewish Christianity and of Marcion, without requiring one to follow either in the status they attributed to the Hebrew scriptures. It also provided a key to understanding the scriptures as a whole and a basis for perceiving how the gnostics impose an alien system on the scriptures.[20]

19. See von Campenhausen, *The Formation of the Christian Bible* 88-102.
20. See, e.g., *Against Heresies* I.10.1; cf. Greer, *Early Biblical Interpretation* 123-25.

This outline understanding of basic Christian beliefs concerning the work of God the creator, Jesus his Son crucified and risen, and the Holy Spirit was related in content to the baptismal creed but formally distinguished from it. It was the church's "canon of the truth" (so, e.g., Irenaeus, *Against Heresies* I.9.4, 22.1). It provided a framework for understanding scripture, and in particular for avoiding the heresies that could emerge when passages were taken out of their context in scripture as a whole.

The idea of such a rule of the faith (i.e., "canon of the faith")[21] consisting of an outline understanding of the story of God's purpose was developed by Tertullian and used to provide a key to understanding the varying moral demands of scripture.[22] It codified or canonized certain central affirmations of the gospel and thus marginalized others, but also — mostly unconsciously — thereby left open a number of options on the way the affirmations might be understood. Superficially the canon for the faith was not canonical scripture but a canonical summary of the gospel. But a better way to express its nature would be to describe it as a skeleton outline of the faith of scripture itself, because it was considered present within scripture rather than imposed on it from outside as something alien. Scripture in turn provided the flesh for the bones constituted by the rule.

The controversies also drove the catholic church to determine what sources it acknowledged as guides to the true nature of Christian faith itself. In the context of the novelty of the teaching of Marcion and the gnostics and their bold claim that actually it is they who hold the true apostolic faith, Irenaeus affirms the apostolic faith passed on and confessed consistently in the oral teaching and preaching of the worldwide church and expressed in the written Gospel (e.g., *Against Heresies* I.10; III.4-5, 24). He recognizes that the Hebrew scriptures and the church's tradition are no longer enough, but must have Christian writings set alongside them. So a broad collection of "the writings of the evangelists and the apostles" stands alongside "the Law and the Prophets" (I.3.6). They do not replace them; Irenaeus still preaches by setting alongside each other the Hebrew scriptures

---

21. *Kanōn tēs pisteōs* in Greek, *regula fidei* in Latin. See, e.g., Flesseman-van Leer, *Tradition and Scripture* 125-28, 161-70, and references there. The conventional translation "rule of faith" is probably misleading; the phrase surely refers to the faith *in* which one believes, not the faith *with* which one believes. But in this and analogous phrases it is not absolutely clear whether the genitive is objective ("the rule for the faith"), subjective ("the rule that comes from the faith"), or explicative ("the rule that consists in the faith").

22. See Bray, *Holiness and the Will of God* 104-11.

and the facts about Jesus as passed on in the church. But in his theological and apologetic work in the context of Gentile rather than Jewish controversy the written Gospels and Epistles rather than the Hebrew scriptures and the church's tradition — both questioned by his opponents — come to be prominent.[23] Written rather than oral sources maximize safeguards against traditions that claim antiquity but are actually of recent origin, and excludes documents such as the *Acts of Peter*, which were not explicitly gnostic but were used by the gnostics. Eusebius of Caesarea attributes to Ignatius the concern, in the context of the development of the various heresies, to set down the apostolic tradition clearly in writing "for safety's sake."[24] It is an anachronistic comment but one that articulates a concern that does develop through the centuries up to Eusebius's own day.[25]

Marcion's canon is the first formal list of Christian canonical books known to us, and it stimulated the church to begin to devise its own list. The significance of this should not be exaggerated; the church in general already informally recognized Marcion's canon along with a wider range of documents. It was hardly just as a negative consequence of Marcion's exclusive stress on Luke and Paul that people began to value other Gospels and letters. Sooner or later they would perhaps have had to draw up their lists, but Marcion seems to have precipitated this. He thus caused them not merely "to state more clearly what they already believed"[26] but to work out more clearly what they *should* believe.[27] Independently of the link between Marcion and the canon it has been pointed out how manifold are the pointers toward the development of the canon in the most important city in Turkey, Ephesus.[28]

If the catholic church felt it needed scriptures at all, it might have been tempted to devise a collection that kept well away from the paths that led to the various heresies. In fact it did the opposite. The groups regarded as heretical could identify with different strands among documents accepted by the catholic church. Matthew is markedly Jewish Christian. John and

---

23. Von Campenhausen, *The Formation of the Christian Bible* 183-86.

24. Eusebius, *Church History* III.36.

25. R. M. Grant, "The Creation of the Christian Tradition," in *Perspectives on Scripture and Tradition* (ed. Kelly) 16.

26. Grant, *The Formation of the New Testament* 126; cf. Metzger, *The Canon of the New Testament* 99.

27. Von Campenhausen, "Marcion"; cf. *The Formation of the Christian Bible* 147-209.

28. Lemcio, "Ephesus and the New Testament Canon."

Paul can sound rather gnostic. Revelation anticipates Montanism in its assumption that the day of prophecy and vision is not over. Marcion would appreciate both Paul's antithesis between law and gospel in letters such as Romans and Galatians, where Paul does utilize the Hebrew scriptures, and also his omission of reference to the Hebrew scriptures in other letters such as Philippians, Colossians, and Thessalonians (with the deprecatory words about the Jews in 1 Thess 2:15-16).

Over against Marcion the catholic church confirmed that it was committed to a range of material that gave expression to several versions of the apostolic faith. "The particularity (for example, letters addressed to particular churches) and the plurality (for example, four Gospels) of the canonical tradition indicate that faith regards itself as historical: it refers itself to Jesus of Nazareth and it is realized by particular persons in particular times and places."[29] Thus in the context of the production of other Gospels in the second century and of Marcion's adherence to (expurgated) Luke alone — and, he says, of other groups' excessive concentration on Matthew or Mark or John — Irenaeus sides with those who recognize all four of the Four Gospels and develops the grounds for recognizing their witness and not that of others. They are accepted in their separate form rather than conflated into a harmony such as Tatian's, and they appear in the company of one book of acts of apostles.[30] Their plurality witnesses to the richness of Christ, but it is a limited plurality, limited to where the church has sensed an authentic witness to Christ.

The letters of apostles were written with particular churches in mind and in the context of a relationship with those churches. Marcion venerated Paul while some Jewish Christians honored Peter and James the Just, but the mainstream Christian tradition already assumed that in principle all such apostles could belong to all the churches,[31] even if it was selective in the material it affirmed in this way. In the context of Marcion's emphasis on an expurgated Paul, Irenaeus recognizes a longer and unexpurgated Pauline collection and refers to Paul's letters and to Acts as "scripture" (*Against Heresies* III.12.9, 12). He also cites Hebrews, 1 Peter, and 1 and 2 John. In the context of the Montanist revival of prophecy and vision he refers to the Apocalypse of John and the *Shepherd* of Hermas as scripture (IV.20.2; V.30.1-2). Montanism likely discouraged the catholic church from

---

29. Funk, *Parables and Presence* 165.
30. *Against Heresies* III, Preface; III.1-5, also 11, 14.
31. Bruce, *Tradition Old and New* 137, noting 1 Corinthians 3:22.

increasing recognition of apocalypses such as Hermas and the *Apocalypse of Peter*.

Therefore, while Marcion encouraged the catholic church to recognize a broad canon, Montanus encouraged it to set limits to its canon.[32] While not seeking to embrace every view that ever called itself Christian, in general the characteristic of the catholic position was to be willing to hold together a wide variety of views — as well as Paul, Hebrews (with its hesitations about the possibility of repentance), James (with its stress on works, which would enrage Luther), and Revelation (with its millennialism). Admittedly E. Schüssler Fiorenza sees it as not catholic enough because it is affected by a patriarchalism that would include 2 Timothy and other epistles that subordinated women, but not the *Acts of Paul and Thecla,* which told of a woman preaching and baptizing.[33]

The nature of the heresies was to emphasize a strand of truth and take it too far. The nature of catholic Christianity was to affirm what a heresy emphasized but to set it in a broader context provided by the perspectives overemphasized by other heretical groups. By retaining the Hebrew Bible, with the Jewish Christians and against the gnostics, it implied the conviction that Christianity is both historical and particular. By adding Christian documents to the Hebrew Bible, it implied the conviction stressed by Marcion and the gnostics that Christian faith is novel and universal.[34]

Since Harnack it has been customary to see the end of the second century as the single decisive moment in the development of the Second Testament canon. In reaction to this overestimate there is a move at present to postpone the existence of a canon until the fourth century. Irenaeus represents, in this view, one stage in a story. Under the stimulus of the factors analyzed above he encouraged the catholic church to do as its faith and its inclination led it, to give special status to documents that provided it with a definitive understanding of the gospel in narrative form (and — though less formally — in the discursive form of the epistle). Tertullian applied to the two bodies of scripture the phrase "the complete instrument of each testament" and thus came close to providing them with the titles "Old and New Testament," which in due course came into common usage.[35]

32. Metzger, *The Canon of the New Testament* 106.

33. *In Memory of Her* 54. Tertullian (*Baptism* 17) refutes appeal to the *Acts of Paul and Thecla* on the grounds of the disagreement between what Paul is said to allow there and the stance he is said to take in 1 Corinthians 14.

34. Cf. Greer, *Early Biblical Interpretation* 116.

35. See *Against Praxeas* 20 (*totum instrumentum utriusque testamenti,* translated

Brevard Childs has examined how the writings that became the canon often came into their final form in order to fulfill an ongoing normative function,[36] and we have noted how they came to be given this function in the church between the mid-first and mid-second century, so that the developments of the late second century were no more the beginning than they were the end of the canonical process.

Ernst Käsemann suggested that "the New Testament canon does not, as such, constitute the foundations of the unity of the Church; on the contrary, ... it provides the basis for the multiplicity of the confessions."[37] As such the canon seems to reflect more second-century than fourth-century attitudes.[38] By the fourth century, a much tighter understanding of one orthodoxy developed, reflecting a different social, political, and ecclesiastical situation. Yet the Second Testament in its final form maintains its diverse nature; this, too, marks the influence of the second century on it.

A Canon of Second Testament Scriptures

On the usual view the oldest extant actual list of Second Testament books comes from about Irenaeus's time, but from Rome;[39] it is named after its discoverer L. A. Muratori. More a description of the contents of the scriptures than a mere list, it indicates recognition of the Four Gospels, Acts, Paul's letters, Jude, John's letters (it is not clear whether two or three), the Wisdom of Solomon, and the Apocalypse of John. The *Apocalypse of Peter* is disputed, being read in church only by some; the *Shepherd* of Hermas is read but not in church, being "of only recent origin." The list does not mention Hebrews, James, or the letters of Peter; it specifically excludes writings of the gnostic Valentinians, the Marcionites, and the Montanists.

---

loosely in vol. 3 of the Ante-Nicene Fathers series). Here and elsewhere during this period the term "testament" refers to the covenant itself, and in passages such as this and the ones quoted by McDonald (*The Formation of the Christian Biblical Canon* 180-81) it is difficult to be sure when it has become a title for the actual scriptures as opposed to the covenants/testaments to which they bear witness. Cf. van Unnik, "'Η καινὴ διαθήκη."

36. See his *The New Testament As Canon*.

37. "The Canon of the New Testament and the Unity of the Church" 103.

38. Cf. R. A. Markus, "The Problem of Self-Definition," in *Jewish and Christian Self-Definition* (ed. Sanders and others) 1:1-15.

39. See Ferguson, "Canon Muratori," against Sundberg, "Canon Muratori"; also Metzger, *The Canon of the New Testament* 191-201, 305-7.

Parallel to Irenaeus's argument for the propriety of having four Gospels is the list's argument for the propriety of Paul (like John in his Apocalypse) writing to seven churches, a fact that also hints that the Epistles comprise a catholic body rather than a collection of merely local letters. N. A. Dahl suggests that the second-century collecting of letters of Paul to seven churches was the occasion when prologues first came to be attached to the letters.[40]

If we compare Muratori's canon with assumptions about Christian scrip- tures that characterize different churches in the third century or that appear in writers such as Clement of Alexandria, Hippolytus, Cyprian, and Origen we find that there is broad agreement on the scriptural status of the Four Gospels, the Acts of the Apostles, the Pauline corpus, 1 Peter, and 1 John. There are varying views regarding whether this status attaches to further Gospels (e.g., the *Gospel of the Hebrews*), letters such as 2 Peter, James, 2 and 3 John, *Barnabas*, Jude, *3 Corinthians, Laodiceans*, Hebrews, and *1 Clement*, and writings such as the *Acts of Paul*, the *Didache*, the *Preaching of Peter*, the Apocalypses of John and Peter, Hermas, and Enoch. Nor should the broad agreement be exaggerated. The church in eastern Syria used Tatian's harmony rather than the Four Gospels. Individual writers ask questions about John or the Pastorals and continue to refer to sayings of Jesus that do not appear in the Four Gospels, which apparently came to them orally or in another Gospel.

The fourth century is when the churches are attempting to draw up a definitive list of the contents of scripture. Now there are episcopal pro- nouncements and synodical decisions about scripture rather than theolog- ical arguments.

Early in the century Eusebius of Caesarea distinguishes four categories of books:[41] Universally recognized are the Four Gospels, Acts, Paul's letters (probably including Hebrews), 1 John, and 1 Peter. Eusebius also includes the Apocalypse of John here, though he later implies that there are questions about it. The second category consists of books that are widely but not universally acknowledged: James, Jude, 2 Peter, and 2 and 3 John. The third comprises books that are clearly noncanonical, such as the *Acts of Paul*, Hermas, the *Apocalypse of Peter, Barnabas*, the *Didache*, and the *Gospel of the Hebrews*. These are orthodox but "spurious" — that is, of known post- apostolic origin. The fourth category is heretical books such as the *Gospel of Peter*, the *Gospel of Thomas*, the *Acts of John*, and others.

40. "The Origin of the Earliest Prologues to the Pauline Letters."
41. *Church History* III.25.

Other writers, particularly clearly Rufinus, distinguish canonical books and ecclesiastical books, that is, those that are normative for faith and those that are not normative but may be inspired and edifying and thus may be read in church. As the Articles of the Church of England would do later, he puts the Hebrew canon in the first category, books that have come to be known as the Old Testament Apocrypha in the second — though he uses the word "apocrypha" for books that could not be read in church at all. He then puts the books that make up our Second Testament in the first category and Hermas, *Didache,* and a lost work called *The Judgment of Peter* in the second category.[42]

Fathers of succeeding decades in the East give lists that vary in how many of Eusebius's disputed books they include, some adding others such as Wisdom and Ecclesiasticus, and there is parallel and continuing variation in the more official lists of eastern churches and in their lectionary usage.[43] The Apocalypse of John, for instance, still has no place in the Greek liturgy or the Syrian lectionary. Theodore of Mopsuestia seems to have recognized none of the Catholic Epistles, even 1 Peter and 1 John.[44] Athanasius's *Easter Letter* of 397 lists as the canon the books in our Second Testament. As will have been the case with the Hebrew scriptures from the beginning of the church, however, "it is also significant, judging from the total number of surviving copies, that only a very small proportion of Christians could ever have owned, or even seen, a copy of the complete canon of the New Testament."[45]

In the West we may take Cyprian's list from about 250 as a starting point. It corresponds to Eusebius's list of universally acknowledged books except that the Apocalypse of John has an undisputed place, whereas Hebrews does not. The Fathers of the fourth century then vary in a way parallel to those of the East in the number of the disputed books they recognize, until Jerome and Augustine approve a list that includes all the works in Eusebius's first two categories, the universally acknowledged and the disputed. This list was recognized by synods at Hippo in 393 and at Carthage in 397 and 419 and was the standard list from that time in the Western church, though for some centuries the pseudonymous letter to the Laodiceans was sometimes regarded as canonical. Subsequently Luther and other continental figures treated Hebrews, James, Jude, and Revelation as

42. *Commentary on the Apostles' Creed* 37-38.
43. See Metzger, *The Canon of the New Testament* 201-28, 309-14.
44. See Bruce, *The Canon of Scripture* 214-15.
45. *Ibid.,* 217.

of questionable status, but they were expressing strong personal views about such books rather than proposing that the canon be revised.[46] This canon was reaffirmed by the Council of Trent in 1546, appears in a number of Reformed confessions, and is implicitly accepted in the Thirty-Nine Articles. It corresponds to the New Testament in modern Bibles.

46. Cf. Althaus, *The Theology of Martin Luther* 84.

12

The Bounds of the Canon

What are the implications of the history of the canons' development, with its probabilities and uncertainties? What determined whether books were accepted into either Testament? Where should the bounds lie?

Which Books Belong in the First Testament?

With regard to the Jewish scriptures questions are raised by the existence of more than one canon. Three inferences have been drawn from the history of how this came about. The traditional Protestant view is that the right canon is that of the Hebrew Bible. The traditional Roman Catholic and Orthodox view is that the longer Greek canon in one of its forms is the right canon. The more modern liberal view is that this diversity points to the falseness of the dilemma: Let us abandon the idea of a canon and profit from whatever writings are informative or edifying.[1]

Postbiblical Jewish writings, the works often referred to as the intertestamental literature, have great importance as a bridge between the Testaments and between the Hebrew Bible and Jesus.[2] Their developed beliefs in resurrection, final judgment, and the role of angels became part of the beliefs taken for granted by the early Christians. Paul's teaching presupposes the understanding of the origin of sin and the interpretation of Genesis 1–3 found in some of these works. The Second Testament's answers are addressed to questions framed by Jews in the postbiblical period. And the

1. Cf. Dungan, "The New Testament Canon in Recent Study."
2. Cf. Barr, "Le Judaisme postbiblique et la théologie de l'Ancien Testament."

use of scripture in the Second Testament presupposes the way scripture was read in that period. Postbiblical Jewish writings are of key importance to an understanding of the Second Testament. Yet that is not to imply that the Christian canon should include these writings (if it should, it would be difficult to determine how many of them). Still less is it the case that their importance in this connection puts a question mark alongside the idea of there being a more circumscribed canon of pre-Christian Jewish writings. Not everything that influences one of the scriptural writers is itself part of scripture.

Acceptance of an "open canon"[3] would be historically closer to Judaism and Christianity in their early periods. It would also be attractive in a pluralist age: It is not only with regard to scripture that for many people in our time the idea of a canon with fixed limits has lost its attractiveness.[4] It is precisely this attractiveness of the idea in a pluralist age that makes it suspect, but at least it draws attention to the possibility of living with an open canon. The reasons for defining the canon precisely are in part practical ones, such as the need to know which documents to put in a printed Bible.

Sundberg suggests that we should follow the church's instinct in validating the wider Greek canon rather than the canon established by people who did not believe in Jesus.[5] It was an understandable mistake, he suggests, for the Protestant churches to confine their Christian canon to a selection of books whose limits were fixed only after Jesus' day and in reaction to the early Christian movement. That mistake now needs to be corrected.

Sundberg's argument is weakened if the boundaries of the Hebrew canon, even if they were reconsidered at Yavneh, were already established by that time. Indeed, whenever the canon's boundaries were defined, the argument hardly holds. There is little indication that the works that eventually belonged to one of the Greek canons belonged even informally to the scriptures in the first Christian century, and if we receive the Jewish scriptures from the hands of Jesus and the Second Testament writers, it would be odd to include among them a substantial number of works that they never accepted as scripture. Furthermore, whenever the canon was determined, there is no actual evidence that this took place as part of Christianity crystallizing its identity over against Judaism and that this explains (for instance) its exclusion of the Jewish apocalypses.

---

3. Ackroyd, *Studies in the Religious Tradition of the Old Testament* 209-24.
4. See Steiner, *On Difficulty* 1-17, with regard to the classical and literary canons.
5. See "The Protestant Old Testament Canon."

In one sense the addition of the deuterocanonical scriptures of the Greek and Latin canons to the writings of the Hebrew canon would seem to make little difference, despite Luther's discovery that occasionally a theological point could hang on them. A. Weiser suggests that Ecclesiasticus was appropriately excluded from the canon because of its identification of Wisdom and Torah,[6] but such distinctions are subtle, and one suspects that the outsider would find the similarities between canonical and deuterocanonical wisdom books as striking as the differences. As an argument based on the canons' content it may be more significant that the longer canons have a different balance as wholes. The Hebrew canon is dominated by the Torah and the Prophets, whereas the other books comprise half the canon in its Greek version. But the practical effect of the church recognizing a longer canon would chiefly be to add to the material within the Jewish scriptures that the church ignores.

Another question of principle might be considered. We have emphasized that the Bible is predominantly a story, a story about Israel that comes to a climax in Jesus. Christianity finds its background and origins within the history and faith of Israel, and its acceptance of the Jewish scriptures reflects its awareness of the rock from which it was hewn. It is therefore appropriate that the daughter faith should accept its mother's definition of her scriptures. It is the Jews who were given "the covenant, . . . the law, the worship, and the promises" (Rom 9:4).[7] Even if their definition of scriptures was in part designed to distinguish mother and daughter, that only incorporates in the constitution of the canon an ambiguity over the relationship of mother and daughter that is reflected in other ways in the two communities.

Israel's canon simply exists; to try to reopen it is to try to rewrite history or reportray the identity that Israel developed for itself. The Hebrew Bible is what Israel itself wanted to say, what Israel's tradition resulted in.[8] Barr extends this argument to apply to acceptance of the Masoretic Text as "the last faint impulse of the great movement of Israelite tradition that formed our Old Testament."[9] This fits with indications from the Second Testament that Christian Jews and other Jews had the Jewish scriptures in common. Sundberg's theological argument for acceptance of the Greek canon is that

6. *Introduction to the Old Testament* 409.
7. Childs, *Biblical Theology of the Old and New Testaments* 65, following Jerome.
8. Barr, *The Scope and Authority of the Bible* 14-17.
9. Review of J. K. S. Reid, *The Authority of Scripture* 92.

it is the church's creation. The theological argument *against* his view makes the same point: To recognize the Greek canon is to preempt the independence of the Jewish scriptures' pre-Christian witness.[10]

Criteria for Inclusion: Canon, Prophets, and Apostles

The process through which the canon came into being was as situational as the process by which the individual books came into being or that by which any word comes from God.[11] "In sacred Scripture we never confront God speaking outside of human media, outside of the horizontal perspective and of history."[12]

In the case of the Hebrew Bible we have hardly any hard evidence regarding the process by which it came to be and the factors that led it to be what it is. In the case of the Second Testament the dynamics of the situation and the factors involved in the recognition of books varied between the three main stages of the story (see above, chapter 11). For most of the first two centuries Christians simply presupposed that key significance attached to the gospel tradition, then to certain apostolic letters, then to some written Gospels. That reflected assumptions about the nature of the gospel, that the figure and the words of Jesus were of key significance for Christians, that Paul and other figures had been commissioned to expound and apply that gospel and had done so effectively, and that in due course a written form of the story would best keep them in touch with Jesus. But the matter was not very controversial and not cause for close reflection.

The controversies that led to the making of sharper distinctions among gnostics, Marcionites, Jewish Christians, Montanists, and catholics made that reflection necessary at stage two, later in the second century, because all these groups might have agreed with the assumptions outlined above without agreeing on the nature of the gospel itself. It is here that concern with apostolicity has its significance.

First, apostolicity suggests that documents are recognized because they express the apostolic faith or the rule of the faith, the apostolic gospel as

10. Brett, *Biblical Criticism in Crisis?* 180.

11. Achtemeier, *The Inspiration of Scripture* 122.

12. Berkouwer, *Holy Scripture* 73. Berkouwer compares Samuel's tardiness in realizing that God was speaking to him, 1 Sam 3:2-10; cf. John 12:29.

preached from the beginning and continuously affirmed by the church. In these writings the catholic church found the Christ in whom they believed. The writings of the gnostics were rejected on the grounds that they preached another gospel, a different Christ. Thus not all purportedly apostolic writings were included in the church's scriptures. Several works that bore the name of Peter were excluded because their contents did not match the faith of the catholic church; Mark and Luke were accepted *formally* on the basis of their link with the preaching of Peter and Paul but *substantially* on the basis of the church's recognition of its own faith in their presentation. It was content that determined whether a document was apostolic. If it preached the apostolic gospel, it could be attributed to an apostolic author. Apostolicity "has to do less with the authorship of particular writings than with the integrity of a shared vision."[13]

In the case of the First Testament, too, it seems likely that during the Israelite and Second Temple periods individual books had commended themselves to the community on the basis of their contents. In due course, to attribute a work such as Proverbs to a person such as Solomon may have been a matter of producing a rationale for accepting documents that had earlier been accepted on a different basis. The original grounds for the scriptural status of Proverbs would have been its content, its relative antiquity, and its wide acceptance; attribution to Solomon is a consequence of those grounds rather than a cause of the book's status. Conversely the mere attribution of the work to a figure from Israel's classical period was not enough to gain a place in the canon for apocalypses such as Enoch, perhaps because their content did not commend them.

Luther's attitude to the canon worked in continuity with this understanding of the significance of apostolicity: "Whatever does not teach Christ is not apostolic, even though St. Peter or St. Paul does the teaching. Again, whatever preaches Christ would be apostolic even if Judas, Annas, Pilate, and Herod were doing it."[14] Luther's canon criterion was whether material preached Christ, and it led him, not unequivocally, to affirm the documents that appear in the Jewish and Christian Bible. It was on the basis of their content that he questioned the place of some, treating Esther as of similar status to Maccabees, and regarding Hebrews, James, Jude, and Revelation as in effect deuterocanonical. He would have approved of the way the church in Rhossus, Syria, gave up reading the *Gospel of Peter* in church

---

13. Green, *Imagining God* 117.
14. "Preface to the Epistles of St. James and St. Jude," *LW* 35:396.

when attention was drawn to its docetic tendencies.[15] It is striking that the books Luther questioned were those that were of uncertain status when the canon was in a more fluid state — Esther before and during the early Christian period, the four Christian books in the discussion that led to the forming of the Second Testament.

To judge from the actual nature of the Second Testament, a second contrasting implication of apostolicity is that the canonical witness is characterized by some diversity (as we noted in chapter 11). The catholic church recognized four Gospels with different perspectives on Jesus, and recognized Hebrews, Revelation, and letters by Peter and John (and in due course James), rather than accepting just one Gospel and letters by Paul, in agreement with Marcion. The apostolic rule of the faith is important as a skeleton, but it can be enfleshed in a number of apostolic ways. Even Tatian's harmony, for some time canonical in Syria, in due course gave way to the individual Gospels, while churches that tended to use one Gospel were invited by their canon to use four.

"The non-canonical texts are vitally important for understanding the immense range of diversity in which the emerging canon was being read, as well as the diversity with respect to which it was produced": They indicate the limits of what is acceptable, so that canons, like texts, both confirm and confront (or limit) the church.[16] The considerations that led the church to formulate its canon over against the beliefs of Marcionites, gnostics, Jewish Christians, and Montanists also continue to play a part in safeguarding it from the subtractions and additions of Protestantism (e.g., Luther's exclusive Paulinism), Roman Catholicism (e.g., Marian dogmas and papal infallibility), and Pentecostalism (especially in the Third World), as well as the gnostic-like philosophical schemes of academic theologians, which transform and traduce Christian faith in the course of setting it within an alien framework. The canon is — against Käsemann — a charter for the unity of the church, but for a unity to be sought by acknowledging that the scriptures are broader than any of our denominations.[17]

The conviction that the apostolic faith indeed represents the faith of the apostolic period suggests a third conviction attaching to the stress on apostolicity, one concerning the historical origin of the documents. As

15. Eusebius, *Church History* VI.12; cf. Bruce, *Tradition Old and New* 142.
16. Keck, "Is the New Testament a Field of Study?" 33, 34.
17. Wainwright, "The New Testament as Canon" 561-65, 569, referring to Käsemann's "The Canon of the New Testament and the Unity of the Church."

usually expressed this is a conviction that they were written by the apostles or by their associates, that is, in a particular period or by particular writers. But this is the formal indication that in their substance they do express the original apostolic gospel. It gives grounds for the conviction that they offer reliable witness to the nature of the Christian faith. The gnostic and the Montanist writings were rejected not only because of their content but because of their novelty. Despite their claims, they were of recent, not ancient, origin.

Superficially it will seem a problem that relatively few of the documents recognized by the catholics were, in fact, written by apostles. Indeed, C. F. Evans declares that "if the word 'apostolic' is to be used of the New Testament at all it can only be in [a] very diffused, if not Pickwickian, sense."[18] But apostolicity of actual authorship was not the criterion for canonicity. The concern of apostolicity was more a chronological matter, involving derivation from the period closest to Christ and thus the period of Christian origins. It signified not so much authorship as antiquity and authentic witness to Christ.

Thus Irenaeus's canon "is not guaranteed and constituted, in the later manner, on the basis of a formal principle, but rather is in the Lukan sense 'historical'" (cf. Luke 1:2); the basis on which Muratori's canon excludes Hermas is similarly that it comes from the postclassical rather than the primitive period, not that it was not written by an apostle, any less than Mark or Luke was.[19] When the First and Second Testaments were described as the Prophets and the Apostles, neither the former nor the latter description was fundamentally a statement regarding authorship.[20] Thus Evans exaggerates when he speaks of "something precious being bolstered by false claims in the effort to make it out to be more than it is" by means of "the accursed mystique of 'apostolicity,' from Papias and Irenaeus to Cullmann."[21]

Recognizing documents as apostolic meant recognizing that they expounded the apostolic faith as it was proclaimed in the decades in which the church began. To conflate the Second Testament writings with those of Clement, Ignatius, or Hermas is to do the opposite of what either set of authors wanted. Admittedly the distinction between apostolic and post-

18. *Is "Holy Scripture" Christian?* 17.

19. Von Campenhausen, *The Formation of the Christian Bible* 330, 206, 254, 259.

20. Against Kümmel, *Introduction to the New Testament* 494, where he disputes von Campenhausen's point just noted.

21. *Is "Holy Scripture" Christian?* 34, 36.

apostolic is not a sharp one. While many of the Second Testament documents were written in the early decades of the church's existence by first-generation figures such as Paul, we know nothing of the authorship of books such as Hebrews, and it seems entirely possible that some extrabiblical documents such as *Didache* antedate some Second Testament documents. Conversely a number of works *not* included in the Second Testament stand under apostolic figures as firmly as and perhaps no less historically than some works within the Second Testament that refer to figures such as Paul or Peter but were not actually written by them. Perhaps we may infer that the church recognized in the latter the apostolic faith as it might now be applied in a new age.

The link between canonicity and authorship may be similar in the case of the First Testament, as the Tosefta speaks of them. Yadayim 2:13 records a rabbinic discussion in which it is asserted that "The Gilyonim [the Gospels] and the books of the Minim [heretics] do not defile the hands. The books of Ben Sira and all the books that were written since that time do not defile the hands." The reference to dating may reflect the view that the period of inspiration was the period from Moses to Ezra. The canonical books *prima facie* claim some connection with that period. Yet we now associate books such as Proverbs and Ecclesiastes at least in their final forms to a period close to that of Ecclesiasticus, and they look no more the product of prophetic inspiration than that book was. We therefore find the rabbis' argument problematic in the same way as that concerning the apostolic authorship of Second Testament writings: It is a principle honored more in the breach than in the observance. But it does not seem to have been at all a universal Jewish view that prophecy ceased early in the Second Temple period, and it is doubtful if this was either a reason for including some books and excluding others, or a compelling reason for affirming or denying the status of particular books subsequently.[22] As we have noted, attributing books to Solomon may reflect the conviction that it expresses classical Jewish faith and wisdom, rather than having generated that conviction.

The stress on strictly apostolic *authorship* of Christian documents may have derived from groups such as the gnostics. The Four Gospels are themselves anonymous. Later Gospels claim more overtly to have been written

---

22. Aune, *Prophecy in Early Christianity and the Ancient Mediterranean World* 103-6. See further Barton, *Oracles of God* 105-16; Blenkinsopp, "Prophecy and Priesthood in Josephus" 240-41; Bockmuehl, *Revelation and Mystery in Ancient Judaism* 84-89; Feldman, "Prophets and Prophecy in Josephus" 400-407.

by apostles and other eyewitnesses, and this claim perhaps led the catholics into the trap of trying to claim apostolic authorship or vicarious apostolic authorship (cf., e.g., Papias) for documents that had long had authority because they were authentic interpretations of Jesus.[23] The gnostic writings were all written in the second century.

The disappearance of the gnostic writings until their twentieth-century rediscovery resulted from the "victory" of church leaders who held what came to be *the* orthodox view.[24] But a reading of the rediscovered texts, with their Jesus who neither suffers nor rises from the dead, does not make one conclude that the wrong side won. Their affirmation of women's roles and of God as mother may preserve or develop authentic Christian insight, but their total interpretation of Jesus is a reinterpretation. They may well include sayings that represent what Jesus actually said, whereas there are sayings in the canonical Gospels of which that is not true. Nevertheless the catholic interpretation of Jesus is as a whole more plausible historically than the gnostic interpretation, which sets him in an alien interpretative framework. "The documents that eventually came to constitute the New Testament were, so far as can be judged, in fact the best and most nearly proximate evidence for Christian origins"; there is a real difference between them and — for instance — the writings of the Apostolic Fathers.[25] "Even the most debatable of the 'disputed' books in the New Testament canon has more of the quality of apostolic authority about it than the letters of Clement of Rome and Ignatius of Antioch or the *Shepherd* of Hermas."[26]

Apostolicity also hints at a fourth factor that in due course produced a further criterion for canonicity. The early Christian documents were of an occasional kind, written to specific churches and addressing local questions. But their apostolicity was one feature that gave them more than local importance. The apostolic faith belonged to the whole church, any one local church would profit from all the perspectives of the apostolic faith, and all subsequent churches needed to be linked to the apostolic churches in their historicity and particularity. The church is one, across time and geography. The church of the second and subsequent centuries is heir to all the apostolic inheritance.

A further factor with which this links, namely the emergence of a

23. Cf. Bruce, *The Canon of Scripture* 257.
24. Pagels, *The Gnostic Gospels.*
25. Moule's review of *Is "Holy Scripture" Christian?* 419.
26. Bruce, *Tradition Old and New* 150.

consensus concerning documents among the churches, belongs especially to stage three of the development of a canon of Second Testament scriptures. Augustine urges that the degree of authority attached to a book should be proportionate to the number and the authority of the churches that recognize it.[27] Rome's caution over regarding Hebrews as scripture, despite a familiarity with it that goes back to Clement, issued in part from hesitation over being out of step with other churches as well as from its anonymity. Another criterion of canonicity was thus catholicity, the wide recognition of a document as authoritative. What gave documents their original recognition was a widely recognized acknowledgment of their contents. The whole church had heard the gospel in them. It may be difficult to imagine Paul (or Jesus) making consensus the basis for canonicity. But on his own Paul (or Jesus) can produce heresy as well as reformation, both possibilities reflecting his stress on revelation and not merely tradition.[28]

We have noted Eusebius's division of potentially scriptural writings into four groups, ones acknowledged by all the churches, ones acknowledged by some, ones that were not of apostolic origin but were apostolic in content, and heretical works. The tendency was for books that were apostolic in their teaching and were not known to be of postapostolic authorship to move from the second category to the first. On this basis Jude came to be generally accepted; Hermas, because it was known to be later, did not. Conversely Jerome, like the later Augustine, takes the view that the authorship of Hebrews is a matter of indifference, given that the book was written by a person of the church and has been long even if not universally recognized in the church as having a status superior to that of extracanonical books.[29]

The Determination and the Openness of the Canon

An implication of this fourth aspect of apostolicity is that the formation of the biblical canon is the work of the church. Theologically speaking the church did not create the canon, but came to recognize it — as it did not make Jesus God's Anointed or Lord but came to recognize that he was that.

27. *Christian Doctrine* II.8 [II.12]; cf. Metzger, *The Canon of the New Testament* 237, 253-54. Von Campenhausen (*The Formation of the Christian Bible* 261) finds this argument already in Muratori's canon.
28. Funk, *Parables and Presence* 163, 164.
29. *Letters* cxxix.3; cf. Bruce, *The Canon of Scripture* 226-27, 232.

"In no sense of the concept could or can the Church give the Canon to itself"; our recognizing the church's canon is not our bowing to the judgment of the church — any more than is the case when we come to believe in Christ — but our agreeing with the church in recognizing that in these works God speaks. Yet the church can only come to acknowledge what the canon is "to the best of its knowledge and judgment, in the venture and obedience of faith, but also in all the relativity of a human knowledge of the truth that God has opened up to men"; in that sense "this establishment of the Canon is the work of the Church."[30] We find that the community to which we belong has made a response of faith to certain scriptures, and we take that fact and what we ourselves find the Holy Spirit doing with these scriptures as a basis for our own response of faith to them.

At one level, then, these books comprise the scriptures because it is they that the church chose. Subsequent Christian generations may seem obliged simply to trust God to have made sure that it made the right choice. The contents of the canon are part of the tradition of the church that subsequent generations inherit, which as such has the right to be treated with respect, though not unquestioningly. There is "reason for greater confidence and greater expectation with respect to the canonical writings than to any other writings, even though this decision, which the church made in faith, cannot be accepted untested."[31] If the church made the decisions about the canon, they must be subject to the Reformation principle that "popes and councils can err."[32] "The question of the canon has never, in principle, been definitely answered, but it is continually being reopened." It is a dogma of the church, which as such is never final or infallible. "The fact that it was the Church of the 4th century that defined the present canon, and created the sacrament of the Mass and the Papacy, must remind us of this truth."[33]

The Reformation made tradition open to question, yet reckoned it acceptable if questioning did not invalidate it. In order to test the church's decision we might ask again whether the scriptures meet the criteria we have noted: We are free to ask once more whether its books proclaim in their content the gospel of the God of Israel and of Jesus, the church's Lord, whether they do so in a way that speaks to the church in its diversity, and

---

30. Barth, *Church Dogmatics* 1/2:473, 474-76.
31. Mildenberger, "The Unity, Truth, and Validity of the Bible" 405.
32. Ogden, summarizing the Church of England Articles 19 and 21 in "The Authority of Scripture for Theology" 249.
33. Brunner, *Revelation and Reason* 131.

whether they represent a witness to the apostolic faith. People do undertake that questioning; in one sense it seems to lead nowhere, though the fact that we are free to ask the question is a gracious gift. One is relieved at least that the canon has not in the event been impoverished by the omission of Esther with its testimony to the hidden God's commitment to Israel, Ecclesiastes with its permission to doubt, the Song of Songs with its enthusiasm for sexual love, Hebrews with its rigorism, James with its stress on works, or Revelation with its vision.

While happy with some notion of tradition, Reformation thinking would have felt uncomfortable with the conclusion that the authority of the scriptural canon depended on the authority of the church, and it developed two further criteria of canonicity. Both involve appeal to the work of the Holy Spirit. One was that the canonical books were ones that were uniquely inspired by God. This novel idea is difficult to justify from scripture itself. The Fathers certainly assumed that the scriptures were inspired, but they also believed this of their own writings.[34] The Second Testament itself sees the whole church as filled with the Spirit and speaking the Spirit's words, rather than implying that inspiration might be limited to certain people or writings. The only uninspired writings are unorthodox ones.[35] Inspiration was a necessary but not a sufficient criterion for regarding something as canonical.[36]

The other approach to the question of the canon associated with the Reformation is the correlative view already noted in chapter 9: We accept these writings because the Holy Spirit who inspired them testifies to our spirits that they are holy scripture. It was Calvin who classically formulated the belief that the deepest conviction that the scriptures came from God derives from an inner working in the human spirit by the divine Spirit, who grants a certainty that does not issue from mere arguments.[37] John Owen describes the scriptures' compelling self-authentication in terms of their capacity to illumine and to do things; the role of the Spirit is, then, not to add to that an inexplicable extra conviction regarding the matter but to enable people to perceive these capacities and respond to them.[38]

But Calvin did not appeal to the Spirit's witness as a basis for conviction about disputed books such as Hebrews, James, 2 Peter, and Jude; nor does

34. Kalin, "The Inspired Community"; cf. Sundberg, "The Bible Canon" 365-70.
35. Metzger, *The Canon of the New Testament* 256.
36. We will consider inspiration further in Part III.
37. See esp. *Institutes* I/7. See further chapter 17 below.
38. *Three Treatises Concerning the Scriptures* 318-29.

the testimony of the Spirit indicate the meaning of scripture, as is sometimes implied.[39] Calvin affirms the authority of the disputed books on the
more classical basis of their containing nothing unworthy of an apostle,
their revealing the majesty of Christ, and their being compatible with the
undisputed books: in other words, on the basis of their contents.[40] Here,
too, the implication of the doctrine of the Spirit's testimony is that the
Spirit opens human eyes so that they can see evidence and be persuaded
by it, though the relation between the work of the Spirit and such evidence
is not as explicit in Calvin as it is in later writers and confessions.[41] Later
Calvinism did claim that the Spirit's testimony establishes the bounds of
the canon: Carl Henry faults Harold Lindsell for appealing to the Spirit's
testimony to establish conclusions that could not be reached otherwise.[42]

The Spirit's witness is what leads us to heed particular books or passages
when we read them, in response to their contents. We may personally never
experience that witness with regard to every part of scripture individually.
The Spirit seems to have failed to give positive witness to Luther regarding
James. Richard Baxter, too, comments,

> I confess, for my part, I could never boast of any such testimony or light
> of the Spirit or reason; neither of which, without human testimony or
> tradition, would have made me believe that the book of Canticles is canoni-
> cal and written by Solomon, and the book of Wisdom apocryphal and
> written by Philo, as some think, or that Paul's epistle to the Laodiceans
> and others is apocryphal, and the second and third epistle of John canoni-
> cal.[43]

Insofar as this happens broadly with scripture, however, it issues in a
conviction regarding scripture as a whole. It may thus be distinguished from
an experience Nineham describes: "You will all have had again and again
the experience . . . of finding that it is only as you go back to the Bible that

---

39. See, e.g., M. Wiles, "The Uses of 'Holy Scripture,'" in *What about the New
Testament?* (ed. Hooker and Hickling) 159.

40. *Institutes* I/8; cf. Ridderbos, *The Authority of the New Testament Scriptures* 11,
84 [²10, 79-80]; Berkouwer, *Holy Scripture* 89.

41. Warfield, "Calvin's Doctrine of the Knowledge of God" 79-130.

42. *God, Revelation and Authority* 4:163. See, e.g., Lindsell, *The Battle for the Bible*
162, 183; also 34 for the claim that this is in effect Calvin's own approach to 2 Peter.

43. *The Saints' Everlasting Rest,* preface to Part 2, as quoted in Orr, *Revelation and
Inspiration* 203, though I have not been able to locate it in any of the editions available
to me.

you regain your balance, . . . — your unfaith is rebuked, your fears and frettings removed, your path made clear."[44] He is speaking of particular passages; he compares Coleridge's declaration that "whatever *finds* me, bears witness for itself that it has proceeded from a Holy Spirit."[45] He makes it explicit that being thus affected by particular passages does not imply accepting everything in the Bible — it could throw you off balance!

It is impossible to offer conclusive external or internal grounds for recognizing one particular form of either canon. The evidence for the Hebrew canon being the form of the Jewish scriptures that Jesus would have acknowledged is strong but somewhat circumstantial. The Second Testament as we know it was widely acknowledged in the Western church but not elsewhere, and there is no external validation for the Second Testament canon such as the one Jesus might be reckoned to give for the Hebrew Bible. The internal grounds for distinguishing all the books within the Hebrew canon from all other Jewish works, and all the books within the Second Testament from all other early Christian books, are not conclusive, as is reflected in the fact that it took the churches centuries to come near a common mind on the matter. The documents were evidently not immediately or even eventually self-authenticating. Both parts of the canon included books that were the subject of dispute and have continued to be so. Perhaps this reflects the fact that we can never expect to prove that something is God's word. Recognizing that is always and inevitably an act of spiritual discernment and an act of faith.

Such facts may require some form of acceptance of an "open canon" in yet a further sense. The canon is not open in the sense that all we have is a wide range of possibly edifying Jewish and Christian religious literature; we do have that resource, but it is not as such a canon. It is open in the sense that there can still be argument about and reconsideration of the way its bounds have been set, and in the sense that one can combine a working certainty about its center with more hesitation about its edges. In general the situation is interestingly similar to one that obtains with literary canons.[46] Literary classics impose themselves as works of truth, illumination, and normativity, rather than being imposed, and they do this corporately and over the centuries rather than in the mind of each person individually. And we find ourselves both hesitant to revise a canon (espe-

---

44. *Explorations in Theology* 1:110.
45. *Confessions of an Inquiring Spirit* 26 [Letter 1].
46. Cf. Tracy, *The Analogical Imagination* 108-9, 115-16.

cially by dismissing what an earlier generation found compelling) and not necessarily certain about the edges of it.

With regard to scripture, uncertainty about the canon can sound alarming. But the early church preached, spread, and grew in theological understanding for at least four centuries without agreement on the matter. Further, where churches are agreed on a canon this does not lead them to agreement on matters of doctrine such as the Trinity, election, sacraments, ministry, or eschatology or on matters of ethics such as observance of the sabbath or Sunday, homosexuality, or pacifism. Conversely, where churches disagree on the canon — for example, the Roman Church over against the Protestant churches — it is not this that constitutes the chief ground for the differences between them. The significance of a canon may be what it excludes as much as what it includes,[47] but this does not in practice seem an illuminating principle for understanding why different canons stop where they do. Further, the idea of an open canon should not be allowed to give too much prominence to the uncertainty on the edges of the canon. The heart of the canon's significance lies in its central message, and the core of the Second Testament, the Four Gospels and the Pauline letters, is a matter of no controversy.[48]

It may be helpful to compare this question with that concerning the text of scripture. In practice churches accept a variety of versions of scripture that vary textually at numerous points, but they all function as versions of one canon.[49] Our inability to justify the precise bounds of the biblical canon is a formidable problem in theory, but less so in practice. Or perhaps the canon's fuzzy edges, which make it difficult to draw a sharp distinction between everything in the canon and everything outside it, is a parable or reflection of the continuity between the activity of God in scriptural times and after scriptural times and thus a sign of grace and a hidden hint of the gospel. Perhaps the untidiness and apparent arbitrariness of aspects of the process whereby the canons came into being is also a sign of that grace, which works through human processes, with their oddities, and declines to bypass them supernaturally.[50]

---

47. Green, *Imagining God* 116.
48. Cf. Berkouwer, *Holy Scripture* 80-81.
49. Metzger, *The Canon of the New Testament* 270.
50. I owe this point to an observation by Peta Sherlock.

13

Scripture as Resource and Norm

Christian life and thinking are shaped by forces other than scripture. These include the church and its tradition, human reason and secular thought, human experience (religious and other), and the commitments we make. In principle that is not something to be regretted or feared as long as we do not pretend that it is otherwise. One bit of evidence for this is that it is also true of the thinking and behavior of the people who appear in and who wrote the Bible. Since the Reformation, however, Christians have been more aware of this variegated shaping as a problem rather than as a richness, realizing more clearly that the church's resources can and have come into conflict. As Aquinas illustrates, the church always assumed that only arguments from scripture carry full authority, the reasoning of philosophers and the teaching of the doctors of the church being valid only as supportive arguments. It seemed to Luther, however, that in practice the Pope did not operate this way.[1] The question then is what is the relationship between the role or status of scripture and that of tradition, reason, our experience, and our commitments?

Tradition

Scripture's witnessing tradition, first oral and then written, is fundamental to the nature of scripture itself, but the people who appear in the scriptures and who wrote them imply that broader traditions and postbiblical tradi-

---

1. See Thomas Aquinas, *Summa theologiae* I/1.8; cf. Stout, *Flight from Authority* 41-44, 107.

tion, too, can have positive value, even though it is also capable of perverting the scriptures (see Mark 7). The Second Testament understands Jesus on the basis of ways of thinking and approaches to interpretation that had developed *from* the scriptures over the years and not on the basis of the scriptures alone. There is no necessary clash between Bible and tradition. Both Testaments began as tradition, in narrative and in other forms. The church established a canon of scripture not to safeguard the church and the truth against tradition but to safeguard authentic tradition over against novelty and perversion.[2]

In at least three ways the church and its tradition may continue to shape Christian attitudes. First, there have been claims for the authority of a body of tradition separate from scripture that provides some other access to apostolic teaching, claims such as were made by the Council of Trent in 1546. In response to these, Article 6 of the Church of England makes the polemical claim that "Holy Scripture containeth all things necessary to salvation." No body of tradition separate from scripture can sustain a claim to mediate the apostolic gospel. In this sense, the Church of England accepted the Reformation watchword "Scripture alone" and affirmed that the Bible had sole authority for the life of the church and of the individual.

Second, the shape of Christian faith and worship is influenced by a doctrinal tradition embodied in the catholic creeds and expressed in the "rule of the faith," which we considered in chapters 11 and 12. This rule is not an oral tradition that rivals scripture in authority but a guide for interpretation used, under the conviction that it crystallizes scripture's own central thread, as a means of ensuring that the church keeps to the apostolic faith.[3] Even in evangelism the church rightly passes on such a rule of the faith rather than leaving people with no map through the scriptures in their marvelous rich diversity and no safeguard against the alternative of an idiosyncratic rule of the faith of some individual or group.[4]

In the Church of England, Article 7 thus calls for wholehearted acceptance of the Apostles', Nicene, and Athanasian Creeds, on the grounds that their contents may be proved by scripture. Their words are not scriptural, but their content is believed to be. They provide us with that map for our theological exploration of scripture. As such they encourage such explora-

2. Muddiman, *The Bible* 10-11. See further the World Council of Churches report "Scripture, Tradition and Traditions," reprinted in Flesseman-van Leer, *The Bible* 18-29; pp. 112-14 above.

3. Cullmann, *The Early Church* 94-95.

4. Abraham, *The Logic of Evangelism* 145-52.

tion, and we will hesitate to assume that their mapwork is mistaken, though it remains only mapwork. The map is answerable to the land, not the land to it, and is measured by it rather than vice versa.[5] Best notes that the rule of the faith contains no reference to grace, a theme on which the Patristic church sometimes became hazy, and also suggests that the rule of the faith began to lose its significance and its authority once there was a collection of scriptures.[6] In the modern age the churches that emerged from the Reformation need to be critical about the Reformation tradition, which has blindspots as well as insights and forms only one element in the total Christian tradition, whose light helps us to interpret scripture.[7] The need for a critical stance is even more pressing with regard to the statements of faith of less catholic bodies such as denominations or parachurch organizations.

Third, other traditions of the church that have developed over the years shape Christian attitudes and practice in a way that in principle can hardly be questioned. The Holy Spirit indwelt the church from the beginning in order to guide it in its ongoing life as it faced new situations and new questions. As time went by the church accumulated beliefs, customs, and practices that did not as such come from scripture, but were — or at least may have been — part of the Spirit's guidance. The church came to observe Sunday in a way partly parallel to Jewish observance of the sabbath and to dedicate particular buildings to worship in a way partly parallel both to the Jewish temple and to the synagogue. It developed orders of ministry, such as the eventual threefold order of bishops, priests, and deacons, partly parallel to the Jewish institution of high priest, priest, and Levite. It has often centered the leadership of a local congregation in one man who is employed full time and paid to fulfill this task as his profession and who alone can preside at Holy Communion.

None of these features of church life appears in any of the churches described in the Second Testament. They are part of the church's tradition, part of the way it believed the Holy Spirit led it after Second Testament times. These aspects of church life need to be recognized as such and honored as attempts to live by scripture. The Church of England's Articles claim that its structure of ministry can be traced back to scripture. Presby-

---

5. See O'Donovan, *On the Thirty Nine Articles* 55-56. For tradition as guide, cf. also Fackre, *Authority* 157.
6. "Scripture, Tradition and the Canon of the New Testament" 279-80.
7. Allchin, "An Anglican View on Scripture and Tradition" 298-99.

terians can treat the Westminster Confession as if it were scripture itself. Members of IVCF/UCCF can treat their basis of faith as if it were something other than a historically rooted tradition. These are all human traditions, but they may be faithful attempts to think and live by scripture.

There are differences in the status attributed to tradition in different churches. At the time of the Reformation Luther made no attempt to purge the church of customs that had a long history in the church and were not directly contrary to scripture, and an acceptance of such traditions became characteristic of the Church of England. A special authority has attached to the Fathers of the first four centuries and to the traditions of the undivided church. The Reformed churches have been more inclined to question any practices that were not directly warranted by scripture, and in England the Puritans campaigned for this stance, to be opposed by Richard Hooker.[8] The Church of England's Article 34 affirms the authority of the church to determine traditions, ceremonies, and rights in whatever way is not actually in conflict with scripture and denies the private individual the moral right unilaterally to change such. The Church of England may seem too firmly insistent on regarding patterns developed in particular social contexts as nonnegotiable. The Christian Brethren (Plymouth Brethren) are one body that aims to follow scripture itself and avoid the influence of extrascriptural traditions. But Brethren author F. F. Bruce points out how even churches who reject such traditions as a matter of principle are shaped by traditions of their own, whether or not they recognize this fact.[9] He also notes, as we have above, that we receive the actual Second Testament canon (and perhaps that of the First) as a tradition of the church rather than from scripture itself.

To accede to the way the church has come to understand and apply scripture over the centuries may seem wiser than trusting in the private judgment of an individual or even a generation. Others have walked the Christian way before us, and we follow in their steps.

> They therefore deserve our careful if critical attention. We can learn much from following what they have left us from their conversation. If, however, we find that one and another of them — not to mention whole generations — have gone astray in some respect . . . then we should first be sure we hear them as they themselves wanted to be heard and understood. Only when we have understood them in this way should we feel justified in

8. See *Laws of Ecclesiastical Polity* II (1594).
9. See *Tradition Old and New*. Cf. Smart, "The Treacherousness of Tradition."

taking issue with them. Responsibility to those behind us calls for us to treat our predecessors as we would be treated by our successors.[10]

"How sorry we feel for those who have lost their memory. It is as if they had had a large part of their personality cut away." "Tradition is the Church's memory."[11]

At the same time it needs to be acknowledged that the church's tradition can in principle work against scripture and against the Holy Spirit, and has done so in practice. Barr notes that the tradition that issued from the First Testament and the ways of interpreting it that were current in Jesus' day led to Jesus both positively and negatively: It enabled him to discover his calling, and it led his enemies to reject him and seek his death. That process was not confined to that moment; it is within the church's tradition, too, that we have to look most seriously for human failure and perversity.[12]

If we discover that scripture contradicts our traditions, we are faced with the question of which to follow. In establishing the canon of the Second Testament the Patristic church was opening itself to subordinating its traditions to The Tradition — even if it was also using its understanding of the gospel to help it to see what canon to establish. We are invited to judge even our most cherished formularies and attitudes by scripture rather than vice versa. The forms of ministry in the church of the first century were developed in response to its social context, and there is no reason to view these forms as normative and thus to fault forms of ministry that do not outwardly correspond to these. But the forms of ministry in the church of the first century were also outworkings of the gospel, and we have an obligation to consider whether our forms of ministry give expression to the gospel. The church tests its tradition — both its teaching and the forms of its life — by scripture.[13]

Reason and Secular Thought

While recognizing that human insight can go wrong, scripture itself shows an unself-conscious confidence in human insight; the approach of the

10. Van Buren, *A Theology of the Jewish-Christian Reality* 1:47.
11. H. Chadwick, "Reflections on Tradition in Fact and Belief," in *Scripture, Tradition and Reason* (ed. Bauckham and Drewery) 289.
12. Barr, *Old and New in Interpretation* 27-32.
13. Cf. the Anglican-Orthodox 1976 Moscow agreement (see Evans, *Authority in the Church* 11).

wisdom books and that of an author such as Luke to writing his Gospel provide illustrations. While the Torah emphasizes its God-given nature, its contents largely match the religious and ethical writings of other peoples and those of human wisdom. Scripture's affirmation and utilization of reason suggests that a concern for biblical theology does not mean one has to be opposed to philosophical theology or natural theology.

The discoveries of empirical science and of secular thought in general have a significant influence on the Christian church. The study of humanity and of the world in which we live generates insights that shape our thinking in a variety of ways. We understand more than previous generations did about subjects such as the nature of the physical universe and of humanity, about aspects of the human mind, emotions, and will and the relationship between these, and about the effects of heredity and environment on the human personality. This influences the way we interpret passages of scripture such as Genesis 1. As embodied in secular educational, sociological, psychological, and counseling theory and practice, such study has transformed important aspects of the church's theory and practice.

In our journey through history we have carried as well as the scriptures books by writers such as Plato and Aristotle, and "whether acknowledged or not, these too have been turned to as authorities."[14] Within the Church of England, especially since Richard Hooker, reason has been placed alongside scripture and tradition as one in a threefold strand of authorities for the church. The dominance of reason in secular thinking has tended to give it the final word. But reason itself is culturally shaped, not an objective absolute. Thus "the careful theologian is the one who understands the consensus of the day and fights against being infiltrated by it":[15] Scripture has the capacity to enable that process. When it says things that seem odd, threatening, or even irrelevant, it is especially deserving of attention.[16] Scriptural authority is characteristically of the "soft" kind, which gives reasons and can expect to make sense and earn our willing agreement, but it will not be surprising if there are occasions when we cannot see the sense in what God says. At moments when scripture clashes with our own reason, we have to decide whether scripture has misunderstood God or whether we have. For scripture to be our authoritative canon means that we assume that the latter is more likely, refusing "to reserve the right to pass an

---

14. Van Buren, *A Theology of the Jewish-Christian Reality* 1:23.
15. Schaeffer, "Race and Reason" 60.
16. Countryman, *Biblical Authority or Biblical Tyranny?* 96.

unfavourable verdict on whatever a fair exegesis of Scripture would lead one to suppose God says."[17]

Human Experience

Both Testaments assume that people not only learn of God from scripture but also have direct experiences of God. The theology of the First Testament is in large part a theology of experience; the exile, for instance, broadly and deeply shaped Israel's religious, theological, and national understanding. The Psalms invite us to learn from the religious experience of Israel, while Paul expects churches to learn both from their own religious experience (e.g., Gal 3:2) and from his (e.g., Phil 3). It is quite possible to be committed to studying scripture carefully and submissively but miss what it is pointing to (John 5:39), and God's direct speaking to someone may help the church break out of this vicious circle. The wisdom tradition and the teaching of Jesus in the parables and elsewhere (e.g., on God's fatherly love in Matt 5) illustrate scriptural confidence in what can be learned from more general empirical human experience, while both Testaments are willing to utilize concepts and forms derived from other religions to enable them to express more clearly the nature of their own faith.

For all human beings their own experience (religious and otherwise) also exercises a significant influence on them. People who emphasize scriptural authority characteristically also emphasize the reality of the individual's personal relationship with God, within which God may speak and guide individuals in their lives. In charismatic renewal circles this receives an extra dimension: As well as speaking to me for my own sake, God may also give me messages for other people. People who become involved in charismatic renewal may well find that they are more motivated to listen to God through scripture, not less so, but scripture does have a less dominant significance in circles where God is expected to speak to people directly than it has where God is mainly expected to speak through scripture.

The prayer and testimony of people who belong to other religions may also seem to bring illumination to people who confess Christ, as may the traditions and teachings of the culture in which we are brought up.[18] Feminist theology encourages theology to take account of women's distinc-

17. Helm, review of Barr's *Bible in the Modern World* 23.
18. Pui-Lan, "Discovering the Bible in the Non-Biblical World" 36.

tive experience, of menstruation, conception, pregnancy, giving birth, nursing, and menopause — and of men's distinctive experience.[19] Further, it insists that we take account of women's distinctive experience of living in a male-dominated world.[20] Indeed, Katharine Doob Sakenfeld suggests that "the place of women's experience (and the proper definition of 'experience') in appropriating the biblical witness is . . . the central issue around which feminist discussion of approaches to biblical authority revolves."[21] Pamela Dickey Young discusses women's experience in terms of "source and norm of theology."[22] For a reformist feminist, women's experience is a means of understanding the tradition, but for a revolutionary feminist, it is a means of creating a *new* tradition.[23]

More generally, as reason replaced tradition as scripture's chief theological rival, so experience has now replaced reason. Experiencing things for ourselves seems the supreme or the only way to guarantee their reality. Carl Rogers expresses a characteristic conviction of our age, influencing theology as much as other areas of conviction: "Experience is, for me, the highest authority. The touchstone of validity is my own experience."[24] Subjective certainty is a more assured and a more promising starting point than anything external to ourselves. R. Bellah and his associates have characterized the basic American attitude toward life as "expressive individualism," which holds that "each person has a unique core of feeling and intuition that should unfold or be expressed if individuality is to be realized." The good life is one rich in experience, the right act is one with the most exciting challenge or the best feeling, the key values are those intuitively and freely affirmed by the choice of the individual.[25] Such attitudes naturally find expression in the religious sphere. We emphasize expression of and reflection on our own feelings and our religious journey. Present-day human experience may seem a better starting point for theology than scripture and tradition.[26] Current educational theory also places great em-

19. See, e.g., V. Saiving Goldstein, "The Human Situation: A Feminine View," *JR* 40 (1960) 100-12 = *Womanspirit Rising* (ed. Christ and Plaskow) 25-42.

20. E.g., R. R. Ruether, "Feminist Interpretation," in *Feminist Interpretation of the Bible* (ed. Russell) 114; cf. Dickey Young, *Feminist Theology* 53-56.

21. "Feminist Perspectives on Bible and Theology" 6-7.

22. *Feminist Theology* 49-69.

23. Christ, "The New Feminist Theology" 203-4.

24. *On Becoming a Person* (Boston: Houghton Mifflin, 1961) 23, quoted by Bloesch, *Essentials of Evangelical Theology* 2:240.

25. R. Bellah, et al., *Habits of the Heart* (Berkeley: U California, 1985) 333-34.

26. See Schillebeeckx, *Christ* 29; cf. Thomas, "Theology and Experience" 180.

phasis on general human experience as a resource for people in their learning.

Discussing the role of experience in theology and its relationship to scripture is problematic. Experience is currently much emphasized, but the concept is an elusive one, one of the most obscure we have, according to Gadamer.[27] In some usage its subjective side is prominent, as when we speak of the deep inner awareness of self and world to which Rogers refers and of our inner sense of what truly matters, has value, and deserves our commitment. In other usage its objective side is prominent, as when we refer to what has happened to us or to what we can personally check. Either way "experience means learning through 'direct' contact with people and things."[28] "Religious experience" is often spoken of in such a way as to imply that it ineluctably belongs to the subjective realm of inner feelings, but Nicholas Lash protests at this assumption and insists that religious experience involves the whole person, thinking and acting as well as feeling.[29] The appeal to experience in theology has its objective as well as its subjective side. People's experience of whether prayer for healing achieves something has some influence on their beliefs about God as healer.

So what is the relation between what we learn through experience and what we learn through scripture? Is "experience of life" "the primary text," as some liberation hermeneutic assumes?[30] How does scripture function as resource and a norm for experience?

We make a conceptual distinction between experience and interpretation and often see these as successive occurrences. First we experience, then we interpret; different people may have the same experience but interpret it differently in the light of their beliefs. Experience comes first, finding language in which to express the nature of the experience comes second. Real authority, it might seem to follow, lies with the experience; the means of interpreting it (e.g., scripture) comes second. Some feminist theology and interpretation speaks about women's experience in this way,[31] though Carol Christ defines experience in terms of feeling and perception, action

---

27. *Truth and Method* 310; cf. Thomas, "Theology and Experience" 179, who adds a quotation attributed to A. N. Whitehead that "the word 'experience' is one of the most deceitful in philosophy."

28. Schillebeeckx, *Christ* 31; cf. O'Collins, *Fundamental Theology* 33-34.

29. *Theology on the Way to Emmaus* 143-53.

30. Rowland and Corner, *Liberating Exegesis* 45.

31. See Green's criticism (*Imagining God* 121, 129-30) of McFague's work in *Metaphorical Theology*.

and reflection, body and mind, and individual and community, not in terms of prereflective immediacy.[32]

An influential current strand of thinking questions whether it is true that we first have an experience and then decide to interpret it as an experience of God or of love. Do experience and interpretation follow each other in this way? "Trying to use prelinguistic experience as a theological criterion involves an implicit contradiction: it is like wanting to remove one's glasses in order to check their reliability against a 'direct' view of the world."[33] Experience does not come to us raw; like reason it reflects expectations and categories that we bring to it and our own cultural and religious tradition. Even the objective side of experience, the interest in objective realities that we can personally see or touch, has a historical side to it, and we must be wary of thinking that it does not.[34] The basic human experiences of women and men, noted above, take different shapes in different cultures: Paul's arguments from nature (1 Cor 11:14) are from nature as enculturated in a particular context. "People with different paradigmatic commitments characteristically have different experiences."[35]

Experience and understanding are then two sides of one coin. When the same thing happens to people with different beliefs, it is not the same thing that happens to them. One may encounter more, or less, than was objectively there.

> Not only does the religious man interpret in a different way from the non-believer, he lives in a different world and has different experiences. Thus for the believer the exodus through the Red Sea can in fact be taken as an expression of an *experience* and not as a secondary interpretation or a superstructure that can be detached from the context of experience.[36]

Adherents of different religions do not conceptualize the same experience in different ways. They have different experiences.[37]

On this theory "interpretation" comes before experience, in the sense that a framework of thinking formed in the light of a resource such as scripture makes it possible to have experiences of certain kinds. "To become

---

32. See "The New Feminist Theology" 212.
33. Green, *Imagining God* 129-30.
34. Gadamer, *Truth and Method* 310-11.
35. Green, *Imagining God* 133.
36. Schillebeeckx, *Christ* 50.
37. Lindbeck, *The Nature of Doctrine* 40.

a Christian involves learning the story of Israel and of Jesus well enough to interpret and experience oneself and one's world in its terms"; more broadly, "language (or, more generally, some conceptual and/or symbolic interpretive scheme) is a condition for religious experience."[38] From a feminist perspective Mary Ann Tolbert also notes that "experience itself is interpreted. The data of our existence is filtered through some organizing matrix in order for us to categorize it, order it, and make it sensible."[39]

There seems to be some plausibility about both these views: There is surely a dialectical relationship between language and experience. "Our experience is moulded by our understanding, and our understanding is modified by our experience."[40] Not merely individually but collectively "we are not passive recipients of identical impressions"; we "both bring to and extract from experience a variety of attitudes, presuppositions, and schemata of interpretation, which change from age to age."[41] The early Christians were influenced both by the transforming character of their experiences of Jesus and by the categories within which it was natural for them to interpret him. They could experience salvation through Jesus because that was how they understood salvation, but their experience of Jesus and of salvation through him outgrew their categories.[42] "Thought makes experience possible, while . . . it is experience that makes new thinking necessary."[43]

Christian experience is subjective, individualistic, restricted, arrogant, diverse, and introspective.[44] Scripture as canon shapes expectations and provides categories for experience. It provides a resource for critical reflection on experience. Human religious and inner experiences are of very varied kinds, and not all can be affirmed. Some religious and inner experiences take classist, racist, sexist, or other forms that are in conflict with fundamental Christian affirmations regarding love and justice, and of course the prophets and Jesus are often critical about their hearers' experiences.[45] So we bring our experience to the Psalms, and look at the psalm-

---

38. *Ibid.*, 34, 37.
39. *The Bible and Feminist Hermeneutics* 120.
40. Wiles, *The Remaking of Christian Doctrine* 57. Cf. the discussion between Don Cupitt and C. F. D. Moule in Cupitt, *Explorations in Theology* 6:27-41.
41. Hebblethwaite, "The Appeal to Experience in Christology" 265.
42. Wiles, *The Remaking of Christian Doctrine* 53.
43. Schillebeeckx, *Christ* 32.
44. Miller, *The Authority of the Bible* 70-91.
45. Thomas, "Theology and Experience" 196.

ists' experience in the light of ours and at ours in the light of theirs, in order that we may permit ours to be "disciplined by the speech of the Psalms" and let the latter "reshape our sensitivities."[46] The tension between our religious experience and that of which we read in scripture is resolved not by reinterpreting scripture in the light of our experience but by seeking to have our experience conformed to that of which scripture speaks.

Our Commitments

Whether we *see* the truth depends on whether we *do* the truth (John 7:17). Presenting ourselves to God and being willing to be transformed lead us to discernment of God's will, rather than vice versa (Rom 12:1-2).[47] A fourth source of influence on us, capable of leading us into truth or untruth, is the commitments and vested interests that we already have. "All theology knowingly or not is by definition always engaged for or against the oppressed."[48] Liberation theology has especially noted that commitments come first and articulation of belief second, but the phenomenon can be observed elsewhere. How the Church of England sees marriage and divorce is heavily influenced by the fact that it is an established church, whose practice has to come to terms with the state of society. How minister and people understand the theology of ministry reflects what practice of ministry and congregational life they are committed to. How I evaluate critiques of theological education reflects my instinct to safeguard my job.

The relationship of scripture to praxis is similar to its relationship to experience; commitments also reflect attitudes, values, and opinions that have been shaped by something. Commitment to God's ways makes it possible to understand God's words, but on what basis do we undertake some action as in accordance with God's ways? Liberation theologians can speak as if an act of commitment contained its own justification. Hence "the inescapable importance of the ethical leap, the political choice."[49] The agonizing of Mathieu, the philosopher-hero of Sartre's trilogy *The Roads to Freedom*, hovering between inability to commit himself and commitment without reason, illustrates more realistically the dilemma of finding a basis

---

46. Brueggemann, *Praying the Psalms* 39.
47. Hays, "Scripture Shaped Community" 51.
48. E. Schüssler Fiorenza, *Bread Not Stone* 45.
49. Assmann, *Practical Theology of Liberation* 105.

for commitment. Some ideology or faith must lie behind an act of commitment.[50] Actions are not self-authenticating, and theology involves "critical reflection on praxis in the light of the Word."[51] In his *Critique of Pure Reason* Immanuel Kant "elevated moral practice into the canon [!] by which the interpretation of all biblical and ecclesiastical traditions is to be judged."[52] Mere dogma counts for nothing, but a vision of God (for instance, a triumphalist God or a suffering God) makes a difference to a person's praxis.

Actions may appear so clearly right that they carry intrinsically self-evident justification, because we do not come to them with empty head and heart. We come to them with a set of assumptions about God and the world, truth and life, love, mercy, and justice, whose guiding lines embrace those particular actions unambiguously. Although commitment may lead to new insights and to the refining of previous assumptions, commitment itself operates on the basis of a framework of insights already assimilated, as the hypotheses that scientists or historians bring to their evidence presuppose a view of reality as a whole. Scripture as canon is resource and norm for such a vision of God in the light of which we decide how to act and judge events. It is normative resource before the event, and measuring line after it.

Karl Marx declared that "the philosophers have only *interpreted* the world, in various ways — the point, however, is to *change* it." Ironically Marxism has exercised its greatest influence in the world by its vision, its interpretation of history, rather than by its actual activity. "The most powerful way to change the world is precisely by interpreting it."[53] Hence "identification of the issues is as important as fighting in the streets or in the mountains."[54] If Christians have a clearer understanding of the world, they ought to be in a position to develop a more adequate concrete praxis than Marxism.[55] It is right to suspect and question the assumption that the only way to do theology is to infer contemporary application from objective

---

50. Cf. Segundo, *Liberation of Theology* 101.

51. Gutiérrez, *A Theology of Liberation* 13 (noted already at the beginning of chapter 8 above).

52. Moltmann, *The Trinity and the Kingdom of God* 6.

53. Green, *Imagining God* 152. Cf. Miranda, *Being and the Messiah* 5-6.

54. A. Mafeje, "The Problem of Anthropology in Historical Perspective," in *Canadian Journal of African Studies* 10 (1976) 332, quoted by Mosala, *Biblical Hermeneutics and Black Theology* 121.

55. Cf. Kirk, *Liberation Theology* 200-201.

exegesis or systematic theology. Critical reflection on praxis in the light of the word and critical reflection on theology in the light of praxis complement each other in a necessary and vital dialectic.

Scripture as Resource and Norm

We have noted in chapters 8 and 9 that the scriptures have a foundational and final role in Christian faith because it is a faith that concerns historical events and that emerged in a particular historical context. The authority of scripture is the authority of the gospel, which speaks with authority out of scripture. That intrinsic argument is buttressed by the christological consideration that Jesus treated the Hebrew Bible this way, so that following Jesus involves following him at this point. Recognizing the two Testaments as the church's authoritative resource and norm is in keeping with the nature of Christianity and with the attitude of Jesus, while declining to do so is more difficult to reconcile with either.

It is for this reason that scripture has a significance for an understanding of Christian faith that tradition, reason, human experience, or Christian commitment cannot have. By their nature they cannot inform us of the gospel. It is the Bible that tells us of the key events that form the foundation for the faith and that offers us the classic interpretation of their significance. It thus determines the nature of our worldview in the sense that it shapes our theology and life as a whole. It thereby provides us with the framework that helps us to perceive the kind of political, social, and economic policies that deserve Christian commitment. It provides us with the set of assumptions about the nature or meaning of the world within which scientific reason can operate. Scripture has a final role as well as a foundational role in Christian faith, in that it provides us with a measuring line by which to check decisions that we have made. Tradition, reason, commitment, and experience can all help to open our eyes to the meaning of scripture itself, but they can also obscure its meaning, impose meanings on it, or can come into conflict with it. For scripture to be the church's canon is for it to be the measure of tradition, reason, commitment, and experience rather than vice versa.

The directness with which it can fulfil this function varies. It does not refer to every subject on which we have to make judgments. In that connection, we need to return to the fact that its central significance is that it preserves the memory of the events on which the faith is based and the classic formulation of that faith in Israelite and early Christian times. To say that scripture contains all that we need for our salvation (Church of England Article 6) is not to pretend that it offers direct guidance on every issue on which we need to come to a Christian mind. It is to say that it contains an adequate account of the events and the faith for us to live by that account and to make decisions in the light of it. It can lead men and women of God to full maturity (2 Tim 3:17). To say that we rely on scripture alone is not to pretend that we are independent of other resources in every connection but to affirm that scripture is clear in its message and adequate in its account of those foundational matters.

PART III

SCRIPTURE AS INSPIRED WORD

14

The Words of God
in Human Words

To speak of the inspiration of scripture is fundamentally to claim "that in some way the Bible comes from God, that he has in some sense a part in its origin."[1] In what sense, and to what end?

The model of scripture as God's inspired word has its background in the prophets. In the Bible as a whole the *witnessing tradition* comes first in order, first in extent, and — if the setting of priorities is appropriate — first in importance. This witnessing tradition incorporates, especially in the Pentateuch, extensive material by way of direct maxim regarding belief and behavior, and this suggests the *authoritative canon* as a second model for scripture. Next in order come the prophetic books with their suggestion of this third model, scripture as an *inspired word*. Through the prophets God *spoke* (Heb 1:1). They experience the activity of the Spirit of God and speak the word of God. They bring a transcendent divine word, yet one that comes through their human personality.

The Word of God at the Critical Moment: Jeremiah 36

The fourth year of King Jehoiakim's reign was when things began to catch up on Judah and when the Babylonians (and God) began to catch up on Jehoiakim. He had been put on the throne by the Egyptians as their puppet, but the Egyptians had just suffered a humiliating defeat at the hands of the

---

1. Barr, *The Bible in the Modern World* 17.

Babylonians. It was one of the first triumphs of the great Nebuchadnezzar, the Babylonian king who eventually destroyed Jerusalem. 604 BC was a year of great significance, like 1812 or 1914 or 1989. Anyone could see which way the wind was blowing.

In that year Jeremiah sensed that Yahweh was telling him to make one last attempt to persuade the king to turn back. Jeremiah was to write down the prophecies he had delivered over the twenty-three years of his ministry and send them to the king. This meant producing what may have been in effect the first edition of the Book of Jeremiah. During those years Jeremiah had been telling people they must turn to Yahweh or be cast off, and all that time they had been ignoring Jeremiah — or rather laughing at him — because the disaster he warned of never actually came. For them, and at times for Jeremiah himself, that seemed to indicate that God's word could not be believed in. It never came true. Jeremiah's feelings as he received this commission may therefore have included a sense of relief that the critical moment had finally arrived. The political situation seemed finally to be proving that he was right. Yahweh was at last acting in accordance with those words uttered through Jeremiah.

So Jeremiah summoned his colleague Baruch. Baruch could write, so he could take Jeremiah's words down; perhaps Jeremiah could not write. Further, Baruch was free to visit the temple. Everyone used to go there to rejoice at festivals and to pray on fast days, but Jeremiah could not; apparently the authorities had become weary of him causing trouble by telling everyone that the king and the priests were ignoring God's words to them, and they had banned him.

Baruch was just as committed to Yahweh as Jeremiah was. Not that this made identifying with Jeremiah easy; he had seen what people had done to Jeremiah over the years, putting him into prison and threatening to kill him. He had seen what God had done to Jeremiah, the price Jeremiah had paid for being a prophet. He knew that, in a situation like the one they were in, declaring God's word cost something. Jeremiah in turn knew that Baruch feared for his own life. Indeed, he gave Baruch a word from God especially for him, a promise that he would be safe (Jer 45). Coming from a man who himself had experienced some escapes over those two decades, the promise carried conviction. Somehow a natural feeling of being scared stiff and a conviction about the trustworthiness of Jeremiah's God coexisted in Baruch's heart.

So they set about the task of putting Jeremiah's prophecies into writing. Some months elapsed, perhaps not merely because the task took some time, but because they were waiting for the right occasion. Eventually it presented itself. Nebuchadnezzar's army marched down the west coast of Judah, past where Tel Aviv now is. It attacked and sacked the Philistine port of Ashkelon. The Babylonians were breathing down Jehoiakim's neck. The people came together in Jerusalem to fast and pray.

At that moment Baruch took the scroll that he and Jeremiah had produced to the temple court, where people wandered about and talked in the way we hear of in the Gospels later. He gathered people around him and began to read Jeremiah's warnings about the Babylonians bringing death and desolation to the land. People on the temple staff of course heard about this, and someone decided that they had better tell the state authorities, who in turn sent for Baruch. They cross-examined him and thus discovered how Jeremiah had circumvented the ban on his own presence in the temple court. They were presumably frustrated that their plans to silence him had failed, and they knew that they had to tell the king what was going on. But they also knew that once they did that, they had signed Jeremiah's and Baruch's death warrants. So they warned Baruch that the two of them would be wise to disappear.

The authorities' action perhaps proves that they did not feel very loyal to Jehoiakim, the king foisted on them by the Egyptians. It also hints that in their heart of hearts they knew Jeremiah was right. They *had* gone away from Yahweh. They still attended the temple, but spiritually and morally they had moved miles away. When Baruch caught them off-guard with the word of God, however, they proved themselves to be the spiritual sons of those officials in Josiah's day who knew how to respond to the scroll read in the temple on that occasion. (The story in Jer 36 parallels the one in 2 Kgs 22 at a number of points — or makes a pointed contrast with it — and seems to have been deliberately constructed to do so.)

Nevertheless they also confiscated the scroll and reported to the king what had happened. He sent for the scroll and got a member of his staff called Jehudi to read it out. It was December and was evidently cold in Jerusalem, as it can be (it snows there sometimes). Jehoiakim was in his winter quarters and had a fire going. Jehudi read systematically through the scroll, column by column — it would be more like reading a microfilm than reading the kind of books we are used to. But the king did not let Jehudi wind the scroll onto the equivalent of a take-up reel. Each time he had finished three or four columns the king would reach out and hack it off, so that the scroll dropped section by section into the flames of the fire.

Perhaps this was partly an act of bravado on Jehoiakim's part, designed to show that it took more than a prophet and his tin-pot assistant to put King Jehoiakim off. But there would have been more to it than that. Now that Jeremiah had put all those prophecies into writing, the situation really was much worse. Spoken words are all very well, but they can be lost in the wind; a person cannot necessarily be held to them. Putting things into writing makes them definite and fixed. All the more so when things are put into writing in the name of God. Even a king who liked to think of himself as a cool and worldly-wise politician will have found it a little threatening to have there in writing God's declared intention to bring disaster upon him. Jehoiakim's act was one designed to stop Jeremiah's words from coming true, by destroying them.

Of course it was naive for Jehoiakim to think that he could frustrate God's purpose by burning God's words. In any case, it was only too easy for Jeremiah and Baruch to start again, perhaps looking after the scroll better this time. Not only that, Jeremiah knew that Jehoiakim had crossed a line. He had gone too far. The wets in the cabinet had been caught unaware by God's word and had let themselves be convicted by it. The king was not going to let himself be tricked, exhorted, or reasoned into a change of policy. He would rather rend the scroll than rend his garments (36:23-24: the same Hebrew word each time). He was not for turning. His father Josiah knew how to respond to the word of Yahweh, but Jehoiakim did not (compare again the story in 2 Kings 22; also Jer 22:13-19 for the explicit contrast). The new scroll included some extra words about Jehoiakim himself (36:29-31).

It is a story full of suggestiveness about the inspired word of God: about the cost some people paid to deliver the words that we now have in scripture, about God's faithfulness to those who declare the word of God faithfully, about how much of the Bible is warning of judgment hanging over the people of God, about the way God's word can sometimes get through to people when their defenses are down, when they are unprepared to be hit by it, about how awesome it is that we have God's word in writing, about how taking that for granted is as effective as burning it, about how dangerous it can be to ignore God's word, and about how God's word cannot be destroyed, silenced, banned, or drowned, because it will keep resurfacing.

Prophecy as the Inspired Word of God

Like other models for scripture, inspiration has a broader and a narrower application. In the extended sense of the phrase, the whole of scripture is

God's inspired word. Josephus uses the idea of inspiration in this way, and sees the opening chapters of Genesis as obtained "by inspiration from God."[2] Second Testament writers describe as the word of God both laws in the Pentateuch and the gospel message preached by the first Christians (e.g., 1 Cor 2:9-13). "*All* scripture is God-breathed . . ." (2 Tim 3:16).

In the narrower sense, the idea of inspiration is most at home with the Prophets. It is here that inspiration has its specific background and origin. It is the prophets who characteristically claim to speak under divine prompting and to speak words framed by God rather than by them. Paul begins "I Paul . . ."; they begin "thus says Yahweh."

> The word inspiration has received more numerous gradations and distinctions of meaning than perhaps any other in the whole of theology. There is an inspiration of superintendence and an inspiration of suggestion; an inspiration which would have been consistent with the Apostle or Evangelist falling into error, and an inspiration which would have prevented him from erring; verbal organic inspiration by which the inspired person is the passive utterer of a Divine Word, and an inspiration which acts through the character of the sacred writer; there is an inspiration which absolutely communicates the fact to be revealed or statement to be made, and an inspiration which does not supersede the ordinary knowledge of human events; there is an inspiration which demands infallibility in matters of doctrine, but allows for mistakes in fact. Lastly, there is a view of inspiration which recognises only its supernatural and prophetic character, and a view of inspiration which regards the Apostles and Evangelists as equally inspired in their writings and in their lives, and in both receiving the guidance of the Spirit of truth in a manner not different in kind but only in degree from ordinary Christians.[3]

Doctrinal discussion of inspiration has been in difficulty for at least a century. An important factor in the impasse that this discussion has reached has been confusion over whether and at what point we are discussing inspiration in terms that apply to scripture as a whole or to the Prophets in particular. Statements about inspiration can be too specific to apply comfortably to scripture as a whole or too general to provide a satisfying account of the Prophets in particular. It has thus been argued that we should consciously cease making the Prophets our starting point for discussing inspira-

---

2. *Against Apion* I.8. "Inspiration" is *epipnoia*.
3. Jowett, "On the Interpretation of Scripture" 417-18.

tion.[4] But because the origin of the model lies with the Prophets, it seems
more appropriate to move in the opposite direction and seek to consider the
model in the light of its intrinsic meaning in this original connection. As with
other models for scripture, in understanding inspiration we do best to begin
with the original narrower application of the term and move from there to its
extended application to scripture as a whole. We will not initially concern
ourselves with an understanding of inspiration that can be applied to the
whole of scripture. We will, rather, look for the distinctives of the model that
emerge in its original connection, with the Prophets.

The phrase "the word of God" appears first in scripture as a term to
describe a particular spoken message that comes to a prophet or is transmitted by a prophet to people (1 Sam 9:27; 2 Sam 16:23; 1 Kgs 12:22; 1 Chr
17:3). The parallel phrase "the word of Yahweh" is much more common
and applies to others as well as prophets (e.g., Gen 15:1, 4; Exod 9:20-21;
Num 11:23-24; 1 Sam 3:1, 7; 15:10; 2 Sam 7:4; 24:11; 1 Kgs 2:27; 6:11;
12:24). Some Psalmists evidently also exercise a ministry that involves
bringing people words from God (e.g., Pss 12; 46; 50; 75; 81; 95).

The word of Yahweh characteristically takes the form of a promise or
warning regarding what Yahweh will be and do in relation to people. Sometimes it includes explicit instructions regarding the action that is required in
response to the word; it may even focus on such a word of instruction (e.g.,
Josh 8:8, 27; 1 Sam 15:13, 23, 26). Sometimes the plural "words of Yahweh" is
used, still to refer to one prophetic message of promise and commission; the
broader notion of God speaking words appears more generally in connection
with Yahweh's issuing commands at Sinai and subsequently (e.g., Exod 20:1;
24:3; Num 12:6; Deut 4:10, 36; 1 Sam 15:1, 11).

The First Testament also sometimes connects the *spirit* of God with
prophecy. Balaam utters an oracle when the spirit of God comes on him
(Num 24:2), as do Amasai (1 Chr 12:18) and other figures in Chronicles. The
spirit of Yahweh speaks through David (2 Sam 23:2). A number of passages
describe the spirit of God coming on people with the result that they "prophesy" (Num 11:25-29; 1 Sam 10:10; 19:20) — apparently some nonrational or
nonverbal activity, perhaps parallel to speaking in tongues. The spirit of
Yahweh is especially involved in the ministry of Elijah and Ezekiel, though
here it relates in particular to extraordinary experiences that come to them or
feats that they perform rather than specifically to their words (e.g., 1 Kgs

---

4. So, e.g., Achtemeier, *The Inspiration of Scripture* 75; also Abraham, *The Divine
Inspiration of Holy Scripture;* contrast, e.g., Sanday, *Inspiration* 128.

18:12; 2 Kgs 2:16; Ezek 3:12, 14; 8:3). All these passages reflect the fact that the activity of Yahweh's spirit inspiring the Prophets is a subset of that tumultuous, extraordinary, unpredictable, invisible activity of the spirit of Yahweh related especially in the stories of Othniel, Gideon, Jephthah, Samson, and Saul. The First Testament sees the activity of the spirit of God where the extraordinary happens. To speak of the scriptures as inspired thus hints that they are unpredictable and irresistible, free and mysterious.

It is striking that the prophetic books are the ones that most explicitly speak both of their divine origin and also of their human and historical origin. They characteristically open with some variant on a formula that points to these two fundamental aspects of their nature and of the way they need to be read. The Book of Hosea, for instance, is introduced as "the word of Yahweh that came to Hosea the son of Beeri, in the time of Uzziah, Jotham, Ahaz, and Hezekiah, kings of Judah, and in the time of Jeroboam the son of Joash, king of Israel." The Book of Jeremiah is introduced as "the words of Jeremiah the son of Hilkiah, of the priests who were in Anatot in the area of Benjamin, to whom the word of Yahweh came in the days of Josiah the son of Amon, king of Judah, in the thirteenth year of his reign . . . ." The formula varies, but it commonly draws attention to these two characteristics of the prophetic books. They are the words of Yahweh; they are also the words of particular human beings.

In these opening words to prophetic books it is not the prophet who speaks. The formula speaks *about* the prophet, and is presumably the work of editors who provided information such as this to guide later generations in their reading of the prophets. But these guidelines correspond to indications that appear in the prophetic oracles themselves. On the one hand, prophets urge people to "hear the word of Yahweh" (Hos 4:2; Jer 2:4). Prophets often speak as if they were God speaking: Thus throughout Hosea 5 the "I" that Hosea uses is God, not Hosea. Or they declare "Yahweh says . . ." (e.g., Jer 2:2, 5), speaking as messengers of Yahweh the divine king, whose words they bring in the way that a human king's messenger brings his words. As the word of God, inspired speech compares with the nature of the Qur'an as it has traditionally been seen, as received verbatim in its Arabic language without the vehicles of its reception contributing at all to its nature.[5]

The prophets, however, are also capable of speaking their own words,

5. See, e.g., Zaehner, "Why Not Islam" 176-77; Cragg, "How Not Islam" 390-91; also " 'According to the Scriptures,' " in *Ways of Reading the Bible* (ed. Wadsworth) 24-25, 34-35.

acting as go-betweens for Yahweh ("he") and people ("you"), or speaking for themselves to Yahweh (see notably Jer 15:15-21). Further, when they do speak the actual words of Yahweh, those words are ones that reflect the historical situations in which they are uttered — a time such as that of Jeroboam or Josiah, a place such as the northern or the southern kingdom. The prophets reflect a background in the traditions of Israel and Judah that shape what they say in significant ways, and they use genres that reflect the speech forms of their day. They speak as Hosea the son of Beeri or Jeremiah the son of Hilkiah of the priests who were in Anatot in the area of Benjamin and contribute to what they say as Yahweh's messengers by who they themselves individually are, by the experiences that they bring to their calling and that their calling brings to them, and by their reflection and creativity. Then their words reach us through the work of groups of human redactors.

The words of the prophets thus claim more explicitly than any other parts of scripture to be words deriving from God; they also draw as much systematic attention to their human and historical origins as any part of scripture. That gives a double focus to our attempt to analyze their nature and to the task of interpreting them.

• 15 •

An Effective and Meaningful Word

W. J. Abraham suggested that discussion of inspiration should start from the everyday meaning of the word in contemporary English.[1] It is surely more appropriate to begin with the pointers suggested within scripture itself regarding the significance of its being the inspired word of God. The First Testament, and the Second in its references back to the First, point to two key implications of inspiration.

The Word of God: Certain to Come About

In the prophetic books themselves, to draw attention to the divine origin of a message is to declare that it is certain to come about. Part of the idea's background lies in the power that can reside in human words. In the right circumstances, when a person says "I love you," "I hate you," "I baptize you," "I commission you," "I promise you," or "I forgive you," those words have power. They effect something or guarantee something. In scripture Isaac's words of blessing effectively convey the firstborn's privileges to Jacob (Gen 27).

It is a powerful person who utters effective words. Naturally the words of the all-powerful God have an unequalled effectiveness.[2] It was by speaking that Yahweh brought the world into being (Gen 1; Pss 33:6, 9; 148:5-8) and it is by uttering words that Yahweh redeems and keeps Israel (Pss 33:4; 107:20;

---

1. *The Divine Inspiration of Holy Scripture* 63.
2. On this theme see, e.g., von Rad, *Old Testament Theology* 2:80-95, with the nuancing of Thiselton, "The Supposed Power of Words in the Biblical Writings."

cf. 147:12-20). Yahweh's words issuing from the mouth of a prophet are a sword that slaughters the people (Hos 6:5), a missile that devastates them (Isa 9:8), a fire that consumes them like wood (Jer 5:14), or a sledgehammer that shatters them (Jer 23:29). To declare God's word is not merely to convey information but to implement a decision; the recipients of the word are permitted to overhear the declaration so that they may align themselves with it by trust or repentance. They are not forced to do so, as the story of Jeremiah and Jehoiakim shows. Amaziah, too, had warned Jeroboam about the words of Amos because "the land cannot bear all his words": He would have to be silenced so that the events his words announced could be short-circuited (Amos 7:10). Paradoxically, while such attempts to frustrate words from God make it necessary that the words be effective, when people align themselves with such words, then those words can be reconsidered.

The account in the Book of Jonah of God's dealings with Nineveh shows how the words of God are not irrevocable in the manner of the laws of the Medes and Persians. Ultimately, however, God's declared purpose *will* stand; the intention God has announced *will* be achieved. At either end of Isaiah's prophecies regarding Babylon (Isa 40:8; 55:10-11) there is a particularly powerful affirmation of this point in a context in which it did not seem to be true, as exile dragged on and Yahweh seemed to lack either the power or the inclination to stand by that announced purpose.

The word of God is a reality that effectively shapes history. This is an important motif in the books from Genesis to Kings and in the recapitulation of the story in Chronicles. It is the word of God that calls creation into being in Genesis 1 and that imposes curse, enmity, pain, toil, mortality, banishment, and destruction in Genesis 3–6. It is the word of God that renews and recreates the world and guarantees its security in Genesis 8–9 and that imposes confusion in Genesis 11. It is the word of God that promises Abram land, increase, blessing, fame, and protection and that he will become a blessing. The story from Genesis 12 to Joshua is in large part the account of how that word of God is effective in shaping the history of Abram's people, granting them those gifts that it promised. The covenant made at Sinai (see especially Exod 19–34) and reaffirmed in the Plains of Moab (see Deuteronomy) reinforces the principle that the word of God gives its pattern to the history of the people of God: It gives detail to the words concerning the blessing and curse that will attend Israel's life as Israel either keeps its side of the covenant or neglects it (the words of God in these two contexts are also commonly words of command).

The story from Joshua to Kings continues to depict the way the word of God at work in history achieves God's purpose, as the later reflection on this period in Daniel's prayer in Daniel 9 notes. Within that story, the promises and warnings given to Abraham and Moses are supplemented by God's promise to David, which becomes a key statement forming the history of Israel and Judah (2 Sam 7:25, 28; 1 Kgs 2:4; 6:12; 8:15, 20, 24-26). For the first time this promise from God is specifically a word uttered by a prophet. As such it is supplemented by a sequence of prophetic words from God that join it in shaping the history of Israel and Judah (see 1 Kgs 2:27; 12:15; 22). Yahweh's effective promise to David reappears in Chronicles' retelling of this story (see 1 Chr 17; 2 Chr 1:9; 6). Here, too, the "prophetic" word of God — though not always uttered by "prophets" — shapes the history of Judah (e.g., 2 Chr 12:5-8; 13:4-12; 20:14-17; 21:12-15). In a parallel way within the Prophets themselves, warnings such as those of Isaiah 6 and promises such as those of Ezekiel 37 are not merely factual predictions but implementations of God's purpose. There is a terrible example in Jeremiah 28:16-17, where Jeremiah pronounces an effective death sentence on Hananiah (cf. Hos 6:5).

The language of the prophets is performative:[3] They effect that to which they refer. When the voice of Yahweh sounds, things happen (Amos 1:2: a motto for the Book of Amos and for prophecy as a whole). Yahweh's words uttered through the prophets are dynamically effective for both negative and positive ends (Jer 1:9-10). To call scripture the word of God, then, is to suggest that it is effective and brings people to death or to new life. "The language of the biblical text is prophetic: it anticipates and summons realities that live beyond the conventions of our day-to-day, take-for-granted world. . . . It shatters settled reality and evokes new possibility in the listening assembly."[4]

In Psalm 119 the second characteristic form of the word of God, alongside command, is promise, and a characteristic response to the word of God is thus joyful hope. It is purely in response to this word that hope arises. Psalm 119 is a prayer under pressure, like most Psalms. It is spoken

3. J. L. Austin's term, in *How to Do Things with Words;* cf. Evans, *The Logic of Self-Involvement.* For the application to prophecy, cf. W. J. Houston, "'Today, in Your Very Hearing': Some Comments on the Christological Use of the Old Testament," in *The Glory of Christ* (ed. Hurst and Wright) 41; more broadly Caird, *The Language and Imagery of the Bible* 20-25.
4. Brueggemann, *Finally Comes the Poet* 4; he adds, "Preaching continues that dangerous, indispensable habit of speech."

by someone who is under attack despite — or because of — a life committed to God's ways. No doubt it also presupposes an internal pressure that corresponds to that external pressure, namely, the question whether God's word is really true. When it affirms that suffering is good for you or that God is certainly just and faithful (vv. 71, 75), one wonders whom the psalmist is trying to convince. In this context it emphasizes the word of God, which takes the form of undertakings regarding how God will behave (e.g., vv. 41-42, 49-50, 147-48). It is the *failure* of God's undertakings that generates the psalmist's anguish (vv. 81-84) and lead to the recurrent plea, "renew my life" (cf. vv. 25, 37, 50, 88, 154). Theologically, God's undertakings lie behind and undergird the undertakings that God expects regarding how human beings will behave — as is implied by the Psalm's appeal to grace (v. 58). To say that when we fulfill the commands God fulfills the promises risks imperiling the stress on God's grace and mercy, but it is the case that our hope that God will fulfill the promises, along with our experience of that fulfillment, has to lead us into fulfilling the commands (cf. vv. 26, 88, 146). Promises as well as commands come from God and also reflect "laws" of God's working in the world; both offer us "comfort" (vv. 50, 52). They stimulate an obedience that is awed but joyful and a trust that is joyful but awed (vv. 7, 38).

It is as promise that the word of God is infallible: It does not fail to come true and thus it does not deceive. "Does his word fail?", a psalmist asks rhetorically (Ps 77:8): It cannot be that the promise of God will ultimately fail to be fulfilled and thus deceive the one to whom it is given. "Not one word has failed of all his good promise," Solomon confesses (1 Kgs 8:56; cf. Josh 21:45; 23:14; 2 Kgs 10:10). A statute that God makes "does not fail" (Ps 148:6) and cannot be superseded. God's teaching "never fails" (Ps 19:7 NEB): It can be relied on to bring new life to a person.[5] Scripture will cease to be infallible only when God ceases to keep his word.[6]

In scripture, then, talk of the infallibility of the word of God implies a claim about its truth, not in the sense of factual correctness, since it is likely to be a statement that is not at present factually correct, but in the sense of its reliability and effectiveness. Scripture's own way of understanding the infallibility of God's word takes it as a statement of what will be, not of

---

5. The verbs are *gamār* ("come to an end"), *nāpal* ("fall"), *'āman* (n-stem, the positive expression "be reliable"), and *'ābar* ("pass over").

6. Cf. Loretz, *The Truth of the Bible* 86-89, as quoted in Burtchaell, *Catholic Theories of Biblical Inspiration* 267.

what is. It is reliable in the sense that it is guaranteed to come true — guaranteed by the very truthfulness of God — not in the sense that it is necessarily true at the moment. To say that scripture is inerrant is to say that it does not wander, go astray, or lose the path; it is undeviating.[7] The inerrancy 2 Timothy is explicitly concerned for is also an avoidance of swerving from the truth about the gospel and upsetting the faith of others (2 Tim 2:18); the problem with humanity is error in the sense of deceitfulness, not error in the sense of factual limitations (Rom 3:4).[8]

To complement the negative affirmation that it never fails, scripture also contains the positive declaration that God's word is utterly reliable. Israel's story is an account of how God made this word stand (Deut 9:5; cf. 1 Sam 1:23; 2 Sam 7:25; 1 Kgs 2:4; 6:12; 8:20; 12:15). It is the story of how the divine word is (ful)filled (1 Kgs 2:27; 8:15, 24). Yahweh's "statutes stand quite firm" (Ps 93:5): The declaration that the world will be secure is certain to be effective (cf. 111:7). The prayer "may your word come true," referring to God's promise to David (1 Kgs 8:26), has a firm basis and will be granted (cf. 1 Chr 17:23; 2 Chr 1:9; 6:17). The reliability of Yahweh's word follows naturally from Yahweh's own reliability (e.g., Deut 7:9; Pss 98:3; 100:5; 143:1; Isa 49:7).

The Hebrew words for truth or truthfulness[9] are also used to refer both to the truth(fulness) of Yahweh's word and to the personal truth(fulness) of Yahweh. The word "true" can be applied to a statement regarding present realities or past events, thus suggesting the sense of "factual," but such uses of the word are less common. Statements that are "true" characteristically refer to the future; they are promises, warnings, or ethical injunctions. Reliability and truth attach to God's word through Elijah or Micaiah (1 Kgs 17:24; 22:16) in the sense that the word of these prophets comes true. The oath that Yahweh swears in truth is one that Yahweh will see comes true (Ps 132:11). It is in accordance with this that David acknowledges that Yahweh's words are true (2 Sam 7:28). Another way to make the point is to declare that Yahweh's word has been "proved," as silver is. That is the nature of Yahweh's promises (Pss 12:6; 18:30; 119:40; Prov 30:5).

Isaiah 52:13–53:12 is too complex, unusual, controversial, and difficult a text to form a starting point or test case for an approach to hermeneutics. But it is striking that this passage offers a complex and unusual illustration

---

7. Burtchaell, *Catholic Theories of Biblical Inspiration* 299, 304.
8. Berkouwer, *Holy Scripture* 181, 240.
9. ʾ*emet* and ʾ*emûnâ*; they are etymologically related.

of the nature of the word of God as a supernaturally effective word. Its failure to identify its referent encourages its successive audiences to apply it in various directions: to Israel, to Jesus, to Paul, to the church, to various subsequent groups and individuals. To "close" its meaning by determining once and for all that it refers (for instance) to Jesus is to imperil its effectiveness as a word of God.[10] The Second Testament, of course, did not do that; while it used the passage to help it understand Jesus, it also saw it as having significance for the calling of the church. The passage's own openness as the word of God enables it to effect that to which it refers; it is indeed a performative utterance.[11]

The theme of the effectiveness of God's word reappears in the Second Testament. God's word is God's means of creating, sustaining, and judging (2 Pet 3:5, 7; Heb 1:3; 11:3). It does not fall or fail (Rom 9:6): The reference is to that same agelong promise to Abraham that had shaped the story of Israel before Christ and will still shape that story in Christ. Torah and Prophets will be fulfilled; not the slightest element in them will fall or fail (Matt 5:17-18; Luke 16:17). "The scriptures *must* be fulfilled," says Jesus (e.g., Mark 14:49; cf. Luke 22:37; 24:44; Acts 1:16). Certain events happen or happened "that the scripture might be fulfilled" (John 13:18; 17:12; 19:36; cf. 12:38; Matt 1:22; 2:15, 23; 8:17; 13:35; 21:4). The word of God addressed to people is "alive and powerful," sharp and penetrating, dividing and sifting (Heb 4:12). The warnings of the prophets, or of a prophetic psalmist such as the one to whom Hebrews is referring here, are effective in bringing about the judgment of God — or in bringing about blessing of people if they respond to the warnings that accompany invitations to return to Yahweh, and thus make it unnecessary for the warnings to be implemented. The same applies to the words God gave Moses. They were words that were alive (so Acts 7:38) and could thus bring life as people lived by them, in accordance with Moses' own claim to set before people the way of life and the way of death (Deut 30:19).

Jesus does not speak like a prophet saying "Thus says the Lord." While he acknowledges the words of the Torah and the Prophets, he adds to them his famous "But I say to you. . . ." He speaks his own words of power. It is now *his* words that will not pass away. His words effect healing, forgiveness,

---

10. Cf. Croatto, *Biblical Hermeneutics* 25-28; Croatto does use it as a sample text to illustrate his theses regarding interpretation, but its distinctive nature makes it a difficult text to use in this way.

11. Clines, *I, He, We, and They* 53.

freedom, stilling, and withering (e.g., Matt 8:8, 16; cf. Peter's words in Acts 5:3-5). Jesus *is* the word of God (John 1:1-18). The Second Testament is interested in "truth" in the sense of correspondence to present or permanent reality; Romans 1:18 and 25 speak of people suppressing such truth about God.[12] But Jesus is also the truth in the sense of the one who can be relied on.

The Inspired Word: Significant beyond Its Original Context

In the Second Testament the divine origin of prophetic words has a second significance for people beyond their effectiveness for those to whom they are first given. It further suggests that these words are meaningful, indeed make special demands, in a later context than the one in which they were originally uttered. That conviction also no doubt underlies the fact that the words of the prophets were preserved: There was something about those words that gave them a significance beyond their original context. Hebrews hints at this point by using the present tense when referring to God's speaking of scripture. This is not merely a word that God *said* but one that God *says* (e.g., 3:7; 12:5). The whole argument of the Epistle is an outworking of the conviction that in scripture God is speaking *now*.

The Fathers attach the same connotation when they speak of the Holy Spirit's involvement with scripture. It is when they believe that the scriptures directly address issues of their own day that they find it natural to refer to the Spirit speaking in the biblical passage: so Irenaeus with regard to how Matthew's birth story disproves the views of the gnostics, and Tertullian with regard to how 2 Timothy's requirement that a bishop be "the husband of only one wife" confutes those who claim unlimited license for bishops — and more generally to how the scriptures confute the heresies of his day.[13] Passages of such foresight reflect the Holy Spirit's foreseeing. The Holy Spirit is also seen behind other passages that evidence a knowledge that the writers could not have had by natural means, such as Moses' acquaintance with pre-Mosaic history and the Gospels' insight into the supernatural aspects to events accompanying Jesus' baptism.[14]

---

12. Vawter, *Biblical Inspiration* 152.

13. Irenaeus, *Against Heresies* III.16.2; Tertullian, *On Monogamy* 12; *On Fasting* 15; *Against Marcion* V.7, referred to by Sanday, *Inspiration* 34-35, though not to note this point.

14. See Origen, *Against Celsus* I.44.

The conviction that the First Testament has a significance beyond what it had in Israelite times also underlies the classic Second Testament reference to the inspiration of the First Testament in 2 Timothy 3:15-17. The historic significance of this passage in the discussion of inspiration means that we must give it some consideration here.

Talk in the broad framework of inspiration was common among Jews of the Roman period, among the Second Testament writers, and among the Fathers, though the actual terms "inspiration" and "inspired" occur on only a few occasions in English translations of the Bible. 2 Timothy 3:15-17 refers to the scriptures first as "sacred writings" that are capable of conveying the wisdom that leads to salvation through faith in Christ Jesus. Among Greek-speaking Jews such as Josephus and Philo, phrases such as "sacred writings" were standard terms for the Hebrew scriptures in Greek translation.[15] In due course they became standard terms among Christians for the Gospels and Epistles.[16] To say that these pre-Christian sacred writings can lead people to salvation through Jesus Christ presupposes the conviction that they have a significance beyond the significance they had in Israelite times. The passage in 2 Timothy then expresses that conviction in a further connection: These scriptures have a role in the teaching, rebuking, training, and equipping of the servant of God in Christ.

The single word translated "inspired by God," *theopneustos,* appears nowhere else in the Second Testament. This may, in fact, be the first surviving occurrence of it. The translation "inspired by God" is dependent on the rendering in the Latin Vulgate[17] and is questionable. Etymologically the English word "inspired" suggests that scripture is "breathed into by God," whereas *theopneustos* rather implies "breathed out by God."[18] The NIV translation "God-breathed" thus corresponds more closely to the word's etymological meaning. Scripture is the product of God's creative breath.

Terms, such as this one, that refer to inspiration were normally applied to people rather than writings, until Fathers such as Clement of Alexandria began to follow 2 Timothy's usage and applied *theopneustos* to the Gospels and Epistles as well as to the Hebrew scriptures.[19] Talk in terms of *writings* being inspired by the Spirit is in fact logically odd, and it may be that in

---

15. E.g., Josephus, *Antiquities* X.10.4 (210); *Jewish War* VI.5.4 (312); Philo, *Life of Moses* II.51 (292).

16. See, e.g., Clement of Alexandria, *Miscellanies* I.20; II.11 (I.98; II.48).

17. *Inspirata.*

18. Warfield, *The Inspiration and Authority of the Bible* 133.

19. *Miscellanies* VII.16 (101, 103).

2 Timothy 3:16 the scriptures are described *by metonymy* as "inspired" — it is really the writers that the passage has in mind.[20] The significance of the expression is then not that the writings were breathed out by God but that they were the result of someone being blown over by God. This would fit with the way in which the prophetic books themselves link the Spirit and prophecy.

For the Second Testament writers the importance of the fact that scripture is the inspired word of God is that it speaks beyond its original context. This is not to imply that we redefine "inspired" so that it comes to mean "inspiring." The English expression "the inspiration of scripture" could refer to the inspiration scripture brings to people, but in 2 Timothy 3:16, at least, *theopneustos* is not a subjective statement about scripture's effects but an objective statement about its origin: so classically Warfield[21] against H. Cremer, who argued that *theopneustos* meant full of God's Spirit and therefore redolent of it.[22] Yet one reason that works came to be reckoned inspired was that they had been found to be inspiring,[23] and the objective statement is of interest because the inspiredness of God's words makes them inspiring.

There are other questions about the translation of this key passage, though they do not necessarily affect its fundamental meaning. The common translation "all scripture is inspired by God/God-breathed" takes the clause as a whole[24] to refer to the entire First Testament, in parallel with "sacred writings."[25] But "scripture"[26] can refer to an individual passage of scripture, and the phrase here may rather mean "every passage of scripture is God-breathed." In Greek as in English we would in fact expect a "the" if the phrase in question denoted "the whole scripture"; there is somewhat of a parallel in 2 Peter 1:20, which also lacks "the": "every prophecy in scripture. . . ."

NEB renders the clause in 2 Timothy as "every inspired scripture has its use. . ." This might imply a distinction between parts of the scriptures

---

20. Newman, *Biblical Inspiration* 63.
21. *The Inspiration and Authority of the Bible* 245-96.
22. *Biblico-theological Lexicon of New Testament Greek* (ET Edinburgh: Clark, 1878; [4]1895) 730-32; he is following H. Ewald. Cf. more recently Trembath, *Evangelical Theories of Biblical Inspiration;* Lampe, "Inspiration and Revelation" 713.
23. Hoffman, "Inspiration" 457.
24. *Pasē graphē theopneustos.*
25. So Warfield, *The Inspiration and Authority of Holy Scripture* 237-38.
26. *Graphē.*

that are inspired and useful, and others that are not. Now it may be that Jews in the early Christian period distinguished between parts of scripture that were received by inspiration and other parts that were just as authoritative and binding but came into being by other means.[27] The distinction is suggestive for our effort to distinguish between scripture as a witnessing tradition, as an authoritative canon, as an inspired word, and as an experienced revelation. Further, 2 Peter 1:16-21 may indicate that there were Christians (or Jews) who did not believe that the scriptures as a whole were inspired. But 2 Timothy's reference to "sacred writings" already indicates that this letter, like 2 Peter, reflects an orthodoxy that would take the traditional view, affirming the status of all the scriptures. So if we render the phrase "every inspired scripture has its use," we must do so with the understanding that this means "every scripture, being inspired, has its use . . . ,"[28] not that it implies that there are uninspired or useless scriptures. If anything, 2 Timothy is controverting aspersions that were being cast on some parts of the First Testament and is affirming that, as scripture, all of it is inspired.[29]

The passage presupposes that inspiration is verbal or propositional. That statement can be misinterpreted. To say that the actual words of scripture are inspired is not to imply that individual words in isolation from their context can be treated as carriers of divine meaning. Words have their meanings in the context of sentences. Nor is speaking of propositional revelation to imply that the Bible is a system of timeless dogmatics; the Bible's propositions were formulated in relation to historical contexts and have to be understood in connection with those contexts. Nor is it to say that all scriptural inspiration is exclusively a matter of propositions. Scripture indeed contains propositions, statements that represent in the third person what is to take place or what has taken place. But it also contains self-expression, statements in the first person that disclose what the speakers feel. It can also beckon, in the second person, calling to the listeners.[30] To affirm that nevertheless inspiration is indeed a matter of words is to acknowledge that words are the characteristic vehicles of meaning: "If the verbal form of the Bible were different, then its meaning would be different."[31] No one who has struggled to find the right words to bring an insight

27. So Leiman, *The Canonization of Hebrew Scripture* 127.
28. So Barrett, *The Pastoral Epistles, ad loc.*
29. A. T. Hanson, *Studies in the Pastoral Epistles* 44.
30. Alonso Schökel, *The Inspired Word* 134-50.
31. Barr, *The Bible in the Modern World* 178.

or an experience to verbal expression "will say that the choice of words is an unimportant and accessory feature of authorship: he is more likely to say that authorship is best defined as the selection of words."[32] God's entrusting the choice of words to human authors is, then, an act of notable self-denial.

While the words of scripture thus involve propositions, the function of these propositions is of key importance. 2 Timothy 3:15-17 starts from the presupposition that the scriptures "have already shown their power," their power to bring people to salvation in Christ, and goes on to indicate that "the same Scriptures have now become the object of expectation. . . . Scripture was able and it will be able for what is said about its meaning for the life and activity of the reader both before and after."[33] The intervening declaration regarding its nature as inspired links the two affirmations of scripture's power. To call scripture "inspired" is to promise that it has things to say beyond its own day — to promise that it will speak to us.

The Inspired Speaker of God's Word

We have noted that 2 Timothy 3:16 has a further distinctive feature in that it attributes inspiration to scripture itself rather than to its authors. In this it contrasts with the further classic passage in another of the later Epistles, 2 Peter 1:21: "It was not on any human initiative that prophecy came; rather, it was under the compulsion of the Holy Spirit that people spoke as messengers of God" (REB); "they were carried along by the Holy Spirit" (NIV). The verb translated "under compulsion" or "carried along" is a strong one; it is used in Acts 27:15 of a ship being carried along irresistibly by the wind. The prophets were not merely guided, directed, controlled, or led, but were conveyed by another's power to the goal that that one had chosen. They spoke "an immediately Divine word."[34] Other more mainstream Second Testament documents, and the words of Jesus, also refer to the Holy Spirit's involvement in the uttering of words preserved in the scriptures. Thus in Mark 12:36 Jesus refers to David speaking "in the Holy Spirit" (RSV "inspired by the Holy Spirit"; cf. Acts 1:16; 4:25). Psalm 95:7-11 consists of

32. McKenzie, "The Social Character of Inspiration" 122.

33. Barth, *Church Dogmatics* I/2:504.

34. Warfield, *The Inspiration and Authority of Holy Scripture* 137, though Abraham notes that these passages do not actually describe it as a word that God speaks (*The Divine Inspiration of Holy Scripture* 93-95).

words that "the Holy Spirit says" — God's words, not the Psalmist's (Heb 3:7; cf. 9:8; 10:15-17). Hebrews incorporates scores of quotations from the First Testament but *never* refers to their human authors or speakers. Where the author or speaker is mentioned, it is always God, Christ, or the Holy Spirit (4:7 mentions the human mouthpiece, but even here God or the Holy Spirit is the author).[35]

Such talk in terms of the *author's* inspiration is like Philo's descriptions of the prophets. Jeremiah, for instance, speaks as one who is "inspired and possessed by God."[36] Moses is "carried along" by God when he utters his oracles; indeed, "every prophetic soul is divinely inspired and prophesies many future things not so much by reflecting as through divine madness and certainty."[37] It is also like the Talmud's assumption that the prophets spoke through the Holy Spirit and the idea sometimes mentioned that the disappearance of the prophets meant the Holy Spirit's ceasing from Israel.[38]

The Second Testament author whose experience most nearly takes this form is John, the author of Revelation, a Christian "prophecy" (1:3; 22:7, 18, 19; cf. 10:11; 22:6), who emphasizes that he received his visions when he was "in the Spirit" (e.g., 1:10; 4:2; 17:3; 21:10). It is the Spirit who speaks his words (e.g., 2:7, 11; 14:13). Inspired prophecy resembles speaking in tongues. The Fathers apply such phraseology to the authors of the Gospels and Epistles as well as to the First Testament writers: They are "carried along by the Spirit"[39] or "carried along by God in the Spirit."[40]

What we need to note here is that when the Second Testament refers to either the text or the person being inspired, it does so to undergird the central claim that the text has special meaning and makes special demands on a later audience. It thus affirms a prophecy's certain effectiveness and

---

35. Westcott, *The Epistle to the Hebrews* 474-75; cf. Warfield, *The Inspiration and Authority of the Bible* 319-20.

36. *Katapneustheis enthousiōn, The Confusion of Tongues* XII (44). Philo is referring to Jeremiah 15:10.

37. *Life of Moses* II.48 (264) (cf. I.31 [175]), referring to Moses' words in Exod 14:13; *Questions on Exodus* II.49. "Carried along by God" renders *theophoreutheis;* cf. *hypo pneumati hagiō pheromenoi* in 2 Peter 1:21.

38. Cf. b. Yoma 9b; b. Soṭa 48b; b. Sanhedrin 11b; see Davies, *Jewish and Pauline Studies* 4; Feldman, "Prophets and Prophecy in Josephus" 400-419.

39. *Pneumati theophorēthenta;* so Clement of Alexandria, as quoted in Eusebius, *Church History* VI.14.7.

40. One word combining key terms from 2 Peter 1:21: *pneumatophoroi;* so Theophilus of Antioch, *To Autolycus* 2.9, 22; 3:12. I assume that "carried along by the Spirit" rather than "Spirit-bearing" is the right translation.

ongoing meaningfulness. "Whatever was written in former days was written for our instruction" (Rom 15:4). This meaning and these demands may have been unknown to the text's human author.

It is thus characteristic of Second Testament references to the inspiration of scripture — and fundamental to the intrinsic significance of this model — that inspiration is a hermeneutical category. The passages referring to inspiration do not link the text's inspiration and its inerrant truthfulness. While they do assume that the texts had human authors and had to be understood in the light of what they would mean to that author, their central aim in listening to the scriptures is to listen to God speaking in them. The scriptures are God's word. That is not merely a statement of their authority or truth but an indication of a way to read them.[41] In some churches scripture readings are prefaced by the admonition "Listen for the word of God!" It is as one listens to scripture for the word of God that one hears it speak as the word of God.[42] The word of God is by definition something dynamic and active, so that there is a sense in which written scripture has to *become* the word of God.[43] This is not to deny that it always has the objective status of God's word but to acknowledge that something further needs to happen if it is to speak to me. The fact that the scriptures are God's inspired words is the guarantee that this further event can indeed take place.

41. See Wood, *The Formation of Christian Understanding* 39.
42. Green, *Scriptural Authority and Narrative Interpretation* 92-93.
43. Barth, *Church Dogmatics* I/2:530.

• 16 •

Forms of Inspiration

Behind the human beings who speak words of prophecy is a divine initiative and speaking, but the Holy Spirit speaks and works through human agents "in many varying ways" (Heb 1:1); there are a number of different forms of inspiration.

Theologians have sometimes spoken of variety in the *degree, depth,* or *extent* of inspiration,[1] implying that some biblical texts or types of texts or biblical authors are more inspired than others. In speaking of variety in how the authors were inspired I do not imply variety in how inspired they were. The point which that way of speaking is reaching after is better made by speaking in terms of degrees or depth or extent of *revelation.*[2] All inspired scripture shares in the fundamental qualities of the inspired word of God, its effectiveness, and its capacity to speak beyond its own day. All forms of inspiration ensure that God's word is heard and uttered. But what inspiration means and how it works can vary from person to person and from text to text. This is true even among the prophets, who are our starting point for discovering what is the significance of seeing scripture as God's inspired word.

Scripture itself offers a considerable number of hints regarding the forms that inspiration can take. Warfield observes that 2 Timothy 3:16 with "God-breathed" declares "that the Scriptures are a Divine product, without any indication of how God has operated in producing them."[3] Yet such early Christian talk of inspiration was one with the Jewish understanding

---

1. So, e.g., Beegle, *Scripture, Tradition, and Infallibility* 205-6, quoting Sanday, *Inspiration* 398.
2. Cf. Ramsey, "The Authority of the Bible" 6.
3. *The Inspiration and Authority of the Bible* 133.

of the day; there was nothing controversial about it. Jewish writers had noted a number of the features of inspiration that are implicit in references in the Hebrew scriptures to inspiration, even though at some points they may have assimilated their understanding to that of classical Greece. Philo offers a still serviceable categorization of Moses' prophetic utterances: In some Moses speaks in God's name or God speaks through him. Others involve a conversation between him and God. Yet others involve him speaking in his own person but bringing words of such power (e.g., the promise of Exod 14:13-14) that it is clear that God is behind his words.[4]

Discussion of inspiration often proceeds on a basis of inference from how one might have expected it to work rather than from material within scripture itself that relates to the question. Partly because they are concerned from the beginning with an understanding of inspiration that will cover narratives such as Genesis as well as prophets such as Isaiah, both more liberal and more conservative studies of the nature of inspiration are preoccupied with denying that it involved anything supernatural that would have infringed the freedom of the human author. They emphasize that inspiration works through natural processes. There is thus a rationalist streak in both approaches; indeed, Abraham describes the conservative understanding of inspiration as rather "sophisticated," "speculative," and "intellectualist," as well as "rationalist," in tone.[5] Philo's categorization is unembarrassed by the fact that references to inspiration within scripture belong within the totality of its references to the activity of the Holy Spirit, which more commonly witness to the extraordinary activity of God, which enables people to do things they could not normally do.

Inspiration as God Using an Instrument

Philo's first category of prophecy involves God using someone as an instrument. This corresponds to references in the First Testament to God speaking "by means of," literally "by the hand of," Moses or one of the prophets (e.g., Num 36:13; Hag 1:1; Zech 7:7). In parallel the Second Testament declares that "The Holy Spirit spoke by the mouth of David" (Acts 1:16; cf. 4:25; 28:25; Matt 1:22; 2:15).[6] The idea seems to be that God uses these human

---

4. *Life of Moses* II.35 (188); cf. II.35-51 (188-292).
5. *The Divine Inspiration of Holy Scripture* 5.
6. Packer (*"Fundamentalism" and the Word of God* 81) takes these as instances of

beings as instruments in a way that did not involve their minds even as receptors of the divine message.

Philo conceives such inspiration in these terms: "No pronouncement of a prophet is ever his own; he is an interpreter prompted by Another in all his utterances, when knowing not what he does he is filled with inspiration"; it is "the Divine Spirit that plays upon the vocal organism and makes sounds on it that clearly express its prophetic message."[7] The idea of the prophets being God's instruments is taken up in a famous passage by the second-century Christian writer Athenagoras, who says that the Spirit "moved the mouths of prophets like musical instruments."[8] According to Hippolytus "God compelled the prophets to give utterance through the Holy Spirit."[9] Gregory the Great pictures the human writers as the Spirit's pen: Who asks questions about the pen when they know the author?[10] Augustine pictures them as the hands of Christ's body that Christ uses as if they were his own.[11] Calvin describes God as controlling Balaam's tongue and thus making effective use of this corrupt instrument, Balaam delivering words put into his mouth without his mind being involved in the process.[12] The nature of an instrument is to be the actual and effective means of its user fulfilling some purpose. The instrument indeed does the work, but this achievement depends on the activity of the user; the instrument is only a means.

Talk in terms of God using the human mouth to utter words that are purely God's own or using the human hand to write words that are purely God's own must contain a degree of metaphor. The word of God as the prophets declare it is of human and historical origin, as the prophets themselves point out. The words of different prophets reflect their backgrounds and personalities as well as their speech patterns; they are refracted through their minds and spirits. Calvin says of Psalm 88 that "The psalm

---

the concursiveness of inspiration whereby the words of the Psalms are both David's and God's; but Acts describes them only as God's words spoken through David's mouth.

7. *Special Laws* IV.8 (49); cf. I.11 (65); cf. *Who Is the Heir* LII (259-60). "Inspiration" here is *enthousia*.

8. *Plea for the Christians* 7. Cf. Hippolytus, *On the Antichrist* 1; Pseudo-Justin, *Exhortation to the Greeks* 8.

9. *Against Noetus* 11:4. "Compel" is *anankazō*.

10. *Morals on the Book of Job,* Preface I.2; cf. Alonso Schökel, *The Inspired Word* 60.

11. *Harmony of the Evangelists* I.35 (54).

12. *Commentaries on the Four Last Books of Moses* 4:203-4, on Numbers 23:4-6; cf. his comments on Acts 1:16 (*The Acts of the Apostles 1–13,* 41) on the Spirit using the tongues of David and the prophets as instruments.

contains very grievous lamentations, poured forth by its inspired penman when under very severe affliction, and almost at the point of despair," but he adds — understanding it through the prophetic paradigm — that "the Spirit of God, by the mouth of Heman, has here furnished us with a form of prayer for encouraging all the afflicted."[13] The former statement suggests that the latter's instrumental language is metaphorical.

To say this is not to assimilate this first form of inspiration to others that we will consider. It is a well-established feature of religious experience for people to utter words that they have not formed in their conscious minds. Although their words also no doubt reflect their personality and speech patterns, these words are ones that (they feel) they would not and could not have uttered without at the very least God causing material to emerge from otherwise inaccessible depths of their personalities. Their mouths, they might well say, are indeed God's instrument.

With talk of inspiration that involves human beings being used as God's mouth or hand or limb we can associate talk of their speaking "by the Spirit" (Mark 12:36) or being "carried along by the Holy Spirit" so that they "spoke from God" (2 Pet 1:21). We have noted that a number of the prophets offer descriptions of their own experience that match terms such as being "carried along by the Spirit." Ezekiel especially speaks thus and also speaks of the effect of Yahweh's hand upon him (see, e.g., 1:3, 22; 3:12, 14, 22, 24; 8:1, 3; 11:1, 5, 24; 37:1-2; 40:1; 43:5; also Isa 8:11; and cf. 1 Sam 10:6). Amos says, "Yahweh took me" (7:14-15), while Isaiah describes himself as compelled to speak by Yahweh's strong hand (8:11). Jeremiah refers to a divine compulsion to prophesy, which he was powerless to resist (Jer 20:1). The human will is ignored if not overridden.

Josephus takes up this way of speaking. He describes Balaam saying to Balak, "Do you think that it is in our power to speak or be silent about such things when the Holy Spirit takes possession of us? For he causes us to utter words such as he wills and speeches without our knowledge. . . . When he has entered into us nothing that is in us is any longer our own."[14] Josephus, too, speaks at least *partly* in metaphor, since the actual words of those who were inspired in this way do reflect their distinctive individual personalities; indeed, this can become *largely* metaphor, to express the conviction that in some sense what is said is of divine origin. But we must also note the intrinsic central affirmation that without God's personal

13. *Commentaries on the Book of Psalms* 3:405-6, 407.
14. *Antiquities* IV.6.5 (119, 121).

intervention and compulsion the words in question would never have emerged from these human spirits.

In this connection Josephus speaks of inspiration in terms of possession by the Spirit. An underlying assumption here is that like the human body the human personality is not a self-contained and impregnably bounded entity but one capable of being entered by other forces, in particular by the dynamic of God. That transforms what a human being is capable of doing, as the stories of extraordinary leaders such as Samson and Saul show. Turning someone into a mouthpiece of Yahweh is another possible result of this event, when "the divine energy thrusts itself intrusively into the person's soul, filling it with a new rich content and endowing it with unusual gifts. . . . The message was the result of the divine life or spirit operating with explosive effects in his own consciousness. . . ." "The flash of inspiration in which the message is born implies the working of the divine within the human consciousness."[15]

But even Ezekiel does not describe himself as possessed by God. J. Lindblom distinguishes between an inspiration in which "the deity itself . . . takes its abode within man, penetrates him, acts and speaks in him, so that the divine *ego* . . . more or less pushes out the human *ego*," and inspiration in which there continues to be a clear distinction between the divinity and the self.[16] In both forms the inspired person may be understood as the mouthpiece of the deity. Even Ezekiel clearly belongs in the second category. He is driven rather than possessed.

A. T. Hanson likens prophets thus understood to mediums,[17] while J. I. Packer speaks in terms of the possibility of inspiration sometimes involving a trance.[18] One might compare inspiration in this form with ventriloquism or ghostwriting, in either of the senses of that term. On the other hand, there is no actual necessity that uttering words one believes are directly given by God must involve a state that is trance-like or in any other respect mentally or spiritually or emotionally exalted. Within scripture this is sometimes hinted at, but commonly not; and outside scripture, people who believe they see visions or receive words from God *may* do so in an unusual state of mind, or they may not. There is no reason to assume that mediating a message from God normally involves the mystical element of "an intense act of exalted imaginative perception or vision, which quite transcends the

15. Knight, *The Hebrew Prophetic Consciousness* 64, 65, 66.
16. *Prophecy in Ancient Israel* 33.
17. *Studies in the Pastoral Epistles* 45.
18. *"Fundamentalism" and the Word of God* 78.

measure of the everyday consciousness with its multiple interests and distractions": The words are H. Knight's,[19] but he himself goes on to note how essential in the prophets' experience the concrete, cognitive, rational, verbal aspect is, in contrast to the experience of the mystic. A prophet may sometimes have a visionary experience (e.g., Isa 6), but this is not offered as the norm of prophetic experience.

Inspiration as God Dictating to a Messenger

Philo's second category of prophecy, that which involves a conversation between a person and God, points to the idea of God's dictation of material to a prophet. The prophets transmit God's word as a result of hearing God speaking, not in this instance because God takes over their mouths. Their familiar "thus says Yahweh" itself suggests that their inspiration took the form of verbal communication of messages by God. Here the human mind is consciously engaged even if not creative (cf. 1 Pet 1:10-12).

Chrysostom, Jerome, and Augustine seem to be the first theologians to use the explicit language of dictation with reference to the scriptural writers. The Holy Spirit "dictated" Romans through Paul; the Evangelists put down what they had come to know at the dictation of the Head.[20] Calvin speaks of the Holy Spirit "dictating" the scriptures of both Testaments.[21] He emphasizes that in basing their teaching on the First Testament priests and teachers teach "from the mouth of the Lord" (Mal 2:7), and he connects the Spirit's ministry to the Second Testament writers with Jesus' promise that the Spirit would bring to mind what Jesus had taught by mouth (John 14:26). In his commentary on Jeremiah 36:4-6 he uses the same verb both of God dictating to Jeremiah and of Jeremiah dictating to Baruch, adding that Jeremiah did not dictate anything that came to his mind merely as his own thoughts but only what God "suggested" to him.[22] John Wesley describes the author of Psalm 22 as like a prophet "thrown into a preternatural ecstasy" and as one who thus speaks "what the Spirit dictated."[23]

19. *The Hebrew Prophetic Consciousness* 95-96.

20. Jerome, *Letters* 120.10; Chrysostom, First Sermon "On 'Greet Priscilla and Aquila,'" PG 51:187; Augustine, *Harmony of the Gospels* I.35.54 (here "dictation" is *dictis*, "words").

21. *Institutes* IV.8.6, 8.

22. *Commentaries on the Book of the Prophet Jeremiah and the Lamentations* 4:329.

23. *Explanatory Notes upon the New Testament* 383; cf. Abraham, *The Divine Inspiration of Holy Scripture* 115.

Again a degree of metaphor can be involved when people speak of parts of scripture being dictated. The verb may simply be a way of expressing the conviction that, whatever the actual process of inspiration, the statement that results corresponds exactly to what God wanted said or written.[24] It is possible, after all, for the Fathers also to speak of the scriptures as *written by* the Holy Spirit,[25] and this is clearly metaphor. Within scripture itself, too, it may be that the prophets' "thus says Yahweh" is sometimes a metaphorical way of affirming the certain truth of a prophetic word. When we are told of "the word that came to Jeremiah from Yahweh, 'Stand at the gate of Yahweh's house and proclaim this message there . . .'" (Jer 7:1-2), the impulse to speak may have been an inner prompting rather than an audible voice, as the content of what Jeremiah said may have been his own formulation.

If so, however, such usage likely goes back to and trades on a more literal meaning of the phrase. That literal meaning is certainly implicit in the story of the call of Samuel, which presupposes the audibility of God's voice, and in other accounts of conversations between God and prophets It is implicit in the prophets' references to taking part in consultations between Yahweh and other supernatural beings concerning the divine purpose (e.g., 1 Kgs. 22:19-22; Jer 23:18, 22). It is implicit in the reference to God putting words into Jeremiah's mouth (Jer 1:9; cf Isa 59:21), an idiomatic expression for the communication of the specific words that a person is to say (such as Joab's to the woman from Tekoa in 2 Sam 14:3, 19), and in Jeremiah's criticism of prophets who use their own tongues and yet claim that what they say is what Yahweh says (Jer 23:31). It is implicit in Isaiah's talk of God speaking "in my ears" (5:9; 22:14; cf. Ezek 9:1, 5) as a human person speaks in someone's ears (36:11; 37:29). It is implicit when the relation between Yahweh and a prophet is compared with that between Moses and Aaron, Moses' spokesman (Exod 4:15-16; 7:1). It appears also in some Psalmists' testimonies to prophet-like experiences of hearing God speak (Pss 49:4; 62:11; cf. 85:9). A number of other passages refer to people

---

24. See Rogers and McKim, *The Authority and Interpretation of the Bible* 29, and notes, on Augustine; J. I. Packer, "Calvin's View of Scripture," in *God's Inerrant Word* (ed. Montgomery) 103; and Vawter, *Biblical Inspiration* 59-60, on the post-Tridentine Roman Catholic writer Melchior Cano.

25. Chrysostom, *Homilies on Genesis* XXI (on 5:1-2) (and cf. *Homilies* II on 1:1); Jerome, *Commentary on Isaiah* IX (on 29:9-12); cf. Origen, *Homilies on Numbers* XXVII.1. On the sense in which they also speak of God as the scriptures' "author" (perhaps suggesting "cause"), see, e.g., Vawter, *Biblical Inspiration* 22-24, and references.

hearing God speak while they are in a trance-like sleep (Gen 15:16; Job 4:13; 33:15; Dan 8:8; 10:9). The Second Testament also describes people hearing God speak in a trance (*ekstasis,* Acts 10:10; 11:5; 22:17), though we have noted that the conviction that one has heard God speak does not presuppose a trance-like or even exalted religious experience. Still less does it presuppose an ecstatic experience, despite Second Testament use of *ek-stasis;* the English word "ecstasy" has such varied meaning as to be inevitably misleading unless one defines it each time one uses it.

Given such material in scripture itself, it is striking to find that conservative writers are inclined to reject the giving of dictation as a way of conceiving the process of inspiration. Warfield does note that "it is a process of nothing other than 'dictation' " that the prophets describe, but he then comments that "the question may remain open of the exact processes by which this dictation is accomplished."[26] Dictation is not an appropriate model for understanding the origin of the whole of scripture, but it is one form of inspiration to which the prophets testify. Abraham objects that among evangelicals "inspiration continues to be approached as if it were some kind of complicated speech-act of God."[27] In doing so, they follow the prophets and the Second Testament.

As with the words uttered through God's use of the prophet as an instrument, however, we must take account of the fact that the words that God is said to have dictated reflect the personalities of the human speakers. Alonso Schökel suggests that the right analogy for Yahweh's relationship with a prophet is thus an executive who outlines ideas to a secretary or speechwriter who, the executive knows, will then compose a letter or speech that expresses those ideas well, rather than an executive who uses a junior simply as a copy-typist.

> In these cases, there is a close collaboration, a union of mind and will, in order to produce the end result. The executive gives the general theme, sketches its development and some of its leading ideas, and perhaps proposes one or two good phrases which ought to be incorporated. The secretary then draws up the document. . . .[28]

Even a passage such as the ten commandments, which are portrayed as quite directly God-given, may be illumined by being considered in this way.

26. *The Inspiration and Authority of the Bible* 87, quoted by Abraham, *The Divine Inspiration of Holy Scripture* 34.
27. *The Divine Inspiration of Holy Scripture* 36-37; cf. 62.
28. *The Inspired Word* 72.

Both versions of the commandments in Exodus 20 and Deuteronomy 5 are said to have been dictated by God at Sinai, but they are not identical, which suggests that human beings were involved in putting God-given ideas into words.[29]

A prophet speaks in the name of Yahweh, declaring "thus says Yahweh."[30] Such expressions have their background in the relationship between a messenger and a king, and this background may also help our understanding of the phrases. In a passage such as 2 Kings 18:19-25, we need not assume that the field commander's speech was dictated by Sennacherib word-for-word. A messenger will say "thus says the king" when he is putting the king's message in his own words, which then have quite the same authority as words that are actually dictated. A messenger acts as his king's plenipotentiary whether it is the messenger or the king who composes the actual sentences he utters. So a prophet of Yahweh prophesies "in Yahweh's name" (e.g., Jer 11:21), being commissioned as Yahweh's representive before other people, and in effect bringing Yahweh's own presence. The message is Yahweh's and is effective as Yahweh's. The actual words are formulated by the prophet.

There is therefore no need to assume that this form of inspiration submerges the personality of the prophet. When Ezekiel is given a scroll containing the message he is to proclaim, he is commanded not to read it but to eat it (2:8; cf. Jer 15:16). That may imply that he is to "assimilate what it held, and then from this interior fullness utter his message. There is nothing mechanistic about the prophetic activity; it is vital, dynamic, and interior"; the message is the word of *Yahweh,* but *Ezekiel* provides it with its onomatopoeia, assonance, chiasm, rhythm, and imagery.[31] Calvin thus contrasts the way God deals with Ezekiel or Jeremiah, illuminating their senses before guiding their tongues, with what happens to Balaam.[32]

To suggest this is not to offer a way of separating divine truth and human misunderstanding within the text. Over the past two hundred years scholars have experimented with various ways of distinguishing between the inspiration at the core of what a scriptural author perceived and said and the outward form of the author's words, which did not in the same sense come from God. These attempts have aimed at finding a way of

29. Brown, *The Critical Meaning of the Bible* 10-11.
30. On this "messenger formula" see, e.g., von Rad, *Old Testament Theology* 2:36-37.
31. Alonso Schökel, *The Inspired Word* 93, 96; and further 188-98.
32. *Commentaries on the Four Last Books of Moses* 4:203-4.

ascribing apparent errors in the text to its human author, while preserving an affirmation that its core is inspired (see, e.g., Burtchaell's survey of nineteenth-century Roman Catholic approaches[33]). The distinction between the divine and the human contribution may well be hinted at by scripture itself, but not with the intent or the implication of such modern explorations of this theme. Indeed, Alonso Schökel[34] warns against the attempt to divide between the divine and the human contributions on the basis of analogies such as that of a secretary. Their usefulness in the present connection is rather that they help us to envisage how a prophecy could be expressed in words devised by the prophet, yet be exactly what God wants said and therefore have the effectiveness of God's word.

It is appropriate to say that the scriptural text *contains* the word of God if we mean that in the sense that the bottle contains the wine or that this book contains my words. But the expression is apt to suggest that the text contains the word of God in the sense that the wine bottle contains alcohol or that this book contains many quotations. In this sense the expression presupposes that it also contains much else and is thus a misleading expression. The entire text is the word of God.

Inspiration as God Standing behind a Prophet's Own Words

The prophets themselves sometimes hint in another direction at a process whereby they provide the words to express God's ideas, when they alternate between words explicitly uttered by them in their own person and words uttered more directly in the name of God. This takes us to Philo's third form of inspiration, which involves someone speaking in their own person, yet speaking words of such power that God must lie behind their words. Their teaching brings divine wisdom, but this is formulated through the creative exercise of their own human minds rather than independently of it. Isaiah explicitly himself composes his bizarre love song on behalf of Yahweh (Isa 5:1-7). Other prophets utter a number of words of exhortation, dirge, or accusation as themselves, speaking of Yahweh in the third person (e.g., Amos 5:1-2, 6-15; 7:16; Mic 1:2-5, 8-12; 2:1-2, 6-11).

When the prophets said "I" (e.g., Amos), not "he" (i.e., Yahweh), they were still inspired. Human beings spoke, but from God, carried along by

33. *Catholic Theories of Biblical Inspiration* 88-229.
34. *The Inspired Word* 66-72.

the Spirit (2 Pet 1:21). As Justin Martyr put it, prophets may speak as if they were doing so in their own person, but it is actually the divine Word who moves them.[35] They may formulate their words through their own reflection, yet they mirror God's thinking. In formulating what they say they have made the decisions, and in this sense "verbal inspiration" is an inappropriate phrase to describe the origin of their words; yet they work under the supervision of the Spirit, who is prepared to own the result, and in this sense it can be described as "verbally inspired."

This understanding of inspiration came to be normative in the "scholastic synthesis,"[36] which continues into modern conservative accounts of the doctrine of inspiration. Human authors speak their own words, yet they are "completely controlled by the Holy Spirit." God is not "constrained, hampered and . . . frustrated" as a result of speaking through human mouthpieces; the Spirit's activity is *concursive,*" that is, "exercised in, through and by means of the writers' own activity, in such a way that their thinking and writing was *both* free and spontaneous on their part *and* divinely elicited and controlled, and that what they wrote was not only their own work but also God's work."[37] God and a human being can both be free agents involved in the same action. God is manifestly and publicly behind an event such as the exodus and the activity of a prophet such as Ezekiel and more covertly behind an event such as the Jews' deliverance from Haman and the activity of a scribal figure such as Luke. In events and messages, divine and human may interweave in a wide variety of ways between these extremes.

Inspiration, then, may involve the supervision of a person by the Holy Spirit. Warfield defined inspiration as "a supernatural influence exerted on the sacred writers by the Spirit of God, by virtue of which their writings are given Divine trustworthiness."[38] *The* importance of inspiration is that it safeguards a writer from error. And one aspect of supervision indeed involves ensuring that the person avoids errors. A driving instructor normally leaves the pupil in control of the car, but overrides the pupil's action

35. *First Apology* 36.
36. Vawter, *Biblical Inspiration* 44.
37. Packer, *"Fundamentalism" and the Word of God* 80.
38. *The Inspiration and Authority of the Bible* 131. He reasserts the point with regard to the trustworthiness of the prophetic word referred to in 2 Peter 1:19; but here the reference is precisely to reliability in the sense of effectiveness, proved by the events that fulfill it (if the traditional translation is right, but see Bauckham, *Jude, 2 Peter,* on the passage).

or inaction when necessary, in a way that the pupil may or may not sense, to prevent a costly mistake.

Scripture itself, however, links inspiration with certain effectiveness and ongoing meaningfulness rather than with the prevention of error. Perhaps, then, the research supervisor is a more illuminating embodiment of this model. That role involves being a resource for ideas that the student may investigate, develop, and make his or her own; it may well involve having been the stimulus to the work in the first place. Preachers, too, may believe that they receive from God key insights for a sermon, but they then develop these by their own insight and creativity toward a result that reflects God's giving and providence but is distinguishable from the drafting of a speech or a letter on behalf of an executive, which we have considered in connection with the dictation model. Preachers speak in God's name, but speak as an "I." Secretaries sometimes compose letters and send them out in their own name, but with the authority of the executive. Prophets sometimes explicitly speak their own words, but compared with what they would normally be capable of, they may speak in a way that reflects, not so much a heightening of their gifts or necessarily the possession of concrete facts that they would not otherwise have access to, but a deepening of their insight.

The process of receiving such an insight might be thought of as intuition or telepathy, "the communication of impressions of any kind from one mind to another, independently of the recognized channels of sense" (*Oxford English Dictionary*).[39] The intuition may reflect a special degree of insight that is an essentially natural gift. But at this point the fact that scripture associates the Holy Spirit with the "natural" as well as the "supernatural" is significant. "Natural" gifts are to be seen as gifts from God the Holy Spirit that give a person, by virtue of his or her creation, the potential to see and say things that others might be incapable of. That that person is then chosen by God and given over to God makes it possible for this potential to become actual, through the special work of the Holy Spirit.

This form of inspiration may be illumined further by another way in which we are used to speaking of inspiration in contemporary English, the notion of a person being inspired by someone else, that is, provoked or influenced by the person's acts or words, to speak or act or speak in a similar but still distinguishable way: That person's spirit is breathed into the one who is inspired. These are modern connotations of the notion of inspiration; as far as I know, the first writer who discusses them in connection

39. Quoted by Abraham, *Divine Revelation* 22.

with scriptural inspiration is J. H. Newman.[40] They can hardly be treated as *the* key to understanding scriptural inspiration,[41] but they do suggest an aspect of the nature of God's influence on people such as the prophets as they work under the inspiration of the acts that reveal the heart and mind of God, which is involved in this world in love and for our salvation.

Such talk of inspiration facilitates further allowance for the individuality of the work of the person inspired.

> Since the pupils vary in ability, temperament and interests, the teacher's influence will show itself in varying degrees and in a fragmentary fashion. Some of them will understand him better than others and they will differ from each other in emphasis and scope. Other influences, beside that of the teacher, will be present and discernible. Yet it is not impossible to discover what his teachings must have been.

This analogy allows equally for God's activity and for the scriptural writers' use of their creative power. Indeed, "the most successful teacher is one who enables the pupil so to stretch his own intellectual powers as to grasp what he otherwise would not."[42]

There are further variants on the notion of inspiration that suggest that God's person lies behind human words of power. How are we to conceive of a prophet's inspiration when he tells a story (Jer 36) and, even worse, when he records prayers (Jer 14), complaints (Jer 12), reflections (Jer 17:9), accusations (Jer 20), or dialogues with God, including dialogues in which God contradicts him (Jer 15)? As Sanday notes,[43] such passages make clear that the prophets themselves are capable of drawing a sharp distinction between what comes from God and what comes from themselves. Yet the latter is also prophetic and inspired. While this excludes any mystical merging of human and divine, it does imply that God can speak *through* as well as *to* human experience.[44] In a famous passage (Jer 9:2-3) the identification of Jeremiah with Yahweh is so complete that we are not quite sure whose feelings we are reading of, or whether it matters. But here, too, the union is not one of mysticism or possession but of something more

---

40. *On Biblical Inspiration and on Infallibility* 75, cf. 60.

41. Against Abraham, *The Divine Inspiration of Holy Scripture* 62; see further 58-75; also Trembath, *Evangelical Theories of Biblical Inspiration;* Mitchell, "Does Christianity Need a Revelation?" 105-6.

42. Mitchell, *The Justification of Religious Belief* 153, 154.

43. *Inspiration* 148.

44. Robinson, *Inspiration and Revelation* 166-67.

like empathy.[45] The words of God do not have the purely external relationship to their human speaker that a king's may have to his messenger's; the messenger's person contributes to the thoughts and the words.

Thus Isaiah presents his Vineyard Song (5:1-7) as a song of his own sung *for* Yahweh as a vinedresser. In the middle of the song there are words sung by the vinedresser himself, but as a whole the song is specifically not God's word. A prophet's insight, a prophet's creativity, and a prophet's receiving communication from God interweave; and the incorporation of the result in the Book of Isaiah implies a recognition of the whole as a word from Yahweh. The prophetic words spoken in the form of the speech of a messenger are explicitly Yahweh's words, but they are prefaced by other words by means of which the prophet himself sought to win people's attention for his message; by being incorporated within the prophetic book, these also are taken to be in some sense part of the word of Yahweh.[46] The prophets' usual introduction to their oracles, "thus says Yahweh," is not Yahweh's word in the same sense as what it introduces, yet it is part of the inspired word of God as the prophetic book presents it.

One approach to some passages such as those we are considering is to see them as indeed explicitly human productions subsequently accepted by God; the model for their origin might be a government minister on his or her own initiative drawing up a document or proposal that the monarch then endorses and signs. The Holy Spirit accepts these words of human composition and certifies their reliability and significance. N. L. Geisler criticizes Berkouwer for expressing the view that the Bible is human words taken into service by the Holy Spirit, and words expressing human questioning and doubts.[47] But there is no need for him to see the reflection of Hobbes, Spinoza, Hume, Hegel, and Nietzsche (!) in that view. It is, after all, implicit in what Luke and John directly say about their work as human writers. Geisler's view, expounded in the name of scripture, involves ignoring the testimony of scripture.

The prophetic words we are considering come as explicitly human words that need to be taken as divine words. So it is with the words of Jesus. He affirms the presence of God, proclaims the demand of God, declares the forgiveness of God, and promises the rule of God, all in ordinary human words that demand to be taken as divine words — those of a

---

45. Cf. Heschel, *The Prophets* 1:115; Heschel actually uses the word "sympathy."
46. Bartlett, *The Shape of Scriptural Authority* 17.
47. *Biblical Errancy* 232-33, referring to Berkouwer, *Holy Scripture* 143, 145, 167, 203.

prophet, or rather more than a prophet. "God's word has become one with the simplest human word — that is, in fact, the mystery of the entire message of Jesus."[48] That mystery continues in the ministry of Paul, who speaks of the Thessalonians receiving his words as the word of God (1 Thess 2:13) — the words of an unimpressive, unsuperlative preacher put in the shade by other wonder-working apostles. "The one who hears you hears me, and the one who rejects you rejects me" (Luke 10:16). The words are divine, but also entirely human, as humanly created and uttered as any human words. "Even when one ponders the words 'not taught by human wisdom but taught by the Spirit' (1 Cor. 2:13), it is indisputable that these are *Paul's* words (1 Cor. 2:13a)."[49] There is continuity rather than discontinuity between the speech of God and human speech, and here, at least, inspiration is not a supernaturalist concept. "God's word is intended to be delivered humanly, and its divinity is to be proclaimed and grasped in its humanity."[50] "The word is near you" (Rom 10:8) — because the *Word* is near you.

---

48. Bornkamm, *Early Christian Experience* 6.
49. Berkouwer, *Holy Scripture* 152.
50. Bornkamm, *Early Christian Experience* 8.

Understanding the
Inspiration of a Text

Inspiration involves God working on, with, and through human beings in such a way that they utter human words that have the effectiveness and meaningfulness that attaches to words that God utters. Inspiration is open to both a "prophetic-personal" and a "poetic-textual" understanding.[1] We have considered the process whereby God may speak through a person. But what of the words and texts that result? How may we conceive of these being both human and divine?

This question is an instance of the broader theological issue concerning how we can understand something as embodying both the human and the divine or as brought about by both supernatural and natural causation. The issue surfaces in a number of aspects of Christian theology, each of which may help our thinking about inspiration in particular: the person of Christ, the Holy Spirit's involvement with the church in connection with charisms and other aspects of Christian experience, the phenomenon of ordinary human creative inspiration, the working of the sacraments, and the shaping of historical events so that by God's providence they play a part in the fulfillment of God's purpose. In each case it is easy to emphasize one or the other of the causalities, either the divine or the human. Disagreements among Christian traditions often arise from variations of overemphasis on one or the other.[2] One framework for discussing this recurrent issue is Michael Polanyi's notion of "boundary control" or "marginal con-

1. Muddiman, "The Holy Spirit and Inspiration" 132.
2. So Burtchaell, *Catholic Theories of Biblical Inspiration* 279-80.

trol," derived from quantum mechanics.[3] In a human being cellular processes and neuromuscular processes, for instance, have their own inherent order and the former cannot be reduced to the latter, but as the higher order of reality the former supplies boundary conditions to the latter and harnesses it. Similarly God harnesses human activity without undoing its self-determination.

The Inspiration of Scripture in the Light of the Incarnation

The classic analogy or model for understanding the nature of inspired scripture is the nature of Christ himself. While there are clearly limitations in comparing a book and a person, the opening comparison and contrast in the Epistle to the Hebrews between God speaking through the prophets and through Christ presupposes that there is some similarity between these two; so does John's description of Christ as the word of God become flesh. A number of the Fathers take up the comparison, and it is summed up in Barth's statement that scripture is like Jesus Christ himself in that "in its own way and degree it is very God and very man."[4] R. Pache suggests that Christ and scripture have in common that they are eternal and Spirit-conceived, that they become earthly, that they are accommodated to human comprehension, perfect, authoritative, rejected, triumphant, accessible to faith, and mutually witnessing, and that they reveal the Father.[5]

We may be helped in our approach to the divine-human word, then, by understanding it in the light of the divine-human Word. Orthodox christology involves, for instance, a firm awareness of the unity of the person of Christ, an insistence that we do not attribute some acts to the divine person and some to the human, and a recognition that we relate to the divine Christ only by relating to the human Christ and never get beyond him, yet that we relate to the human Christ for the sake of meeting the divine Christ. It is possible to understand Jesus Christ by starting from the human person with his background as Abraham's descendant (Matthew), as an object of John's baptism (Mark), or as Mary's son (Luke). Or it is possible to understand him by starting from the divine person who is the

---

3. See Milavec, "The Bible, the Holy Spirit, and Human Powers" 215-21, following Polanyi, *Tacit Dimension* (London: Routledge, 1967) 35-45; also Dulles, *Models of Revelation* 147, 203.

4. *Dogmatics* I/2:501. Cf. Young, *The Art of Performance* 21-25.

5. *The Inspiration and Authority of Scripture* 35-42.

Word incarnate (John). Similarly it is possible to understand scripture by starting from the fact that it is God's word and from that base investigating its humanness, or by starting with its humanness and letting the human word speak as a divine word.

The analogy with the incarnation helps us to see that the words of God in scripture can be expressed in a context and be culture-relative, and could yet have absolute significance; their contextuality need not imply that they are limited to their context. When God speaks, by a prophet or by a Son, inevitably this speaking takes place in a context, and any generalizations of absolute validity have to allow for that historicality. In becoming a member of a certain race at a certain time, the Word undertook a self-emptying that involved speaking as someone of a particular day and culture.

When God speaks, cedar trees may break, people recoil, and kings make for their exile (Ps 29:4-5; Exod 20:18; Dan 4:31). Yet it is not generally so with the speaking of Jesus. His words can easily be ignored; the manner of their impact is different. The words of scripture resemble in this way the words of Jesus. The warnings of the prophets did not compel recognition or turning. Like Jesus, scripture takes the form of a servant.[6] His incarnation "was not a dazzling manifestation of God in barely human form, but a willing obedience to the limitations of a true humanity. . . . If Scripture is 'inspired', it is inspired by the same God who accepted the constraints of the incarnation."[7] The word of God does not come in manifestly divine form any more than the Word of God did. It comes in human form, in scandalously human words, appropriate to its concern with a divine Word who took human form.

Like a man of his day Jesus spoke in terms of the sun "rising" (as it appears to do), and he could be aware of his own ignorance even about important theological matters (Mark 13:32) — though his awareness of the limitations of his knowledge protects his inerrancy rather than imperiling it. He expressed himself by means of the eschatological concepts of his day.[8] He spoke in relation to questions that surfaced in a particular historical context, yet addressed these in such a way that his words transcend that context. The inspired word does the same.

6. Berkouwer, *Holy Scripture* 196.

7. A. E. Harvey, "Attending to Scripture," in *Believing in the Church* (a report of the Doctrine Commission of the Church of England) 36.

8. Rahner, *Theological Investigations* 4:338, quoted by Berkouwer, *Holy Scripture* 177.

A number of debating points can be made on a basis of the analogy between inspiration and incarnation. Conservative writers suggest that it is their doctrine of scripture that corresponds to orthodox Alexandrian christology, because it asserts the true but infallible humanity of scripture that parallels the true but sinless humanity of Christ. J. I. Packer,[9] further, likens the critical view to Nestorian christology, which distinguishes too sharply between the human Jesus and the divine Son. The view that the Bible is a human book that God condescends to adopt and affirm[10] would presumably count as adoptionism unless safeguarded by the stress on the prevenient grace of God in the formation of scripture, which we have considered above[11] — though it might be asked whether adoptionism might be appropriate with scripture even if not with christology.

J. R. W. Stott warns against a docetic view of scripture that overemphasizes the divine at the expense of the human.[12] Packer, however, wishes "to start by recognizing the unity of Our Lord's Person as divine and to view His humanity only as an aspect of His Person," and correspondingly to start from the idea of the scriptures as "the oracles of God" and "to study their character as a human book only as one aspect of their character as a divine book."[13] In both christology and hermeneutic this stance is impeccably Alexandrian and Augustinian, but in both christology and hermeneutic it is subject to correction by the Antiochene interest in beginning from the humanity of Jesus and the humanity of scripture and not compromising either by an overemphasis on the divine.[14] Thus A. G. Hebert sees critical scholars as safeguarding the real humanity of scripture over against an overemphasis on its supernaturalness, which is an attitude corresponding to a monophysite christology, which denied Christ's true humanity.[15] D. F. Wright[16] locates evangelical study of the doctrine of scripture in a post-Nicene but pre-Chalcedonian phase, one that has affirmed scripture's divine aspect but not its human aspect, so that we need safeguards against both

---

9. *"Fundamentalism" and the Word of God* 83, comparing Warfield, *The Inspiration and Authority of the Bible* 162-63.

10. Anderson, "The Bible in the Church Today" 5; cf. Brown, *The Critical Meaning of the Bible* 6.

11. See chapter 16 (pp. 222ff.) above.

12. *The Authority and Relevance of the Bible in the Modern World* 4.

13. *"Fundamentalism" and the Word of God* 83, 84.

14. See Loretz, *The Truth of the Bible* 141; cf. Burtchaell, *Catholic Theories of Biblical Inspiration* 266.

15. *Fundamentalism and the Church of God* 76-78.

16. "Soundings in the Doctrine of Scripture in British Evangelicalism."

Apollinarianism and (in reaction) Nestorianism. Vawter locates the importance of scholastic study of the doctrine of scripture in its formulation against an Aristotelian rather than a Platonic background, a background that was monist rather than dualist in its christology and in its approach to scripture. Philosophical presuppositions made it natural to believe in the indissoluble unity of the divine and human Word of God and word of God and to interpret the latter accordingly (and thus less allegorically).[17]

The analogy with incarnation has also suggested an approach to the question of the relative significance of inerrancy in relation to inspiration. Whereas many Roman Catholic and Evangelical writers have viewed inerrancy as *the* significant implication of inspiration, Alonso Schökel invites us to imagine a formulation of the doctrine of the incarnation that is preoccupied with stating the impeccability of Christ and handling apparent objections to it. He notes that the central significance of the incarnation would thereby be obscured. It may have been necessary to protect scripture by a wall of arguments for its inerrancy, but "we must stop to consider whether or not the wall is the essence of the city" or whether the city itself is something else.[18]

Debating points can thus be made, though the debaters recognize that there are limits to the analogy between inspiration and incarnation. There is not such an intrinsic link between the nature of Christ and the nature of scripture that one can argue directly from the one to the other.

The Inspiration of Scripture in the Light of the Spirit's Involvement in the Church

In formulating his understanding of inspiration, Charles Gore began by formulating his understanding of the Holy Spirit, and specifically of the Spirit's work in the church.[19] James Barr more recently argued that "the true analogy for the Scripture as Word of God is *not* the unity of God and man in the Incarnation; it is the relation of the Spirit of God to the People of God"; as God elects that people into existence, without precluding their exercise of their freewill, so God elects into existence (i.e., inspires) their tradition, without precluding them from writing of themselves.[20] Without

17. *Biblical Inspiration* 45-47.
18. *The Inspired Word* 311.
19. "The Holy Spirit and Inspiration."
20. Barr, review of Reid, *The Authority of Scripture* 89, 91; cf. Barr, *Escaping from*

necessarily agreeing to choose one analogy rather than another we may gain insight through seeing the Spirit's involvement with scripture as a subset of the Spirit's involvement with Israel and the church. G. Turner suggests a number of the Spirit's characteristics, described in John 14–16, that scripture shares: It comes from the Father, is permanent and irreplaceable, is true, is not received by the world, has an intimate effect on us, teaches us, brings Jesus to our memory, witnesses to Jesus, judges us, guides us, declares our final destiny, glorifies Jesus, and declares Jesus.[21]

In scripture itself, Joel looked to a day when the spirit of God would be poured out widely on people and prophecy would be a very common phenomenon (2:28-29). Acts 2 sees Pentecost as the arrival of that day. Henceforth the Spirit is active in the whole church. Anyone who makes the fundamental Christian confession "Jesus is Lord" shows thereby that they are "in the Spirit" (1 Cor 12:3). This belongs to their baptism. Believers choose to utter the words of confession, but the Spirit draws them out. Henceforth the Spirit is given to them, lives in them, drives them, and speaks in and with them (Rom 5:5; 8:11, 14, 15, 16). The Spirit distributes various charisms to people in the church (1 Cor 12:11; RSV uses "inspire" here). The promise that the Holy Spirit will give to disciples the words to say when they are put on trial (Mark 13:11) surely applies to other disciples beyond the Twelve. Even Paul's allusion to speaking in words taught by the Spirit rather than by human wisdom (1 Cor 2:13) may refer not exclusively to his experience as an apostle but to the normal experience of (mature) Christians. In general, the Second Testament uses terms to speak of the Spirit's normal activity within the church similar to those it uses for the inspiration of the scriptures. It is the Spirit of Christ who was active within the prophets; it is the same Spirit through whom Christian Evangelists preach the gospel of Christ (1 Pet 1:11, 12). The scriptures are the oracles of God (Rom 3:2); "stewards of God's grace" in the church also speak "oracles of God" (1 Pet 4:11).

Among the early Fathers, Clement of Rome and Ignatius of Antioch as readily speak of their own words as given by the Spirit as they do those of the prophets. Justin Martyr and Irenaeus make more explicit the conviction that precisely the activity of the Spirit once found in the prophets now manifests itself in the gifts that the Spirit gives to Christians.[22] In due

---

Fundamentalism 127-28. Farley systematically questions the incarnational analogy: See, e.g., *Ecclesial Reflection* 78-79.

21. See "Biblical Inspiration and the Paraclete."

22. E.g., *1 Clement* 45, 59, 63; Ignatius, *Philadelphians* 7; Justin, *Dialogue with*

course a distinction came to be made between, on the one hand, the involvement of the Spirit with scriptural writers and others in the first-century church and, on the other hand, the Spirit's work in the church in post-apostolic times. That provided a way of safeguarding the church from the excesses of those who claimed to be inspired and of giving account of the fact that empirically there came to be a difference between the two involvements: The mainstream churches did not experience many people claiming to speak under divine inspiration. The way the Second Testament speaks and the occurrence of such phenomena elsewhere in the church make that distinction now difficult to sustain, though it also requires us to develop Barr's insight in a less rationalistic direction.

The belief that there was a unique charism of inspiration confined to prophets of the biblical period looks like a hangover from the dispensationalist view, which confined charisms to the first century. A better starting point is to assume that God's working in prophets in biblical times was essentially analogous to God's working among other prophets and inspired persons, rather than essentially different from it. This makes it easier to make sense of the way in which the Second Testament speaks of the Spirit's activity in the church and to draw out its implications for our understanding of inspiration.

The varied and tumultuous activity of the Spirit in the people of God embraces a range of charisms, some of which are "higher," some presumably therefore lower, but none to be despised (1 Cor 14). The involvement of the Spirit is apparently not in itself a guarantee of the exalted theological or moral significance of what it generates; what it signifies is that something extraordinary and far-reaching takes place. The Holy Spirit's activity in Israel and in the church operates through human beings in their individuality and their lopsidedness. It does not bypass their distinctive humanity but uses it. They do not have to be perfect, nor do their words have to be models of balance, free of rawness or solecism, in order for God to work through them. The grace of God is such as to be entirely prepared to speak through skewed human agents and quite relaxed enough to trust that their eccentricities will do more good than harm, set as they are in the context of all that the Spirit says and does. That is true of the Spirit's activity in Israel and in the church, and it is suggestive for our understanding of the Spirit's activity in inspiring the eccentricities of Ezekiel and Obadiah.

Trypho 82, 87-88; Irenaeus, *Heresies* I.15.6; II.32.4; III.11.9; and further Sundberg, "The Bible Canon and the Christian Doctrine of Inspiration."

The Inspiration of Scripture
in the Light of Creative Inspiration

The activity of God by the Holy Spirit in the church is in turn an aspect of the Spirit's total activity in the world and is not discontinuous with it. Phenomena such as teaching, prophecy, tongues, and healing in the church are distinguished from the same phenomena in other religions or in secular contexts not by their intrinsic nature or psychology but by the purpose they are consecrated to serve. Scriptural inspiration may thus be seen as a subset of general creative inspiration.

Scientists, poets, and musicians often testify to a sense of being driven by forces that transcend themselves or to a sense of receiving their insights or their actual works from some source outside themselves. Verses may leap unbidden and fully formed into the mind, so that the poet is hard put to it to get them onto paper quickly enough — though on other occasions an idea or theme or image will mull around the mind over a long period and the creative process will be a much more consciously active one in which the poet struggles to give adequate expression to the poem within. Inspiration makes possible and demands a corresponding application and effort.[23] Both recall some prophetic psalmists' descriptions of their creativity, the mind bubbling over (Ps 45:1), the fire burning as one muses and then the tongue speaking (39:3), the mind expressing its insight and the mouth speaking wisdom as the song within the psalmist becomes words and music (49:3-4).

The point of such psalms is to give human testimony and to pray human prayer, and as expressions of joy and lament they thus need to be manifestations of fully and truly human responses to God. They are words directly spoken by human beings to and for God, not words directly spoken by God. The inspiration of essentially human words connects with the understanding of inspiration as a way of speaking of the origin of secular works of art. In a reverse movement writers such as G. Hebert[24] have applied the artistic notion of inspiration to scriptural works. Their inspiration is that of great religious teachers; God speaks through them, as through other works of art. As an event or an experience may inspire someone to write or tell a story about it, so the Christ event inspires the Evangelists to write their Gospels. As a musician or lyricist may feel that he or she received

---

23. Gunton, *Enlightenment and Alienation* 91.
24. *Fundamentalism and the Church of God* 76-78.

a song rather than actively composed it, so prophets may feel that they have received their words rather than having personally composed them. As a modern poem or novel may seem to demonstrate depths that point beyond mere human insight and experience, so may an Israelite poem (Song of Songs), drama (Job), collection of sayings (Proverbs or Ecclesiastes), or story (Ruth), with the result that it comes to be preserved and regarded as scripture.

It is common to argue that the unique truth and significance of the *content* of scripture, that it conveys the gospel through which we are put right with God, argues against there being an analogy with the way artists "receive" their works, which do not have that significance.[25] There is certainly a uniqueness about inspired scripture that needs safeguarding, but there are no grounds for locating the basis of this uniqueness in the manner of its inspiration; the grounds lie elsewhere (as we have noted in Parts I and II). Preaching and teaching, whether in scripture or in the church, use the same methods to communicate life-or-death truths, and less important truths and error. It is thus not self-evident that the unique importance of scripture required a unique method of producing scripture. Similarities in the *process* by which God brought the oracles of the prophets into being need not imply a similarity in the *value* of what was produced.

The indications that scripture itself gives point toward this similarity rather than to any distinction between scriptural inspiration and inspiration of a non-Israelite, non-Christian, or secular kind. Scripture uses the same terms to describe prophetic inspiration as Philo uses, and many of these terms parallel descriptions of inspiration and prophecy in non-Jewish Greek writers referring to nonscriptural writings. It uses the same terms to describe the processes of "true" inspiration as it uses for false inspiration. Jeremiah's struggle to establish the authenticity of his message over against that of other prophets makes no appeal to the distinctiveness of the form of his experience; what was unique was the content of his message. Scripture associates the work of the spirit of God with the workings of the human spirit by virtue of God's creation.[26] We have noted above the contribution that the prophets' own human creativity makes to their work.[27]

25. So, e.g., Packer, *"Fundamentalism" and the Word of God* 77; cf. Berkouwer, *Holy Scripture* 161, quoting H. Bavinck, *Gereformeerde Dogmatiek* (Kampen: Kok, [4]1928) 1:395-96. See also Abraham's critique (*The Divine Inspiration of Holy Scripture* 49-51), which effectively stems from the difficulty of linking this understanding with his own approach to inspiration.

The possible phenomenological parallels between inspired prophecy and inspired creative art suggest a further insight. Many artists do *not* experience their creativity as involving "receiving" their works from elsewhere. It is indeed a matter of their own creative activity — though they may also acknowledge that in another sense their gifts and the fruits of these gifts are exactly that: gifts. It seems possible that something similar is true about prophecy. We have noted that prophets do not *always* claim a sense of having "received" their words. They were often quite aware that they themselves formulated them.

It is commonly said that inspiration, rather than annulling the faculties of the human personality, raises these faculties to their highest activity and freest exercise.[28] Much is clarified if we assume that the processes or experiences of inspiration by which the prophetic books came into existence were essentially similar to the processes involved when God speaks to people outside scripture. The belief that scriptural inspiration is essentially but unanalyzably distinctive in its processes can be sacrificed to Occam's razor.

The Inspiration of Scripture
in the Light of the Nature of the Sacraments

Jesus is the living bread; people share in his life by hearing his words and by partaking of his body and blood (John 6). The word of Christ effects or has a part in effecting his people's cleansing (Eph 5:26): It "has sacramental force."[29] Word and sacrament belong together as means by which God reaches out to us, so that the inner links between word and sacrament would be expected to imply resemblances between them. "Just as Christ's body and blood are given under the elements even though the bread and wine are not transformed, so the divine Word is given through the temporally and historically conditioned Scriptures."[30] The words of scripture are not immediately or directly God's speech,[31] but neither are they only the speech of human beings responding to God or giving an account of

26. Cf. Vawter, *Biblical Inspiration* 8-13.

27. See pp. 231-36 above.

28. So, e.g., Orr, *Revelation and Inspiration* 169.

29. Bultmann, "The Word of God in the New Testament," *Faith and Understanding* 297.

30. R. Bring, summarizing Luther, in *How God Speaks to Us* (Philadelphia: Muhlenburg, 1962) 30, as quoted by Bloesch, *Evangelical Theology* 2:272. Young (*The Art of Performance* 21, 85) finds a sacramental understanding in Origen.

their human experience of God or reaching out to God. Immediately and directly they are humanly created, uttered, and written, but they are expressions of God's love and grace reaching out to us and are meant and used by God as the means in and through which God speaks to us, and to which we respond. Like the sacraments, scripture is not merely a means of grace in a purely objective sense, but a means of personal encounter between God and people.

J. H. Newman quotes (though in order to query it) the view that "the inspiration of Scripture consists in its quasi-sacramental power. It has a force, an influence, and an operation, which is simply supernatural. . . . A blessing and a success will go with the use of the sacred text, which will not follow from any mere words of man."[32] Scripture is a means of grace, capable of communicating God's own resources to people. It is not that special power attaches to these forms of words as if they were magical formulas. But special power attaches to the message they express as it grasps people and is grasped by them, and even as it is rejected by them and becomes instead a means of judgment.[33] Paul's comments on the sacrament as a means of judgment (1 Cor 11:29) offers a parallel.

As with the sacraments, scripture has an objectiveness that makes reading and even preaching it effective independently of the holiness of its ministers. As with the reception of the sacraments, however, reading of scripture does not have an automatic effect on people. The Spirit who inspires scripture has to perform the additional work of witnessing to the minds, hearts, and spirits of its readers that it is God's inspired word, so that they receive it as such.[34] In turn readers have to respond to it in trust and hope. Receiving eucharistic bread and wine as if they were ordinary food brings the recipient only physical benefit, and reading scripture as a source for historical information brings only historical edification. Scripture is designed to lead people to eternal life, but it does not inevitably do so (John 5:39). Conversely receiving ordinary bread and wine cannot bring the recipient the spiritual benefit that eucharistic bread and wine conveys, and reading other books does not bring the spiritual benefit that scripture brings.

---

31. Against Warfield, e.g., *Revelation and Inspiration* 104.
32. *On Biblical Inspiration and on Infallibility* 61.
33. Alonso Schökel, *The Inspired Word* 371.
34. Calvin, e.g., *Institutes* I.7.4: see chapter 12 above.

The Inspiration of Scripture
in the Light of God's Acts in History

The working of God's providence in human affairs suggests another analogy for the inspiration of scripture. The idea of providence is of key importance to the classical evangelical exposition of the doctrine of inspiration by writers such as Warfield and Packer. It is also implicit in the approach of Barr, who takes it to mean that God "was present in the formation of their [Israel's and the early church's] tradition and in the crystallization of that tradition as scripture"; "the Spirit *accompanies* human thought and action; the human thought and action, however, can be given human and historical description, without resort to supernatural interventions at any points of difficulty."[35]

Israel understood the events of history in general as under the control of Yahweh, but portrayed this sovereignty as working itself out through the processes of human decision-making. The fall of Jerusalem and the exile came about by divine agency, but by a divine agency that operated through human beings. The story of these events could be told without mentioning Yahweh's involvement — as it was by the Babylonians. In the Second Testament, Peter's description of Christ's death in Acts 2:23 encapsulates particularly neatly the notion of the concurrence of the divine and human will in the exercise of God's providence: "This Jesus, delivered up according to the definite plan and foreknowledge of God, you crucified and killed by the hands of lawless people." The dual divine and human responsibility for such events might be compared with the dual responsibility of author and characters for the acts in a play.[36]

In a parallel way God's speaking through a prophet such as Ezekiel came about through the overarching providence that ensured that a man like him was among the exiles to minister to them. Both preaching and prophecy are "truth through personality."[37] Inspiration involves a providential oversight of the development of the person whom God will call to be a prophet and of the speaking and writing that that person will actually do. The result is that they speak and write as they are inclined to do, not necessarily aware of special divine prompting or authority, but with the effect being that exactly what God wants is said and written. It can even thus be said that the writers are "completely controlled by the Holy Spirit"[38]

35. *The Bible in the Modern World* 18, 132.
36. C. S. Lewis, *Miracles* 183.
37. Cf. Phillips Brooks, *Lectures on Preaching* 5-34.
38. Packer, *"Fundamentalism" and the Word of God* 77, 78.

— though "controlled" is a risky verb to use, since it could imply that their words are not genuinely theirs. "The biblical authors . . . were authors of their books in the full sense of the word, not with a weakened but a heightened activity through the impulse of the Spirit."[39] As the words uttered by Hamlet belong both to him and to Shakespeare, the words uttered by Isaiah belong both to him and to God, and each depends on the other.[40]

The doctrine of providence thus helps to interpret some aspects of the work of God in the world and some aspects of the inspiration of scripture. It does not account for other aspects, indeed for key aspects. The exodus story involves an act of God in a different sense from what applies when we speak of the exile in that sense: The events as the Book of Exodus relates them simply cannot be told without bringing in divine causation. In order to tell *that* story at all without that aspect, Yahweh has to be demythologized out of it.[41] Peter's account of the resurrection is quite different from his account of the crucifixion: The resurrection is not an ordinary event with extraordinary significance. It is, rather, simply an act of God (Acts 2:24). The doctrine of providence by its very nature draws attention to and seeks to give a theological account of the *regularities* in God's involvement in the world, and it enables us to speak meaningfully of the whole of history as the act of God. Yet this brings a paradoxical element into the discussion because the notion of acts of God was originally designed to provide a way of thinking about *extraordinary* events, not about all events. These extraordinary events do not *have* to be miraculous, in such a way that the account of them *must* be of a God-of-the-gaps kind,[42] but they *are* extraordinary, not ordinary, events.

The same is true with the notion of inspiration. Ezekiel's prophesying required the providential presence of a person such as Ezekiel, so that he could see and hear the things that the particular initiative of God could show and speak to him on Israel's behalf. Providence is a necessary but not sufficient condition for God's inspired word to be spoken. The prophetic word belongs in the realm of the extraordinary. Inspiration, strictly speaking, "always has the character of the irruption of something new."[43] That

39. Berkouwer, *Holy Scripture* 171, following H. Bavinck, *Gereformeerde Dogmatiek* (Kampen: Kok, [4]1928) 1:402-3.

40. Alonso Schökel, *The Inspired Word* 73-77.

41. Cf. Croatto, *Exodus* 25-26.

42. This is Barr's concern in *The Bible in the Modern World* 132.

43. Lindblom, *Prophecy in Ancient Israel* 34.

aspect of its nature is reflected in everyday speech when someone declares, "What an inspired idea!" What is meant is that the idea is both insightful and unexpected. It breaks out of the parameters within which people have been thinking with a novel and illuminating suggestion. To describe a poem or a painting as inspired is, again, to imply that it is sublime and profound and also surprising and striking. One of the functions of prophecy was to be the means whereby God could speak to Israel from outside the parameters of its habitual thinking. It was God's way of finding elbow room in a context of institutional constraint. The inspired word is an extraordinary word. While prophetic books incorporate the work of anonymous preachers and scribes who in part act as representatives of the community in which the Spirit of God dwells, they overtly emphasize the creative contribution of inspired individuals such as Isaiah or Jeremiah, and the modern reader commonly finds much of the books' creative insight in the work of these great originators.[44]

N. L. Geisler criticizes Berkouwer for noting that God's word does not come to us in miraculous form, suspecting that Berkouwer is "shying away from the supernatural."[45] The accusation is no more applicable to Berkouwer than it is to writers such as Warfield and Packer, who especially stress the link between providence and inspiration. Significantly, Warfield notes that his definition of the normal nature of inspiration as involving God working through the personal initiative of a human writer is one that does not apply to "prophecy, properly so called."[46] It is unsatisfactory that the inspiration/word of God model, which derives from prophecy, receives a normative definition that distances it from prophecy. Despite the advantages of the scholastic approach to scripture, which enabled it to take more seriously the unity of Christ and the unity of scripture, this is also true of Thomas Aquinas's interpretation of the phenomenon of prophecy using the categories of Aristotelian philosophy rather than of Hellenistic Judaism.[47] Although the categories of Hellenistic Judaism were also affected by Greek thinking, their Neoplatonism happened to be nearer to the prophets themselves at this point.

One can extend the application of the analogy with providence and the acts of God in this connection. The exile, along with the excesses

---

44. J. Barr, *Holy Scripture* 90, 93.
45. *Biblical Errancy* 232, referring to Berkouwer, *Holy Scripture* 145, 170, 207.
46. *The Inspiration and Authority of Holy Scripture* 95.
47. Collins, *Introduction to the New Testament* 331.

brought about by Israel's enemies, shows that the acts of God do not necessarily work out flawlessly. God works though human agents. The events brought about through those agents may be affected by their sin, and thus those events do not necessarily correspond to the ideal will of God. In the same way, to affirm that scripture came into being through acts of God's providence does not suggest grounds for affirming the flawlessness of scripture. God condescends to work through the limitations of writers and hearers. If there is an argument for the flawlessness of scripture, it does not lie here.

• 18 •

Scripture as a Whole
as Inspired Word

For Paul, the Hebrew scriptures as a whole are "the oracles of God" (Rom 3:2). In Hebrews 5:12, "God's word" includes the Torah as well as the Prophets. According to Acts 7:38, the actual commands in the Torah came as "living oracles" to Moses, as to a prophet. In Matthew 19:5, Jesus cites the narrator's statements in Genesis as what God says. "Scripture says" and "God says" are entirely equivalent.[1] As it is possible to see the whole Bible as Torah so it is possible to see the whole as prophecy; a term that applies strictly to one part is extended to the whole. "*All* scripture is God-breathed . . ." (2 Tim 3:16). Among the Fathers, Clement of Rome describes the scriptures as a whole as "the true utterances of the Holy Spirit," Irenaeus as "spoken by the Word of God and his Spirit."[2]

Extending the Model of Inspired Word of God:
Its Application to Narrative

To discover how the model of God's word applies in this broader connection, we need to recall what it means to affirm that something is the word of God. The primary implications of this affirmation will also be significant when the prophetic model is stretched to apply to the rest of scripture. The

---

1. Warfield, "'It Says:' 'Scripture Says:' 'God Says,'" and "'The Oracles of God,'" in *Revelation and Inspiration* 283-391 = *The Inspiration and Authority of the Bible* 299-407.
2. See *1 Clement* 45; Irenaeus, *Against Heresies* II.28.2.

implication of the stretching is that scripture as a whole resembles prophecy in its certainty to be effective in achieving God's purpose and in its promise to be full of significance beyond its original context. We *can* declare in the liturgy that an excerpt from the life of Peter or the agonizing of Job or the questioning of Ecclesiastes is the word of the Lord, because such passages *are* designed to do something to the life of the people of God and because there *is* something profound and relevant to us about the way they portray a world before our eyes and ears. When we declare that the Bible as a whole is the word of God so that what the Bible says, God says, or when we express belief in the plenary inspiration of the whole of scripture, we imply that those key features of God's word, its effectiveness and its ongoing meaningfulness, apply to all of it. They apply to the parts that may not seem effective or relevant at all, to Leviticus, Esther, Jude, and Revelation, as well as to Isaiah and Jeremiah. So the critique of writers such as T. G. Baker[3] is only superficially valid.

Effectiveness and ongoing meaningfulness are central to the significance that scripture itself attaches to something being God's inspired word. It will be an open question whether other implications of that confession apply to parts of scripture beyond prophecy. Warfield, for instance, in the light of the nature of prophecy sees the whole of scripture as "the immediate word of God himself, speaking directly as such to the minds and hearts of every reader," who therefore "does not require to make his way to God, painfully, perhaps even uncertainly, through the words of His servants, but can listen directly to the Divine voice itself speaking immediately in the Scriptural word to him."[4] In a similar way, in an often-cited sermon J. W. Burgon defines the inspiration of scripture as implying that "every Book of it, — every Chapter of it, — every Verse of it, — every word of it, — every syllable of it, *(where* are we to *stop?)* — every letter of it — is the direct utterance of the Most High!"[5]

Statements such as these may be appropriate to prophecy, where the human speakers understand themselves as mouthpieces for the God who speaks through them directly to their hearers. They do not seem so appro-

---

3. " 'This Is the Word of the Lord.' "
4. "The Biblical Idea of Inspiration," *Revelation and Inspiration* 104 = *The Inspiration and Authority of the Bible* 158 = *Biblical Foundations* 70.
5. *"Inspiration and Interpretation"* 89 (1905 ed., 86); see, e.g., A. Richardson, "Fundamentalism," *Chambers's Encyclopaedia* (new ed., London: Newnes, 1959) 6:114; Packer, *"Fundamentalism" and the Word of God* 180; Huxtable, *The Bible Says* 61; Berkouwer, *Holy Scripture* 23.

priate to narrative, wisdom, psalmody, or epistle, which explicitly offer the words of human beings, so that one hears the word of God through these human beings speaking to other human beings (or, in the case of the Psalms, speaking *to* God). It is not immediately and directly God who says "Yahweh our Lord, how majestic is your name in all the earth" and "Yahweh, God almighty, God of Israel, arise to punish all the nations, do not be gracious to any villainous traitors" (Pss 8:1; 59:5) or "I don't remember if I baptized anyone else" and "I have been a fool" (1 Cor 1:16; 2 Cor 12:11) or "I have fought the good fight" and "bring the cloak that I left with Carpus at Troas" (2 Tim 4:7, 13). No doubt Burgon's point was that the whole of scripture is *truly* God's word, and this is not affected by how far it is *directly* so.

"Not all Scripture is God's word in the way that prophetic words are."[6] To affirm inspiration was not even specifically a way of making a statement regarding divine authorship, though it implied that. The inherent nature of narrative, in contrast to prophecy, is to conceal the author (divine as well as human) by letting the events tell the story. We must not "generalize in univocal fashion the concept of inspiration derived from the prophetic genre and assume that God spoke to the redactors of the sacred books just as he spoke to the prophets,"[7] any more than we should flatten the notion of inspiration so that the way it applies to such redactors determines the way it applies to prophets. The experience of evangelists and psalmists was unlike that of prophets. Their words are just as much God's words, just as effective and relevant, but they did not come to and through their writers in the same way.

To declare that narrative in particular, then, is God's inspired word is to say that it is effective and of ongoing relevance. This is true of scriptural narrative as an extension of the fact that it is true about the gospel itself. "You have been born anew . . . through the living and enduring word of God," which (Isa 40:8 says) "endures for ever" and consists in "the good news that was preached to you" (1 Pet 1:23-25). Isaiah 40 affirms the nature of the word of God as the declaration of Yahweh's promise and purpose, which is guaranteed to achieve its purpose because it is Yahweh's. These are characteristics originally attributed to the word expressed in prophecy, the prophetic "thus says Yahweh." In 1 Peter 1 the model of prophecy as the

---

6. Bauckham, "The Limits of Inerrancy"; the preceding paragraph is dependent on this paper.

7. Ricoeur, "Toward a Hermeneutic of the Idea of Revelation," *Essays on Biblical Interpretation* 77, 92.

word of God is stretched to apply to a message expressed in a story, in the gospel. The characteristics of the word of God are thus extended to the proclamation that has brought a new life to people in Christ. That proclamation consists in the gospel message preached, the narrative message embodied for us in the witnessing tradition in scripture.

As we have noted, the phrase "the word of God" is not used in scripture to describe scripture as such, but it is commonly used in the Second Testament to refer to the gospel message preached, the story of Jesus' coming, life, death, resurrection, and continuing activity in the mission of the church (e.g., Acts 4:31; 6:7; 11:1; 1 Thess 2:13; Heb 13:7; also Jesus' own words in passages such as John 14:24; 17:14, 17).[8] 1 Peter itself summarizes the gospel message in terms of Jesus being chosen and revealed, dying to redeem people from an empty life, and then being raised from the dead and glorified (1:18–21). That narrative good news is "the word of God," a declaration of God's promise and purpose bound to find fulfillment. By extension the Gospels and Acts themselves, and the narratives of the First Testament with their declaration of God's promise and purpose at work in history, are also the word of God. Paul, too, thus speaks of his message as expressed in words "taught by the Spirit" (1 Cor 2:13). To judge from what he himself says, he does not see his letters as inspired or as the word of God (though we may believe they are), yet he does see his witness as inspired. He preaches the gospel, the word of God, and people receive it as that, not as human words (1 Thess 4:13).

As with any word of God, then, to describe in these terms the story of what Jesus has done for people is to imply the expectation that this story will be notable for its power and fruitfulness (cf. Acts 6:7; 12:24; 19:20). It does things. It is the means by which people receive new birth and salvation (Jas 1:18, 21). It builds people up and gives them an inheritance (Acts 20:32). The assumption that as God's word scriptural narratives do something can be illustrated from Charles Wood's observation that the aim of a statement such as "God was in Christ reconciling the world to himself" (2 Cor 5:19), a narrative statement in a work of theological reflection, was not so much to "resolve a Christological puzzle" as to "transform the relationship between God and humankind."[9] The word of God is the word of reconciliation (2 Cor

---

8. Bultmann, "The Word of God in the New Testament," *Faith and Understanding* 298; Bultmann later adds that "the relation to history" is also "a constitutive characteristic of the Word in the Old Testament" as the prophets utter it (305-6).

9. *The Formation of Christian Understanding* 71.

5:19): It both concerns reconciliation and effects reconciliation. It is a reliable and effective, powerfully performative statement.

The narratives of scripture thus share the characteristics of the word of God that scripture itself attributes to prophecy. The gospel story does its work and brings new life to people. The gospel of God is the power of God (Rom 1:16): It effects things. In Part I we assumed that treating biblical narrative as a witnessing tradition implies the conviction that these stories do reflect God's story. If at points their world has been imagined, that does not in itself mean that it is merely imaginary — that these are stories that have sense but lack reference. It may mean that "the sense of the text is not behind the text, but in front of it"; it "points towards a possible world."[10] Indeed, it effectively brings that world into being.

The second significance of describing something as the inspired word of God, suggested by the Second Testament and the Fathers, was that it drew attention to what might be called in modern parlance the depth dimension in the text and its capacity to carry on speaking. Applied to narrative, the model of inspiration draws attention to the profundity and ongoing significance of its interpretation of events or of its creation of a new world before its hearers' eyes and ears, both of which speak far beyond the dreams of its authors. Inspired scripture, narrative as well as prophetic, is meaningful in a far-reaching way beyond the context in which it was first written. The telling of the biblical story is not a mere recounting of events from the past but a reenacting of a drama that involves people in the present.[11] Connecting with that, the gospel story has ever new significance for new generations.

The biblical text "has generative power to summon and evoke new life." It is prophetic in that it "anticipates and summons realities that live beyond the conventions of our day-to-day, take-for-granted world." It calls a new world into being. That includes its narratives, and specifically its fictional narratives, which as such probe to a new world rather than being limited to the experienced world and offer "impossibly daring visions of the possible."[12] "The fictions of God are truer than the facts of men."[13]

10. Ricoeur, *Interpretation Theory* 87; cf. "Response" (to essays by Crossan and others) 79; *Time and Narrative* 2:77-82; also Greenwood, "Poststructuralism and Biblical Studies"; Lentricchia, *After the New Criticism;* Lischer, "The Limits of Story."

11. Cf. McKnight, *Post-Modern Use of the Bible* 200, quoting Sternberg, *The Poetics of Biblical Narrative* 45, 122.

12. Brueggemann, *Finally Comes the Poet* 4, 5.

13. Green, *Scriptural Authority and Narrative Interpretation* 94; cf. Brueggemann, *Finally Comes the Poet* 6.

The authors of biblical narrative do not claim to write by inspiration; if anything, what they say about their work excludes that, as they describe the "ordinary" process by which they work. They make no claim to the "thus says Yahweh" of the prophets, yet neither do they themselves generally appear in their work, and a paradoxical result of this is that it enhances their claim to divine insight, a narrator's omniscience that extends to the mind of God. "The biblical narrator, quite unlike the Prophet, divests himself of a personal history and the marks of individual identity in order to assume for the scope of his narrative a godlike comprehensiveness of knowledge that can encompass even God Himself."[14] Although biblical narrative makes no claim that God was involved in its coming into being, we may conclude that God was so involved; it is thus that it has the effectiveness and the power that comes from being part of the inspired word of God.

Authoritative Canon and Experienced Revelation as Inspired Word of God

Inspiration is a model that is applied to command material as well as narrative. The law of God can be spoken of as the word of God (Mark 7:13). The implication is that God's commands also share in the characteristics of the inspired word: They are effective and they speak beyond their day — sometimes in regrettable ways, as happened when biblical material affirming slavery delayed the abolition of slavery.

The link between inspiration and the authoritative canon became important as a result of the Reformation. We have noted that the notion of inspiration has been reapplied in varying ways in response to a number of questions over the Christian centuries. In the context of the Reformation it came to be related to the question of the authority of scripture. The question of scriptural authority had not previously been controversial; in theory, at least, the whole church was committed to it. It became a matter of controversy when the fundamental importance of scripture's supreme authority, affirmed by the Reformers, did not seem to be acknowledged by other Christians. On one side, the Reformers were in conflict with a Catholic Church in which they identified a fundamental flaw: It was willing in practice to attribute such authority to certain postbiblical traditions and to

14. Alter, *The Art of Biblical Narrative* 157.

the teaching authority of the church itself that the authority of scripture became fatally compromised. On the other side, the Reformers also came into conflict with the latter-day Montanism of the radical reformation, which was willing to attribute such authority to what the Spirit might be saying now that the authority of scripture itself was again compromised. In such a context the Reformers needed a basis for the previously unquestioned belief that scripture had unique authority in the church. John Calvin responded to that need by making scripture's inspiration the basis for its possession of a unique status over against postbiblical tradition, the teaching authority of the church, and latter-day Montanism.[15] His successors went further in declaring that scripture alone was inspired. They took up the idea that in First and Second Temple times there had been a period during which God spoke through prophets, a period that came to an end, and they used this idea to justify rejection of the Apocrypha and also applied it to the Christian era to buttress the distinctive status of the Second Testament writings.[16]

The link between inspiration and authority thus derives from the Reformation. To make the inspiration of scripture the basis for its unique authority in this way was a novel theological move, even though Calvin saw himself as merely restating the church's traditional belief about scripture. The fact that his move was novel did not in itself make it wrong; theology proceeds in part by seeing how the old faith can speak to new questions. But attributing new significance to inspiration in this way led to an obscuring of the significance scripture itself attaches to inspiration. Further, we have noted that the Bible itself does not seem to see the Spirit's involvement with its authors as phenomenologically distinctive. It does imply that scripture has special authority, but the grounds it suggests for this authority do not lie in its inspiration. Perhaps it could not have this authority if it were not inspired, but there are other inspired statements as well as those in scripture, and the mere fact of being inspired does not convey this distinctive authority. Inspiration may be a necessary ground, but it is not a sufficient ground, for attributing special authority to scripture. Nor do the grounds for the special authority of scriptural words of God lie in their reaching a higher level or depth than other inspired words of God; at least it is not self-evident that *every* scriptural prophecy is of a higher level than *every* postscriptural prophecy.

15. See *Institutes of the Christian Religion* I.9; IV.8.
16. See Sundberg, "The Bible Canon" 370-71.

The supreme authority of the words of God in scripture derives from the same source as the supreme authority of the stories in scripture, their link with the gospel events. These are words that God gave in connection with the fulfillment of that purpose of salvation that came to a climax in Christ. The point is not merely a formal one. Barth comments that the inspiration of scripture is not comparable with other forms of inspiration, in that "it rests on the relationship of the biblical witnesses to the very definite content of their witness. It is indeed this content that inspires them."[17] It is the historical nature of the gospel and the witnessing character of scripture that give it unique authority over against church tradition, the teaching authority of the church, and extrascriptural prophecy, and also over against human experience and human reason.

The prayers of the Psalms, the reflection embodied in Israel's wisdom books and in some early Christian letters, and the revelations reported in the biblical apocalypses also belong to God's inspired word.

According to the Second Council of Constantinople in 553, Theodore of Mopsuestia described Proverbs and Ecclesiastes as books that Solomon "composed from his own experience[18] for the benefit of others, since he had not received the grace of prophecy but rather that of prudence, as blessed Paul has said."[19] In the case of a work such as Ecclesiastes, in particular, the book's statements are explicitly expressions of human opinion; to speak of it as inspired might seem perverse since its author "would surely deny that he had received the word of God; he was writing out of collective human experience."[20] His way of speaking is "I said to myself" (e.g., 1:16, 2:1), on the basis of what can be seen empirically, not "thus says Yahweh."[21]

It is particularly clear that the Psalms are also human words to God, not divine words addressed to human beings. Yet they share in the effectiveness of God's word and in its continuing relevance and capacity to speak. Indeed, to say that they are human words rather than divine words is an oversimplification. The psalmists describe an experience of inspiration like that of a prophet (Pss 45; 49; 78). They have heard God speak (Pss 2; 50;

---

17. *Church Dogmatics* I/2:520.

18. *Ex sua persona.*

19. J. D. Mansi, *Sacrorum conciliorum nova et amplissima collectio* (reprinted Graz: Akademische, 1960) 9:223; cf. Vawter, *Biblical Inspiration* 163-64; Zaharopoulos, *Theodore of Mopsuestia on the Bible* 33.

20. Brown, *The Critical Meaning of the Bible* 7.

21. Alonso Schökel, *The Inspired Word* 97-98, 327.

81:5; 85:8; 110). The very fact that the Psalms are poetry, like the words of the prophets, may be evidence that they come through divine inspiration.[22] The Second Testament's many references to the Psalms begin from the identification of them as God's inspired word. In Hebrews, with two exceptions, "all the primary passages that are quoted to illustrate the true nature of the Person and Work of Christ are taken from the Psalms" (e.g., Heb 1:5, 7, 8-9, 10-12, 13).[23] Two imprecatory Psalms are taken up in Acts 1:16, 20 (Pss 69:25; 109:8) — with enthusiasm rather than embarrassment because their prayer for punishment is fulfilled in the fall of Judas from his place in the Twelve. The application of these words to Judas stems from their having been spoken by the Holy Spirit: They are the word of God in the sense that they have significance beyond their original day.

In general, however, to affirm that wisdom books and psalms are the word of God may imply that here we may have recourse to the classic notion of God providentially working through the human personality so that words devised by a human author are words that express the mind of God and fulfill God's purpose — a notion that is less well fitting to much of prophecy itself. It is also appropriate to the Epistles. Paul speaks as the mouthpiece of the Spirit, yet not as one who receives his words directly from God. He believes his words reflect the concerns and promptings of the Holy Spirit working through his own mind and heart, which he has given over to Christ, but he devises the words. "The Divine *acts through* the human"; his letters "bear the stamp of an individual mind. . . . The theology of St. Paul is a reasoned system."[24] Paul thinks through theological issues in essentially the same way that we do, the Holy Spirit being involved in all the aspects of that process. Sometimes he makes it explicit that a particular part of his teaching is *not* the word of the Lord (1 Cor 7:10, 12, 25). But even this does not stop it from being the word of God, that which effects the will of God in the Corinthians' lives and which continues to be meaningful for us.

22. Mowinckel, *The Psalms in Israel's Worship* 2:92.
23. Westcott, *Hebrews* 473.
24. Sanday, *Inspiration* 355.

• 19 •

Inspiration and Inerrancy

The narratives in scripture are part of the inspired word of God. It has been inferred that their inspiration by God is a guarantee of their historical truth, or — to put the matter more strongly — of their *inerrancy*. Is inspired scripture inerrant?

Attitudes to Factual Accuracy over the Centuries

It is a matter of debate when a strict affirmation of inerrancy came to be associated with belief in inspiration. The debate is keenly fought. At a superficial level it is merely an argument about historical theology or church history, but underlying this argument are rival claims regarding who are the heirs to Christian orthodoxy.

From the Fathers to the nineteenth century it was possible for orthodox scholars to combine strong statements of scripture's inspiration, inerrancy, and truthfulness, with occasional apparent acknowledgments that scripture is sometimes not factually accurate. Newman, for instance, suggested that the Fathers indeed believed that the scriptures were inspired and inerrant, but that the error that they said was not in the scriptures was the significant type of error that endangered faith or morals, not error over mere matters of fact.[1] The difficulty with this understanding is that the Fathers seem capable of combining their recognition that scriptural narratives are sometimes unhistorical with specific declarations elsewhere regarding the detailed reliability of them.

1. *On Biblical Inspiration and on Infallibility* 91.

Neither is it the case that the Fathers see scripture as incapable of intentional error or of seeking to deceive us, as wholly truthful in aim, yet capable of accidental error. Augustine declares that "the Evangelists could be guilty of no kind of falsehood, whether it was of the type designed intentionally to deceive or was simply the result of forgetfulness."[2] Commenting on Matthew's account of the healing of two blind men at Jericho and noting the differing parallel accounts in Mark and Luke, Origen asserts: "If we believe for certain that the Gospels were written with the cooperation of the Holy Spirit, those who wrote them could not have had any lapse of memory."[3] In his Gospel commentaries Origen sometimes goes out of his way to compare narratives in the four Gospels in order to harmonize them. In comparing John 1:27 ("worthy to *untie*") with Matthew 3:11 ("worthy to *carry*"), he comments that the Evangelists cannot have "made any mistake or misrepresentation" or expressed themselves loosely, so John must have said both things at different times.[4]

On the other hand, in discussing John 2:12-25 and the difficulty of reconciling it with the first three Gospels, Origen emphasizes that the Gospels contain many a "discrepancy" of this kind, which he declares to be insoluble if we have to take each Gospel as attempting a historical account. All four are true, but "their truth is not to be sought for in the outward and material letter" but under the assumption that some statements that appear to make historical claims are actually included to bring home a spiritual truth, not a historical truth.[5] Gregory of Nazianzus, too, stresses how every detail of a Gospel narrative has something to teach us, and excludes the possibility that there are mistakes in scripture;[6] he is no allegorist, but he is referring to the detail of the Gospel *story,* and to make him thereby assert that every detail is historical is to impose an anachronistic distinction on him. Augustine believes that the Spirit led Matthew to refer to Jeremiah rather than Zechariah (Matt 27:9) because this emphasizes that all the prophets are the same and encourages people to put Jeremiah and Zechariah together.[7] He both suggests that John must have spoken of car-

2. *Harmony of the Evangelists* II.12 (29); cf. Pinnock, "Limited Inerrancy," in *God's Inerrant Word* (ed. Montgomery) 143.

3. *Commentary on Matthew* XVI.12, quoted by Sanday, *Inspiration* 37.

4. *Commentary on the Gospel of John* VI.18.

5. *Commentary on the Gospel of John* X.1-4. He does also allow a spiritual interpretation of the passages about sandals.

6. *Orations* II.105.

7. *Harmony of the Gospels* III.7 (30-31).

rying as well as of untying and also comments that an approximate statement can be just as reliable as a precise one.[8] Chrysostom combines a stress
on the precision of scriptural narrative with a stress on its considerateness,
which leads it to make allowance for our limitations.[9] Within scripture
itself, we might note the observation on Melchizedek's lack of parents in
Hebrews 7:3, which is surely an argument from the way the story in Genesis
14 is told rather than one that infers that historically Melchizedek had no
parents.

Origen also comments on the order of events in Genesis 1, where the
sun, moon, and stars are not mentioned until after three days, with their
evenings and mornings, have passed. He assumes that this can hardly be
the historical order of events; it has to be treated allegorically. It is theologically true but not historically true.[10] Augustine similarly warns people
not to bring discredit on the Christian faith and the Bible by treating the
Bible as a source for astronomical information that non-Christians know
is incorrect.[11] Calvin also declared that Genesis 1 was not designed to teach
scientific truth. He and his contemporaries were quite aware that the Genesis creation story did not correspond to the findings of science: Astronomers
knew that Saturn was a more significant light than the moon even though
the moon is described in scripture as one of the two great lights. Calvin
rebukes people for seeking astronomical information from Genesis, which
speaks of things only as they appear.[12] His attitude contrasts with that of
inerrantists such as H. Lindsell, who specifically affirms that scripture must
be factually reliable in what it says about astronomy, though not with that
of J. I. Packer, who takes the opposite view.[13]

Luther describes scripture as "God incarnate."[14] Yet he is untroubled by
irreconcilable "discrepancies" in scripture: "Let it pass, it does not endanger
the articles of the Christian faith."[15] Calvin also indicates that he was aware

8. *Ibid.* II.12 (29).

9. E.g., *Homilies on Genesis* XV.7-8.

10. *Principles* IV.1.16.

11. *Genesis according to the Literal Sense* I.39; quoted by Polman, *The Word of God According to St. Augustine* 61 and by Rogers and McKim, *The Authority and Interpretation of the Bible* 26-27.

12. See *Commentaries on the First Book of Moses Called Genesis* 1:79, 85-87.

13. Lindsell, *The Battle for the Bible* 18; Packer, *"Fundamentalism" and the Word of God* 96-98.

14. See chapter 17 above.

15. *WA* 46:727, cited in Rogers and McKim, *The Authority and Interpretation of the Bible* 87.

of trivial inaccuracies in scripture such as the seventy-five rather than seventy people in Acts 7:14 and the posture of Jacob in Hebrews 11:21,[16] but he does not assume that this compromises belief in the writers' total honesty and the writings' full inspiration, which covers their facts as well as their doctrine.

A further approach to inaccuracy is instanced in subsequent Protestant writers. Historical method in the ancient world did not focus on the kind of critical examination of sources that is essential to modern historiography, but on the preserving and developing of traditions handed down to the writer. Matthew Henry understood that scriptural writers were not seeking to undertake a critical task and so should not be faulted for failing to complete such a task. He remarks of the author of 1 Chronicles 8:1-32, "This holy man wrote as he was moved by the Holy Ghost; but there was no necessity for the making up of the defects, no, nor for the rectifying of the mistakes, of these genealogies by inspiration. It was sufficient that he copied them out as they came to his hand. . . ."[17] John Wesley, while observing that "If there be any mistakes in the Bible, there may well be a thousand. If there be one falsehood in that book, it did not come from the God of truth,"[18] nevertheless makes similar observations to Henry's regarding errors in the sources underlying the genealogy in Matthew 1.[19]

Even in the mid-nineteenth century at Princeton Theological Seminary, where B. B. Warfield later taught, Charles Hodge showed a similar apparent inconsistency. In his *Systematic Theology* he affirms that all the scriptures are inspired and thus infallible in what they teach in matters of scientific, historical, and geographical fact as well as matters of moral and religious truth. He goes on to minimize the significance of errors in scripture, but thereby grants their existence:

> The errors in matters of fact which skeptics search out bear no proportion to the whole. No sane man would deny that the Parthenon was built of marble, even if here and there a speck of sandstone should be detected in its structure. Not less unreasonable is it to deny the inspiration of such a

16. *The Acts of the Apostles 1–13* 181; *The Epistle of Paul the Apostle to the Hebrews* 175.

17. *An Exposition of the Old and New Testament* (reprinted London: Nisbet, 1886); quoted by Orr, *Revelation and Inspiration* 181.

18. *The Journal of the Rev. John Wesley* 6:117 (entry for 24 July 1776); quoted by Pinnock, *A Defense of Biblical Infallibility* 2.

19. *Explanatory Notes upon the New Testament,* on Matt 1:1; cf. Abraham, *The Divine Inspiration of Holy Scripture* 116.

book as the Bible, because one sacred writer says that on a given occasion twenty-four thousand, and another says that twenty-three thousand, men were slain.[20]

Writers from the Fathers to the nineteenth century thus combine an affirmation of inerrancy with an acknowledgment that scriptural narrative includes factual errors. Now it might be suggested that comments of the latter kind should be seen as aberrations, inconsistencies incompatible with such writers' doctrine of inerrancy, but it is more plausible to see them as indicating that the logic of affirming inerrancy had not yet been thought through. As we have noted, the question regarding inerrancy is one that was not clearly formulated until the nineteenth century, the period that saw the development of critical approaches to the origins and nature of the biblical books and brought discussion of the doctrine of inspiration to its heyday.[21] The humanity of scripture was a postulate accepted before the development of critical theories, but not one whose implications the church had had cause to think through. The development of critical theories brought a more systematic examination of the humanness of the process whereby scripture came into being and of the parallels at the level of its literary nature with other writings from the ancient world. That made it more difficult to affirm that it manifested inerrant truth, which the received understanding of inspiration implicitly or explicitly claimed for it without having thought through the implications of scripture's humanity.

Even critical theologians sometimes suggest that when conservative Christians insist on the inspired inerrancy of scripture they are only con-tinuing to affirm what Christians had believed from earliest times.[22] But the modern affirmation made in the light (or in the face) of more recent study has a different significance from the old affirmation. Christian doc-trine is an ineluctably historical and developing phenomenon. Evangelical apologists cannot claim that their doctrine of scripture is nothing more and nothing less than what was always maintained by the church; while they may claim to be the heirs of earlier figures, they cannot claim identity with their position in a different century or millennium.[23]

20. *Systematic Theology* 1:163, 170. Warfield (*The Inspiration and Authority of the Bible* 221) takes this as only an *ad hominem* argument.
21. See Maarten van Bemmelen, *Issues in Biblical Inspiration*, on Warfield, Sanday, and other nineteenth-century writers.
22. So, e.g., Burnaby, *Is the Bible Inspired?* 28.
23. Wright, "Soundings in the Doctrine of Scripture in British Evangelicalism"

The Nineteenth-Century Elaboration

The specific context in which the category of inspiration was elaborated in the nineteenth century was the development of critical study of scripture's historical origins and historical accuracy. This led to the stretching of the model of inspiration so that it could suggest a theological response to questions raised by that study. Among nineteenth-century Protestant discussions particular historical importance attaches to the work of B. B. Warfield, which had decisive influence on evangelical approaches to inspiration for the next century. Subsequent conservative writers such as J. I. Packer[24] rightly see themselves as restating Warfield's position in the continuing context of questions that had first come into prominence in the nineteenth century, especially concerning the relationship of the inspiration of scripture to its human origin. It was through Packer's work that Warfield's approach to the questions raised by critical study came to replace the native British approach of James Orr with its stress on progressive revelation.[25]

Warfield was Professor of New Testament at Princeton Theological Seminary. In the mid-nineteenth century at Princeton Charles Hodge had expressed the conviction that "the whole end and office of inspiration is to preserve the sacred writers from error in teaching."[26] The Princeton approach to the doctrine of scripture and its inerrancy built on the work of the seventeenth-century Genevan theologian Francis Turretin, a figure of great influence on Princeton theology in general.[27] Like Hodge, Warfield saw the significance of inspiration as lying in its making the biblical writers' words also the words of God "and *therefore* perfectly infallible."[28] "Infalli-

---

88. Contrast the stress on the identity of the views of (e.g.) the Fathers, the Reformers, Wesley, Warfield, and Spurgeon in Nicole, "The Inspiration and Authority of Scripture" I:199-200.

24. See his *"Fundamentalism" and the Word of God.*

25. Cf. Wright, "Soundings in the Doctrine of Scripture in British Evangelicalism" 105; Marsden, "Fundamentalism as an American Phenomenon."

26. "Inspiration" 685; so also Warfield's colleague A. A. Hodge, "Inspiration," 225-26 (quoted by Rogers and McKim, *The Authority and Interpretation of the Bible* 282, 350).

27. See Rogers and McKim, *The Authority and Interpretation of the Bible* 172, 268-69, 279-81, 377. The novelty of Warfield's view should not be exaggerated; see J. D. Woodbridge and R. H. Balmer, "The Princetonians and Biblical Authority," in *Scripture and Truth* (ed. Carson and Woodbridge), 251-79; also Woodbridge, *Biblical Authority* 119-40.

28. *The Inspiration and Authority of the Bible* 420 = *Revelation and Inspiration* 396; my emphasis.

bility" in this context has the same meaning as "inerrancy"; the latter term has recently come into more consistent use because "infallibility" can be used in a softer sense. The Chicago Statement on Biblical Inerrancy thus distinguishes infallibility and inerrancy,[29] and H. D. McDonald distinguishes between "the inerrancy of biblical facts and the infallibility of the biblical truth."[30]

A major concern underlying the development of the classic evangelical doctrine of inspiration was thus the undergirding of conviction regarding the complete factual truth of scripture, an inference from inspiration that had not been so stressed in earlier periods when concern with inspiration had other interests. Warfield's emphasis was that something inspired is thereby guaranteed free of error.

This development within Protestant thinking in the centuries up to the late nineteenth century followed a parallel course to that of Roman Catholic thinking. According to Vawter, the actual identification of inspiration and preservation from error was first made by J. Jahn (1792), who defined inspiration as "the divine assistance for avoiding errors."[31] It is explicit in Pope Leo XIII's encyclical on scripture, *Providentissimus Deus*, of 1893.[32] Thus Hoffmann's comment that "the identification of inspiration with inerrancy . . . seems to be at the heart of the Protestant difficulty" over formulating a doctrine of scripture[33] refers to a problem that was not in origin an exclusively Protestant problem. Catholic and Protestant writers have in common an important development in thinking about inspiration that makes it a means of undergirding convictions regarding the complete factual truth of scripture by emphasizing an inference neither stressed in earlier periods, when concern with inspiration had other interests, nor drawn in scripture itself.

Whereas critical study sought to determine the nature of biblical narrative from the narrative itself, Warfield took his clues for determining the nature of biblical narrative from statements about that narrative elsewhere

---

29. Cf. Boice, *The Foundation of Biblical Authority* 11; Henry, *God, Revelation and Authority* 4:217.

30. *I Want to Know What the Bible Says about the Bible* 75.

31. *Einleitung in die göttlichen Bücher des Altes Bundes* 1 (Vienna: Wappler, 1792; [2]1802 [ET *An Introduction to the Old Testament*; New York: Carvill, 1827]) 91; as quoted by Vawter, *Biblical Inspiration* 69 and Burtchaell, *Catholic Theories of Biblical Inspiration* 50-51.

32. Vawter, *Biblical Inspiration* 72-73, 132.

33. "Inspiration" 450.

in scripture (e.g., 2 Tim 3:16). In this sense he was taking a deductive approach, starting from scripture's more theoretical statements about the nature of scripture and arguing that study of its detailed form must work within the framework that such statements provide.[34] He then put particular stress on the conviction that these statements include an implicit claim that scripture is factually true at every point. Critical theories that point in any other direction must therefore be wrong. It is thenceforth taken for granted that there is an intrinsic and inevitable link between scripture's inspiration and its inerrancy. The ambiguity in writers such as Origen, Augustine, Luther, Calvin, Henry, Wesley, and Hodge is resolved.

As we have noted, Warfield believed he was merely restating the church's traditional beliefs about scripture, though in fact his doctrine (or more broadly that of the Princeton school) was innovative and was developed in response to the questions of his day. No one had previously asserted a doctrine of inerrancy that had not either turned a blind eye to minor apparent errors in scripture or interpreted them allegorically. There is thus a parallel between the work of Warfield and that of Calvin. As Calvin had redirected the significance of inspiration to make it the basis for scripture's authority, so Warfield redirected it to make it the basis for a stress on inerrancy. Like Calvin, Warfield wrote in the conviction that he was merely restating the church's traditional beliefs about scripture, but by finding a new significance for inspiration he was risking obscuring the significance scripture itself attaches to inspiration.

Difficulties with Inerrancy
and Approaches to Solving Them

If Warfield's inference from inspiration to inerrancy were correct, we might expect it to mesh with the nature of scripture as we find it when we study it in detail. It does not in fact do so. As writers from the Fathers to the nineteenth century had perceived, scripture does not give the impression of being factually inerrant. Extreme measures are required to vindicate the attribution of detailed inerrancy to it. By normal standards of evidence it contains a large number of factual slips, such as the attribution of Goliath's death to both David (1 Sam. 17) and Elnathan (2 Sam. 21:19) and the

---

34. He describes his approach in *The Inspiration and Authority of Holy Scripture* 220-26 = *Revelation and Inspiration* 220-26.

attribution of the quotation in Matthew 27:9-10 to Jeremiah rather than Zechariah. Such slips are no more than one might expect in any human document, but neither are they remarkably less.

Nearly all these "apparent errors" are long known and have had resolutions proposed for them, but accepting such resolutions often "means disregarding standards of evidence that are relied on in our normal lives."[35] Warfield declares that "no single error has as yet been demonstrated to occur in the Scriptures,"[36] and this is true insofar as no amount of evidence can turn an "apparent difficulty" into a "proven error." Thus A. T. Hanson and R. P. C. Hanson paraphrase Warfield to mean "no single error has yet been found in the Scriptures that cannot be explained away by the exercise of the inventive imagination and the acceptance of the most improbable conjectures," of the kind involved in maintaining the Ptolemaic cosmology in the light of the evidence that the planets do not revolve around the earth.[37]

R. E. Brown claims that it is a regular philosophical principle to infer the possible from the actual rather than the other way round; we have assumed this principle with regard to arguments concerning the resurrection that rule out such an event *a priori*. So "if historical errors exist, they must be possible."[38] In contrast, K. Nielsen comments (in connection with an argument about the incoherence of the idea of revelation) that "what is not possible cannot be actual."[39] It is likely that Warfield and the Hansons actually presuppose the position of R. Swinburne, who observes that

> if your background knowledge of what the world is like shows some detailed historical claim to be quite likely, then you will need little in the way of historical evidence in order rationally to believe it. Conversely, if your background knowledge shows some detailed historical claim to be rather unlikely, then you will need a lot in the way of historical evidence in order rationally to believe it.[40]

Where Warfield and the Hansons (with Brown) differ is over whether the quantity of "evidence" (for the presence of errors in scripture) is sufficient

35. Abraham, *The Divine Inspiration of Holy Scripture* 25.

36. *The Inspiration and Authority of the Bible* 225 = *Revelation and Inspiration* 225.

37. *The Bible without Illusions* 54.

38. *The Critical Meaning of the Bible* 16.

39. "The Primacy of Philosophical Theology" 169; cf. Griffin, "Is Revelation Coherent" 278.

40. *Responsibility and Atonement* 4.

to compel the conclusion that scripture contains errors, given how "un-likely" this conclusion is (in Warfield's view). And whether someone who takes Warfield's view is prepared to change their mind will likely depend on whether they can see an acceptable alternative view. If such a person does not regard the Hansons' view as an acceptable alternative, he or she may rationally stick with Warfield no matter how much detailed evidence the Hansons come up with.

Awareness of the fact that there do seem to be statements in scripture that are scientifically or historically untrue has led to a number of attempts to nuance a statement of scripture's inerrancy in order to produce a satis-factory alternative view. Many inerrantists recognize that Genesis 1–3 is not a factual account of creation. They may seek to preserve the narrative's inerrancy by "restricting inerrancy to the sense intended by the inspired writer"[41] and by then suggesting that this author was not intending to teach history or science. The difficulty here is whether we can make this move without falling foul of the "intentional fallacy."[42] We have no access to the author's intention except in the text in which it is embodied,[43] and we risk reading into the text the authorial intention that suits us.

To circumvent the appeal to intention it is possible to seek to preserve the text's inerrancy by declaring that it is history expressed in parabolic rather than literal form, a possibility allowed for by D. Kidner in his treatment of Genesis 1–3.[44] A parallel move is to confine scripture's inerrancy to what it actually affirms, as "The Lausanne Covenant" does:[45] What scripture merely mentions without actually affirming need not be expected to be inerrant.

Within Genesis 1–3 there are some pointers toward a parabolic under-standing, but this approach to the difficulty, which arises from apologetic rather than literary considerations, again risks reading into the text what we want to discover. In the fashion of allegory it involves moving arbitrarily from a more literal to a more figurative method of interpretation wherever the former threatens the inerrancy of the text.[46] A writer such as Calvin

---

41. So Pinnock, "Limited Inerrancy," in God's Inerrant Word (ed. Montgomery) 148-49. I once argued this myself, in "Inspiration, Infallibility, and Criticism."

42. Montgomery, God's Inerrant Word 30-31, against Fuller, "The Nature of Biblical Inerrancy."

43. J. S. Feinberg, "Noncognitivism: Wittgenstein," in Biblical Errancy (ed. N. L. Geisler) 194-96.

44. Genesis 66.

45. Paragraph 2; see Let the Earth Hear His Voice (ed. Douglas) 3.

46. Barr's opening substantial point in Fundamentalism.

recognized that God spoke in scripture through narratives that express the cosmological understanding of the writers' day. God did not choose to reveal a more adequate cosmology to the readers.

J. W. Montgomery argues that there is an unacceptable dualism involved in the suggestion that scripture can be theologically true even if it is historically or scientifically false.[47] But Calvin regards Genesis 1 as theologically instructive without being scientifically true,[48] and it is difficult to categorize Calvin as a dualist. He implies the view that Genesis 1 is not a scientific treatise, that its theology is therefore not dependent on it having scientific accuracy, and that its perspective is therefore not dualistic. It is only an extension of this position to maintain that in the same way subsequent biblical narratives are not historiography that get their history wrong, but narrative complexes incorporating material with varying relations to history; as such their theology, too, is only partly dependent on their historical accuracy. Calvin's relaxed attitude to inaccuracies in passages such as Acts 7:14 and Hebrews 11:21 suggests that he might have been willing to draw this inference, as is indirectly witnessed by John Murray's need to observe that Calvin expressed himself unwisely on these passages.[49]

The question is whether we can, indeed, argue that all that Genesis 1 was affirming is that God created the world and that its authors were not actually affirming belief in a three-decker universe; certainly the contemporaries of Copernicus assumed they were. We cannot "save" the factual inerrancy of Genesis 1 simply by an appeal to literary forms. We need some principle for deciding that at certain points a narrative is not making the historical assertion that it appears to be making. Unprincipled movement between literal and nonliteral readings of narrative implies risks to the authority of scripture and to the gospel much greater than the admission that some historically intended statements in scripture are factually inaccurate. Appeal to literary genres can be "an unconscious mechanism for allowing the exegete to adopt what opinions he chooses while formally progressing to acknowledge the truthfulness and inspiration of the New [or Old] Testament writings."[50] Barton calls this "salvation by hermeneutics."[51]

47. *God's Inerrant Word* (ed. Montgomery) 24-25.

48. See J. I. Packer in the same volume, "Calvin's View of Scripture" 106.

49. *Calvin on Scripture and Divine Sovereignty* 31.

50. See M. Dunnett, "A Remarkable Consensus," *New Blackfriars* 68 (1987) 809, as quoted by R. Trigg, " 'Tales Artfully Spun,' " *The Bible as Rhetoric* (ed. Warner) 117. Cf. Lohfink, *The Christian Meaning of the Old Testament* 46-47.

51. *People of the Book?* 6.

Some difficulties can be approached by suggesting that they entered the text subsequent to its original writing, during the process of its textual transmission. Since Warfield inspiration and inerrancy are generally predicated not of the text we have but of the original, now inaccessible text of scripture, scripture "as originally given."[52] But "it follows that the Scriptures as we now have them are neither infallible nor inspired."[53] Yet it was certainly the scriptures as they had them, not some hypothetical originals to which they had no access, that Paul and his fellow believers regarded as God-breathed and to which 2 Timothy 3:16 refers.[54] There are theological as well as critical grounds for having confidence in the biblical texts that we have: It is difficult to imagine God inspiring scripture in the first place and then letting its text fail to be reasonably preserved.[55] It is also difficult to maintain that the textual transmission of the scriptures was both careful enough to ensure that we really have the word of God and hazardous enough to permit such mistakes as would explain errors in the text as we have it.

Again, inerrancy may be preserved by associating it only with matters of significance for belief and behavior, with what directly relates to "salvation through faith in Christ Jesus" and to the maturing of the man or woman of God (2 Tim 3:15-17). The error scripture is concerned with is swerving from the truth and leading others into such error (2 Tim 2:18; cf. Rom 3:4). Statements such as Wyclif's description of scripture as "the infallible and necessary rule of truth" indeed suggest that a major focus of belief in inerrancy lies in scripture's doctrinal truth rather than the accuracy of its historical detail. It might be possible to infer that God's involvement in the origin of scripture precludes errors that would interfere with its purpose to lead people to salvation and maturity; it thus precludes major historical unreliability, but not other errors, such as slips over detailed matters of fact.[56]

One difficulty about this suggestion is that it may seem to resolve only

52. See Letis, "The Protestant Dogmaticians and the Late Princeton School." John Owen's *Treatise* on the "Integrity and Purity of the Greek Text" illustrates the Protestant affirmation of the copies of the text that they actually possessed as reliable in their letters and pointing.

53. Lindsay, "The Doctrine of Scripture" 291, quoted by Rogers and McKim, *The Authority and Interpretation of the Bible* 384.

54. Beegle, *Scripture, Tradition and Infallibility* 164.

55. Packer, *"Fundamentalism" and the Word of God* 90-91.

56. So Orr, *Revelation and Inspiration* 162; cf., e.g., Berkouwer, *Holy Scripture* 179-81; Marshall, *Biblical Inspiration* 61-65.

part of the problem of the inerrancy of scripture, and perhaps the lesser part. While discussion of the problem focuses on factual inerrancy, accepting scripture's *theological* inerrancy arguably raises bigger difficulties (consider, for instance, 2 Kgs 17:25). Thus S. Davis seems not to notice that if the Bible is mistaken in saying that God told Israel to kill the Canaanites,[57] it is mistaken theologically or morally or both, and not merely historically. From a more conservative perspective, there is another difficulty with this view. The Bible essentially interrelates the theological and ethical with the historical and factual. It is therefore difficult to maintain that it can be fully reliable in matters of doctrine and ethics without being fully reliable in matters of history.[58] The essence of scriptural narrative lies in the fact that it is a unity of interpreted event or incarnate interpretation rather than bare chronicle or timeless truth.[59]

Difficulties in Principle and Disadvantages in Practice

Warfield's inference that scripture must be without error was derived deductively from the fact of scripture's inspiration. The inerrancy of scripture is not directly asserted by Christ or within scripture itself. It has only the status of a deduction from direct statements regarding inspiration. It is therefore questionable whether Warfield's deductive approach to the nature of scripture should overrule an approach that looks at its phenomena more empirically. The empirical facts about the detailed contents of scripture drive us to ask whether Warfield's deduction is valid. "Our views of inspiration must be determined by the phenomena of the Bible as well as by its didactic statements."[60]

Implicitly Hodge is commending an approach to a doctrine of scripture that has inductive as well as deductive features. N. L. Geisler criticizes such views: "Doctrines are not based in the data or phenomena of Scripture; they are *based* in the teaching of Scripture and *understood* in the light of

57. So *The Debate about the Bible* 94-95.
58. So most trenchantly F. A. Schaeffer in, e.g., the pamphlet *"It Is Essential for the Truth of Christianity that the Bible Relates Truth about History and the Cosmos, As Well As about Spiritual Matters"*; it quotes the support of leading British inerrantists J. Wenham, O. R. Barclay, J. A. Motyer, D. Jackman, R. Clements, and J. R. W. Stott.
59. Weber, "The Promise of the Land" 3-4.
60. Hodge, *Systematic Theology* 1:170; quoted by Abraham, *The Divine Inspiration of Holy Scripture* 38.

the phenomena of Scripture."[61] Geisler does not offer reasons for this statement beyond its purely formal parallel with Francis Bacon's contrast between deductive and inductive reasoning in science. The distinction between "basing" a doctrine and "understanding" it seems in any case to be a difficult one. Further, Geisler's view that scriptural material can be divided into that which teaches and that which constitutes phenomena seems to contradict the statement in the classic passage on scriptural inspiration that *all* scripture is profitable for teaching (2 Tim 3:16).

Admittedly one must equally query the deductive argument that stands opposite to Warfield's, expressed forcibly by Barth.[62] "The prophets and apostles as such, even in their office, even in their function as witnesses, even in the act of writing down their witness, were real, historical men as we are, and therefore sinful in their action, and capable and actually guilty of error in their spoken and written word." Barth's assertion is not made on the basis of the phenomena of scripture but on the basis of inference: He wants to underline "the miracle" that "sinful and erring men as such speak the Word of God." If we resist this truth we "resist the sovereignty of grace." "If the prophets and apostles are not real and therefore fallible men . . . then it is not a miracle that they speak the Word of God." But "human therefore sinful" is as questionable as "inspired therefore inerrant."

The *fact* that the Bible is inspired provides our thinking with a starting point. The *nature* of the Bible's inspiration we must learn from scripture itself. "Most inspiration theory has not been talk about the Bible. It has been talk about talk about the Bible. Rather than examine the Book itself . . . they have preferred to erect elaborate and risky constructs of formula upon formula." We need to "scrutinize the Bible to see what it shows of its own nature and origins. . . . How, despite our preconceptions, has inspiration really worked?"[63]

As we have noted, stretching the idea of inspiration so that it applies to genres other than prophecy is in principle unobjectionable, but it is hazardous. Care is needed in inferring significances from models. We may extend their application in a direction that loses touch with their original significance and emphasizes implications that do not belong to them. This seems to have happened with inspiration and the stress on scripture's inerrancy, and in particular on the factual inerrancy of scriptural narrative.

---

61. *Biblical Errancy* 21, emphasis original.
62. *Church Dogmatics* I/2:521-22.
63. Burtchaell, *Catholic Theories of Biblical Inspiration* 283-84.

That stress began from and encouraged a stretching of the inspiration model that lost touch with the original objectives for describing scripture as the inspired word of God.

"The Bible is inspired, therefore it is inerrant" is an argument parallel to "Christ's death paid a ransom for us, therefore we can ask to whom the ransom was paid" or "God chose some people for salvation, therefore he chose others for damnation" or "God is Father, therefore he is male rather than female." It is at this point that models (in this case, models for scripture) may act as checks on each other, barring the way to false inferences. If Warfield's inference were correct, we might expect it to be more directly justified by other models or by other more direct statements in scripture, and this does not seem to be so.

The fundamental difficulty with Warfield's approach thus lies in his "therefore." To apply the model of inspiration to narrative involves stretching the inspiration model, and this is justified by scripture itself. But to infer that inspired narrative must be inerrant involves a second stretching of the model, one *not* justified by scripture. The description of scripture as inspired was not designed to make a statement regarding its accuracy. Scripture itself does not make a special connection in either direction between inspiration and factual or propositional truth. To say that something is true does not imply that it is inspired, and to say that something is inspired is not a way of guaranteeing that it is true: The point of the affirmation lies elsewhere. Warfield's whole approach involved questionable inferences regarding the significance of inspiration. The development of the doctrine of inspiration in relation to new questions cannot be faulted in principle, and in seeking to safeguard the factual truth of scripture Warfield was concerned about a matter of importance. But by handling this issue by linking scripture's accuracy with its inspiration he lost sight of the significance scripture itself attaches to inspiration. Warfield's stress on inerrancy removes the emphasis from the heart of the matter, inspiration itself, to an emphasis on something that is a possible corollary but not the thing itself.[64]

The prophets did believe that they spoke God's words and may have believed themselves inerrant. There is force to the deductive argument from *dictation* to inerrancy.[65] What God says is without error, so if God dictated scripture, then scripture is without error. But the claim that inspiration

---

64. Collins, *Introduction to the New Testament* 343.
65. Abraham, *The Divine Inspiration of Holy Scripture* 32-33.

implies inerrancy rests on the prior identification of inspiration with dictation, which inerrantists do not maintain. The focus of the debate on inerrancy is the narrative parts of scripture, and these parts make no claim to be dictated by God. They are inspired but not dictated, and therefore their inspiration is not an argument for their being inerrant.

In principle, then, the affirmation of scripture's inerrancy labors under difficulties. It also has some practical disadvantages that are the reverse of the advantages its advocates claim for it.

First, it cannot safeguard the historical factuality of the gospel in the absence of associated interpretative principles to establish at what point narratives are making historical claims. Some conservative or evangelical writers have concerned inerrantists by accepting that there are midrashic, nonhistorical elements in the stories of Jesus' birth and infancy in Matthew 1–2, that is, that the stories in part result from meditation on the prophecies that they quote rather than indicating that the events they narrate actually happened.[66] Perhaps less controversially, at least one of the Second Testament accounts of Judas's death, commented on in chapter 5 above, has been seen as the result of meditation on scripture of this kind and thus as a true but not factual account of Judas's end.

It is possible to describe parts of the Second Testament as midrashic and nonhistorical without denying their inerrancy. "Infallibility and inerrancy . . . are not hermeneutical concepts, and carry no implications as to the character or range of biblical teaching."[67] The Chicago Statement on Biblical Inerrancy explicitly affirms that scripture's inerrancy extends to statements on matters such as science, history, and authorship, but it goes on to qualify that assertion by allowing that scripture can be imprecise, phenomenological, hyperbolic, and topical rather than chronological in arrangement, and it makes that qualification without offering any criteria for determining when straightforward factual statements are being made. It thus seems to remove the possibility of safeguarding the assertion about facts in scripture that it wishes to safeguard. What is needed to this end is not a principle of inerrancy but some principles of interpretation; but these, too, are more slippery than inerrantists often acknowledge, and it may be

66. See Winter, *But This I Can Believe,* especially 61-63; more systematically Gundry, *Matthew.* The pamphlet by Schaeffer mentioned in n. 58 above is a response to Winter.

67. Packer, *"Fundamentalism" and the Word of God* 98. I am not clear how Packer can, in the light of this statement, state elsewhere that "the confession of inerrancy . . . does make a full and faithful articulation of biblical Christianity possible *in principle*," as quoted later in this section.

that the only way of safeguarding the factuality of events such as the virgin birth and bodily resurrection of Jesus is to require commitment to some such specific interpretative conclusions, as the creeds do. To say scripture is inerrant is not to say how far it is historically factual.

Second, a commitment to inerrancy cannot safeguard objectivity in interpretation.[68] Inerrantists of impeccable pedigree disagree on how far a crucially important passage such as Genesis 3 is to be understood as literal history,[69] on the degree to which the Gospels tell us Jesus' actual words,[70] on whether the literary device of placing one's words in the mouth of someone else occurs in scripture,[71] and on the nature of scripture's teaching on subjects such as election, baptism, and eschatology.

Third, the stress on inerrancy does not contribute to taking the text of scripture itself with great seriousness. It tends to divert energy from the task of interpreting scripture to a preoccupation with harmonization, which hinders rather than helps an understanding of particular texts. Packer argues that it "does make a full and faithful articulation of biblical Christianity possible in principle";[72] the inerrancy of scripture is the only principle for interpretation that keeps us facing all the problematic places of scripture. But the same result could surely issue from believing in the inspiration of scripture, and the history of biblical interpretation suggests that abandonment of a doctrine of inerrancy has often enabled interpreters to come to a more satisfactory understanding of a passage. In contrast, believing in inerrancy has often led interpreters into strange harmonistic exegesis. H. Lindsell in his book *The Battle for the Bible* offers excellent examples, such as the suggestion, which we noted already in chapter 4, that Peter must have denied Jesus six times in order for the Gospel accounts to be harmonized.[73] Such efforts at harmonization are not the accidental result of a sound approach but the inevitable result of an unsound approach.

68. Against Jones, *The Bible Under Attack* 27-30.

69. Contrast Packer, *"Fundamentalism" and the Word of God* 98; Kidner, *Genesis* 66; with Young, *Genesis 3* 7-8.

70. For Jones, "to uphold inerrancy does not demand that we regard the Gospels as presenting verbatim accounts of what the Lord actually said" (*The Bible Under Attack* 26); other inerrantists insist that we do have Jesus' actual words, so that Synoptic variants must reflect Jesus speaking in slightly different ways on different occasions.

71. See Boer's illustration from E. J. Young, *Above the Battle?* 48-49.

72. "Encountering Present-Day Views of Scripture," *The Foundation of Biblical Authority* (ed. Boice) 78.

73. *The Battle for the Bible* 174-76. On classic attempts at harmonization of the Gospels, see Childs, *The New Testament as Canon* 145-47.

They are not evidence that the interpreter has faced the text of scripture, problems and all, with the seriousness that it deserves as the word of God.

Fourth, a commitment to inerrancy fails to bolster the status of scripture as the truth. There are, after all, many inerrant statements outside scripture; the present sentence is one, as is the Nicene Creed.[74] If scripture is inerrant, it only parallels many other writings that are not the inspired word of God. If our stress on scripture as the inspired word of God takes up the implications of inspiration drawn within scripture itself, such as its effectiveness and meaningfulness, we are more likely to bolster that status.

Fifth, a stress on inerrancy cannot safeguard people from a slippery slope that carries them from abandoning inerrancy to an eventual reneging on all other Christian doctrines. Indeed, it more likely impels them toward such a slope. The claim that scripture is factually inerrant sets up misleading expectations regarding the precision of narratives and then requires such far-fetched defenses, such as those of Lindsell just noted, that it presses people toward rejecting it. The associated claim that stressing inerrancy is the only way to take the authority and inspiration of scripture seriously then presses people toward the conclusion that therefore they cannot maintain these convictions at all.

Sixth, it is easy to make the confession of inerrancy a banner under which one stands, and for it nevertheless (or consequently) to become a replacement for serious interaction with scripture rather than an indication of thinking and living by scripture. "Thousands . . . kiss the book's outside, who ne'er look within."[75] Further thousands may read it devotedly but not let it be the means of making their thoughts captive to Christ in practice.[76] The people of God need to be encouraged and helped to take the whole of scripture seriously, but they are more likely to make that commitment by being helped to hear scripture speak and to meet Christ through scripture than through being provided with solutions of ever-decreasing plausibility to an ever-increasing range of problems of ever-increasing triviality.

---

74. Cf. Burtchaell, *Catholic Theories of Biblical Inspiration* 52.

75. W. Cowper, *Expostulation* 1:386 (see *The Complete Poetical Works of William Cowper* [Edinburgh: Gill and Inglis, 1853]); McDonald, *I Want to Know What the Bible Says About the Bible* 144.

76. Berkouwer, *Holy Scripture* 34-35. Cf. Barr's comments on the way scripture can function as a religious symbol, noted in the discussion of Matt 4:1-11 in chapter 7 above.

The God-Givenness of a Broadly Accurate Text

The wide range of difficulties involved in the doctrine of inerrancy makes us consider resolving the ambiguity present in writers from the Fathers to the nineteenth century in a direction opposite to that taken by Warfield. Bauckham's paper "The Limits of Inerrancy" could be seen as such a resolution. He notes that it is possible for a scriptural author explicitly to speak with approximation or uncertainty or in a way that is subject to minor correction; Paul does so in 1 Corinthians 1:14-16, where he first declares that he baptized only Crispus and Gaius, then apparently recalls that he also baptized Stephanas's family, then finally safeguards his position by granting that he cannot remember whether he baptized anyone else. Any inspiration and inerrancy that we can appropriately attribute to Paul is apparently compatible with uncertainty or with the possibility of minor inaccuracy regarding what actually happened, features that inevitably derive from his working on the basis of human knowledge with its gaps, which the Holy Spirit does not choose to fill as part of inspiring Paul's work. As far as Paul's argument is concerned, if it turned out that he baptized scores of people, his argument would fall, but if his recollection is only slightly at fault, the argument is not affected.

In this passage Paul has cause to make it explicit that he may be subject to correction. That is actually built into any human writing undertaken on the basis of recollection. Bauckham's point is that this implicitly applies to all human writing, including specifically historiography. It is the nature of historiography to allow for the possibility of some error in what is stated; it is written with an implicit qualification along the lines of "This is as accurate as my sources allow" or "This is a history written on the basis of the traditions available to me." It is of the nature of history that it is written in acknowledgment of the aphorism "Ten percent of what I say is wrong; the trouble is, I do not know which ten percent." The presence of that degree of error does not make the historian's work cease to be valid historiography. The aphorism is not printed at the head of a historical work, but it is implicit, and this may be so in scripture as elsewhere. Some judgments in scripture likewise have the implicit character of firm assertions, others that of judgments of probability or personal opinion; to trace God's activity behind their formulation does not change their nature as judgments of probability or personal opinion.

While scripture sometimes aims at precision (perhaps so in John 21:11), it is commonly satisfied with approximation, with the accuracy of a portrait rather than that of a photograph. The former, after all, may convey the truth more accurately than the latter by underplaying some features of its subject and exaggerating others. If there are particular unhistorical elements in a fundamentally historiographic book such as Luke's Gospel, the appropriate response is not to feel that one has to seek to vindicate Luke's historicity at these points lest belief in its inspiration be imperilled. Nor is it to assume that at these points Luke was aware that he was writing legend rather than fact. Luke was seeking to write history, in an ancient form. But history is always subject to the "ten percent" rule, always involves reliance on sources, and in its ancient form involves passing them on less critically than is the case with historiography as we practice it today.

F. A. Schaeffer declares that if Paul is wrong in his apparently factual statement that Eve came from Adam (1 Cor 11:8), then "there is no reason to have certainty in the authority of any New Testament factual statement, including the factual statement that Christ rose physically from the dead."[77] This seems not to follow. To find that at certain points a historian is mistaken in no way discredits the historian's work as a whole or suggests that it is unreliable as a whole. We do not take that approach with Thucydides or Plutarch or with any modern witness to some event. It is only when we have made up our minds in advance that the history must be inerrant that the discovery of one mistake in it imperils its authority[78] or raises questions about its inspiration that have a false starting point in the assumption that inspiration suggests a claim about accuracy when in fact it suggests a claim about effectiveness and meaningfulness. As Matthew Henry saw, divine inspiration does not change the way a narrator works.

One does not have to be under the influence of existentialism to infer from a comparison of Genesis 1 with creation stories of some other peoples that inspiration did not provide the scriptural author with extra information about history, cosmology, or science.[79] The occasions when the scriptures consciously speak approximately or profess ignorance (e.g., Luke 9:28; John 6:19; Acts 4:4; 2 Cor 12:2; Rom 15:24) indicate that inspiration did not make up for lack of ordinary human knowledge. As S. T. Coleridge remarks, there is no reason to believe that the biblical writers "were divinely informed as well as inspired."[80]

---

77. *No Final Conflict* 33-34.

78. A. T. Hanson and R. P. C. Hanson, *The Bible without Illusions* 42.

79. Against Geisler, *Biblical Errancy* 234; he is criticizing Berkouwer, *Holy Scripture,* e.g., 178.

80. *Confessions* 27 (Letter 2).

The nature of biblical narrative indicates that God is content to speak through narratives that express the historical understanding of the writers' day. It indicates that God could inspire the biblical writers and use them to utter words to put a purpose into effect and to speak meaningfully far beyond the speaker's own day, without providing them with the extra information that would be needed if their words were to be inerrant. God did not choose to reveal a more adequate history to them, but spoke through the kind of historiography that they would write. It is *that* which is the inspired word of God. It is that which emerges from a real acting of God in history and through real historical human beings. The "faults" in that history witness to the gracious condescension of God in working through us as we are and using the human word as it is, notwithstanding any factual errors, as was noted in Vatican II's debate on revelation.[81] Errors in scriptural narrative are not present because of God's oversight; God knew they were there but was prepared to work through them. This may be a peculiar, even objectionable, way for God to act; to judge from the actual evidence of scripture, it is the way God has acted.

We may draw a comparison with Jesus' comment on the Mosaic divorce regulation. He sees certain biblical laws as given by Moses as a consequence of human hardness of heart (Mark 10:5). We may view such laws as divinely inspired, but nevertheless they are not statements of what God would ideally want to say. Similarly, divine inspiration does not change the nature of narrative written by humans, which as such is subject to the ten percent rule. It is not the nature of divine inspiration to alter that; divine inspiration is concerned with effectiveness and meaningfulness, and factual error need not hinder effectiveness and meaningfulness. It may even help it in some ways by drawing attention to the genuine and "unfixed" nature of the human testimony that the narrative offers. Given the erraticism of much that the Holy Spirit inspires according to scripture, it is certainly not difficult to imagine the Holy Spirit inspiring writings with factual errors in them![82] We must hold back from inferring too surely what God may have been prepared to accept in the course of inspiring scripture, given the preparedness for self-denial that God has shown for the sake of our salvation, given that God is One whose thoughts are not our thoughts, and given that omnipotence is not something God needs to worry about.[83]

---

81. See "The Council Debate on Revelation," *Herder Correspondence* 2 (1965) 20-22; cf. Burtchaell, *Catholic Theories of Biblical Inspiration* 268.

82. Reid, *The Authority of Scripture* 165.

83. Brown, *The Critical Meaning of the Bible* 17-18.

The God who inspires scripture does not lie or repent, in the manner of a human being. God's words are always matched by deeds (Num 23:19; cf. 1 Sam 15:29). Unlike lying human words, God's words are flawless and stand forever (Pss 12:6; 18:30; 119:89; Prov 30:5-6). It has been suggested that this excludes error from inspired scripture.[84] We may note first that the focus in all these passages is on God or human beings making reliable statements about the future, not about the past. Second, other related passages of scripture affirm that God does repent (e.g., 1 Sam 15:11[85]), though not that God lies, so that the question of the link between God's word and deed is more complex than these passages indicate. While always acting consistently and with reason, God can have a change of mind in response to human deeds. Third, it may be questioned whether working with the ten percent rule that is built into narrative counts as lying in the context of inspired prophecy. Fourth, we may note that Acts strongly implies that Stephen spoke as a man full of the Spirit at his trial (see 6:5, 10, 15; 7:55), but he did not speak inerrantly.

To describe scriptural narrative as the word of God is not directly to attribute to it a particular historical accuracy. It may be that it is marvelously accurate, but this is not implicit in the mere fact that it is God's word. For scripture to be adequately factual but not inerrantly factual is not at all puzzling or worrying.[86]

The implicit claim of biblical narrative is to be reasonably accurate, not inerrant, and accepting it in its own terms and on its own evaluation involves accepting it as such and not as purporting to be quite free of error. In a rationalist, historicist age it is easy to infer that material that is not factually historical cannot be taken seriously. When people come to acknowledge that there is such material in scripture it easy for them to lose their trust in scripture as God's word, to lose the warmth of their attachment to it as a gracious gift of God, and to abandon their openness to hearing it speak. But there is no need for all this to follow. Material that is unhistorical is not uninspired. The whole text is God's inspired word. If certain points in Luke are unhistorical, those parts of this inspired Gospel also contribute to an inspired portrait of Jesus that can be effective and mean-

84. So W. A. Grudem, "Scripture's Self-Attestation," *Scripture and Truth* (ed. Carson and Woodbridge) 28-35, though many of his references have little relevance to the question of historical reliability.

85. NIV translates the same verb (*naḥām* niphal) differently here.

86. Against R. A. Finlayson, "Contemporary Ideas of Inspiration," *Revelation and the Bible* (ed. Henry) 226.

ingful for its hearers. We do not dismiss them because they are unhistorical but let them continue to function effectively and meaningfully to render Jesus for us. Writers such as Origen were right in saying that we pay attention to the whole, not merely those parts that we believe to be factual. Each detail, whether historically factual or not, contributes to the true picture that the narrative sets before us and deserves our attention. The whole narrative, including any nonfactual elements, as it is and not as we might expect it to be, is God's inspired word, and as such does its work and speaks to us.

• PART IV •

SCRIPTURE AS EXPERIENCED REVELATION

• 20 •

Revelation in Theology
and in Scripture

Scripture is the product of divine revelation, human experience, and human reflection. These three ways of looking at scripture do not form as simple a model as those examined earlier. They form a triptych or a trio of overlapping circles like those in a Venn diagram.

Revelation is the most familiar of these terms in discussion of a doctrine of scripture. Within scripture revelation commonly links with human experience: It may follow involvement in prayer or a period when experience of God and of grace seems to have been denied, or it may lead to the experience of enthusiastic worship such as that in the Revelation to John.[1] Revelation may sound like the most supernaturally absolute of the models for scripture, but even divine revelation comes through human experience. Therefore, its supernatural content and truth are apprehended only by one who pays attention to its human character. The links between revelation and human reflection are illustrated by Paul. When he thinks through questions theologically, he utilizes insights that he attributes to direct revelation. In general, indeed, theology's task is to reflect on revelation.[2] Experience and reflection in turn have links of their own: The wisdom books are the fruit of interaction between experience and reflection.

---

1. Craddock, "Preaching the Book of Revelation" 278; cf. Brueggemann, *Finally Comes the Poet* 152-53.
2. Brunner, *Revelation and Reason* 3.

Revelation as a Theological Theme
and as a Scriptural Theme

While revelation has a long history as a theological category, it came to prominence when it was set over against reason.[3] During the medieval period reason and revelation were categories used within the context of orthodox belief. Both denoted aspects of the propositional content of the faith, distinguished uncontroversially from each other as natural revelation and special revelation.[4] The eighteenth century set reason and revelation over against each other, and the controversy with Deism required orthodoxy to make a distinctive affirmation of revelation over against a stress on reason that involved surrendering key Christian truths that could not be based merely on reason. At the same time theologians were concerned to protect the reasonableness of that affirmation of revelation, and it was this in part that led to the understanding of revelation as personal rather than propositional and as in some sense mediated through history.

Like reason, experience can be set in antithesis to revelation. David Hume especially pressed the view that truth must be derived from what can be empirically verified, a view that Friedrich Schleiermacher modified in substance if not in form by including human religious experience within the realm of the empirical.[5]

The notion of revelation has in fact thus been used in theology in a bewildering variety of ways.[6] It is not a concept of univocal meaning, and discussion of it is confused and confusing. As we noted in chapter 1, revelation is actually itself a model, which as such has been open to use in varying connections. It is a term that long had value-status in theology, and Christians who believed that *scripture* was of key significance to Christian faith naturally therefore wanted to affirm that scripture was the locus of God's special revelation. Irenaeus was the first writer to apply the term "revelation" to scripture as a whole.[7] More recently, "a sense of revelation-weariness has settled over theology."[8]

---

3. D. A. Pailin's "Reason in Relation to Scripture and Tradition," in *Scripture, Tradition and Reason* (ed. Bauckham and Drewery) 207-38, offers a nuanced account of the history of this relationship.

4. Cf. Latourelle, *Theology of Revelation* 155; Persson, *Sacra Doctrina* 19.

5. Henry, *God, Revelation and Authority* 1:80.

6. Cf. Dulles, *Models of Revelation.*

7. *Against Heresies* I.3.6

8. Thiemann, *Revelation and Theology* 1; cf. Brett, *Biblical Criticism in Crisis?* 161.

How, then, does scripture itself refer to revelation? In everyday contexts it does so in connection with human beings revealing secret facts (1 Sam 20:2, 12, 13; Prov 20:19) and with the public proclamation of an official edict (Esth 3:14; 8:13). It also speaks of people coming out of hiding or darkness and thus revealing themselves (1 Sam 14:8, 11; Isa 49:9) and of the uncovering of things that should and normally do remain hidden (Lev 18; 2 Sam 6:20; Luke 2:35). This can include human wickedness (Ezek 21:24; Hos 7:1).

These everyday connotations of revelation language carry over into religious use of that language. Scripture speaks of God revealing facts or promises about the future (1 Sam 9:15; 2 Sam 7:27; 1 Chr 17:25; Amos 3:7; Luke 2:26). It speaks of secrets that belong to God and of other things that are revealed to Israel for the sake of their obedience (Deut 29:29). It speaks of theological secrets that *are* revealed, notably regarding God's purpose for the Gentiles (Rom 16:25; Eph 3:3, 5). It speaks of the known but invisible God being revealed person-to-person (Gen 35:7; 1 Sam 2:27; cf. John 21:1; Gal 1:16) and making evident in earthly history the wrathful power and saving justice of God (Isa 53:1; Ps 98:2; Luke 2:32; Rom 1:17, 18; Rev 15:4). It also speaks of God revealing Jesus, apparently in the sense of causing the penny to drop about his significance (Matt 11:25; 16:17). With similar meaning it refers to the revealing of the gospel message (1 Cor 2:10) and of aspects of Christian truth not currently grasped by people (Phil 3:15).

God's revelation comes through the working of the human mind and spirit (John 1:4, 9), through the natural world (Rom 1:19-20), through the processes of human experience (Rom 1:18), through events of human history and of Israel's history in particular (Ps 98:2), through theophanic appearances (1 Kgs 3:5), through the declaration of God's name(s) in Israel's midst (Exod 6:2-3), through words spoken to people such as prophets (1 Sam 3:7; Amos 3:7), through commands that express God's will (Deut 29:29), through traditions that preserve memories of Israel's experiences (Mic 6:5), through the declaration of such experiences in the world (Isa 12:4-5), through the person and life of Jesus (John 1:14), through the gospel message about him (Rom 1:17), through scripture and the light it throws on him (Rom 11:25; 16:25-26), through specific messages given to the church (1 Cor 14:6, 26, 30), and through the End, which will finally clarify all that can be clarified (1 Pet 1:5, 7, 13).

Compared with and in relation to this final revelation, all intermediate revelations — such as the private appearances of the risen Jesus, which contrast with his public crucifixion — are but anticipatory prereflections.[9] Revelations that scripture gives concerning the End do not make it less of a mystery, calculable and therefore manageable; "revelation is not the bringing of what was once unknown into the region of what is known, perspicuous and manageable: it is the dawn and approach of the mystery as such."[10] Indeed, all our knowledge is a matter of stumbling discovery rather than certain omniscience. It is at the End that we will know as we are known. Enlightenment is not possession in the present but the promise of the End. We live with the promise of knowledge — and therefore we grope confidently forward.[11]

In Jesus Christ and in the gospel the justice of God is revealed, making salvation available to both Jews and Greeks on the basis of faith in Christ (Rom 1:16-17). Here God's secret purpose to bring about the world's obedience is revealed (16:25-26). In a sense, then, the profound human desire for closure, for answers, for revelation, has been met — a consolation that the Hebrew Bible refuses.[12] Yet this, too, turns out to be an anticipation of a final revelation that still remains future. Even Mark, if it does not move from clarity towards mystery, at best moves between revelation and mystery and "forestalls closure."[13] The cross is the climax of revelation but also of incomprehension, and the resurrection does not resolve the tension between revelation and incomprehension.[14] God's supreme act of unveiling leaves the divine glory veiled in flesh in the form of a servant; it is seen only with the eyes of faith.[15] Even the person of Jesus is not a self-evident revelation. It takes a revelation from God to recognize even the significance of Jesus (Matt 16:17; cf. 11:25-27; Eph 1:17).

The passages mentioned above include some that use not the actual words "revelation" and "reveal" but associated terms such as "secret," "manifest," and "show."[16] In theological study it has been common to

---

9. Moltmann, *The Trinity and the Kingdom of God* 84-85.

10. Rahner, "The Hermeneutics of Eschatological Assertions" 330.

11. Gunton, *Enlightenment and Alienation* 50-51, 150.

12. Josipovici, *The Book of God* 89.

13. W. H. Kelber, "Narrative and Disclosure," in *Genre, Narrativity, and Theology* (ed. Gerhart and Williams) 3; see also other essays in the same volume; T. F. Berg, "Reading in/to Mark," in *Reader Perspectives on the New Testament* (ed. McKnight) 200-201; and Kermode, *Genesis of Secrecy*.

14. Marcus, "Mark 4:10-12 and Marcan Epistemology."

15. Richardson, "Gnosis and Revelation in the Bible" 32.

16. E.g., as well as Hebrew *gālâ* and Greek *apokalyptō/apokalypsis,* Hebrew *rā'â* and *sôḏ* and Greek *phaneroō* and *mystērion.* See also Schillebeeckx's study of the use of *charis* with the meaning "revelatory grace" (*Christ* 117-19).

extend the presumed semantic field of "revelation" farther so as to include all divine-human communication, including — for instance — any occasion when Yahweh speaks to a prophet. There can indeed be a close relationship between revelation of person and revelation in words: Yahweh reveals himself by speaking words (1 Sam 3:21; Isa 22:14). Further, in the common perception the essence of prophecy itself is often assumed to be the knowledge of things that could not be known by normal means.[17]

Léon Morris thus derides Gerald Downing for concentrating his study of revelation on the narrower field of terms, though such a procedure avoids the risk of diluting the specific and distinctive connotation of revelation as the unveiling of a secret.[18] It is ironic that Morris accuses Downing of imposing his own categories on the text when it is Downing who focuses his study of revelation on the text's actual references to revelation. As with other models for scripture, we will need in due course to stretch the model of revelation, but it will be more illuminating to consider its narrow sense initially.

Wolfhart Pannenberg and his associates treat the biblical data on revelation as insignificant because the Bible does not use the terms in question in keeping with their definition of revelation as "the complete self-disclosure of God."[19] One might have expected this to make a study of the theological significance of the biblical data the more compelling; again it is ironic that Ulrich Wilckens, a member of this group, accuses Rudolf Bultmann of "a total neglect of the terminological data," while Pannenberg elsewhere offers a parallel though gentler criticism of James Barr.[20]

Downing suggests that "befriending" is a better model for the activity of divine self-manifestation for which theologians such as Brunner use the term "revelation."[21] "Befriending" clearly refers to a personal event that involves both words and acts without being confined to them, it avoids implying an as yet unrealized face-to-face clarity about God's self-manifestation, and it sheds much of the confusing historical freight of the word "revelation."

In scripture as in theology the language of revelation is thus used in a

17. Barton, *Oracles of God* 128-31.

18. See Morris, *I Believe in Revelation* 20-22; Downing, *Has Christianity a Revelation?*

19. *Revelation as History,* e.g., 8, 9, 27, 57.

20. Wilckens, in *Revelation as History* (ed. Pannenberg) 115; W. Pannenberg, "Revelation in Early Christianity," in *Christian Authority* (ed. Evans) 76, 79-80.

21. See his review of Dulles's *Models of Revelation* in *Theology* 87 (1984) 295-97.

variety of ways, but it is much less prominent in scripture than in the theological usage of the medieval and modern periods, and of course does not have the concerns that emerged during these times, which are largely foreign to the situation of the scriptural writers. It is misleading to try to relate such concerns directly to that situation.

Barr notes that in the First Testament and other Jewish writings actual revelation language, while rarely used with regard to historical events or prophecy, is used quite frequently in the apocalypses, not to refer to the revealing of God but to refer to the revealing of mysteries.[22] This puts us on the track of the appropriate specific starting point for relating the Bible and revelation. If we ask what sense it makes to use the term "revelation" of written documents, the natural place to start is with *the* revelatory books in scripture. Those books are Daniel, the part of scripture in which revelation language is most prominent (especially 2:19, 22, 28, 29, 30, 47), and the Revelation to John, which opens by describing itself in terms of the revelation that John saw and the voice that he heard (1:1-2, 10-12).

Revelation in the Apocalypses

The Jewish and Christian apocalypses in general have often been seen as predominantly focused on revelations concerning the future, but their interests are much broader. They concern any matters about which human beings could have no knowledge except by divine disclosure. They thus unveil things above and below, things in front and behind (cf. Mishnah Hagigah 2:1).[23] They speak, that is, of heaven and hell — and of enigmatic aspects of earthly life here "below." They also speak of future and past — or rather of past and future: Hebrew actually and logically speaks of the past as what lies in front of us so that we can see it and of the future as what lies behind us so that we cannot see it; it understands life as like rowing a boat, with our eyes on where we have been and our back to the invisible future.[24]

It is instructive to consider the biblical apocalypses against this grid, and Daniel 10–12 provides a convenient focus for this.[25] (a) Daniel 10 is particularly concerned with the realm above and with an experience of

22. *Old and New in Interpretation* 88-90.
23. Cf. Rowland, *The Open Heaven* 75.
24. Schofield, *Introducing Old Testament Theology* 26-27.
25. For what follows, see Goldingay, *Daniel* 268-334.

contact between that realm and our world. In this respect it is comparable to the revelations referred to in 2 Corinthians 12, though the two are differently conceived in that Daniel 10 involves heaven coming to a human being while the experiences in 2 Corinthians 12 (like some apocalypses outside scripture) involve a person being taken into heaven. Daniel sees a human-like figure of supernatural splendor. The figure is dressed in linen, the clothing of a priest; as in Ezekiel 9–10 a servant of the heavenly temple appears in connection with the affairs of its earthly equivalent.

The specific purpose of this revelation is to introduce the revelation that follows in chapter 11, but in doing so chapter 10 gives Daniel insights into aspects of heavenly realities beyond the realities that directly affect him. These insights include allusive references to the leader of the Persian kingdom, with whom the speaker must fight, to the leader of the Greek kingdom, who will come in due course, and to Michael, one of the supreme leaders and the leader of Daniel's own people. Michael will later be described as one who stands by those who belong to Daniel's own people (12:1); he has a mutually supportive relationship with the figure who speaks to Daniel. As in other ancient Near Eastern writings and other parts of the First Testament, the revelation assumes that the results of battles on earth reflect the involvement of heaven, though it is not clear how far the supernatural leaders to which the revelation refers are in opposition to the will of the one God. What is clear is the assumption that there is a more-than-earthly dimension to earthly changes of empire and earthly conflicts.

This feature of Daniel 10 makes clear that its concern relates closely to that of the main body of the revelation that follows. The reason that events from Alexander to Antiochus unfold as they do, with their pattern of frustration and failure, is that behind earthly conflicts are the heavenly conflicts described in chapter 10. The significance of these heavenly conflicts in this connection is underlined by the reappearance in 12:5-8, after the revelation concerning things past and things to come, of two celestial figures, presumably the same ones who have already appeared in chapter 10 — though the passage is not explicit regarding their identity.[26]

A converse to this portrayal of earthly events as reflecting heavenly relationships is the portrayal of earthly acts as having implications in the heavenly realm. An assault on the temple in Jerusalem and its offerings is an attack on the heavenly temple and on the One to whom the offerings are made (11:36; see further 8:9-12).

26. See Hall, *Revealed Histories* 94.

(b) The main body of Daniel's revelation (11:2-39) alludes to the reality of the world above, but its main concern lies elsewhere. If we may say that Daniel 10–12 draws attention to worlds above and below and to future and past, in chapter 11 the greatest attention is given to the world of the past, to events that led up to the second-century crisis in Jerusalem, to which Daniel 10–12 as a whole speaks. This in itself raises questions about the assumption of much modern study that the apocalypses offer pseudo-revelations about the past only in order to validate their revelations concerning the future.[27] Their revelations about the past have inherent theological and parenetic significance of their own.

"Revealed history" was a common genre in the Mediterranean and Near Eastern worlds.[28] In connection with the distant past, even the bare facts can only be gained by revelation, as is the case with revelation concerning the future or the realms above and below. In connection with events of the more recent past, the facts may be accessible, but the presupposition of revealed history is that their meaning may not be transparent. Furthermore, if anything, God's involvement in history increases the mystery of that meaning. Unaided human intellect cannot grasp history's significance. One who reckons to understand the past implies a claim to God-given insight into the matter. This assumption may underlie one understanding of the description of the narrative from Joshua to Kings as "the Former Prophets": It was written on the basis of insights derived from the prophets' interpretation of events.[29]

Among the material from the Mediterranean and Near Eastern world that purports to offer revelation regarding history, some examples do so anonymously, others in the name of their actual authors, and others attribute their revelations to persons who lived long before their actual authors' day. The Book of Daniel takes up this last convention. Traditionally its revelations have been understood to derive from the sixth-century Mesopotamia in which Daniel's own story is set, but author and readers would have been familiar with other "prophecies" from the ancient world that derived from later than the period that they "predicted" and actually offered quasi-predictions of events from before the author's and recipients' day; toward the end these prophecies then go on to speak of the actual future. The revelations in Daniel parallel these. I assume that the actual

---

27. Cf. Davies, "Apocalyptic and Historiography" 21.
28. Hall, *Revealed Histories* 12-13.
29. Hall, *Revealed Histories* 22, following the work of J. Neusner.

authors and first recipients of Daniel 10–12 themselves lived in the midst of the crisis in second-century Jerusalem, to which the book brings God's message. On any hypothesis regarding the origin of the vision, however, the revelatory aspect to Daniel's insight into history lay chiefly in its insight into the significance of the events it narrates, rather than in the mere factuality of these events.

Chapter 11 gains and expresses its insight into history by looking at events in the light of scripture. The Qumran scrolls "conceive of new revelation as received by the Teacher of Righteousness and a leading council of priests through a process of exegesis."[30] In its theological method, too, Daniel thus shares its approach with other believing Jewish communities of its day. The revelation uses scriptures that emerged from earlier periods in the people's history to cast light on the crisis of its own day. In our terms, the events that came to a climax in the time of Antiochus are perhaps being understood typologically as a recapitulation of those crises in earlier centuries, so that the earlier Assyrian enemy from the north stands for the Syrians and Sargon for Antiochus. Alternatively they are perhaps understood as the fulfillment of prophecies from passages such as Numbers 24, Isaiah 8 and 10, Ezekiel 7, and Habakkuk 2. As in Matthew 1–2, the author perhaps has no particular theory regarding the hermeneutical link between scripture and the events of recent decades; the key fact is that the former is open to being used to cast light on the latter.

By providing the means for interpreting events, use of scripture in this way also suggests the conviction that the puzzling, painful, and in due course horrifying events of the present crisis are within the parameters of God's sovereignty over Israel's history. In the Babylonian period, the books of Joshua to Kings had expounded a theology of history according to which loyalty and disloyalty to the Torah generally receive their reward. This had been taken to its logical conclusion in the Persian period in the renewed historical survey in Chronicles. But this seemed to offer little illumination on the Greek period, and the revelation in Daniel 10–12 seeks to fill this vacuum.

The conviction that the puzzling events of the Greek period are within the parameters of God's sovereignty is further underlined by the use of phrases such as "at the set time" (11:29) and by the revelation's quasi-predictive form. According to the portrayal of matters in Daniel 11, during the exile a heavenly being unveiled events to take place over the coming

30. Bockmuehl, *Revelation and Mystery in Ancient Judaism* 56.

four centuries, up to the End, from the contents of "a reliable book" (10:21). To say that history was prewritten was to affirm that it was under control, so much so that it could be pictured as predetermined. If the revelation is a quasi-prediction, that is only a picture. It was after the events of that history had happened that the history in 11:2-39 was declared to have been prewritten. Events were described as inevitable (e.g., 11:36) only when they had become inevitable by virtue of having taken place. The quasi-predictive form, which declares that what is actually past history was prewritten, makes the point that God is in control even of the inexplicabilities of history, including the successes of the godless and the sufferings of the faithful, and even at moments when evil is asserting itself in a particularly oppressive way. Given the difficulty of viewing history as it actually unfolds as the direct will of God, the revelation declares that it is in some sense foreknown by God and in some sense willed by God. History is part of a pattern and a purpose rather than being random and meaningless.

(c) With Daniel 11:36-39 we reach the end of the material in the revelation that can be correlated with historical events of the period up to the 160s B.C. Daniel 11:40–12:13 looks forward to the actual future from the perspective of the Antiochene era. Here the vision's utilization of scriptural phraseology becomes more systematic. As in the earlier part of the chapter it reflects not some "second-sight" foreseeing of mere historical facts, but the revelatory potential of scripture itself. The quasi-prediction in 11:2-39 has shown that one can make sense of the known but senseless past by relating it in the light of scripture. When the revelation regarding the future in 11:40–12:13 portrays the actually unknown future in the light of the same scripture, that gives grounds for believing in its portrait — not in the sense that scripture gives grounds for believing that the mere facts are accurate, but that it gives grounds for believing in this vision of how things will turn out. When the revelation speaks of the past, it does so on the basis of having historical data, and of having the scriptural text as a means of interpreting them. When it speaks of the future, it has only the scriptural text, and it is providing an illustrative, possible embodiment of that text, which is not to be pressed to provide historical data but to provide a scriptural revelation of what the events to come will *mean.*

At the point where the revelation reads really future events out of God's book, those events are ones associated with the End, with the final defeat of evil and the final establishment of God's rule in the world, which is part of the purpose for history that God is determined to achieve. There is indeed a fixed inevitability about history, in that human beings cannot frustrate

God's ultimate purpose. In that sense they cannot alter what is determined by God's will. Drawing a possible scenario provides a way of imagining the End. Its reliability — as an imaginary scenario, not as a forecast of how things must literally be — is supported by the fact that it is drawn in the light of scripture. As the Assyrians fell, so will the Seleucids. As the desecration of the First Temple was reversed, so will the desecration of the Second Temple. The affliction of Israel will give way to triumph as the affliction of Yahweh's servant in Isaiah 53 did. Antiochus is portrayed in the light of prophecy's depiction of Nebuchadnezzar's final defeat of Egypt: All he does is precipitate prophecy's last great battle, in which he must fall. That the revelation is expressed in words and images from earlier scriptures points up its significance as relating to the End. This aspect inherent in the earlier scriptures is taken up in 1 Peter 1:10-12: It had been revealed to the prophets that their words concerned things that would remain hidden until Christ came.

The scriptures in the light of which the future is imagined are scriptures that have already proved true in Israel's experience. Israel's picture of the future "must always be read as an assertion based on the revealed present and pointing towards the genuine future, not as an assertion pointing back from an anticipated future into the present."[31] The revelation's predictions are not mere anticipatory pronouncements of fixed future events. Like the promises and warnings of the prophets they offer an imaginarary scenario regarding the kind of issue that must come from present events. They do not correspond to the actual events that brought the downfall of Antiochus, but it is not the nature of biblical prophecy to reveal the literal nature of events before they take place — as is illustrated by the fact that the Christ event does not correspond to passages such as Isaiah 9:1-7. It is also because these are "imaginative portrayals" that they cannot be harmonized with each other in their imagery, though this does not imply that the content of their actual assertions cannot be seen as part of a consistent picture.[32]

To infer that the visions are designed to encourage rather than to convey information[33] is to put the point too sharply. Imaginary portrayals of the future, like the imaginary portrayals of the past we have considered in Part I, offer a parabolic account of events. There can be arguments over which

31. Rahner, "The Hermeneutics of Eschatological Assertions" 337.

32. *Ibid.* 335-36.

33. Collins, "Inspiration or Illusion" 33, though he later notes that "fiction and truth are not mutually exclusive" (36).

events they "refer" to, and they can have the advantages and disadvantages of being rarely falsifiable and therefore rarely verifiable. But their account is not devoid of reference to actual events, even if we cannot tell from the "parable" what the events were or will be.

Antiochus attacks both the people of God and God. His fall likewise has a heavenly side as well as an earthly side (12:1). He is defeated because in heaven his representative is opposed (in court, as in Jude 9?) by Michael, the supreme leader. Michael establishes that his own people's names are written in the citizen list of the true Jerusalem, and his victory there means that Antiochus must lose on earth and that Michael's people must escape. Those martyrs who have already lost their place in the people of God will have it restored to them. Daniel's description of their vindication and of the shame of the apostate, the blasphemers, and the persecutors again comes from the scriptures, from Isaiah and the Psalms. The conviction that the righteous flourish and the wicked get their comeuppance, enshrined in the books from Joshua to Kings and in Chronicles, is reaffirmed: It will be shown true in the long run, "in the End." The longer pattern of history illustrates that conviction even when events in the short term seem to deny it.[34]

(d) Daniel 10–12 offers revelation concerning things above, things past, and things future. In speaking of these three realms it is also concerned with things below, with human experience in this world, particularly in its enigmatic aspects as these found expression in the afflictions of the Antiochene period. In describing things below, it also refers to the realm of death, but only allusively, noting simply that the dead sleep in a land of earth (12:2). Perhaps one is to infer that the answer to Yahweh's question of Job, "Have the gates of death been revealed to you, or have you seen the gates of deep darkness?" (Job 38:17), is still negative. The Bible is in no doubt that God controls Sheol, Gehenna, and the powers of Death and Hell, but it is reticent in describing them. In this respect it contrasts with apocalypses elsewhere, which apparently share the Christian instincts, which have had to build up a doctrine of the nature of hell and of the fall of Satan by remythologizing material such as Isaiah 14 and Ezekiel 31. The biblical revelation is much more restrained.

34. Hall, *Revealed Histories* 118.

21

Revelation: Personal, Propositional, Historical, and Reasonable

Theological study of revelation over recent centuries suggests a second grid against which we may read Daniel 10–12, asking how far revelation is personal, propositional, historical, and reasonable.

Personal Revelation?

Daniel 10 describes a person-to-person visionary experience that prepares the way for the message in chapters 11 and 12. A religious act of preparation on Daniel's part leads into this person-to-person revelation. Such religious observances are not a sufficient cause of someone receiving a revelation or even a necessary cause, to judge from other revelations in the book. But they are an actual precursor of this revelation, and as far as we can tell, there would have been no revelation if Daniel had not sought one in this way. Experience and revelation interact in a second way in that the receiving of the revelation is a highly charged emotional and physical experience for Daniel. It brings fear, trembling, enfeeblement, confusion, collapse, insensibility, turmoil, breathlessness, and convulsion.

Other quasi-predictions comparable to Daniel 10–12 suggest that this account of a revelatory experience is not a straightforward transcription of something that took place during the sixth century. The chapters derive from second-century Jerusalem. How "real," then, is the experience that they describe? The revelation might be a "literary vision," a composition that puts God's message into the literary form of a visionary experience but did not itself actually result from such an experience. If so, it still reflects the reality and nature of such experiences and the interaction between experience and revelation. But it does so indirectly rather than directly.

If these chapters reflect an actual visionary experience, the attribution of the revelation to Daniel may indicate a sense of identification with Daniel, whose own experiences were in some sense the inspiration for this revelation.[1] It may also, or alternatively, indicate a specification of the sense, reported by some visionaries, that their experiences somehow or in some sense happened to someone else: They were only watching.[2] The vision account also reflects the accounts in Isaiah 6, Ezekiel 1–3 and 9–10, and elsewhere. As already existing scripture provides the patterns by which history is interpreted, so it provides the patterns that help make revelatory experiences possible. It becomes "in the imaginations of the apocalyptic visionaries a door of perception in which the text could become a living reality as its details merged with parallel passages to form the distinctive visions of heaven now found in some of the apocalypses."[3] Jewish sources suggest that the pseudonymous apocalypses do reflect visionary or "mystical" experiences on the part of their authors; their links with earlier visions are means to such experiences rather than indications that these are purely literary visions.[4]

In Daniel 10 the author implicitly claims a similarity between his experience and those of Isaiah and Ezekiel, perhaps a re-seeing of their visions, which might suggest that his message could be accepted as theirs were. In Daniel 9 reflection on prophetic scripture and prayer concerning its meaning are the explicit background to the revelation, which coheres with the idea that reflection on material such as that in Daniel 2–7 was also background to the link between Daniel and a real revelatory experience on the part of the visionary in Daniel 10–12. At the same time the differences between the original and the new "text" and the impressionistic nature of the latter's dependence on the former also point to the reality of the vi-

---

1. Russell, *The Method and Message of Jewish Apocalyptic* 134-39; Russell links his discussion with views of Hebrew psychology that are now questioned, but it may not be inextricably dependent on such views.

2. Cf. Lindblom, *Prophecy in Ancient Israel* 43-44.

3. C. Rowland, "Apocalyptic Literature," in Carson and Williamson (ed.), *It Is Written* 173.

4. Gruenwald, *Apocalyptic and Merkavah Mysticism* 29-72.

sionary's personal experience, as does the emphasis on an experiential seeking of God in both Daniel 9 and 10.[5] Revelation is a person-to-person experience.

John's revelation is more radically scriptural than Daniel's. Although it contains no formally introduced scriptural quotations, not a paragraph would survive intact if all the scriptural allusions were removed from the book. A. M. Farrer suggests that this shows that it is more a God-given, scripture-inspired meditation than a revelation that came by surprise fully-formed to John. It parallels the visionary experience brought to Jewish mystics by meditation on Ezekiel 1. Thus in Revelation 4, John "sees his way into heaven by the use of Ezekiel's and of several overlapping scriptural texts. . . . He looked at the written records of these ancient visions until they fused into fresh shapes, expressive of a fuller truth. . . . He seeks new inspiration by drawing old texts into fresh combinations" — a literary process, yet also a visionary process.[6]

A further question is raised by Daniel 10–12. The vision certainly involves one or more heavenly beings, though it is not clear whether God is one of them and thus whether God is revealed to Daniel. Ironically, it transpires that in this person-to-person revelation the identity of neither person is absolutely clear. As regards the heavenly being, the allusiveness partly reflects the fact that the revelation, as the word suggests, is a visual experience, involving the unveiling of realities that were otherwise invisible and whose appearance can be ambiguous. But a theological issue underlies this ambiguity. While the First Testament can affirm that someone has seen God, elsewhere it declares that this is either impossible or fatally dangerous, and such considerations lie behind the reticence of Daniel's vision concerning the identity of the heavenly figure. Paradoxically, to declare that revelation refers primarily to God's self-revelation rather than to the revelation of historical or doctrinal information threatens to make it a motif without a referent. While scripture does speak of God revealing things (about realities such as the person, the world, and the will of God) it is inclined to see God's own self as remaining veiled. What God has revealed is the way we are to walk.[7]

5. Rowland, *The Open Heaven* 214-47.
6. Farrer, *The Revelation of St. John the Divine* 26, 28, 30.
7. Van Buren, *A Theology of the Jewish-Christian Reality* 1:40.

Propositional Revelation?

As in some other apocalypses, the content of the revelation in Daniel 10–12 is actually expressed as an audition, as a verbal message concerning the four realms we have drawn attention to. Despite its visual connotations, revelation commonly suggests the conveying of information, truths about past and future, the realm above and the realm below. It is verbal as well as personal. Indeed, it is verbal as part of being personal: A person's statements reveal the person. They may do this directly, as when someone says "I am depressed," or indirectly, insofar as any statement reveals something of the person who makes it. The acts of a person do not alone reveal the person. Their words are needed to reveal the meaning of their acts; it is doubtful whether there can be *personal* revelation without speaking.[8]

Daniel 10–12 indicates, then, the presence of propositional revelation in scripture and its nature as that which conveys theological information about the realm above and the realm below, about the future and about the past. By implication Daniel 10–12 also presupposes something about the revelatory status of propositional scripture that existed already when these chapters were composed, because that scripture, as well as providing patterns for the revelatory experience in Daniel 10, was a major source of the revelation's theological insight regarding the four realms. These three chapters presuppose not so much that scripture is revelation but that scripture contains and enables revelation. The task of interpreting scripture so that it provides insight on the Antiochene crisis lies at the heart of the ministry of the "discerning ones" who "enlighten the multitude" (11:33) by means of the teaching expressed in a revelation such as Daniel 10–12, and enable the members of that multitude to look at their experience in the light of scripture.[9] The present seems to be a meaningless enigma. Scripture unveils the mystery, providing the key to understanding past, present, and future. The teachers' gift is to be able to see the revelatory significance of scripture for the present. Thus Walter Wink speaks of dialogues with scripture as "among the . . . most consistently revelatory exercises one can do."[10] They enable us to discover ourselves as we discover God.

---

8. See Abraham, *The Divine Inspiration of Holy Scripture* 79-80, with his reference to an unpublished paper by P. Helm; also Abraham's *Divine Revelation* 14-16, with his quotation from Mitchell's "Does Christianity Need a Revelation?" 108-9; and Barr, *Old and New in Interpretation* 21-22, 77-78.

9. Cf. Fishbane, *Biblical Interpretation in Ancient Israel* 506-11; *The Garments of Torah* 67-69.

10. *Transforming Bible Study* 117 ([2]111).

This assumption matches the way scripture is approached in Psalm 119:18, which asks for the opening of the eyes so that one may see wonders there in scripture, even as visionaries have their eyes opened to see some wonder (Num 22:31). Sirach offers a similar portrait of scribes who devote themselves to the study of Torah: They seek the Lord in prayer in connection with their study so that in due course they can share mysteries that have been unveiled there (39:1-8).

Sometimes interpretation requires a revelatory opening of one's eyes because the text itself is characterized by obscurity rather than by revelatory clarity, as is the case with the prophecy of Jeremiah taken up in Daniel 9. What once seemed clear can become obscure, and interpretation is a revelatory act.[11] This can be so even when the text has not become obscure: The interpretative seer can perceive new significance in the text.

Daniel 10–12 combines wonder, interpretation, and vision in reporting a vision of wonders (12:6) unveiled through the study of scripture — as scripture becomes a means of revelation. Psalm 119 speaks of "consulting" written Torah (vv. 45, 94, 155; cf. 1 Chr 28:8; Ezra 7:10) in the way that one "consults" God through a prophet or medium (2 Kgs 8:8; 22:8; Isa 8:19). This way of speaking, too, might suggest that interpretation is understood as revelatory,[12] though the references to "consulting" written Torah make complete sense taken in the more straightforward way (cf. also Isa 34:16).

Sometimes interpretation is a matter of the revelatory unveiling or releasing of the text's hidden potential. When a revelation that has communicated something of concrete, expressible content is put into writing and becomes part of a people's written tradition, this written revelation can seem to become dehistoricized, abstract, and lifeless. It nevertheless retains its creative potential. Applied to a new situation by the scribe's human creativity it can be the means of a new revelation. In this sense the creative interpretative process is understood as the discovery of what was always there in the revelation.[13] Scripture is a deposit of propositional revelation that also becomes a means of propositional revelation.

Van Buren defines revelation as an acknowledged reinterpretation of the believing communities' tradition in response to Jewish history. This at first sounds reductionist, but he is able to give as examples the revelation at Sinai, where Moses professes to stand in the tradition that goes back to

---

11. Cf. Kugel, *Early Biblical Interpretation* 58-59.

12. So Fishbane, *The Garments of Torah* 65-67; cf. *Biblical Interpretation in Ancient Israel* 539-41. The verb is *dāraš*, from which the noun midrash ("interpretation") derives.

13. Scholem, "Revelation and Tradition as Religious Categories in Judaism" 282-89.

Abraham and to offer a new interpretation of what the God of the ancestors is doing and expects, and the revelation through Jesus, through whom the whole existing Jewish tradition is reinterpreted. At both points revelation involves a reinterpretation of the tradition. At both points, and in the scriptural material as a whole, this reinterpretation takes place, indeed, in response to historical events such as the exodus and the Christ event, and also more painful or puzzling experiences such as the exile and the gospel's failure among Jews and success among Gentiles.[14] This takes us to a consideration of the relationship between revelation and history.

Revelation in History?

Daniel's extensive treatment of the past in the course of the revelation in chapters 10–12 itself raises the question of the relation between revelation and history. Some recent theology has especially emphasized revelation in events rather than in word. Wolfhart Pannenberg famously affirmed that "history is the most comprehensive horizon of Christian theology"[15] and edited the symposium called *Revelation as History,* to which we have referred. Scholars such as James Barr have exposed the limitations of this emphasis in general, while C. F. Evans once observed that 1 Maccabees in particular has a better reputation than Daniel as a historical document but that Daniel with its images for interpreting history is much preferred as a document of divine revelation.[16]

In principle, the acts can in part reveal the person, but only on the basis of an already existing set of assumptions regarding the meaning of the acts. That is implicit in Hebrew narrative, which often relates the acts without commenting on the inner person and its motivation, not on the assumption that these are obscure, but on the assumption that the acts make them clear. When Abraham, Joshua, Hannah, or Hezekiah get up early in the morning (Gen 22:3; Josh 6:12; 1 Sam 1:19; 2 Chr 29:20), this is taken to reveal something about the inner person, because the stories' hearers know the meaning of "getting up early in the morning." Given some knowledge of the general significance of different human acts, what I do

---

14. *A Theology of the Jewish-Christian Reality* 1:37-39.

15. *Basic Questions in Theology* 1:15.

16. See Barr, "Revelation through History" and *Old and New in Interpretation* 65-102; Evans, "The Inspiration of the Bible" 14.

reveals who I am. So it will be with God. "If, then, we . . . know God in His relationship to us (to history, to our world), then this is to know God as He is."[17]

The stories in Daniel certainly see history as the sphere of God's activity. The book begins with a God involved in history, giving the Judean king into the hands of Babylon. This God controls historical eras and removes and sets up kings, rules human kingdoms and freely controls and distributes power among them, evaluates the rule of kings and puts them down when they fail this assessment. The perspective on history compares with that which characterizes the rest of the First Testament, though it emphasizes how the process of international history, and not merely that of Israelite history, has meaning as the outworking of God's grace, mercy, purposeful-ness, justice, and zeal.

In the visions the perspective on God and history is more ambiguous. Even in heaven there are conflicts among the agents of God's will, who personify earthly powers in conflict with one another in history, though there is no suggestion, as in *1 Enoch,* that such conflicts in heaven and in history result from a rebellion of heavenly beings near the Beginning. God indeed controls history, but more in the manner of the prison governor who still controls the prison during a riot, in the sense that the prisoners can only go so far. Neither the stories nor the visions see history as a whole or see it as progressing toward a goal.

Daniel 11 in particular, one of the most detailed portrayals in scripture of the unfolding of historical events over nearly two centuries, sees no positive intrinsic or revelatory significance in those events. The details of Persian and Hellenistic history have no constructive theological meaning. Events unfold as a pointless sequence of invasions, battles, schemes, and frustrations, a tale of selfishness, irrationality, and chance. History is neither the implementation of human purposes, the outworking of a principle of order and justice, the unfolding of a plan formulated in heaven, nor the reflection of the sovereign hand of God at work in the world. Often it seems to be the tale of human beings' unsuccessful attempts to be like God, though for the most part the true God appears to be sitting in the gallery watching history go nowhere. "The power of the world empires is inevitably self-limiting," following "a pattern that amounts almost to a natural law govern-ing the rise and fall of nations."[18] Meaning belongs to the End, not to the

17. Van Buren, *A Theology of the Jewish-Christian Reality* 1:87.
18. Newsom, "The Past as Revelation" 48.

historical process: History takes its course and God lets it do so until the moment comes to pronounce judgment on it.[19] The interpretation of history in Daniel 11 matches the way we experience history.

According to Rudolf Bultmann,

> in Jewish apocalyptic history is interpreted from the view of eschatology. In Paul history is swallowed up in eschatology. . . . While the history of the nation and of the world loses its interest, another phenomenon is detected, the true historical life *(Geschichtlichkeit)* of the human being. The decisive history is not the history of the world, of the people Israel and of the other peoples, but the history that everyone experiences himself.[20]

In Daniel 11 the history of the world, of Israel and other peoples, is of great interest, but the decisive matter is the act of God at the End. But the effect of the latter is to affirm the significance of Israel's destiny, not to turn everything into individual history. The difference between stories and visions in Daniel suggests that there are times when the hand of God can be detected in the processes of history and times when it can only be looked for at the End.

The First Testament commonly expresses the conviction that God is at work in history and that history provides evidence that Yahweh is God. It also affirms that God's revelation belongs to the future as well as to the past and present (so regarding God's saving justice, Isa 56:1; God's glory, 40:5; peace and faithfulness, Jer 33:6). This is a particular emphasis of the Second Testament's talk of revelation (Luke 17:30, the Son of man; Rom 2:5, God's just judgment; 8:18, glory; 8:19, the children of God; 2 Thess 2:3, the man of lawlessness; 1 Pet 1:5, salvation; 1:7, 13, Jesus Christ). What can be perceived regarding the significance of history is little in extent (cf. Rom 1:18–3:20).

It is striking that *the* Book of Revelation is the last book in the Second Testament and that Daniel, *the* revelatory book in First, is the latest book in the Hebrew canon. Only at the end does the murky and confused become clear light, denouement, and closure; in the meantime even within scripture people's lives are often characterized by uncertainty, and "God appears to order, guide, promise, and argue — but never to explain, to make every-

19. Noth, "The Understanding of History in Old Testament Apocalyptic," *The Laws in the Pentateuch and Other Studies* 214.

20. "History and Eschatology in the New Testament" 13.

thing clear."[21] There is relatively little that can be called revelation in Hebrew narrative, which is generally written from a limited human perspective rather than that of an omniscient narrator, a role not even fulfilled by Yahweh, who like a visionary sees in part but asks many questions and receives many surprises.[22] Indeed, the First Testament moves from clarity to mystery as often as vice versa (this is so with Daniel and also with Genesis, Saul, David, Job, Jonah . . .).

And not even to the eyes of faith is the Second Testament's revelation self-evident in events. Luke-Acts is a further instance of "revealed history": The events it narrates are known by ordinary means, but their significance often depends on revelation by means of prophecy or by means of scripture.[23] The nature of God's secret purpose to bring Jews and Gentiles into one body in Christ, and through this one body to make that secret purpose known to the heavenly powers, was known only through a special revelation to Paul (Eph 3:1-11). Paul assumes that the events of history may be extremely unrevelatory. Who could have seen God at work in Israel's failure to recognize Jesus? The matter was a complete mystery, and one that threatened to reduce all else to mystery, until Paul saw that this was an aspect of the way God was planning to bring salvation to the Gentiles. As Romans 9–11 indicates, it is reflection on history in the light of scripture that makes this revelatory penny drop; those chapters testify to "revelation by exegesis," the dynamic interaction of scripture, exegetical tradition, and religious experience in the light of the need to solve a problem.[24]

Karl Popper protests "the poverty of historicism," which includes the view that it is possible to interpret history and know its meaning — unless this is by means of some specific revelation.[25] Within scripture itself, earlier scriptures are a resource for people seeking to understand history. Revelation is historical in the sense that it is a historical event, calls for a historical decision, and embodies historical occurrences,[26] but in itself history is a

21. Josipovici, *The Book of God* 88; cf. 76-77, 87-89.
22. Gunn, "Reading Right," in *The Bible in Three Dimensions* (ed. Clines, et al.) 58, 60.
23. Hall, *Revealed Histories* 171-208; Hall looks at John in the same way.
24. Bockmuehl, *Revelation and Mystery in Ancient Judaism* 174-75.
25. Popper, *The Poverty of Historicism*. Cf. C. S. Lewis, "Historicism," *Christian Reflections* 100-113; also Rogerson's comment that we have access to past events only insofar as they are presented in narrative form ("Can a Doctrine of Providence Be Based on the Old Testament" 539); and Hayden White's works on narrative (see bibliography).
26. Gloege, "Offenbarung und Überlieferung" 220, 223; cf. Bartsch, *Kerygma and Myth* 2:75.

means of neither revelation nor redemption. "The revelation of mighty deeds of God without revelation of the meaning of those deeds is like a television show without sound track": It throws us back on guesswork if we are to know the meaning of what is happening.[27] Intelligible silent films are exceptions that prove the rule, for even in this case, the casting of events into narrative is the means of making these events intelligible. It is doubtful whether meaning can ever be discerned in history considered in itself. We discern its meaning by considering it in the light of convictions in terms of which we give unity and purpose to life in general.[28] Events do not speak unless they are interpreted by a narrator or a prophet. Revelation as expressed in the biblical message provides a basis for understanding the meaning of history rather than vice versa.

Pannenberg himself in part affirms this point, noting that events gain their meaning through their links with the traditions and expectations with which people live. Thus the prophetic word precedes the historical event and makes it understandable as an act of Yahweh, the word of command follows on the event as act of Yahweh, and (in the Second Testament) the word of proclamation reports the act of God in Jesus. But Pannenberg insists that it is the act that is the revelation; the word only shares in this status insofar as it is part of the history of revelation.[29] One may compare Brunner's comment that "the inspiration of the Holy Scriptures is not *the* revelation, but one of the forms of revelation, namely, the incarnation in written form of the living personal revelation of the Living God in the history of revelation and salvation,"[30] or Bavinck's that "Scripture is therefore not the revelation itself, but the description, the record, from which the revelation can be known."[31]

The way of looking at the matter suggested by the First Testament's own way of speaking is that there is first a verbal revelation, a word to a person such as Moses, then a redeeming or judging event that confirms the

---

27. K. S. Kantzer, "The Christ-Revelation as Act and Interpretation," in *Jesus of Nazareth* (ed. Henry) 252; cf. Pinnock, *Biblical Revelation* 33. Cf. Alonso Schökel's examples from films, *The Inspired Word* 35-37; also O'Collins, *Fundamental Theology* 74-75.

28. Rogerson, "Can a Doctrine of Providence Be Based on the Old Testament?" 541-42, following F. Platzer, *Geschichte-Heilsgeschichte-Hermeneutik* (Frankfurt: Lang, 1976).

29. *Revelation as History* 152-55.

30. *Revelation and Reason* 12.

31. *Our Reasonable Faith* 95.

revelation rather than constituting it, then a further revelation that draws attention to the event and interprets it further, and/or the telling of a story of word and event that preserves the whole and makes them accessible as revelation or as source of revelation for the future. Revelation is thus the means of understanding history first prospectively, then retrospectively. Exodus and the Gospels may be described as records of revelatory events. They are also revelatory interpretations of events, in the sense that the events would not necessarily have been revelatory for people unless they were narrated in an interpreted form.

History interpreted in the light of revelation is what Cullmann calls prophetic history.[32] He thus sees the whole narrative line from Beginning to End as revelation (or as prophecy, in the terminology he more often uses), with the central section distinctive for also containing material open to historical verification. As he notes, Bultmann treats the whole as myth and thus consistently wishes to demythologize the section with historical reference as well as the sections that lack it. In contrast, Cullmann's own move logically takes place in the opposite direction: The temporal character of the events at the center of this narrative points to the temporal character of Beginning and End.[33]

Barton thus notes that the formal distinction between narratives about the past and predictions of the future easily misleads us into missing what they have in common, symbolized by the Jewish designation of both as the Prophets with a merely subordinate distinction between Former and Latter that ignores the distinction of genre between them. "The same inspiration is needed to look into the past as into the future" and neither past nor future is of interest for its own sake but for what it tells us in and of the present.[34]

For all that, there is a dialectic relationship between scripture and history. Scripture makes it possible in Daniel to interpret second-century history; yet it is second-century history itself that makes it possible to see the significance of earlier texts for second-century history. The First Testament makes it possible to understand the Christ event but the Christ event opens people's eyes to aspects of the meaning and significance of the First Testament. The First Testament points to the gospel applying to the Gentile

32. See *Christ and Time* 94-106.
33. *Christ and Time* 100. Cf. Barth's comments, *Church Dogmatics* III/1:84-90.
34. *Oracles of God* 225, with his quotation from Barr, *The Scope and Authority of the Bible* 36.

world, but only the response of the Gentile world led the church to read scripture in this way. The Second Testament envisages a longer church age than was originally expected because events showed that Jesus was not returning as quickly as expected. The First Testament puts words in the mouth of Moses, and the Second puts words on the pen of Paul, in the light of history as people experienced it later than Moses' or Paul's day. This process continues. "Better understanding of the Bible . . . rarely comes because renewed Bible study has initiated a new theological breakthrough. Such mythical hagiography has no place in reality. Rather, historic events overtake the world and the church, making it painfully obvious that past interpretation of the Bible is untenable." The development of religious tolerance, the interpretation of Genesis 1, the move for the abolition of slavery, and now the move for the abolition of racism and for the equality of women, all illustrate the way in which in practice "we cannot understand biblical revelation apart from historical revelation."[35]

When revelation and scripture have been correlated, it has commonly been inferred that revelation was limited to the scriptural period. As is the case with the limitation of inspiration to the scriptural text and the scriptural period, this seems to conflict with scripture itself and to be a mistaken way to protect the special significance of scripture. God has continued to reveal things since the end of the scriptural period, and historical events are one means of that revelation as it reorients the mind of the church. In the present age, along with the events just referred to, van Buren suggests that the Holocaust and the founding of the State of Israel are one such complex of events.[36] Liberation theology insists that "*human* events must be deciphered as the locale of *God's* revelation."[37] But such events are of ambiguous significance and illustrate the way in which history only becomes revelatory as it leads to renewed study of scripture and renewed insight emerging from scripture. In interpreting anything we inevitably begin from our own situation and move from there to the text we wish to understand. But that point should not be made so sharply as to resolve the dialectic relationship between scripture and history. As well as the movement from perceiving God's activity in current events to understanding scripture better, there is a complementary movement from deepening our study of scripture to gaining clearer insight on God's activity in current events.[38]

35. *Verdict* 27 (1987) 4, 5.
36. *A Theology of the Jewish-Christian Reality* 1:39, 42-44.
37. Croatto, *Exodus* v, emphasis original.
38. Against Croatto, *Exodus* 8, 11.

Revelation and Reason

If revelation conveys information, what is its relationship to other sources of information? The overlapping circles we are considering in Part IV give us the opportunity to consider the relationship between revelation and experience and that between revelation and reason or reflection.

In chapter 13 we considered the sense in which scripture and reason might be rival norms for theology, and in chapter 20 we considered how revelation and reason came to be seen as rivals: If revelation makes assertions that cannot be established by reason, it will then seem that one has to choose between revelation and reason. Alternatively revelation may be seen as built on reason, or vice versa.[39]

Scripture implies that revelation and reason complement each other in a variety of ways. It takes for granted the reality of God as naturally as the existence of humanity. Neither is proved through reason or established by revelation, except in the sense that those truths may be seen as the fruit of general revelation. Reason enables us to think critically about the God who exists and whose reality we grasp by that intuition that belongs to us by virtue of our being made in God's image, but it hardly enables us to verify or falsify God's existence any more than to verify or falsify our own existence. The wisdom books illustrate the potential and the limitations of human reason applied to understanding the meaning of human life. The links between the wisdom, the praises, and the prayers that appear in the Bible and those outside it indicate that other peoples do have some truth about God and humanity.

The necessity of revelation emerges in part from the human sinfulness that has spoiled the operation of human reason in a way more vividly analyzed over the past century by Nietzsche, Marx, and Freud. But even unspoiled reason would need the resource of revelation. Revelation complements reason by giving information to the scriptural authors about the four realms that reason could not provide. Neither intuition nor reason could provide information about the redemptive purpose of God executed through the story of Israel and the story of Jesus. This information is then so fundamental for an understanding of God and humanity that it may make what intuition and reason can achieve seem trivial, and it explains some key differences between biblical wisdom and worship and those of other people. But reason does set to work on understanding these events, as the theologizing of someone such as Paul illustrates.

39. So Brunner, *Revelation and Reason* ix.

Is there a reasonable basis for Daniel's purported revelation to have been accepted by people? The revelation itself suggests a series of considerations; all raise problems considered individually, but they may nevertheless have a cumulative effect.

The revelatory experience through which the revelation was received is part of the basis on which the author commends his message to his hearers. Heavenly beings had been in touch with him, beings so impressive and awesome that one of them might have been God. Admittedly neither author nor audience will have viewed this as a conclusive argument for the acceptance of his message. While believing that his message came by God's gift, he and at least some of his contemporaries knew that it did not come directly from the exilic Daniel in the way described here. Perhaps he was inviting people to believe that the message was received through a revelatory event translated into, or actually experienced as, an experience of the exilic Daniel. Even so, the author and his hearers also knew that a claim to revelatory experience is not to be accepted purely on the basis of the claim (cf. Jer 23:15-32). Conversely, if this message did not come from a revelatory experience on the part of Daniel in the way that the matter has traditionally been understood, this does not imply that it was neither a revelation nor true. If the author knew of the historical events in the revelation by the same means as other scriptural writers knew of the events they relate, this leaves quite open the question whether this author's understanding may have been God-given and true in the same way as theirs. Nor does it follow that the revelation's material on the realm above, the realm below, and the future realm reflects merely the writer's subjective ideas; this, too, can be as God-given as other material on such matters in scripture.

The claims of a vision that purports to have come through a revelatory experience are buttressed by its presentation as an experience of a person of proven discernment and faithfulness. In the book these are characteristics of Daniel himself. In the book's context they are characteristics of the actual recipients of the revelation, who become fleetingly visible as the discerning teachers who pay the price for their ministry (see 11:32-35; 12:10).

Piety and faithfulness are no guarantee of truth. More obviously the message is grounded in the scriptures and they provide the basis for its acceptance. It takes the form of scriptural exposition or of theological reflection on a situation in the light of scripture. But use of scripture in this way is also not a guarantee of the truth of a message. Other Jews of the second and first centuries offered quite different scriptural accounts of the Antiochene crisis.

The Torah suggests that an important test for whether a prophecy has been spoken by God is whether it comes about. Daniel might seem to fail that test, though those who preserved it likely did so on the basis of the view that the deliverance that did take place in 164-63 B.C. did vindicate its prophecy and was also the guarantee that other aspects of it would come true in due course. The message of 11:40–12:3 was more promise than prediction, an encouragement to keep on living in faith and hope in God.

The final test of Daniel's revelation was whether it could be lived with and what kind of living it supported. Daniel's presence in scripture is an indication that people believed that they could live through the crises that came to them in the light of this perspective on crises, which looks at the End promised as well as threatened in them. Daniel's vision brought about the End, the End of an old order's power to lord it over its fellows, because it opened up an alternative world, which people were prepared to believe would endure as the old order would not, a world in which what seemed at present to be weakness was revealed to be true power and what seemed like death was revealed to be the gateway to life.[40] It invited people to live this life in the light of such convictions about that life.

40. D. L. Barr, "The Apocalypse as a Symbolic Transformation of the World." Cf. Collins, "Inspiration or Illusion" 36.

22

The Truth of Revelation

The realms above and below, ahead and behind are the subject of revelation because they are not present to our immediate perception. For the same reason much of our description of them has to involve "describing the other side in the terms of this side." Jesus commented that there are times when literal speech is impossible and one has to be content with "figures" (John 16:25).[1] Revelation may not give literal descriptions of the realities it treats. In what sense is what it says true? What is the nature of its theological and religious language?

The Place of Imagery in Scripture

The Bible is in large part a work of literature, not an analytic systematic theological treatise. Its theology and ethics are expressed in poems "about the weather, trees, crops, lions, hunters, rocks of refuge and human emotions such as love and terror and trust and joy."[2] The interpreter who fails to appreciate scripture as imagery and poetry will not interpret it adequately. Much of scripture's imagery and insight is common to other cultures in the Middle East and elsewhere, or, indeed, is derived from them. While scripture is a body of truth, much of its content was not revealed supernaturally but discovered or imagined in the same way as happens with truth and insight outside scripture.

Like reason, imagination is an ambiguous faculty. To say something

1. *Paroimiai* (NJB "veiled language").
2. Ryken, *Triumphs of the Imagination* 22.

stems from a person's imagination can imply that it is illusory or fanciful, or can suggest the creatively far-seeing and realistic ability to see what actually is there or actually is possible. In this second sense imagination is the point of contact between divine revelation and human experience. Imagination does not generate revelation, but as in science a leap of imagination makes possible a discovery about reality that would not otherwise be made. Developing a definition from Kant, Garrett Green describes this process in terms similar to ones we have utilized in connection with revelation: Imagination makes accessible what would otherwise be unavailable — temporally, because it is past or future, spatially, because it is far away or too small or too big (the microcosmic or macrocosmic), or logically, as with metaphysical realities such as God. It enables us to recognize in something accessible a figure that can truly represent something inaccessible and incapable of direct representation.[3] And what it is representing is something that objectively exists: The language is referential.

Verbal images concentrate meaning in such a way that they express and make it possible to appropriate more meaning than can be articulated and expressed in analytic concepts and words.[4] Their central function is "to connect the clear and focused area of our experience with a dim but insistent kind of experience that is constituent of consciousness but is, nevertheless, not clearly apprehended."[5] Ricoeur emphasizes that they provide us with our only way of articulating the experience of evil: Something with a literal meaning such as stain or pollution, deviation or wandering, burden or bondage, is a means of expressing the experience of evil and its converse — purity, forgiveness, and freedom.[6]

Captivity was a literal reality for Jews in the sixth century B.C., but in the Second Testament the experience of dispersion becomes a symbol; Ricoeur sees captivity as one of our elemental symbols.[7] 1 Peter addresses itself to the exiles of a metaphorical dispersion in the provinces of Turkey, displaced persons who are not really at home where they live, aliens without proper status there (1:1, 17; 2:11). They are encouraged to make the most

---

3. See Green, *Imagining God* 41-80.

4. So Kant in *Critique of Judgment,* as summarized by Tracy, *The Analogical Imagination* 140.

5. Beardslee, "Narrative Form in the New Testament and Process Theology" 303, following A. N. Whitehead.

6. *The Conflict of Interpretations* 315; cf. *The Symbolism of Evil.*

7. E.g., *The Confict of Interpretations* 269-86; cf. Keegan's illustration from the music of Bruce Springsteen in *Interpreting the Bible* 87.

of the fact that joining the Christian community provides "a home for the homeless," as John H. Elliott has called it in his "sociological exegesis of 1 Peter."[8] That notion of gaining a home in Christ has sometimes been as important to subsequent people under oppression as 1 Peter expected it to be to its alienated audience: "This world is not my home, I am just a'passing through."

Modern believers in Europe and North America may also identify with 1 Peter's feeling of not really belonging to this world. They may sense that they live in a world that constitutes an alien environment, one with different hopes and fears and different standards and commitments, one that is always pressing us into its mold and requiring of us that we discern the point at which we have to make a stand and prove that God can be with us and enable us not only to survive but to triumph in exile. Elliott insists that the homelessness of 1 Peter's audience is not merely figurative or "spiritual." Yet our own experience as I have just described it may provide a way into one aspect of the story's significance. Indeed, Elliott also quotes from Alfred Schultz's reflection on the depth and power of the archetypal image of "home," noting how home-leaving, homelessness and homecoming have shaped the drama of the human story since Odysseus.[9] 1 Peter is utilizing the symbols and the experience of dispersion, homelessness, and alienation as ways into understanding and expressing the gospel. If these are elemental symbols, it may be that even the stories in Daniel, which on the surface relate to an entirely literal exile, are doing the same at another level. It would not be surprising if the experience of alienation provided a way into the stories in Daniel.

In general imagery has to be understood historically. Northrop Frye describes the city, the garden, and the sheepfold as the great organizing images of the Bible.[10] The significance of the realities and experiences to which such images appeal varies in different cultures. At the same time they are particular cultural embodiments of widely known archetypes. So particular occurrences of an image need to be interpreted both in relation to the archetype and in relation to the historical context. In using imagery writers are fitting their work into the larger whole comprised of reality as God constitutes it, creates it, sees it, and orders it. They are seeking to be

8. *A Home for the Homeless.*

9. See *A Home for the Homeless* 236, quoting Schultz, "The Homecomer," in *Collected Papers* 2 (The Hague: Nijhoff, 1964) 106-17.

10. *Anatomy of Criticism* 141 (he actually describes these as "metaphors"); cf. Fisch, *Poetry With a Purpose* 1.

open to God. Imagery trades on the familiarity of the down-to-earth, but it also trades on the fact that realities such as vines, coffee, and concrete have their own place in God's scheme of things. It is for this reason that they can bring to expression other realities of which we are only more vaguely aware, or of which we only become aware through them.

Metaphor thus shares with symbol both the capacity to convey "what ideas feel like" and the capacity to give us means of seeing and articulating what we could not otherwise see or articulate. In some ways of using the terms "metaphor" and "symbol" it may be difficult to distinguish them. I would do so by seeing metaphor as specific whereas symbol is archetypal, and by seeing symbol as characteristically familiar whereas metaphors are essentially innovations. Individuals create metaphors, whereas symbols belong to communities and are figures that acquire "a stable and repeatable meaning or association" and enable a community to evoke indirectly what cannot be articulated as powerfully in a direct way.[11] While symbols cannot be freely invented but "are bound within the sacred universe," metaphor depends on creativity: "There are no live metaphors in a dictionary."[12] Indeed, metaphor is inclined to be shocking; it invites us to look at something in the light of something else that we thought was quite dissimilar. Amos addresses cows from Bashan who turn out to be women from Samaria, and laments the death of a young woman who turns out to be Israel itself. In Hosea one who speaks as a mother-bear robbed of her cubs turns out to be Yahweh.

Metaphor facilitates "semantic innovation," which produces "new semantic pertinence by means of an impertinent attribution."[13] Simile compares one thing with another; metaphor more forcefully identifies the one with the other so that they "interanimate each other."[14] We noted in chapter 1 that a metaphor communicates in such a way as to so extend language and generate new insights. It "tells us something new about reality." Metaphor

> brings to language aspects, qualities, and values of reality that lack access
> to language that is directly descriptive and that can be spoken only by

11. Perrin, "Wisdom and Apocalyptic in the Message of Jesus" 553.

12. Ricoeur, *Interpretation Theory* 61, 52.

13. Ricoeur, *Time and Narrative* 1:ix, taking up the approach of his *The Rule of Metaphor*. See also Martin Soskice, *Metaphor and Religious Language* (with some critique of Ricoeur); Hawkes, *Metaphor*.

14. Wren, *What Language Shall I Borrow?* 85.

means of the complex interplay between the metaphorical utterance and the rule-governed transgression of the usual meanings of our words,

and it does so "to redescribe a reality inaccessible to direct description" and thus express something that can hardly be said in another way. In this way, "'seeing as,' which sums up the power of metaphor," can become "the revealer of a 'being as' on the deepest ontological level."[15]

Metaphor and symbol with their openness and potential are not the only or sufficient ways of speaking of God, as Sallie McFague TeSelle implies.[16] Metaphor and symbol are intuitive, experiential, self-involving, allusive, plurivocal, holistic, open-ended, and dynamic, while conceptual thinking is analytic, cerebral, distanced, defined, measured, and nuanced. The creativity of the former is complemented by the discipline of the latter, which clarifies and tests metaphor and symbol. Ricoeur, with whose approach McFague TeSelle identifies herself, recognizes this, noting that one can see taking place in scripture itself a move from symbol to system and conceptualization. "Symbol gives rise to thought" and the importance of symbolism does not mean that we give up rational thinking.[17]

This is not to imply that conceptual thinking is more advanced than symbol; the two complement each other, and the latter is parasitic on the former. Indeed, Ricoeur argues, the move from symbol to conceptual thinking can be one that encourages a rationalistic theology of the kind that in combating Gnosticism became quasi-gnostic itself, replacing images and symbols such as captivity, fall, wandering, lostness, and rebellion with abstract pseudoconcepts such as original sin, which are characterized by an apparent clarity but lack the depth attached to symbols.[18] So we move from a naive first exposure to symbols, by way of reflection on them, to a second naiveté in which we no longer think in symbols but still think with symbols as our starting point.[19] Translating the images of scripture into closely

15. Ricoeur, *Interpretation Theory* 53; *Time and Narrative* 1:xi.

16. E.g., *Speaking in Parables* 29. This is a particularly unfortunate view when combined with the conviction that metaphors are also affective *rather than* actually depictions of a reality that exists (see Martin Soskice's critique in *Metaphor and Religious Language* 108-12).

17. Ricoeur, *The Conflict of Interpretations* 288, 296; cf. "Biblical Hermeneutics" 129-35. See also Ebeling, *Word and Faith* 93-94; and Wicker, *The Story-Shaped World* 1-32 on the distinction between metaphor and analogy.

18. See Ricoeur, *The Conflict of Interpretations* 269-72, summarizing work in his *The Symbolism of Evil*.

19. Cf. Jeanrond, *Text and Interpretation* 41.

defined analytic concepts cannot preserve all that the images communicate and effect. "Metaphors are potential concepts; concepts are petrified metaphors."[20] Analyzing a metaphor, even if this involves speaking at much greater length and lesser effect than the metaphor itself does, may help us to ensure that the creativity of metaphor is partnered with the discipline of reflective conceptual thinking. But the analysis does not make the metaphor redundant. Like criticism in relation to a poem, it sends us back to the metaphor able to appreciate it more fully.[21]

The Logic of Scripture's Language about God

Talk about God has to be analogical; it involves applying to God the language that applies to human beings. We say God acts, speaks, or feels, knowing that these expressions cannot apply to God as unequivocally as they do to human beings, but reckoning that there is enough overlap between God's personhood and ours to make it possible to apply these terms to God with appropriate safeguards and qualifications. Scripture's language about God is anthropomorphic, but as such it is analogical and factual rather than mythic in the sense of fictional.[22] God is more than human, but since God is a person, God's being overlaps with ours as human beings, so that talk of God's "love" and "wrath" are true talk of God. Indeed, such personal talk of God is logically and essentially prior to its application to human beings since God's personal being is prior to ours and all our experience of personhood is secondary to God's (cf. Eph 3:14-15). "God's true revelation comes from out of itself to meet what we can say with our human words and make a selection from among them to which we have to attach ourselves in obedience."[23]

Talk about God also involves the use of imagery, and it requires us to take account of the considerations arising from scripture's general use of imagery and of considerations attaching to analogical language. Images applied to God are necessary and fruitful but must have their boundaries respected. Setting images alongside each other may enable us to see where

20. Green, *Imagining God* 17, 70.
21. Cf. Wren, *What Language Shall I Borrow?* 95, 107.
22. On myth and demythologizing, see *Models for Interpretation of Scripture* (the companion to the present volume) chapter 14.
23. Barth, *Church Dogmatics* II/1:227; cf. Hunsinger, "Beyond Literalism and Expressivism" (which this paragraph more broadly follows) 215.

their applications begin and end. God is, for example, like a father in holding together loving commitment and decisive authority, but unlike a father, God is not physical. God is like the wind in being powerful but invisible and unpredictable, but unlike the wind God is personal. These two images qualify and safeguard each other. We can affirm that Jesus is the real vine but not go on to ask what soil he grows in. We can describe God as our Father without implying that God is male or that someone else is our Mother. One image taken in isolation may be misleading; complementary images, as well as more analytic concepts, may help us perceive when we have taken an image too far.

We need to be equally wary of underinterpreting scriptural images. When John describes Jesus as the real vine, he uses a figure to which a variety of significances and resonances from the First Testament attaches, whether or not Jesus or John was immediately aware of them. When we describe God as our Father, a range of experiences of fatherhood and childhood, positive and negative, contribute to the unfolding of the image. Images point to a depth and breadth of meaning that may go beyond what an author perceived. Their language is deliberately open and suggestive rather than totally defined and specific, and overanalysis or intellectualizing of them may sacrifice their power.[24] Admittedly, by their nature they trade on everyday earthly realities. To the urban westerner a vine sounds inherently spiritual. In the Middle East it is no more spiritual than coffee or concrete. It worked as an image because it utilized the everyday and down-to-earth to extend the boundary of the sayable. Interpreting biblical imagery involves hearing everyday statements in their everyday significance and yet with their transcendent overtones.

In everyday religious speech we may be hardly aware that our language about God is analogical or metaphorical. No doubt scripture's language about God is often similarly instinctive and unreflective, but there are indications that in their use of language its writers were less naive and unsophisticated than is sometimes assumed. When they say that God resides in heaven, or that God resides in a material house on earth, their statements are qualified by others such as "heaven and the highest heaven cannot contain you" (1 Kgs 8:27), which deny that God can be so located or confined and which point toward explicitly analogical language in terms of transcendence.

Much of the biblical writers' language is thus consciously metaphori-

---

24. Thiselton, *New Horizons in Hermeneutics* 580.

cal.[25] It is capable of being reexpressed in conceptual terms as an aid to clearer understanding, but it is not thereby replaced, any more than is the case with other symbolic and metaphorical language. When Barth interprets the three-story universe analogically, understanding "heaven" to suggest the transcendent, wholly other,[26] Miegge suggests this is just another form of reinterpretation, asking whether the text made "an ingenuous affirmation of reality."[27] Scripture's capacity to accompany ingenuous affirmations with sophisticated affirmations, even in the same context, as in 1 Kings 8:12-13, 27-30, suggests that Barth need not be merely imposing a twentieth-century view at this point. Biblical writers need not be understanding the former kind of statement literalistically, and whether they are doing so would have to be determined by the examination of particular passages in the context of their writers' work as a whole. Outside scripture, it is doubtful whether the Greeks were literalistic in understanding their tragedies.[28] Augustine and the scholastics discuss carefully (if no more conclusively than moderns) where the literal ends and the symbolic begins.[29] Luther protests at "that heaven of the charlatans, with its golden stool and Christ sitting at the Father's side vested in a choir cope and a golden crown, as the painters love to portray him."[30]

In general, something similar needs to be said about the objective truth and referentiality of "mythic" language, as we said regarding "historical" narrative in Part I. Jesus may or may not have literally ascended into the sky. If he did not, this does not mean the story of his doing so is merely a myth requiring existentialist interpretation. More likely it is then an imaginative way of making a factual statement in connection with the definite end to which Jesus' resurrection appearances in due course came. "There is no sense in trying to visualize the ascension as a literal event, like going up in a balloon," yet the story of Jesus entering the cloud — in biblical thinking a symbol of God's hidden presence and coming revelation — makes the important factual point that at the end of Easter time Jesus Christ

25. Cf. J. D. G. Dunn, "Demythologizing," *New Testament Interpretation* (ed. Marshall) 298.

26. See *Church Dogmatics* III/3:418-76.

27. *Gospel and Myth* 99.

28. F. K. Schumann, "Can the Event of Jesus Christ Be Demythologized?" *Kerygma and Myth* (ed. Bartsch) 1:189.

29. So A. M. Farrer, "An English Appreciation," *Kerygma and Myth* (ed. Bartsch) 1:216.

30. *WA* 23:131, as quoted by J. Schniewind, "A Reply to Bultmann," *Kerygma and Myth* (ed. Bartsch) 1:46.

as a still human person entered that part of creation that is to the rest of humanity still inaccessible and incomprehensible.[31]

Like other aspects of language, talk about God has to be historical, utilizing language and images as they are used in a particular culture. God's choice to become involved with human beings in the particular way and context in which this happened, including the opportunities and constraints of the way in which this involvement would be understood and communicated, suggests that this way was at least adequate. It may even be that the symbolic or "mythic" thinking of the biblical period, far from imposing alien categories on the gospel, allowed the transcendent significance of events to be expressed in a way that modern secular or anthropocentric myths or worldviews do not.[32]

Particular talk about God may then make a different impression in a culture other than the one that generated it. To say that Jesus is seated at God's right takes up the fact that a human king's son or regent would sit at the king's right and the consequent fact that the king of Israel was described as metaphorically seated at God's right. The image is then applied to God and Jesus. It does not mean that the Second Testament envisages two literal thrones in the sky with quasi-human figures seated on them. We must not be prosaic in the way we read its metaphors. We may well need to reconceptualize or resymbolize the Bible's assertions about the realm above and below and about Beginning and End, but not on the basis that these assertions are merely superficial aspects of its message.

> The question then to which demythologizing addresses itself is whether the gospel is forever imprisoned within these first century thought forms, whether it can be re-expressed in 20th century terms. Are we justified in saying that there is a faith and hope which can be expressed in other language and thought forms but that *remains the same faith and hope?*[33]

The Truth of Daniel 10–12

How do such approaches to scriptural imagery apply to the actual revelatory texts of scripture? In general here, too, the paradigm of "myth" obscures

---

31. Barth, *Church Dogmatics* III/2:453-54; cf. IV/2:153.
32. H. Thielicke, "The Restatement of New Testament Mythology," *Kerygma and Myth* (ed. Bartsch) 1:165-72.
33. J. D. G. Dunn, "Demythologizing," *New Testament Interpretation* (ed. Marshall) 301, emphasis original.

the apocalypses more than it illuminates. The paradigm "symbol" is more promising. In the visions in Daniel 7–8 symbols such as animals and human-like figures have a prominent place. In Daniel 10–12 much more space is occupied by code or allegory, which assume a one-to-one correspondence between the figurative expression and the reality to which it refers. But symbolism also contributes to this apocalypse's imaginative picture of past and future, of the realm above and the realm below.

When Daniel talks about the past, he uses the image of a book in which historical events are written down, but turns this image into a doubly metaphorical expression by describing this book as one already written before the events have taken place (10:21). This provides a forceful way of making a true statement deriving from the reality of Israel's God: To say that history is prewritten is to affirm that it has always been under control. This need not imply that it is fixed independently of the will of its participants. The account of history in chapter 11 presupposes that human beings make real decisions that make history happen. The earlier accounts of Daniel's relationship with Nebuchadnezzar and Belshazzar have already portrayed these heathen kings both as standing beneath an overarching determination of God and as responsible to God and to themselves for their destinies. These two presuppositions must be allowed to qualify each other: The idea of human freedom and power is limited by the idea of divine constraint, the idea of divine determination by that of human initiative and autonomy.

Daniel's revelation regarding the world above and below, with its symbolism, similarly excludes two ways of looking at the present relationship between earth and heaven, the dualistic way and the monistic way. On the one hand, it speaks of no Satan, no heavenly adversary who might frustrate the purpose of God. God is sovereign in heaven and on earth. God's power can be opposed and delayed but not frustrated. Nor is it the case that the real decisions are made in heaven, so that human acts make no difference to what happens. In this connection, too, it is significant that Daniel 11 takes for granted that human beings are responsible for history. Armies have to fight as if the battle on earth alone counted. P. D. Hanson contrasts the apocalypses with the prophets by suggesting that the apocalypses have ceased to translate the vision of Yahweh's sovereignty into the terms of "plain history, real politics and human instrumentality," because of the historical constraints of the visionaries' own experience.[34] While these con-

---

34. "Jewish Apocalyptic against Its Near Eastern Environment" 35.

straints have influenced the way in which the apocalypses express the matter, Daniel 10–12, at least, does seem to present both the heavenly and the historical.

Daniel also excludes monistic thinking. History is not the outworking of human decisions alone. Like other parts of scripture, Daniel assumes that free human decisions unwittingly contribute to the outworking of God's purpose. What Daniel says about the heavenly leaders of the nations presupposes, beyond this, that the purposes of kings and nations are more then merely their own decisions. Something in the realm of the spirit lies behind them.

This portrait of the heavenly leaders of the nations developed from that of the many gods of polytheism. The faith of the First Testament always affirmed that Yahweh was uniquely God, but it also knew that the life of heaven was more complex than talk in terms of monotheism might imply. The idea of the leaders of the nations provided a way of thinking about history as people experience it. More than merely human factors are reflected in its conflicts, with their unexpected defeats and unexpected victories and their frequent upsetting of human calculations. The image of the heavenly leaders of the nations expresses the conviction that there is more to history than we can see. They are not "idealized personifications" of their nations; "they represent the actual spirituality and possibilities of actual entities," the actual nations with their personalities and vocations.[35] These are embodied in their leaders, about whom there is thus something human, earthly, structural, political, and visible, and something heavenly, invisible, suprahuman, immaterial, and spiritual.

Daniel's portrayal of the realm to come is imaginative, like its portrayals of the realm above, the realm below, and the realm of the past. It reflects scripture and symbolism that emerges from human experience. It answers questions that arise in a particular historical context, those raised by the events described in Daniel 11:21-39. It is not concerned with a doctrine of resurrection affecting all times and all peoples. Its theological statement is contextual; it handles questions raised by a particular situation.

The First Testament's standard way of envisaging death and a return to life is to speak of lying down and sleeping, then of waking and getting up. Death is an extreme form of sleep, which therefore provides the metaphor for death. Further, death means joining one's ancestors in the family tomb, so entombment also provides an image for the nonmaterial destiny

---

35. Wink, *Unmasking the Powers* 89, 93-94.

of the person in the company of others in Sheol. Coming back to life means leaving this earthly land (12:2). The whole person, material and spiritual, dies; the whole person, material and spiritual, is restored to life to his or her place within Israel.

In speaking in the terms it does, scripture seems to be making statements about the actual future and about actual present realms other than the one in which we live. On the other hand the references it makes to these realms use symbolism that derives from contemporary experience, as is evidenced by the fact that this symbolism may or may not work as effectively in another culture. In speaking of the realm below, the particular imagery of entities such as the "spirits in prison" in 1 Peter 3:19 may work less effectively in some cultures other than its original one. In contrast, to describe death and resurrection (the latter itself a symbol, of course, because we have no literal way of describing the future event to which we refer) as sleep and waking is a more transcultural metaphor.

The motif of the shaming of the wicked in Daniel 12 also reflects an earthly reality already alluded to in scripture. People were familiar with the way rubbish lay burning and decomposing in the Valley of Hinnom; in Isaiah 66:24 that provided a metaphor for the this-worldly fate of the wicked even in the new Jerusalem. The visible reality and the scriptural image are appropriated in application to a specific body of people in Daniel 12:2. Vindication and exposure in this life can be literally described and can thus become a metaphor for vindication and exposure after death, which cannot be literally described. Again, Daniel 12:2, in a visionary flight into the future, portrays the honoring of those discerning expositors of scripture who had been despised, in the light of the brightness of the stars and in the light of expressions from scripture (Isa 52:13; 53:11). They share in the glory of the new Jerusalem. In a number of ways revelation and human experience again interact in scripture's portrayal of past and future, the realm above and that below.

The resurrection spoken of in Daniel 12:2 also illustrates how a symbol may be both greater and less than the reality to which it refers. It may be greater because it is more naturally open to having more than one referent. It may be less because the reality to which it refers and which we may not be able to describe in a more direct way may require a number of symbolisms to do it justice. The symbol of resurrection can have a number of referents, such as the renewal of the nation, the restoring of some individuals to this-worldly life, and the granting of a new form of life in a new age. Although the apocalypses are rooted in concrete contexts, they characteristically avoid referring specifically to the historical realities of their context and thus facilitate the application of their visions beyond their original referents.[36] In addition, any one referent of a symbol such as resurrection may require other symbolisms alongside that of resurrection to express its significance. The visions in Daniel in fact use a number of symbolisms for the End to which they look, including the granting of authority to the people and the restoration of the sanctuary as well as the restoring of life; indeed, within Daniel 12:2-3 there arguably appear two symbols, elevation to the stars as well as resurrection.[37]

When Daniel speaks of the future, he thus does so in a symbolic or parabolic way, but with factual intent and value. The promise of future vindication (or exposure) is an incentive to faithfulness in the present. It may be that, in J. J. Collins's terms, the *prospect* of transcendence of death makes possible the *experience* of transcendence of death, so that this is both a future expectation and a present depth experience, as Christians begin to enjoy new life now because they know they will rise to new life.[38] The stories in Daniel could be read as expressions of the freedom believers find when they live by the conviction that death is not the worst thing that could overtake them. But this is not explicit in the visions, and Collins notes elsewhere the contrast between the Danielic visions' association of the transcendence of death with the future and the conviction in some of the Qumran writings that it is a present experience.[39] The stress in Daniel's visions is more on faithfulness in the present in the light of a transcendence of death that is promised but not yet experienced.

The Symbolism of Patriarchy

For many people the scriptural symbolism of fatherhood as applied to God, along with the gendered language of which it is an example, has become problematic. R. M. Frye argues that biblical symbolism in general and this symbolism in particular is nonnegotiable. Scripture does not say that God is Mother and only occasionally that God is *like* a mother. It does that deliberately: Canaanite religion and Gnosticism used mother-language for God, and this made them different religions. Scripture could have used this

---

36. Childs, *The New Testament as Canon* 515.
37. Collins, "The Symbolism of Transcendence" 19.
38. "Apocalyptic Eschatology as the Transcendence of Death" 43.
39. "The Symbolism of Transcendence" 10-11.

language, and did not. To call God Mother as well as Father is to presume to name God, which God alone can do; it is to introduce radically different beliefs about God.[40] D. G. Bloesch expresses the argument in another way, suggesting that the description of God as Father, Son, and Holy Spirit is analogical language rather than "mere" metaphor; unlike metaphorical language it is based on divine revelation rather than human experience.[41]

Frye presses the difference between metaphor and simile, perhaps further than it can be pressed. Further, we have to take account of the connotations of the language in both cultures. In an ancient Israelite context it may have been liberating for women that Israel avoided feminine language for God, because of the way in which that language was used in Canaanite religion.[42] The situation might be different in our world — though it might not, insofar as the language is being deliberately given connotations of a Canaanite kind. My own guess is that the latter phenomenon makes the situation and the language ambiguous, and we have to live with that. It is certainly the case that for many people talk of God as Father has inextricably gendered and patriarchal connotations that may not have been attached to it in biblical times, while talk of God as King or Lord neither interacts with human life nor fulfills the positive function it once did, that of setting standards for Israel's lords and kings.[43] The difference between translating *adelphoi* as "brothers and sisters" (Rom 12:1, NRSV) and adding "Mother" to "Father" may not be as great as Frye urges.

Similarly the claim that "Father, Son, and Holy Spirit" is based on revelation rather than human experience seems to involve a questionable antithesis, and to imply that other crucial imagery by means of which scripture describes God's person and activity does not belong to revelation. The Bible itself suggests no distinction between the two sets of terms. All the biblical images function as part of the biblical revelation and are key to it; without these images, there would be no revelation.[44]

What is distinctive of the First Testament is its reticence in calling God Father, let alone Mother, in contrast to the freedom with which other

40. See Frye, *Language for God and Feminist Language*.

41. See *Battle for the Trinity* (Ann Arbor, MI: Servant, 1985), as discussed in Wren, *What Language Shall I Borrow?* 95-102. See further the discussion in Thiselton, *New Horizons in Hermeneutics* 456-60.

42. See, e.g., Hanson, "Masculine Metaphors for God" 317-18; Terrien, *Till the Heart Sings* 59-62.

43. Wren, *What Language Shall I Borrow?* 108.

44. Cf. Farrer, *The Glass of Vision* 43.

religions in the ancient Near East and elsewhere do so. If there is a revelation concerning God's being in the First Testament it is that God is Yahweh (Exod 3), that is, that God is not the father but the liberating actor in Israel's story, the covenant-maker who makes promises, the teacher, and the creator. When all this has been established by revelation, the natural assumption that God is also Father can be allowed to reappear in the Second Testament — though even there it appears more unevenly than is often recognized.[45] As with affirmations regarding the afterlife, this is thus one of the points where, by failing to observe and work with the dynamic within scripture, Christian theology turns into merely an affirmation of what pagans already believe.

Brian Wren suggests that biblical imagery and language with its encouragement of the monarchic metaphor should not control us because it is culture-relative, because it reflects human sin, and because the Holy Spirit has not stopped revealing new things to the people of God.[46] The difficulties in this view arise from the arguments for the normativity of scripture that we have considered in Part II. It seems to me better to argue that the monarchic metaphor, as well as being only one among scriptural metaphors, is actually less dominant there than we usually realize. Because "Lord" is so common in English translations of the Hebrew Bible, we get a false impression of the dominance of this image there. In the Second Testament, the kingship image is in fact more prominent than it is in the First, but there it is turned inside out by the way it is redefined. A large part of our problem with the monarchic metaphor in scripture lies in the way the First Testament has been translated and the way the Second has been interpreted.

---

45. Ricoeur, *The Conflict of Interpretations* 482-91.
46. *What Language Shall I Borrow?* 131.

23

Scripture as a Whole
as Experienced Revelation

Scripture as a whole offers a vision of how things are, have been, and will be. Always implicit and sometimes explicit in the story told by Israel's witnessing tradition is an understanding of the nature of God and of God's ways in the world. That understanding becomes more generally explicit in the Prophets, the poetic books, and the Epistles. For us theological reflection involves considering an issue in the light of the revelation incorporated into scripture, which enables us to look at the present in the light of the past (God's involvement in history) and future (human destiny), what is above (God and the powers) and what lies below (the realm of death). Our ability to do so depends on the unity, reliability, and clarity of the purported revelation provided by scripture.

Revelation Elsewhere in Scripture

While the notion of revelation is most at home in the apocalypses, it also appears in the prophetic books. Yahweh does nothing without revealing the divine secret to prophets (Amos 3:7). The actual words "revelation" and "reveal" are infrequent; reference to seeing a "vision" is more common. Visions are commonly the means whereby prophets learn God's intentions for the future (e.g., Jer 38:21-23), though they may also concern the realm above (e.g., Ezek 1–3). But as revelations can come in words (cf. 1 Sam 3:21; Isa 22:14), so vision language is regularly used of the prophets' more common verbal communication.[1] The whole Book of Isaiah is a vision that he saw (Isa 1:1). In this terminology the work of the prophets also includes revelations concerning the realm of the past (e.g., Ezek 16; 20; 23). Whereas their nature as inspired words of God makes the prophets' messages certain to come true and significant beyond their original contexts, that they are revelations from God undergirds the truth-content of their visions concerning the four realms that revelation is concerned with — past and future, above and below. They are a reliable source of theological insight.

Paul, too, is inclined to claim a revelatory origin for key theological insights that he expresses, which is a guarantee of their truth. Characteristically he appeals to a revelation concerning the events of the past. As we have noted, strictly speaking revelation does not lie directly in the events or the documents that report them. Paul's letters are by nature records of revelations that he has received concerning the theological significance of these events and records of his reflection arising out of them. The acts are the redemption, the insights into the acts stimulated by scripture are the revelation, and the documents are the theology that reflects on the revelation. It is characteristic of the Epistles to look at contemporary issues and problems and to reflect on them in the light of the gospel, of scripture, and of the revelation that has come to the writers in the course of this reflection. Scripture is a deposit of past revelation and a means of future revelation: "not the revelation itself, but the description, the record, from which the revelation can be known."[2]

In Paul there appears another link between the notions of experienced revelation and of witnessing tradition, because he is a witness not only to the facts about Jesus' life, death, and resurrection (Acts 20:24; 26:22; 28:23), but also to what he himself saw and heard at his personal moment of revelation (Acts 22:15; 26:16 — or is the latter for Acts part of the once-for-all work of Christ?). That link also appears in the Psalms, since to acknowledge what God has done is to witness to what God has done.

There are senses in which the witnessing tradition itself may be seen as revelation. Arguably it is that by virtue of conveying good news, for the very idea of "news" suggests the unveiling of something unknown; "news is not something that is logically entailed by what is known already."[3] There

---

1. Cf. Warfield, *The Inspiration and Authority of the Bible* 88-89 = *Revelation and the Bible* 20-21 = *Biblical Foundations* 28-29.
2. Bavinck, *Our Reasonable Faith* 95.
3. H. Price, "Religious Experience and Its Problems," *Faith and the Philosophers* (ed. Hick) 36; cf. Abraham, *Divine Revelation* 85.

is a sense in which this is characteristic of all narrative: Telling a story is a process of revealing, and the later stages of the story reveal the significance of earlier events. Sometimes this involves revealing concealed facts that were chronologically prior and substantially underlay earlier events: Often a story does not unveil events in the order in which they happened but in the order in which they were revealed to a participant, or simply the order in which the narrator chooses to reveal them to the hearer.[4] In scripture's own way of speaking, however, the revelatory aspect of the witnessing tradition lies more in the insight it brings to events that would otherwise be enigmatic. The interpretation of the narratives makes events revelatory.

Authoritative canons are also revelatory. They inevitably reveal something of the one who issued them. Further, material in the Torah that regulates aspects of Israelite ritual and social life but that ceases to be normative for behavior once Christ has come then takes on a new role as a theological resource. It provides categories with which the church thinks through the significance of Christ's death as an act of atonement and means of purification.

Among the wisdom books, Job illustrates the interplay between experience, revelation, and reflection. As a wisdom book its essential nature is to reflect on experience, but a distinctive feature of it is the key place it gives to revelation in the outworking of this reflection. The book recognizes that revelation as such is not of unequivocal significance. Eliphaz appeals to a revelation that came to him, one that confirmed the old truths that Job's experience actually questioned (4:12-21). Elihu reminds Job of the personal revelations that may come to sinners to turn them back into the right way (33:14-18) — another insight that is true but inapplicable to Job. Positively, however, the book begins with a double revelation concerning events in heaven, which, it suggests, provide the theological backdrop to the events on earth in chapters 3–37, and closes with another double revelation offering insight into the nature of God's involvement with the world as Lord of creation and of the forces of disorder within creation. The appeal to revelation in a wisdom book further illustrates scripture's relaxed attitude to the relationship between reason and revelation, which has preoccupied theology since the Enlightenment, and to the relationship between experience and revelation, which is a more recent concern.

The relationships among experience, revelation, and reflection also arise in Psalms. In general, one may presume that the psalms are not merely or not

4. Cf. Culler, *The Pursuit of Signs* 169-87; cf. p. 49 above.

always white-hot expressions of how people felt in the midst of some experience of pain or joy. Like Christian hymnody and poetry they are lyrics that express in retrospect and in prospect the nature of that experience. They look back on that experience in order to turn it into prayer and praise that individuals and communities will also use on future occasions as the vehicles of prayer and praise. They are the fruit of reflection on experience. They also frequently involve revelation, which comes between the experience of pain and the experience of deliverance and on which the psalmist has therefore inevitably if unconsciously reflected before composing the prayer or praise.

A number of psalms make explicit that a word from God was located between lament and praise, a word that indicated how the future would turn out and made possible the transition from lament to praise (see Ps 12). Others make explicit the element of reflection on such a word from God (see Ps 60). Psalm 73 provides a striking instance of the interplay between experience, revelation, and experience. It recalls an experience of affliction despite a life of commitment and of resentment at the contrasting way in which the wicked flourished. It testifies to the insight received in the sanctuary (for "insight" the psalmist uses a term that in Daniel would denote a personal revelation from God, but the psalm can equally be understood to refer to a "penny dropping"). It relates the experience of feeling restored in spirit even if external circumstances are unchanged.

It is the *absence* of an experience of God acting that lies in the background of Ecclesiastes, which witnesses to the patternlessness of human life as we actually experience it. Proverbs, in fact, does the same, though less polemically. Such books have no plot, denouement, or revelation.

Diversity and Unity in the Scriptural Revelation

If the scriptures reflect God's revelation, their contents will cohere; they will point to one consistent reality. "If in fact the Bible in some sense comes from the one God . . . it would seem to follow that the end-product of its effect would have some sort of unity and not be absolutely self-contradictory."[5] Indeed, even insofar as the Bible comes from the church, it reflects the church's conviction that its various parts express the one apostolic faith and suggests an approach to reading it that looks for

---

5. Barr, *The Bible in the Modern World* 99; cf. Packer, *"Fundamentalism" and the Word of God* 84.

coherence. Article 20 of the Church of England declares that the church may not "so expound one place of Scripture, that it be repugnant to another." The part is to be understood in the light of the whole, in the fashion of what later came to be known as a hermeneutical circle. Formulating one coherent understanding of its writings and expecting to reconcile tensions among them is not a concern worked out in scripture itself, but it is consistent with scripture's concern for us to "preach the whole counsel of God" (Acts 20:27).

That these writings are indeed a whole, a unity, is "a postulate that is itself dogmatically founded," and from an eighteenth-century perspective seems to exclude the interpretation of individual parts of scripture in their own right.[6] The sense in which one can clarify a point of Paul's by reference to John or understand Genesis in the light of the Second Testament has thus been qualified by the awareness that each of these writings, while reflecting God's revelation, was put into words by particular human beings concerned to be intelligible in particular contexts. We have discovered that "reading for contrast, rather than simply reading for harmony, can be wonderfully illuminating of the text," bringing an illumination that "depends upon doing precisely what Article 20 instructs us not to do."[7]

That is so because scripture is characterized by variety. "The Bible, and even the New Testament, does not look like a book which conveys a single coherent body of truth."[8] It manifests a rich diversity in the contexts it reflects and the attitudes it takes up. The theologizing of the First Testament revolves round two very different experiences, the triumph of escape from Egypt and the humiliation of exile in Babylon, while that of the Second juxtaposes the shame of crucifixion and the triumph of resurrection. The ethical insights of the Bible embrace both the ideals of creation and of the rule of God proclaimed in Christ and the condescension to Israel's willfulness whereby God adapts the standards of creation and redemption to the human reality. The Bible sees the world both as God's sphere, in which we are to be involved, and as the sphere of evil powers, from which we are to distance ourselves. It sometimes safeguards the divine sovereignty by assuming that God is responsible for all events and sometimes safeguards God's goodwill to us by noting the involvement of other powers in events (cf. 2 Sam 24:1; 1 Chr 21:1).

6. Gadamer, *Truth and Method* 155.
7. O'Donovan, *On the Thirty Nine Articles* 57.
8. Nineham, *Explorations in Theology* 1:98. Vawter begins his *Biblical Inspiration* (2-8) with a forceful statement of scripture's diversity.

There are times when violence is commended and times for turning the other cheek, times for an emphasis on human material needs and times for emphasizing forgiveness and inner renewal, times for a stress on order and times for a stress on conflict, times for a stress on faith in Christ and times for a stress on works of obedience to Christ.

Sometimes passages of scripture are in dialogue with one another, qualifying or elaborating each other as one half-line of a psalm is followed by another, one creation story by another, one story about David or Saul by a variant, Samuel-Kings as a whole by Chronicles (while Ecclesiastes's attitudes and beliefs stand over against those of the same time expressed in Chronicles), one miracle of loaves and fish by another, one Gospel by others, and the First Testament as a whole by the Second.[9] It seems that one version of anything is never enough. Scripture points to complementarities such as creation and redemption, grace and works, divine power and divine weakness, this life and the life to come, oneness and plurality in God, faith and uncertainty, judgment and mercy, nationalism and universalism, individual and community, and Messiah and nonmessiah. Interpreting scripture involves discerning in what way and with what qualifications the various writings make a claim on us when they are considered in the light of each other.[10]

It can seem that the kind of study that identifies tensions within scripture is destructive of belief in scripture's unity and perhaps designed to force us to choose between one voice and another. The appropriate response is not necessarily to dispute the differences between the voices but to affirm that they can be heard forming a harmony. The Bible is a product of human history in its diversity, but this does not preclude that it has its own kind of unity.

> It is somewhat like John James's understanding of the cathedral at Chartres. Chartres is surely the finest expression of Gothic cathedral architecture of all that exist. It is awe-inspiring and breathtaking. . . . And yet James, who spent years studying its every nook, cranny, and detail, says it is in actual fact "a mess."[11]

9. Reed, "A Poetics of the Bible" 161; cf. B. M. Ejxenbaum's comments on literary interpretation in *Readings in Russian Poetics* (ed. Matejka and Pomorska) 17-18; also current discussion of intertextuality, e.g., Culler, *The Pursuit of Signs* 100-118.

10. See Wood, *The Formation of Christian Understanding* 73-74. I have considered these complementarities in *Theological Diversity and the Authority of the Old Testament* 188-99.

11. J. A. Sanders, *From Sacred Story to Sacred Text* 4, quoting J. James, *Chartres* (London/Boston: Routledge, 1982) 9.

Both the cathedral and the Bible are wholes greater than their parts, and both witness to one God. In scripture God worked with people in different contexts and revealed things accordingly; different parts of scripture were confronting different misapprehensions about the nature of faith and obedience and need to be understood and interrelated in the light of that fact. "The 'unity' of the Bible is . . . something to be *sought;* not a starting-point but a goal of the process of study, interpretation and theological thinking."[12] Indeed, like the unity of scripture, its diversity has a basis in the being of God, which is characterized by diversity as well as unity. We cannot argue that the diversity of scripture reflects the explicitly trinitarian nature of God, but at least that diversity coheres with the trinitarian nature of God, while God's trinitarian nature makes the diverse nature of scripture unsurprising and casts light on it.[13]

A further consideration that underlies scripture's nature as characterized by both diversity and unity is that it belongs to God's one history with humanity, extending over time. To talk in terms of scripture and not merely scriptures, holy book and not merely holy books, involves presupposing that in itself scripture's variety does not imply contradiction. Indeed, the view that it does imply contradiction "bespeaks an ahistorical, two-dimensional understanding of the Scriptural texts that conceives of them all as synchronous and competing propositions, rather than dialectically successive and mutually implicating testimonies of God's unfolding self-disclosure."[14] Reading for unity is not merely a reader's strategy but a response to a theological truth about a unity in God's historical dealings with humanity.

We read both for diversity and for unity in the conviction that there is a coherent total picture to be gained from treating individually illuminating insights as having the potential together to form an illuminating whole. Furthermore, while an understanding of the whole depends on an understanding of the parts, the whole also provides a means of understanding the parts and a new context for them that offers some safeguard against taking one element out of proportion or appropriating a single insight on a topic out of the context of the rest of scripture's material on that topic. The rule for the faith, our outline understanding of the Christian faith, provides us with a key to the framework of thinking that emerges from

12. Barr, *The Bible in the Modern World* 99, emphasis original.
13. Gunton, *Enlightenment and Alienation* 140-41.
14. O'Donovan, *On the Thirty Nine Articles* 61.

scripture as a whole. Scripture is a unity in that all of it is expressive of the rule for the faith. But it is expressive of that faith in diverse ways, and the rule for the faith is itself subject to testing by those diverse expressions. If they cannot be understood in terms of the rule, then the rule needs reconsidering. Garrett Green puts this point in different terms by arguing for "a gestalt view of the canon," that is, for seeing the unity of scripture as like the polyphonic unity of a symphony, to which diversity and even dissonance make contributions.[15]

The need to take individual insights in the context of the whole can be illustrated in connection with the study of individual books. Proverbs, for instance, collects a range of material on areas of life such as money and man-woman relationships. A proverb is often designed to be a sharp embodiment of a very specific insight, but that means that it may be unbalanced on its own. Many individual sayings — commending or downgrading wealth, reminding men of their weaknesses or women of theirs — in themselves offer onesided guidance. They belong in the context of the total range of this material, which as a whole recognizes the complexity of the factors that we must take into account in coming to decisions about attitudes and behavior. Observations on the advantages of money and on how to obtain it have to be set in the context of observations about the drawbacks of money and on how to get rid of it (and vice versa). The exhortations to husbands, "Love, don't wander," and to wives, "Do, don't nag," have to be set alongside each other. Individual sayings in Proverbs were of independent origin, but they are now elements in a united whole. Their introduction (1:1-7) invites us to read them as a whole, treating the book as a "text." Something similar may be said of individual psalms in the context of the Psalter.[16]

The collection of books to form the Hebrew Bible and its expansion into the Christian Bible provide a further whole that constitutes a context for the individual books. Each of the books (e.g., Genesis) is both a complete independent text, which provides the context for individual chapters within it, and a constitutive text within the scripture as a whole.[17] On a broader scale, the conviction that we are handling scripture as well as scriptures

15. *Imagining God* 114, 115; Green compares Kelsey, *The Uses of Scripture in Recent Theology* 108.

16. Jeanrond, *Text and Interpretation* 82. Psalms 1 and 150, along with the division into five books, provide similar invitations to a unified reading of the Psalter: see further Brueggemann, "Bounded by Obedience and Praise."

17. Jeanrond, *Text and Interpretation* 91.

suggests the need to look beyond the perspectives suggested on a particular topic within one book, even — or especially — a book that majors on a particular topic, to the perspectives offered on that topic within scripture as a whole, and to scripture's total perspective and scale of values, which suggests the context in which any consideration of the topic needs to be undertaken. What Exodus or the Song of Songs says about sex could be dangerously narrow: Either might give a misleading account of how to look at sex and how to see the significance of sex in relation to other matters.[18]

What Paul (and God) wanted to say to the Corinthians we discover from 1 and 2 Corinthians. What God might want to say to us we learn by considering that discovery in the light of other scriptures. Mark, Paul, and John conceive of the person of Christ in ways that differ from each other, even when they use similar expressions such as "son of God." If we are to take them all as embodying God's revelation, interpreting them involves considering them in the light of each other, once we have established what each writer individually means by this title. They will be capable of becoming part of a coherent whole at the level of thought and concepts if not at the level of their own words. The South African *Kairos Document* formulated an important distinction between "prophetic theology" and "academic theology": The former, like the Israelite prophets, does not pretend to offer a system of general principles and doctrines in the manner of the latter, but concentrates instead on those aspects of the word of God that have an immediate bearing on our situation.[19] These two forms of theology complement each other; either on its own is a danger.

Diverse attitudes to death and an afterlife may be considered in this light. We bring together Proverbs' confident focus on this life, Job's denial of an afterlife, Daniel's affirmation of resurrection, and Paul's basing of this affirmation in the raising of Jesus, all in order to see the significance of each of them. Different Christian groups emphasize the significance of baptism as a sign of God's grace, which is therefore appropriately administered to children, or as a sign of human commitment, one that is therefore appropriate only for adults, and both find a basis for their view within scripture itself.

The diversity of scripture is brought out by a comparison of the First Testament with the Second, and Article 7 of the Church of England thus anticipates the convictions of Article 20 by declaring that "the Old Testa-

---

18. Cf. Childs's treatment from his perspective in *Biblical Theology in Crisis* 184-200.
19. Cf. West, *Biblical Hermeneutics of Liberation* 40.

ment is not contrary to the New." Its claim that in both Testaments everlasting life is offered to humanity through Christ may seem an unfortunate example, but it is less unreliable than the common Christian view that — despite Romans 4 — Israel believed itself saved through observance of the law. Article 7's recognition that some of the law's functions belonged only to pre-Christian times is a further testimony to the diverse places that different parts of the First Testament occupy within one history.

In this connection the diversity within scripture as a whole can be markedly reduced if the particular emphases of the First Testament can be eliminated. Grace can be emphasized rather than law, love rather than justice, forgiveness rather than wrath (especially the annihilation of the Canaanites), and the life to come rather than this life. J. L. Segundo has thus observed that the whole of theology has been conditioned by the attitude it takes — or rather by its failure to formulate a coherent attitude — to the question of the relationship between the two Testaments.[20] Ignoring the First Testament, regarding it as superseded by the Second, or assimilating it to the Second by means of allegory and typology, can thus significantly simplify the complex nature of biblical attitudes. Conversely, that liberation theology treats Exodus as a privileged text and enthuses over the prophets may imply an unthought-out reversion from Second Testament perspectives to those of the First, as if Jesus had not yet come. Both Testaments have to be read in the light of each other, with their relatively greater stress on the material and on the religious. The exodus both explains later events and is explained by them. The danger of biblical theology and biblical interpretation is always that they will simplify the complexity of reality and of scripture.

Theological Inerrancy

Does the whole of the Bible reflect divine revelation, so that scripture is theologically inerrant? We have noted that inerrancy is a questionable quality to attribute to the witnessing tradition: Any witness and tradition need to be fundamentally reliable, but we do not expect to attribute inerrancy to them and may even be hindered from taking them seriously as what they are when excessive claims of this kind are made on their behalf. Inerrancy is a quality more at home with the authoritative canon because the appli-

20. *Liberation of Theology* 113.

cation of that model to scripture does suggest that it is the measure that we apply to our views and lives as we seek to discover whether there are erroneous features in our views and lives — rather than using our views to measure the canon. But still the attribution of inerrancy to the authoritative canon may mask the variety of standards allowed by the canon. Inerrancy is an appropriate quality to associate with the inspired word, insofar as the declared purpose of God is bound to find fulfillment without fail. On the other hand, talk in terms of the inerrancy of the prophetic word tends to obscure the fact that any particular promise or warning is open to nonfulfillment as the implicit conditions attached to it fail to be fulfilled or as God has a change of mind.[21]

Inerrancy is also an odd quality to attribute to scripture as revelation. If we were to say that a telephone directory or a set of printer's proofs was free from error, it would seem a natural remark. We would mean that it is the kind of detailed work that easily contains errors, especially in regard to matters of fact, but that in this case does not. To describe the Nicene Creed or *Hymns of Olney* or *Anna Karenina* as free from error, however, seems less natural. It is not that they contain mistakes, but that this seems a strange category to apply to them. They may be free of error, but their importance to us lies elsewhere, in qualities such as insight and depth. Biblical revelation surely resembles *Hymns of Olney* more than the telephone directory. Inerrancy is an odd quality to focus on.

Nevertheless the question whether scripture is sometimes simply wrong is one that has to be handled. The people of God are ordinary human beings and easily mishear God. Christian vision and theology mix insight and misapprehension. They are limited by the perspectives of the individual and the perspectives of the age. Theological insight, like historical insight, is subject to the ten percent rule ("ten percent of what I say is wrong, the trouble is I don't know which ten percent"). Given another aspect of scripture's diversity, the variety in the levels of insight in different parts of it, it might seem that the ordinary human recipients of God's revelation preserved in the scriptures also inevitably introduced an element of sin and error into what they wrote.

In receiving scripture as God's revelation, however, Israel and the church expressed the conviction that it offers a thoroughly reliable account of the truths about the four realms, past and future, above and below. The explicit conviction of scripture's doctrinal infallibility comes first in No-

---

21. Cf. Barr, *Fundamentalism* 277.

vatian, who in arguing about the Trinity speaks of "the heavenly scriptures, which never deceive."[22] As a Christian I have been grasped by scripture's presentation of God's truth as it once grasped the Jewish people and the early church. I could decide that I am free to distinguish within it between genuine insight and points where the visionary saw things askew. Like the believing communities of old, however, I have been grasped by this vision *as a whole*. I am hesitant to go picking and choosing within it, and I have often learned things by continuing to work at aspects of it that at first seemed odd. So I prefer to assume with those believing communities that God's providence saw to it that their visionary theologians saw things straight, even if they sometimes saw only parts of the picture. It seems a good working hypothesis that material in scripture that seems to raise problems for us is material we need to keep working at to try to hear it aright as sharing in God's truthfulness, rather than material we can feel free to discount as present by divine oversight. The conviction that God's grace and providence lay behind the human words of scripture formed a response to the awareness that these words spoke with the depth, insight, illumination, force, encouragement, and challenge of divine revelation. The belief that scripture is a mixture of true revelation and material affected by human sin sits uncomfortably with the awareness that God, in being involved in the emergence of scripture, so spectacularly and so substantially avoided being circumscribed by the human limitations of its writers.

To deny that scripture offers timeless propositions concerning doctrinal matters is not in itself to accuse scripture of doctrinal error.[23] Scripture is time-bound in the sense that its message is addressed to specific contexts and can only be understood against those contexts, but its significance transcends the contexts in which it came into being. Nevertheless, the arguments of Job or the observations of Ecclesiastes, for instance, are presented to us as comments in the context of a debate, not final conclusions. As we noted in the previous section of this chapter, not only must individual statements be seen in the context of the book from which they come; individual books must be seen in the context of the total scriptural debate. Norbert Lohfink suggests that it is questionable whether we should think in terms of the infallibility or inerrancy of individual statements or books. Only scripture as a whole should be described as infallible.[24] Individual

---

22. *The Trinity* XXX.16 *(nunquam fallunt)*.
23. Against Geisler, *Biblical Errancy* 232-33.
24. *The Christian Meaning of the Old Testament* 33-39.

books are only true or inerrant in that wider context. They must not be silenced by the rest of scripture, but neither must they be seen in isolation from it.[25]

Progressive Revelation and Divine Condescension

R. A. Finlayson speaks of "degrees of revelation" within scripture, varying levels of clarity or light about what God reveals at different moments.[26] As well as reflecting the nature of God, the complexity of reality itself, and the variety of the situations addressed, the diversity of scripture also reflects the differences between absolute truth and rightness and what people can cope with at a particular moment. In seeking to grasp the revelation in scripture as a whole, we must allow for differences in level, but seek to plot these in the light of scripture's own priorities rather than merely in such a way as to reflect the priorities of our culture.[27]

The model of progressive revelation provides a classic way to bring the different levels into relationship, so as to bracket those of the First Testament without formally declaring that its revelation was not revelation.[28] Progressive revelation presupposes that higher perceptions have to build on lower perceptions and that God was involved in the process whereby scriptural writers moved from earlier perceptions to later, higher ones. This has the advantage of enabling us to emphasize the finality of Jesus as God's fullest revelation, and it has provided British evangelicals with a model for interrelationships within scripture that has enabled them to hold onto scripture without going through an equivalent to the American fundamentalist controversy.[29]

But the model of progressive revelation does raise a number of difficulties. First, it is as easy to suggest instances whereby later perspectives are shallower than earlier ones as to suggest instances where they are more profound. The raw material does not fit the model. In general, indeed, it has commonly been reckoned that development within the First Testament

25. Brown, *The Critical Meaning of the Bible* 19-20.

26. "Contemporary Ideas of Inspiration," *Revelation and the Bible* (ed. Henry) 222.

27. Cf. the debate between Barth and Bultmann over *Sachkritik* or theological evaluation of scripture, which I have discussed in *Theological Diversity and the Authority of the Old Testament* 116-21.

28. See Rogerson, "Progressive Revelation," for a history and critique.

29. Wright, "Soundings in the Doctrine of Scripture in British Evangelicalism" 92-93.

and then in the Second took the people of God from a higher level, characterized by the dynamic of the Spirit, to the later, more institutionalized faith of Chronicles or the Pastoral Epistles. Second, the model provides a rationale for abandoning some perspectives within scripture — particularly some or much of the First Testament — rather than a way of seeing scripture as a whole as coherent. It is, after all, a religious version of the evolutionary model of development in thinking, which presupposes that later stages supersede earlier stages. Further, it implies a rather quantitative approach to understanding God's revelation. In reality, the whole of God's person was always revealed to people, even if different aspects of God's truth were perceived with different degrees of clarity.[30]

A more promising model for understanding different levels of revelation in scripture is the idea of God's accommodation. Jesus regards Moses' instructions concerning behavior as subject to the constraint of his audience (Mark 10:5; cf. Gal 3:23-25), and the same is true of Jesus' own teaching about matters such as his own significance and his disciples' relationship with him (John 16:4) and of the teaching of Second Testament writers (Heb 5:11-14). God accommodates the revelation of the truth to the limitations of those to whom it is given. The model of accommodation avoids some of the disadvantages that attach to that of progressive revelation. It makes no assumption about whether material of a higher level is earlier or later.

The idea of God's accommodation is taken up by Fathers such as Origen and Chrysostom, in part as an equivalent to the modern discussion in terms of analogical language. Origen sees the anthropomorphisms of scripture as instances of God's willingness to adapt language to hearers in this way.[31] When scripture talks of God's anger, Origen says, it uses the method of address that suits the ability and benefit of the hearers. God assumes human characteristics for the advantage of human beings. It speaks of hellfire like a parent using the language appropriate to children of a tender age(!).[32] Chrysostom's equivalent term is "condescension" or "considerateness,"[33] which he, too, uses to suggest that the descriptions of God observing that creation is

---

30. Ramsey, "The Authority of the Bible" 7.

31. His word is *symperiphora*, suggesting the way a person adapts when "going about with" someone. The term appears in Philo and Clement of Alexandria (Vawter, *Biblical Inspiration* 40-41).

32. *Against Celsus* IV.71; V.16.

33. The latter is R. C. Hill's preferred rendering of *synkatabasis*: see, e.g., his translation of Chrysostom's *Homilies on Genesis 1–17* (Washington: Catholic University of America, 1986) 17; also "On Looking Again at *sunkatabasis*."

good or forming Adam or walking in the garden in the cool of the day are not intended literally but are designed to give *some* grasp of ineffable mysteries to people characterized by human weakness. The same is true of the references to the Word being in the Father's bosom and to people seeing God.[34] Chrysostom also uses this idea as a more general way of conceiving of God speaking through a human author at all and of seeing how God could speak historically. He can thus sometimes allow for the words of God being relative to particular situations rather than expressions of absolute timeless truth, as they invariably are for Origen.[35]

Speaking through a human being, God condescends to speak through what humans are able to say. Near the beginning of his exposition of John, Augustine comments:

> To speak of the matter as it is, who is able? I venture to say, my brethren, perhaps not John himself spoke of the matter as it is, but even he only as he was able; for it was still a man that spoke of God, inspired indeed by God, but still a man. Because he was inspired he said something. If he had not been inspired he would have said nothing. But because he was a man inspired, he spoke not the whole, but what a man could speak, that he spoke.[36]

Calvin uses the idea of accommodation to explain the differences between forms of worship before and after Christ[37] and other instances in which Jesus seems to be "starting where people are" and not saying what one might expect (e.g., Matt 19:17).[38] Calvin appeals to this notion when the creation story fails to include angels or implies that the sun and moon are the only two planets in our solar system: In both cases God accommodates to speaking from the perspective of an ordinary human being, treating the readers of scripture the way a mother does when she confines her concepts and language to ones her children can understand.[39] Calvin also

---

34. *Homilies on Genesis* III.9-10; XV.8; XVII.3 on Gen 1:4; 2:21; 3:8; *Homilies on the Gospel according to St. John* XV.1-2 on John 1:18.

35. See Vawter, *Biblical Inspiration* 41, for this distinction; Vawter notes that Chrysostom sometimes assumes that scriptural writers share the omniscience of God and are involved in condescension rather than objects of it.

36. *Homilies on John* I.1.

37. *Institutes* II.11.13.

38. *Institutes* II.18.9.

39. *Institutes* I.14.3; *Commentaries on the First Book of Moses called Genesis*, on 1:16. For Calvin accommodation is practiced by God together with the scriptural authors

uses the idea of accommodation to explain statements about God that he cannot take literally, such as allusions to God's repentance, anger, laughter, enmity, yearning, remembering, returning, sleeping, resting, smelling, or planting a garden.[40] H. N. Ridderbos suggests a further instance of this accommodation: The Holy Spirit is content not only with messages that picture the universe in the customary ways of their human authors' day but also with quotations in the Second Testament from the words of God in the First that utilize inaccurate translations.[41]

The model of accommodation may provide a way of approaching other aspects of scripture that raise difficulties for us, such as the Zionism of the First Testament and the anti-Judaism of the Second, or the gendered language for God, which we have considered already (chapter 22 above), along with other aspects of scripture's way of speaking about women and men. There is a risk involved in speaking of Israel as a woman who is rightly punished, since this may seem to legitimate violence against women. And there is a risk involved in portraying Christ as one who accepts the position of a slave, since this may seem to legitimate the institution of slavery.[42] There is even a risk involved in stressing the cross, because this may encourage people to accept the cross of their own oppression and look for no liberation, to indulge in the cult of suffering and fatalism.[43] The scriptural text at this point may reflect liberating or feminist values, but it is open to an ideological patriarchal use as the basis for urging a battered wife to take up the cross and suffer as Jesus did in order to save her marriage[44] or for urging black South Africans to subject themselves compliantly to their oppressors. After going blind, John Hull was curious about whether

---

over against their readers, as is clear in the discussion in Genesis 1 of the size of the planets. Berkouwer comments that only later is the idea of accommodation adapted to express an understanding of the relationship between God and the scriptural authors themselves (see *Holy Scripture* 176-77), but we have seen that the idea appears in this connection in Augustine, even though the actual term is missing.

40. *Institutes* I.17.13; II.16.2; *Commentaries on the First Book of Moses called Genesis,* on 2:8; see also Battles, "God Was Accommodating Himself to Human Capacity."

41. *Authority* 61, quoted in Berkouwer, *Holy Scripture* 173.

42. So R. J. Weems, "Gomer," and S. Briggs, "Can an Enslaved God Liberate?," in *Interpretation for Liberation* (ed. Cannon and Schüssler Fiorenza) 87-104 and 137-53; cf. van Dijk-Hemmes's study of Hosea and the Song of Songs, "The Imagination of Power," and Wren's comments on Hosea 2 in *What Language Shall I Borrow?* 109-10.

43. Segundo, "The Shift within Latin American Theology" 19-20, quoting L. Boff, "Teologia à escuta do povo," *Revista Eclesiástica Brasileira* 41 (1981) 65.

44. So E. Schüssler Fiorenza, *Bread Not Stone* 18.

the Bible had anything to say to him as a blind person, and he did not like what he discovered. "What I found was that God was everywhere described as the God of light. . . . This book, I felt, is for sighted people; I am in another world. Where is the God of my world? Is there a God of the blind?"[45] Any form of speech that speaks forcefully to some people risks conveying silence or error to others.

Many of these examples illustrate how accommodation can become a device to enable us to discount statements that we find disagreeable. More fundamentally, van Buren asks whether the idea of accommodation reflects an inadequate understanding of what was involved in creation itself. It seems to deny that the God who speaks to us or to whom we speak really did create us as beings made in God's image with whom God can thus have natural full personal contact.[46] It remains important to preserve the principle that any theological statement in scripture has some contribution to make in the context of the total perspective on reality suggested by scripture as a whole.

The Clarity of the Scriptural Revelation

The idea of the clarity of scripture received explicit and urgent expression during the Reformation. Scripture was intelligible; it did not need interpretation brought to it from outside (e.g., from the church's teaching) and it can and should be understood literally. According to Luther, "in [the Pope's] kingdom nothing is more commonly stated . . . than the idea that the Scriptures are obscure and ambiguous, so that the spirit to interpret them must be sought from the Apostolic See of Rome."[47] Behind the argument about the clarity of scripture is an argument about whom scripture belongs to and whether it is a means of control. Luther acknowledged that there were mysteries about God that remained mysteries (cf. Isa 40:13; Rom 11:33), that there were more down-to-earth facts that remained as yet unrevealed (cf. Mark 13:32; Acts 1:7), and that there were particular obscurities about some texts (cf. 2 Pet 3:16). He noted that nevertheless scripture presupposed its own fundamental clarity (see, e.g., Pss 19:9; 119:130;

45. Interview in the *Independent* (London), 8 July 1991.
46. *A Theology of the Jewish-Christian Reality* 1:101, 103.
47. "The Bondage of the Will," ET *LW* 33:90; see further 24-28, 89-100. Cf. Althaus, *The Theology of Martin Luther* 76-78.

2 Pet 1:19), and he denied that obscurities over detail compromised this essential clarity on the central doctrines of the faith. Where someone could not see this clarity, the problem lay in their sight (cf. 2 Cor 3:15; 4:3-4). "Scripture is its own interpreter."[48]

In writing this book I am seeking to make its meaning clear. It should not require interpretation; interpretation is needed only when something is unclear. If scripture is clear in meaning, why does it require interpretation?

First, while this particular text seeks to be explicit and patent in its meaning, not all texts do so. An element of polyvalence or irreducible ambiguity characterizes parts of scripture — and all texts, to some degree.

Second, for all readers, to one degree or another, scripture comes from other cultures and speaks in languages other than their own. It requires translation. Because God condescended to speak in human languages to human beings in the contexts of their particular lives, for other people to understand scripture they must understand foreign languages and foreign contexts. To affirm the clarity of scripture is not to claim that it is immediately clear to anyone but to affirm that its meaning is in principle accessible to anyone and to deny the necessity for arbitrary or high-handed interpretation. The church as a whole can check out whether scripture says what it is alleged to say, in the manner of the Jews of Beroea (Acts 17:11). It does not have to defer to religious — or secular — experts. The gift of scripture does not exclude the human activities of research and understanding but rather calls for them.[49]

Third, subjectively scripture may often seem unclear. The disciples on the way to Emmaus were apparently at fault for not being able to understand the scriptures (Luke 24:27), though the same does not seem to be true of the Ethiopian eunuch (Acts 8:31). Both required the right preunderstanding if they were to understand scripture rightly.

Fourth, in a narrower sense questions arise in connection with particularly enigmatic parts of scripture, which seem to require interpretation in the sense of explanation rather than in the sense of translation. 2 Peter laments the difficulty in understanding aspects of Paul's letters (2 Pet 3:16); this plays into the hand of the ignorant and unstable who can twist the meaning of the letters, but Paul did not invent the difficulties. Paradoxically it is the revelatory parts of scripture that are least clear and that most require

48. See *WA* 7:97, as quoted by Ebeling, *Word and Faith* 306.
49. Berkouwer, *Holy Scripture* 271, 272, 285.

interpretation. With a further double paradox they sometimes receive this interpretation within scripture itself, in particular within Daniel, but characteristically the interpretation leaves their truly enigmatic aspects unclear. Opaqueness attaches to such texts in their essence; it is not merely a consequence of passage into alien contexts or times. It reflects the depth of the matters with which the texts deal and our lack of experience of them, which means we cannot have them explained to us. The factors that led to the need of revelation concerning these matters are also the factors that make such matters remain opaque.

Fifth, the assertion that the text is generally accessible is one that could be made about any text. With regard to scripture that assertion also makes a theological point, a point about the contents of scripture more than about its words. The claim is that the message about salvation is clear and intelligible. "The confession of perspicuity is not a statement in general concerning the human language of Scripture, but a confession concerning the perspicuity of the gospel *in* Scripture."[50] The gospel has been clearly revealed, says Luther in dispute with Erasmus over the obscurity of scripture.[51] The basic gospel message is clear to the ordinary person who has never heard of Nebuchadnezzar or Gnosticism.

---

50. Berkouwer, *Holy Scripture* 275; he refers to H. W. Rossouw, *Klaarheid en Interprasie* (Amsterdam: Campen, 1963).
51. See p. 345 above.

24

Human Experience and Theological Reflection in the Two Testaments

The whole of scripture reflects human experience, though material such as the Psalms and some of Paul's letters is more explicit in its relationship with human experience, and specifically experience of God. Consideration of that theme raises questions concerning the relationship between the experience of God to which the First Testament testifies and that which people have in Christ.

Human Experience in Scripture

By virtue of being a human book, the whole of scripture reflects human experience. Its narratives offer little direct information on its authors or intended audience, but even in telling a story, whether more factual or more fictional, scripture reflects the experience of those people. Scriptural narrative grew as a new generation linked its own story with the story of God's dealings with the community in the past. The narrative from Genesis to Kings tells Israel's story up to the exile; Chronicles-Ezra-Nehemiah adapts that story and adds to it the experience of the Second Temple community. In all probability Genesis-Kings itself had developed in this way as succeeding generations updated the story they received. Luke adds part of the story of the early church to his Gospel; here in Acts the "implied author" explicitly introduces himself and his own experience in its "we passages." Paul, too, links his story with the story of Jesus (e.g., 1 Cor 15:1-11).

By their very nature, letters — at least letters such as Paul's — reveal more of the person who writes.[1] Paul's testimony appears in its own right in Philippians 3, while his relationship with particular churches leads him to speak of his experience at some length in 2 Corinthians and Galatians. The ministry of the prophets, too, especially that of Jeremiah, sometimes involves them in explicitly relating their experience with God. Implicitly this is so when they relate God's experiences. We have referred to Jeremiah 8:18–9:6, which famously relates the experience of Jeremiah and God in such a way as to make it difficult to discern which is the one and which is the other. Alonso Schökel notes the difference between a thesis concerning the love of God in a theology manual and the testimony to God's experience in Hosea 11:1-9. It is the latter, as it combines (not replaces) the language of statement with the expressive language of address, which is more "revealing," so that we are invited (in Gregory the Great's words) to "come to know the heart of God in the words of God."[2]

Scripture as a whole, then, reflects the experience of the believing communities. There is no other way to write. Nevertheless there are parts of scripture that are more explicitly and self-consciously the fruit or expression of human experience. They give testimony both to human experience in the sense of what people can learn empirically from what they see in everyday life, truths that anyone can verify from their own experience of life, and they give testimony also to people's inner personal experience and their experience of God. While the commands of the Torah are the foundations of the world (Ps 119) by virtue of the fact that morality provides structure and order for human life, the Torah is complemented by works such as the Song of Songs and the Psalms, which reflect the dynamic power of experience in human life.

In scripture the wisdom books are the great repository of empirical experience, the Psalms that of religious experience. It is immediately noticeable, however, that the wisdom books set the empirical within the context of the reality of God and of ethical values. They attempt to prove neither, and imply that these are part of the reality acknowledged by the

---

1. Cf. Bartlett, *The Shape of Scriptural Authority* 119-25.
2. *Letter to Theodore*, PL 77:706; cf. Alonso Schökel, *The Inspired Word* 140, where he goes on to compare Romans 7 with its revelation in the reaction of human beings confronted by God; also 137-42 generally.

whole world and not just revealed to Israel. They assume that God is real, and they experience life with God as part of it. At the same time, in different ways they recognize that empirical observation does not solve all problems, and the Book of Job provides Job with a way of living with experience only by providing him with a special revelation of the kind that most people never receive and even Job cannot expect to receive again.

In a parallel way the Psalms set religious consciousness within the context of a reality of God defined from outside rather than from within the religious experience of the individual or of one generation. Indeed, ultimately it is grounded not in the inner experience of other people at all but in the events of God's external history with Israel and in the divine word addressed to Israel. At the same time the Psalms make it possible for us to face the reality of the feelings present within us. People are often offended by aspects of the feelings expressed in the Psalms, such as the desire for vengeance, but this taking of offense commonly masks a refusal to acknowledge feelings within oneself that one cannot accept but with which the Psalms resonate.

> The real theological problem . . . is not that vengeance is *there* in the Psalms, but that it is *here* in our midst. And that it is there and here only reflects how attuned the Psalter is to what goes on among us. Thus, we may begin with a recognition of the acute correspondence between what is *written there* and what is *practiced here*.[3]

We understand scripture in the light of our experience, but then the text "becomes a hermeneutic aid in the understanding of present experience."[4] Further, we may then discern a true contrast between our experience and that to which the Psalms witness, when we "bring our own experience to the Psalms" and permit it to be disciplined by their speech.[5]

Gerhard von Rad described the Psalms and the wisdom books in general as Israel's response to God, a way of thinking that James Barr was prepared to extend to scripture as a whole in preference to a too supernaturalist understanding of scripture as the word of *God*.[6] The whole of scripture reflects human experience with God, and the whole of scripture is a resource for

---

3. Brueggemann, *Praying the Psalms* 68.
4. Ebeling, *Word and Faith* 33; cf. Thiselton, "The New Hermeneutic" 315.
5. Brueggemann, *Praying the Psalms* 39; cf. the comments in chapter 13 above.
6. Von Rad, *Old Testament Theology* 1:355-459; Barr, *The Bible in the Modern World* 120.

spirituality. The witnessing tradition relates the gospel story on which our life with God depends. The authoritative canon gives us a rule for life with God. The inspired word makes reliable undertakings to us and promises us that God's word speaks relevantly to us. The experienced revelation offers insight on the worlds that are not before our eyes, which are resources for that experienced life with God. But the phrase "Israel's response to God" or the description of scripture as a resource for spirituality has an especial appropriateness with regard to the Psalms, the nature of which is to speak *to* God rather than about God (in the manner of narrative) or for God (in the manner of Torah or prophecy). The whole of scripture might be described as an acceptable response to God, but the Psalter overtly models that response.

The Experience of Israel and Christian Experience

Many Christians view the uniqueness of their faith as lying not least in a distinctive experience of God through Jesus, one of deeper quality than that which Israel had. They may also view the "Beatitudes," the Blessings that open the Sermon on the Mount, as a particularly deep and moving account of the possibilities and promise of this distinctive Christian life with God.

It is then striking that the form and content of these Blessings derive substantially from the First Testament rather than being a new creation of Jesus. Their initial declaration regarding people of a certain style of attitude and life recalls the beginning of the Psalter (also Ps 128); Jesus' sermon follows the Psalter in beginning by affirming the blessing of people who are open to walking in God's way. The "poor in spirit" to whom the "rule of heaven" belongs are those to whom Isaiah 61 declared good news of freedom, vindication, and restoration long before (cf. Matt 4:23 a few verses earlier). Isaiah 61 was an important chapter for Jesus. He quotes it in his sermon at Nazareth in a passage that Luke includes at an equivalent place in his Gospel (4:16-21) to the Sermon on the Mount in Matthew. He also echoes it in describing his ministry to John the baptizer (Matt 11:2-6). It runs through the Blessings.

Succeeding Blessings recall the First Testament more directly. "Blessed are those who mourn, for they will be comforted" recalls "Yahweh has anointed me . . . to comfort all who mourn" (Isa 61:1-2; also Ps 126). "Blessed are the meek, for they will have the earth as their possession" recalls "The meek will possess the earth" (Ps 37:11; also Isa 61:7 LXX).[7] "Blessed

7. "Earth" and "land" represent the same Hebrew and Greek words. "Land" is right

are those who hunger and thirst for righteousness, for they will be satisfied" recalls "This is the heritage of the servants of Yahweh and this is their righteousness from me, declares Yahweh. Everyone who thirsts, come to the waters. . . . Why do you spend . . . your labour for that which does not satisfy . . ." (Isa 54:17–55:2, RV). "Blessed are the merciful, for they will receive mercy" recalls "With the merciful you will show yourself merciful" (Ps 18:25, RV). "Blessed are the pure in heart, for they will see God" recalls "Who will ascend the hill of the Lord? . . . The person who is clean of hand and pure in heart . . . will receive blessing from the Lord" (Ps 24:3-5 LXX).

The depth of Jesus' insight on spirituality derives to a significant degree from his absorption in the First Testament. Psalms and Isaiah, the books most clearly reflected in these Blessings, are the books most often and most widely quoted in the Second Testament. The Psalter is, of course, the book that most directly concerns itself with our life with God, and Jesus' own example elsewhere in the Gospels directs us to the Psalms as our resource for praise and prayer.

The interweaving of petition and praise in a lament such as Psalm 22 provided Jesus with the means of expressing his own anguish at the experience of betrayal and abandonment (see especially Matt 27:46). Precisely in this psalm he also found the Psalter's characteristic insistence on looking beyond anguish as well as on looking anguish in the face. Claus Westermann exaggerated only slightly (Ps 88 may be an exception) when he declared that in the Psalms "there is no petition . . . that did not move at least one step . . . on the road to praise" as "there is also no praise that was fully separated from the experience of God's wonderful intervention in time of need."[8] Psalm 22 thus holds together three commitments, an openness to God concerning my feelings and needs, a striving nevertheless to maintain faith and praise toward the God who has cared for me in the past and who even in the experience of abandonment is still "my God," and an anticipation of renewed praise for turning to me again at my moment of urgent need. The psalm's successful battle both to look affliction in the face and to look beyond it is reflected in the reference to it in Hebrews 2:12. The anticipatory praise of Psalm 22:22-31, as much as the lament in the opening part of the psalm, belongs on the lips of Jesus.

The resources of the Psalms for our life with God are easily ignored by

---

in Psalm 37:11 and Isaiah 61:7, so why not in Matthew 5:5? Cf. Hill, *The Gospel of Matthew* 110-11.

8. *The Praise of God in the Psalms* 154.

believers who perhaps find it difficult to get beyond the cultural forms, with their preoccupation with bulls of Bashan and Moabite washbasins. But the effort is worthwhile given that in the Psalms we are given scripture's own collection of things God is happy to hear said in prayer and praise.

Yet to say that the Sermon on the Mount draws our attention to resources in the First Testament for our lives with God is to state only a half-truth, as is so with other aspects of the Second Testament's relationship with the First. It is also the case that the arrival of Jesus introduces an element of revolutionary newness into the biblical understanding of spirituality.

This can be seen from the Blessings themselves. While most of their raw material comes from the First Testament, out of that material Jesus creates something fresh and new, a greater whole than the parts it incorporates. What Jesus does theologically — or hears theologically — in bringing together the figures of the anointed king, the beloved son, and the suffering servant (see below, the next section of this chapter) — he does devotionally in the Blessings by creating a new and profound whole from those elements of largely scriptural origin. The Blessings are not a mere anthology of half-remembered aphorisms but a creatively ordered totality. Here, too, the scriptures are the means of a new revelation, a rounded whole that offers its listeners a new comprehensive portrait of that life with God that was already the First Testament's concern and that can now become reality, as the consummation of God's purpose for people becomes a reality with Jesus' coming.

To the shaping of our life with God, however, Jesus' crucial contribution lay not in his teaching but in his life, and especially in his death, resurrection, and giving of his Spirit to his people. Insofar as the Second Testament brings insight and experience that go beyond those of the First, they are insight and experience that can be available now and now only, through those events. It is not that the evolution of human thinking and behavior or the progress of divine revelation has developed to such a point that new statements and experiences can now be added to what was formerly incomplete, but that new events make new statements and experiences possible. Jesus could not speak of the Spirit before the event of the giving of the Spirit (John 7:39). Nor could he speak of taking up the cross or enjoying resurrection life until crucifixion and resurrection had taken place. When those events had happened, the dynamics of life with God could be thought through with new depth, as happens in chapters such as Romans 3–8. Life with God is not now different in its basis. It was only through Christ by faith, in the Spirit, that Israel related to God under the Sinai covenant, and under the sign of that covenant individuals such as Moses and Ruth (along with unnamed hosts of ordinary people) had taken up their cross, experienced new life, and been the vehicles of God's Spirit at work. Now that realities such as cross, resurrection, and giving of the Spirit are events that can be pointed to and explicated, however, life with God can be conceptualized in a fresh way. Our actual experience of life with God is then inevitably affected by our knowing more of why it works the way it does. Our imagination is refigured by what we know, and therefore our lives are changed.

It is instructive to set the "vindicatory" psalms and the Christ event alongside each other. Christian believers are particularly aware of the difference between any prayers we are told Jesus prayed and these prayers for the punishment of our attackers (notably Ps 137). For whatever reasons, these differences do not include shallowness or insensitivity or the lack of a close relationship with God on the Psalmists' part. Christian believers are at other points more likely to yearn for the real experience of God to which the Psalms witness. Theologically, perhaps prayer for one's enemies like that of Jesus on the cross is strictly possible only after the cross, because it is the cross that makes forgiveness available to people. The Psalms' prayers for judgment on the wicked are prayers for God's justice to be at work in the world, and the cross is God's "Yes" to the prayer for wickedness to be punished.[9]

That insight might suggest that such prayers are appropriate before Christ but inappropriate after Christ. Yet one should be wary of drawing too sharply the contrast between the attitude of such prayers and that of the Second Testament. In the Sermon on the Mount Jesus makes it clear that he takes the same stance as John the baptizer to people who resemble trees that fail to fruit and are therefore felled and burned (Matt 7:15-19; cf. 3:7-10). People whose righteousness only matches that of the scribes and Pharisees (!) will be excluded from the rule of heaven; anger, insults, and contempt will mean fiery judgment; adultery, lust, and divorce will mean going to hell (5:20-32). A subsequent saying adds that the heirs of that rule will indeed be thrown into furthest darkness where people cry and groan in anguish (8:12). Nor are prayers for judgment like those of the Psalms absent from the Second Testament: Jesus promises that such prayers will be heard (Luke 18:1-8), and God reassures the martyrs that the moment of vengeance will come (Rev 6:9-11). At this point, as at others, the Testa-

9. Bonhoeffer, *The Psalms* 21-23.

ments correspond rather than sharply contrast — except that the Second Testament's punishments are more devastating.

Theological Reflection and the Christ Event

Theology emerges from reflection on scripture. Scripture suggests images, words, and concepts to shape our thinking and provide us with the framework with which to look at new events. This was so within the scriptural period itself. The Hebrew Bible provided the images, ideas, and words with which to understand Jesus.

The inauguration of Jesus' ministry (Matt 3) provides a telling example. The account of John's activity in baptizing people comes to a climax when Jesus comes for baptism. At the moment when God the Holy Spirit comes to alight on God the Son for his ministry, God the Father speaks from heaven: "This is my son, the beloved, in whom I delight." The words are not devised for the occasion but taken from the First Testament.

Phrases from more than one passage are combined here. "This is my son" recalls Psalm 2:7. Psalm 2 is in origin a royal psalm, a king's testimony to Yahweh's word to him. The king has no fear of being unable to maintain control of subject nations because Yahweh has made him sovereign over them. He recalls Yahweh's words of commission and assurance: "You are my son. Today I have become your father." In the Second Temple period, when Israel had no kings, such a psalm expressed Israel's hope that one day it would again have a king for whom God would fulfill this commitment. In taking up these words and uttering them to Jesus, God the Father declares Jesus to be the anointed one (*mᵉšîaḥ* or messiah) to whom they refer (Ps 2:2).

"The beloved, in whom I delight" recalls Isaiah 42:1. Isaiah 42:1-9 describes the role that Yahweh's servant is expected to fulfill. In some respects this role resembles the king's calling, but the portrait of the servant in Isaiah 40–55 makes clear that this role will be fulfilled not by what we normally see as the exercise of power but by accepting affliction and paying a huge personal price for the restoration of relationships between God and humanity. It is this calling that God puts before Jesus.

These two passages could account satisfactorily for the words that appear in Matthew 3:17. But the middle phrase "my son, the beloved" also recalls Genesis 22:2. There God bids Abraham, "Take your son, your only son, Isaac, whom you love" to make a sacrifice of him. In the end this sacrifice is not exacted, but Abraham shows himself willing to make it. His action and Isaac's implicit willingness to be sacrificed made a deep impression on Jewish thinking, and the passage was much pondered among Jews of Jesus' day. It lies behind Paul's talk of God not sparing his only son (Rom 8:32). Given its importance in Jesus' day, it probably also lies behind God's words in Matthew 3. Jesus is the only son, the one whom God loves but is willing to sacrifice for the sake of the world, and Jesus is called to imitate Isaac's availability.

In Jesus' life and ministry his baptism and anointing by the Spirit was of key importance, and in the gospel tradition the account of this event has a key place. In the words he hears from heaven he receives fundamental guidelines for the way he is to understand himself. He has the authority of the Davidic king, who is given a special relationship with the God of heaven. At the same time he has the calling of the servant with its different form of authority, exercised despite or through affliction. If that point is not explicit enough, he is the beloved son whom the Father is willing to sacrifice for the world's sake. These phrases give Jesus his theological orientation for his ministry. They are "life-texts" that embody central aspects of his calling. They come from the First Testament.

While the explicit utilization of specific biblical phrases to make theological statements of this kind is not frequent in the Second Testament (Hebrews is the great repository of it), the First Testament does pervade the theological background of the Second. The vast bulk of the way the Second Testament pictures God and the world and the relationship between them assumes the way these realities are described in the First. The First Testament is the Second's theological dictionary or its language world. What the word "God" itself meant derived from the Jewish scriptures. "The Old Testament is the greatest single influence in the formation of New Testament theology."[10]

This point can also be illustrated from the story of John's baptizing. He urges repentance on the grounds that the rule of heaven is at hand, exhorts people to flee from the coming wrath, warns them that trees that do not produce are to be felled, and describes one who is coming after him harvesting wheat and burning chaff. All these motifs and themes come from the First Testament, and it is on the basis of his audience's knowledge of

10. Lindars, "The Place of the Old Testament in the Formation of New Testament Theology" 60; cf. I. H. Marshall, "An Assessment of Recent Developments," in *It Is Written* (ed. Carson and Williamson) 1; also Thiselton's comments and references in *New Horizons in Hermeneutics* 148-51.

these scriptures that John appeals to them. It is extraordinary how often an attempt is made to understand "the kingdom of God" by starting from the Second Testament; and the "enigma" of the sense in which the rule of God "is at hand" or "has come" is less puzzling when considered in the light of the speech of the First Testament (e.g., Amos 8:2; Gen 6:13).

The principle that the First Testament provides the theological framework for understanding Christian faith can easily be illustrated from elsewhere in the Second Testament. It is very clear when Paul discusses basic theological questions in Romans. When he outlines his revolutionary gospel in Romans 3:21-26, he shows that he has thought it out in fundamentally biblical terms. He has to face, then, the question whether this gospel can be defended theologically — that is, whether it is biblical enough. He approaches the question in Romans 4 by considering the key case of Abraham and by maintaining that Abraham's relationship with God had a similar basis to the one he speaks of. It, too, was a relationship based on trust. The theology of the First Testament thus illumines and supports the nature of faith in Christ. Romans 3 also alludes to the question what effect this understanding of God's ways has on the position of the Jewish people themselves. This question is taken up systematically in Romans 9–11, where the theological argument is conducted entirely in terms of exposition of scripture.

If the Second Testament treats the First as its major resource for the theological perspective or context for understanding the Christ event, it directs us to a systematic study of the First Testament's concepts, motifs, and images. If Jesus is the Messiah, the only son whom the Father loves, and the suffering servant, this involves us in investigating what these motifs mean in their original contexts. If the First Testament provides the language world in whose terms the Christ event finds its meaning, it involves learning to think and speak in the terms of that language world. If it is the God of Israel whom Jesus calls Father and whose fatherhood he then shares with us, then this involves us in discovering from the First Testament who this Father is. This takes us into the study of the First Testament's symbols and images and of "Old Testament theology," which is the current version of the kind of systematic study of the First Testament to which the Second implicitly directs us.

Jesus and the Second Testament writers understood and handled ideas derived from the First Testament not in their "neat" original form but with connotations received from subsequent exegetical and theological tradition. In the Hebrew Bible the word "messiah" itself had originally referred to

Israel's present anointed king, or to other anointed agents of Yahweh such as priests; now in the Second Testament it is assumed to apply to a hoped-for future king. The human-like figure who represents Israel in the vision in Daniel 7 has become another symbolic redeemer figure. The Second Testament commonly takes up motifs from the First not in their original significance but refracted through their usage in Jewish tradition. This makes a practical difference to the Second Testament's theological use of the Hebrew scriptures, though hardly a difference of principle. Indeed, the Second Testament is in a similar position in relation to the First to our position in relation to scripture as a whole. In both cases, it is the text's own way of looking at reality to which we commit ourselves, even if at points we unconsciously allow our understanding of it to be influenced by subsequent semantic or theological developments.

The Second Testament, then, invites us to interpret the Christ event in the light of the broad theological perspective that emerges from the First, in the light of the latter's language world. The converse point is that we also have to understand the images and theology of the First Testament in the light of the Christ event. As far as we know, no one before had brought together the figures of the powerful king, the beloved son, and the afflicted servant. They are highly diverse figures and it might have been difficult to see how one ought to go about relating them. They are brought together only in the light of the Christ event, which enables one to look back at the story of Israel and the themes of the First Testament and see interrelationships that were imperceptible before the principle of their interrelationship, the one to whom they referred in their "many diverse ways" (Heb 1:1), was himself present. The occasion of Jesus' baptism was a highly creative theological moment. Furthermore, not every aspect of the ministry of John the baptizer derives from the First Testament. Baptism with water and baptism with Holy Spirit or fire have no precise precedent there. The Christ event brought new religious practices and new religious language as well as new collocations of old texts.

The three great moments of this Christ event each generate insights that not only supplement but also refocus and redefine the nature of biblical faith. Christ's incarnation means that "God with us" now means something more radical than was the case in Israel's experience, though something quite consistent with the First Testament's understanding of God and of human beings as created in God's image. Christ's cross brings to clearest external expression that unprecedented paradoxical collocation of kingly glory, fatherly sacrifice, and personal suffering first stated at his baptism.

Christ's resurrection makes the hope of humanity's resurrection central rather than marginal to biblical faith and promises a resolution of the enigma and incompleteness of human life recognized in the Hebrew Bible and instanced by the story of the death of Bethlehem's children and by the prominence even in Jewish history of the likes of Herod and Archelaus.

> Because Christ is the paradigm for the Christian theological imagination, the entire scripture is viewed differently. The focus on Christ alters none of the Old Testament elements, but it defines a new gestalt, a vision of how everything hangs together in a meaningful pattern (cf. Col. 1:17).[11]

11. Green, *Imagining God* 125.

25

Scripture as a Manual
of Theological Reflection

Scripture mediates divine revelation apprehended in human experience. It does so by means of theological reflection on the part of its writers, whose theological reflection provides models as well as resources for our own.

The Reflective Nature of Scripture as a Whole

Scripture is not in the direct sense a body of divine revelation, though sections of it are. Nor is it a manual of theology, a "doctrinal textbook," as Barr notes.[1] Its theological implications have to be drawn out from it. They are on or near the surface in Paul's letters or Job. In Kings or Mark they are farther below the surface, but are there to be mined. Scriptural books issue from and contain theological reflection, though sometimes in forms different from ones we would immediately recognize, and they invite and stimulate theological reflection. In the Bible God's revelation consisted simply in God's letting human beings "state God's own problems *in their language*."[2] Our response to it naturally involves doing the same for ourselves.

In reaction against the predominantly analytic and discursive style that has characterized theological writing, it has become common to stress the

---

1. *The Bible in the Modern World* 89, quoting Vawter, *Biblical Inspiration* 89.
2. E. Fuchs, "The New Testament and the Hermeneutical Problem," *The New Hermeneutic* (ed. Robinson and Cobb) 135-36.

primacy of narrative as the way to do theology.[3] The earlier, opposite move from storytelling to discursive, analytic thought already takes place within scripture, especially in the theology of Paul, which suggests that both have an important place in the church's theological thinking. Christian theology is dependent on biblical narrative because it expounds and puts flesh on the fundamental religious concepts that are normative for the religious community that affirms that narrative.[4] Nevertheless "one can be told once too often that 'God made man because he loves stories.' After the initial enthusiasm over rediscovering the significance of stories, one begins to feel the need for some good old-fashioned arguments that are more scholastic in form," especially when the retelling of the story does not work.[5] Christian theology is parasitic on the Christian story, which gives it its material, and the doctrine of the atonement needs the crucifixion story to give it life. But within scripture itself the crucifixion story was not felt to be enough. Theology is not to be reduced to story.[6]

If scripture is God's revelation, it is equally clearly human words. Human and divine agencies shared in generating this revelation. With any understanding of revelation, however, priority lies with divine agency. That is the nature of apocalypse: The seer perceives what God reveals and hears God speak. Luke, on the other hand, even though in an extended sense he transmits God's revelation to us, describes his work in terms that other narrators could surely echo: "Since many have undertaken to set down an orderly account of the events that have been fulfilled among us . . . I too decided, after investigating everything carefully from the very first, to write an orderly account for you, most excellent Theophilus, so that you may know the truth concerning the things about which you have been instructed" (1:1-4). One might be reading Thucydides or Josephus. Revelation in narrative comes in what we might call scribal rather than visionary mode. Human initiative and reflection are inherently primary in narrative as they are not with prophecy or apocalypse. Biblical narrative is the fruit of human reflection on events that the narrators have witnessed, or that have been

---

3. See, e.g., H. Weinrich, "Narrative Theology," and J. B. Metz, "A Short Apology of Narrative," in *The Crisis in the Language of Faith* (ed. Metz and Jossua) 46-56 and 84-96.

4. Cf. Comstock, " 'Everything Depends on the *Type* of the Concepts . . .' " 233.

5. S. Hauerwas, "The Church as God's New Language," *Scriptural Authority and Narrative Interpretation* (ed. Green) 188.

6. Cf. Ritschl and Jones, *'Story' als Rohmaterial der Theologie;* Lischer, "The Limits of Story" 32-34. Cf. the last few paragraphs of chapter 1 above.

related to them by human traditioning; hence the possibility and the fruit-fulness of redaction-critical study, which seeks to discern the way the reflection of people such as narrators have shaped the text from the source materials that came to them. In this sense "if one wants to use the Word-of-God type of language, the proper term for the Bible would be Word of Israel, Word of some leading early Christians."[7] The formation of the biblical tradition reflects human witness, worship, spirituality, and community life; it is part of a thoughtful and obedient human response to the acts and words of God,[8] as we assume when we go about seeking to understand the Bible as an essentially human, Jewish book.

Visionary and scribe suggest two models for the preacher. Preachers and congregations incline to think of the preacher by means of the prophetic model rather than the scribal model, partly because "prophetic" is a compliment while "scribal" is not. In Matthew, however, Jesus implies that there will be Christian scribes, and Matthew perhaps sees himself as one such scribe.[9] The expositor is a kind of scribe, as is the theologian.[10] The world and the church need both prophets/seers/visionaries and preachers/expositors/thinkers/scribes.

Seers also use reason. If they report nightmares they have seen and dreams they have dreamed, they ask for these to be taken seriously not merely on the grounds of their divine call but on the basis of appeal to reason and order.[11] They use literary forms and share with us their own poetic creations (see, e.g., Jer 14:1-10). They take up the traditions of their people and build on them in ways that are surely self-conscious. Not all prophecy is an extraordinary gift of God, and the process whereby it reaches the written form in which we have it is a human and rational process. Prophecy evidences human experience and reflection.

The nature of wisdom literature is such as to maximize the potential of human reflection in the context of our life before God in the world. The approach of Proverbs and Ecclesiastes is to seek to discover truth from the

7. Barr, *The Bible in the Modern World* 120; cf. Barr's review of Reid's *The Authority of Scripture.*

8. Cf. Achtemeier, *The Inspiration of Scripture* 131-34.

9. M. D. Goulder, *Midrash and Lection in Matthew* 13-15; cf. J. Jeremias, in *Theological Dictionary of the New Testament* 1 (ed. G. Kittel; ET Grand Rapids: Eerdmans, 1964) 742.

10. J. Jeremias, *New Testament Theology* 1:143.

11. J. Barton, "History and Rhetoric in the Prophets," *The Bible as Rhetoric* (ed. Warner) 63.

world and from life rather than to expect it to be supernaturally revealed. They work by reflecting on observation and experience, and they emphasize common sense. They are open to learning from other people, from the wisdom tradition of Israel and the wisdom traditions of other peoples, but even here they are learning from what in principle could be the observation and experience of anyone. They do not expect to discover the answer to every question by this empirical and reflective approach, but they do believe that there is learning potential in it. Nor do they exclude consideration of faith and morals from their reflection. Proverbs' opening description of wisdom presupposes that its empirical observations take place in a context that assumes the fundamental principles of Israel's faith and morals. Most of Proverbs represents nuggets of concrete experiential insight, but in chapters 1–9 in particular it also includes the speculative wisdom that links with what we call philosophy. The fundamental features of wisdom thinking reappear in the words of Jesus (e.g., Matt 6:24-34; 7:24-27; 11:28-30).[12]

The human reflection incorporated in scripture is often corporate in origin. The individual persons of narrators, seers, prophets, and writers of letters was of fundamental importance to the scriptures coming into being. At creative moments such people see something clearly and freshly and express it dynamically and compellingly. But importance also attached to the more anonymous communal contribution of the believing communities. Behind scripture lay a long process of anonymous generation, preservation, and development of material that these individuals then reshaped; and following on their work lay another process of anonymous preserving, refining, adapting, redacting, supplementing, and updating. The anonymity of most of the scriptures reflects the fact that their authors were working on behalf of God or of their people; whichever way it was, apparently their individuality often (though not invariably) felt unimportant. Scripture issued from the life and reflection of the people of God.

In general one may see this origin in the community as reflecting the work of the Spirit in the people of God, though we should not identify this with the notion of inspiration considered above in Part III. The contributions to scripture offered by disciples and editors were not of the extraordinary origin and significance characteristic of the work of the Spirit in inspiring the prophets.[13] But this does not in itself make such anonymous

---

12. Bartlett, *The Shape of Scriptural Authority* 83-98.
13. Cf. A. G. Auld, "Word of God and Word of Man," in *Ascribe to the Lord* (ed. Eslinger and Taylor) 241-42.

contributors less important. Even in the prophetic books a company of people have preserved, commented on, and edited the text so that it expresses the faith of a whole community. One could think of this work as resulting from the inspiration of this community rather than from the inspiration of individuals; but reflection is at least as good a model for understanding what goes on in the community.

Modes of Theological Reflection in Scripture

In Part II we have already noted the famous definition of Gustavo Gutiérrez in his *A Theology of Liberation:* Theology involves "critical reflection on praxis in the light of the Word."[14] Scripture is designed to help us in assessing our own actions and thinking retrospectively. It is a resource for interpreting our experience and a means by which we test our intuitions. In this process,

> it is not the ancient words that are artificially transported into the present in order to become relevant, but it is the present occasion, the situation, which becomes transparent and relevant both to the ancient message and to the hope which permits the interest and concern for ancient texts.[15]

There is more to be said about the nature of theology than Gutiérrez makes explicit in his statement. Theology is proactive as well as reactive, and its resources extend beyond scripture, even if scripture plays a key role in it. Ritschl's focus on the present guarantees relevance, but may well do that only selectively, demonstrating the relevance of some canon within the canon rather than that of scripture as a whole. That achievement is not to be despised, but we will want to utilize the resources offered by the whole canon to this end. Yet insofar as there is some truth in such formulations, how does reflection on praxis, events, or experience proceed?

In a book on supervision and pastoral care, *Helping the Helpers,*[16] J. Foskett and D. Lyall note that reflection on experience has characteristically taken discursive, analytic form, and suggest a move to a more narrative mode in which this reflection would take the form of storytelling. Their suggestion follows the current emphasis on storytelling in a number of

14. *A Theology of Liberation* 13.
15. Ritschl, "A Plea for the Maxim: Scripture and Tradition" 126.
16. See esp. 48-49.

disciplines, noted in the first section of the present chapter. Scripture itself supports both the discursive and the narrative modes. In this book we are considering the way in which the varied forms of the scriptural writings suggest a number of models for a doctrine of scripture. Because scripture is itself a manual of contextual theological reflection they also suggest a variety of complementary approaches to contemporary theological reflection, whether in relation to commitments we have (Gutiérrez's concern), to pastoral experiences (Foskett and Lyall's starting point), or to questions raised by church life (as in my examples below).

We may begin with the discursive, analytic, which appears most systematically in Paul. Paul is *the* great discursive theologian in scripture, but his systematic, analytic thinking characteristically takes the form of contextual theological reflection. This is especially apparent in 1 Corinthians, which takes up a series of issues in church life in Corinth such as divisions within the congregation, aspects of their sexual practice and their worship, and their eating of meat dedicated to idols. What it does is declare the results of reflection on these in the light of a Christian understanding of creation, the story of Israel, the incarnation, the cross, the resurrection, and the future appearing of Jesus.

Contextual theological reflection is also prominent in Romans, superficially the least situational of Paul's letters and the one that most seeks to expound the eternal gospel. At the heart of that exposition and of the letter is Paul's discussion of the place of Israel in God's purpose. Israel's failure on the whole to recognize Jesus as its Messiah is an inescapably urgent contextual problem for Paul. If he cannot give a satisfactory theological account of it, this event fatally undermines his gospel, with its stress on God's promises and lasting faithfulness. It is for this reason that Romans 9–11 has such a central place in the letter. Paul has reflected on the question theologically and in the light of scripture in a more formal sense than in 1 Corinthians. The pocket edition of the *New Jerusalem Bible* normally lists in the margin scriptural references and allusions within passages, but in Romans 9–11 it gives up the attempt and offers only a note that they are too numerous to list. That fact reveals the prominence of scripture in this piece of theological reflection; it was as Paul pored over the scriptures or worked through them mentally that the penny dropped regarding the mysterious purpose that God was implementing, the offering of the gospel to the nations as a result of the temporary defection of those to whom it originally belonged. In 1 Corinthians and in Romans Paul thus models a process of theological reflection that looks at contextual issues in the light of the gospel and in the light of scripture and does so in analytic, discursive form.

When I joined the church to which I now belong, my eyebrows rose at two regular events. One took place each Sunday. As we came to the end of our worship the members of a black-led church began to arrive for their service, which started as we talked together over refreshments in the community center downstairs. The gathering of these two separate congregations for worship and fellowship seemed a contradiction of the gospel with its talk of all ethnic groups being one in Christ. The other event took place each Ramadan, when the local Muslim community was allowed to use the community center for their prayers. That, too, seemed a contradiction of the gospel in the sense of a denial of declarations about people coming to the Father only through Jesus (John 14:6) and about there being salvation through no one else (Acts 4:12). Analytic, discursive theological reflection in the light of the gospel and of direct statements in scripture seemed to put a question mark by the church's policy. Admittedly there is more to be said, as I will note below.

Foskett and Lyall's suggestion regarding theological reflection was that we need to move from a discursive mode of this kind to a narrative mode. Scripture itself models the latter as well as the former. Genesis to Kings is an epic narrative that leads in due course to the exile, and it constitutes, among other things, a tour de force of narrative theological reflection on the experience of exile. It suggests answers to urgent questions: why Israel came to be in exile, what hope it may be able to entertain for the future, and what response is called for to its present experience. The Books of Chronicles retell the same story on a smaller scale and along different lines because the context on which they need to reflect is different: They offer an interpretation of the situation of the postexilic community in narrative form.

The Gospels and Acts are also works of contextual theological reflection, though we know less of the circumstances in which they were written. That perhaps reflects their predominant concern with the facts about Jesus and the beginnings of the church. But they are also concerned to use these to illumine the situation of the churches to which they are written — to offer theological reflection on issues such as the relationship between Jews and Christians and between the life of the synagogue and the life of the church.

The nature of biblical narrative points to a form of theological reflection that involves telling a modern story and showing how it relates to the gospel story and the scriptural story. The relatively recent development of black-led churches separate from white-led churches in Britain has as part of its background the story of the white-led churches' failure to welcome their brothers and sisters in Christ when they began to come to Britain in the 1950s. In her contribution to a symposium "You Have Created Me Black," Eve Pitts gives one humiliating account of this experience (humiliating for a white Christian, that is — particularly one who actually lived at the time in the part of Birmingham where the events took place, as I did).[17] It was this kind of experience that led to the formation of separate black-led churches in Britain. But the scriptural story includes the account of the split between Paul and Barnabas that led to the development of two separate Christian mission ventures in the Mediterranean world. The first story makes it morally impossible for white Christians to criticize black Christians for forming separate churches. The second story gives grounds for hope that even developments that reflect the sin of the people of God can be harnessed to the purpose of God.

The Muslims who say Ramadan prayers in our community center are also people who came to Britain expecting a different reception from the one they experienced. But the growing strength of Islam in Britain needs to be seen against a broader background that coheres with this, the scandalous fact that Islam is a consciously post-Christian religion. The building of the Dome of the Rock on the Temple Mount in Jerusalem expressed among other things an understandable distaste for the Christian religion as people in the Middle East experienced it. The existence and flourishing of Islam are a judgment of God on the state of Christianity. To allow Muslims to say their prayers in a community center attached to a Christian church is perhaps a way of accepting that judgment. It might also be a step on the road of commending Christ to Muslims. Theological reflection in the light of the scriptural story might additionally recall the mixed attitude to other religions expressed by the story told in the First Testament, which includes Abraham's openness to Melchizedek and Elisha's indulgent stance toward Naaman (Gen 14:18-24; 2 Kgs 5:18-19) as well as the strictness of Joshua and Ezra.

The contexts in which we do our theological reflection also offer us ways into perceiving aspects of the biblical story that we have not perceived before. I had always seen Ruth as an essentially pastoral idyll until I read it from the context of the inner city. I then saw that it is the story of a man

17. See *Spirituality and Social Issues* (*The Way* Supplement 63, 1988), pp. 4-5.

who loses his livelihood, his home, and in due course his life before he is even middle-aged. It is the story of a woman who also loses her livelihood, her home, and in due course her husband — so that she is that archetypal inner-city figure, the single parent, until she also loses her sons, and all this by the time she is in her forties (hence her understandable evaluation of the way God has treated her). It is the story of another, younger woman who is the equivalent to the Sikh or Muslim girl next door, marrying cross-culturally and across religious lines, drawn to Naomi's God through Naomi despite what Naomi has to say about her God and thus reflecting how extraordinary are God's ways of reaching people. It is the story of an older man who has everything except a wife and family and who unexpectedly gains both. It is also the story of a baby through whom God gives a lasting significance to four people who look totally insignificant. It is a story about urban people.

Theological reflection within scripture can thus take discursive or narrative form as "an event or occurrence will become an 'occasion of the word of God'" when it "creates an interest in one's memories of the past" and "challenges and renews the creedal affirmation that Yahweh continues to be faithful to his promises."[18] It can also take the forms (among others) of prophecy, policy-making, and worship.

We noted in Part III that the Hebrew prophets' editors draw attention to the fact that the prophets were contextual theologians. They place at the beginning of most of their books a note that indicates in one form or another both the awareness that their work is of divine origin (e.g., "the vision of Isaiah ben Amoz . . .") and the awareness that it came into being in particular contexts ("which he saw concerning Judah and Jerusalem in the days of Uzziah, Jotham, Ahaz, and Hezekiah . . ."). The prophets' work is thus designated as theological and contextual. Their actual oracles presuppose both these features, on the one hand affirming that "this is the word of Yahweh" and on the other commonly drawing attention to the nature of the concrete situations to which they speak.

Their theological reflection took the form of an attempt to drive Israel to face nightmares and to dream dreams. The facing of nightmares is more prominent before the exile, when the prophets are those who can see that calamity is coming on Israel and Judah, who offer a theological interpretation of that calamity in terms of a divine judgment that responds to people's failure of love for Yahweh and love for each other, and who strive to

18. Ritschl, "A Plea for the Maxim: Scripture and Tradition" 125.

persuade them to return to Yahweh before it is too late. They are people who can bring together what they read in the newspapers, what they see in worship and in society, and what they know from Israel's gospel story.[19] When a Bishop of Liverpool warns a Prime Minister that calamity is imminent in his city because of the way in which local government is being exercised, he acts like a prophet insisting that nightmares be faced, without necessarily prescribing what is the detailed nature of the political action that needs to be taken.

With the exile came a transition from the facing of nightmares to the dreaming of dreams, the offering of avenues of hope for a demoralized people. Once again the prophets are confronting their people, but now with unbelievable good news. "Yahweh has anointed me to proclaim good news to the poor, he has sent me to bind up the broken-hearted . . ." says the Isaiah who preaches in Palestine after the exile (Isa 61:1). He sees people who are afflicted, broken in spirit, captive, imprisoned, and cut off from God. His response is not to do anything or to urge anyone else to do anything, but to preach, to talk to people about freedom, grace, joy, rebuilding, and pride. All he does is make promises to people, because what they need is hope. He brings good news, but it is news about the future, about something God is going to do. He is aware that human agencies cannot bring about freedom or grace; these are God's gifts, and therefore there has to be preaching about them as well as action. Pending God's action, the invitation to the people is to dream God-given dreams (dreams that may then inspire human action).

In the contexts in which we minister, hope is commonly people's most pressing need, not least where there may seem to be no room for action. Physical and human desolation is often an obvious reality in urban areas, but the suburbs know as profound a misery, issuing from oppression of people by their wealth and their jobs, and as profound a heartbreak, issuing from their experiences with their children and their marriages. Theological reflection here, too, means discerning God's dreams.

These certainly include dreams for the church such as those expressed in the vision in Revelation 7 of a numberless worshipping multitude. These worshipers come from all ethnic, political, and linguistic groups, and they offer a dream to set against our present reality of Afro-Caribbean Christian worship separated from white Christian worship and of Muslims turning

19. This paragraph depends partly on remarks by John Barton in his "History and Rhetoric in the Prophets," in *The Bible as Rhetoric* (ed. Warner) 51-64.

their backs on the worship of the Lamb. They also help us to see where there is some hint of fulfillment of this dream. There are occasions in urban areas when black, brown, and white, young, middle-aged, and old, women and men, middle-class, artisan, and underclass all meet for worship, and such occasions constitute anticipations of the worship of heaven and encourage the dreaming of dreams.[20]

The prophets invite us to discern what nightmares and dreams scripture encourages. The prophets are not particularly practical people; they are not social reformers. But the Bible does model the translation of story and vision into policy, in the Torah. It pictures the Torah as all given by God through Moses at Mount Sinai (in Exodus and Leviticus) and in the Plains of Moab (in Deuteronomy). It thus declares it to be of heavenly origin and significance. The various bodies of Torah differ from each other, however, and do so because they speak to the needs of different contexts. It is particularly clear that Deuteronomy constitutes a restatement of Yahweh's expectations of Israel as these are expressed in Exodus 19–24. The Pentateuch locates this restatement in the Plains of Moab on the eve of the people actually taking up life in the promised land, but historically it likely reflects the actual experience of life in the land and its pressures. Either way, Deuteronomy is a piece of contextual theology that systematically develops the old theological idea of the covenant so that it becomes a framework for understanding the faith and life of Israel as a whole. It turns theological concepts, stories, and dreams into practical policies, and models the way we may do so.

Scriptural systematics makes me insist that black and white worship together, the dreams of scripture's visionaries promise that they will, and the stories of how things were in scriptural times cause me to make allowances for the fact that they do not yet do so and that God can cope with that fact. Yet this must not allow me to sit back content with a situation that falls short of God's dream. Torah impels me to venture this fourth form of theological reflection, which turns dreams into policies. The drastic policy would be for the white churches to repent, close down the white-led churches, and ask to be admitted to the black-led churches. The less drastic policy is to seek for occasional yet developing means of worshipping and working together that may take us nearer the realization of the dream.

Scripture's fifth mode of theological reflection takes the form of wor-

20. For this point (and one in the next paragraph) see my paper on "The Bible in the City," on which, indeed, the present section is in part a subconscious methodological reflection.

ship. Theology and doxology are closely related: Worship is where the church's vision of God comes into sharp focus. Doctrine is the church reflecting on its worship.[21] Theology is worshippers thinking about their worship, as they must; worship is theologians turning their thought into worship, as they must. Arguably the densest theology in scripture takes the form of worship, in the Psalms.

The Psalms, too, are a contextual theology. Their prayer issues from urgent situations of need on the part of individuals or groups and wrestles before God with the theological questions raised by God's acts and by God's failure to act. The praise in the Psalms issues from concrete experiences of God acting in response to such prayer, of God speaking some word that throws new light on a situation, or of the suppliant seeing afresh some theological truth that enables a situation to be coped with. As Walter Brueggemann has suggested,[22] the Psalms' whole spirituality takes people through a cycle, or spiral, of theological orientation (when they know who God is, who they are, and how life works), followed by disorientation (when some contextual experience shatters those convictions), followed by reorientation (the attaining of some new perspective that does justice to both these earlier sets of experiences and truths). The Psalms are a manual of contextual theology formulated in praise and prayer. They invite us to make our worship part of our theological reflection, and our theological reflection part of our actual life with God. In the light of their pattern we rejoice before God in the fact that the gospel makes one new person out of people of all races, we lament before God about that not being true in experience, we urge God to make it so, and we glory before God in hints of its fulfillment of the kind provided by the occasions described above.

People who are interested in theological reflection are often committed to active work in the church and in the community. They especially need to perceive how incomplete is their theological reflection issuing from and in activity unless it is complemented by theological reflection in the form of worship; though the converse is also true. The fourth and fifth modes of theological reflection in scripture belong essentially together. There are congregations and ministers who are instinctively more involved in community development and those who are instinctively more involved in worship. Each needs to see that both aspects of Christian discipleship are present in their own lives, and each needs to affirm the other emphasis as part of what the body of Christ requires.

21. Cf. Wainwright, *Doxology* 3.
22. *The Message of the Psalms.*

Abbreviations

ATR	*Anglican Theological Review*
BJRL	*Bulletin of the John Rylands Library*
BSac	*Bibliotheca sacra*
CBQ	*Catholic Biblical Quarterly*
CI	*Critical Inquiry*
ET	English translation
EvQ	*Evangelical Quarterly*
HBT	*Horizons in Biblical Theology*
HTR	*Harvard Theological Review*
JBL	*Journal of Biblical Literature*
JETS	*Journal of the Evangelical Theological Society*
JJS	*Journal of Jewish Studies*
JR	*Journal of Religion*
JSOT	*Journal for the Study of the Old Testament*
JTS (n.s.)	*Journal of Theological Studies* (new series)
KJV	(Authorized) King James Version
LW	*Luther's Works* (Philadelphia and St. Louis, 1955-)
ModT	*Modern Theology*
NEB	New English Bible
NIV	New International Version
NJB	New Jerusalem Bible
NLH	*New Literary History*
NRSV	New Revised Standard Version
NTS	*New Testament Studies*
PG	J.-P. Migne, *Patrologiae cursus completus. Series Graeca* (1857-1936)

PL	J.-P. Migne, *Patrologiae cursus completus. Series Latina* (1841-64)
REB	Revised English Bible
RelS	*Religious Studies*
RV	Revised Version
SJT	*Scottish Journal of Theology*
ThT	*Theology Today*
TS	*Theological Studies*
TSC	*The Second Century*
TynB	*Tyndale Bulletin*
U	University of
UP	University Press
VE	*Vox evangelica*
WA	*D. Martin Luthers Werke. Kritische Gesamtausgabe* (Weimar, 1883-)
WTJ	*Westminster Theological Journal*

Bibliography

The bibliography includes works referred to in the text, a few others that I am aware of having utilized but do not happen to have referred to, and articles that I have written from which I have adapted material in this book. In the text, unless otherwise noted, reference is to the latest (British) edition.

ABBA, R. *The Nature and Authority of the Bible.* London: Clarke/Philadelphia: Muilenburg, 1958.

ABRAHAM, W. J. *The Divine Inspiration of Holy Scripture.* Oxford/New York: OUP, 1981.

———. *Divine Revelation and the Limits of Historical Criticism.* Oxford/New York: OUP, 1982.

———. *The Logic of Evangelism.* Grand Rapids: Eerdmans/London: Hodder, 1989.

ACHTEMEIER, E. "The Impossible Possibility: Evaluating the Feminist Approach to Bible and Theology." *Interpretation* 42 (1988) 45-57.

ACHTEMEIER, P. J. *The Inspiration of Scripture.* Philadelphia: Westminster, 1980.

ACKROYD, P. R. "Crisis and Evolution in the Old Testament." *EvQ* 25 (1953) 69-82.

———. *Studies in the Religious Tradition of the Old Testament.* London: SCM, 1987.

ALAND, K. *The Problem of the New Testament Canon.* London: Mowbray, 1962.

ALEXANDER, A. *Evidences of the Authenticity, Inspiration, and Canonical Authority of the Holy Scriptures.* Philadelphia: Presbyterian Board of Publication, 1836(?).

ALLCHIN, A. M. "An Anglican View on Scripture and Tradition." *Dialog* 2 (1963) 294-99.

ALONSO SCHÖKEL, L. *The Inspired Word.* ET New York: Herder/London: Burns and Oates, 1967.

ALTER, R. *The Art of Biblical Narrative.* New York: Basic/London: Allen and Unwin, 1981.

ALTER, R., and F. KERMODE (ed.). *The Literary Guide to the Bible.* Cambridge, MA: Harvard UP/London: Collins, 1987.

ALTHAUS, P. *The Theology of Martin Luther.* ET Philadelphia: Fortress, 1966.

AMIHAI, M., and others (ed.). *Narrative Research on the Hebrew Bible. Semeia* 46 (1989).

ANDERSON, B. W. "The Bible in the Church Today." *ThT* 37 (1980-81) 1-6.

ARCHER, G. L. *Encyclopedia of Biblical Difficulties.* Grand Rapids: Zondervan, 1982.

ARMERDING, C. E. *The Old Testament and Criticism.* Grand Rapids: Eerdmans, 1983.

ARNDT, W. *Bible Difficulties and Seeming Contradictions.* St Louis: Concordia, rev. ed., 1987.

ASSMANN, H. *Practical Theology of Liberation.* ET London: Search, 1975. = *Theology for a Nomad Church.* Maryknoll, NY: Orbis, 1976.

AUDET, J. P. "A Hebrew-Aramaic List of the Books of the Old Testament in Greek." *JTS* n.s. 1 (1950) 135-54.

AUNE, D. E. *Prophecy in Early Christianity and the Ancient Mediterranean World.* Grand Rapids: Eerdmans, 1983.

AUSTIN, J. L. *How to Do Things with Words.* Oxford: Clarendon/Cambridge, MA: Harvard UP, 1962.

BAILLIE, J. *The Idea of Revelation in Recent Thought.* London: OUP/New York: Columbia UP, 1956.

BAKER, T. G. A. "'This is the Word of the Lord.'" *Theology* 93 (1990) 266-73.

BALMER, R. H. "The Princetonians and Scripture." *WTJ* 44 (1982) 352-65.

BARBOUR, I. G. *Myths, Models and Paradigms.* London: SCM/New York: Harper, 1974.

BARR, D. L. "The Apocalypse as a Symbolic Transformation of the World." *Interpretation* 38 (1984) 39-50.

BARR, J. *Beyond Fundamentalism.* Philadelphia: Westminster, 1984. = *Escaping From Fundamentalism.* London: SCM, 1984.

———. *The Bible in the Modern World.* London: SCM/New York: Harper, 1973.

———. "Childs' Introduction to the Old Testament as Scripture." *JSOT* 16 (1980) 12-23.

———. *Fundamentalism.* London: SCM/Philadelphia: Westminster, 1977; rev. ed., 1981.

———. *Holy Scripture: Canon, Authority, Criticism.* Philadelphia: Westminster/Oxford: OUP, 1983.

————. "J. K. S. Reid, *The Authority of Scripture*." *SJT* 11 (1958) 86-93.

————. "Le Judaisme postbiblique et la théologie de l'Ancien Testament." *Revue de théologie et de philosophie* III/18 (1968) 209-17.

————. *Old and New in Interpretation*. London: SCM/New York: Harper, 1966. 2nd ed., London: SCM, 1982.

————. "The Old Testament and the New Crisis of Biblical Authority." *Interpretation* 25 (1971) 24-40.

————. "Revelation through History in the Old Testament and in Modern Theology." *Interpretation* 17 (1963) 193-205.

————. *The Scope and Authority of the Bible*. Philadelphia: Westminster, 1980. = *Explorations in Theology* 7. London: SCM, 1980.

BARR, J., et al. "The Authority of the Bible." *Ecumenical Review* 21 (1969) 135-66.

BARRETT, C. K. *A Commentary on the First Epistle to the Corinthians*. London: Black/New York: Harper, 1968.

————. *The Pastoral Epistles*. Oxford/New York: OUP, 1963.

BARTH, K. *Church Dogmatics*. ET Edinburgh: Clark/New York: Scribner, 1936-.

BARTH, M. *Conversation with the Bible*. New York: Holt, 1964.

BARTLETT, D. L. *The Shape of Scriptural Authority*. Philadelphia: Fortress, 1983.

BARTON, J. *Oracles of God*. London: DLT/Philadelphia: Westminster, 1986.

————. *People of the Book?* London: SPCK, 1988/Louisville: WJK, 1989.

————. *Reading the Old Testament*. London: DLT/Philadelphia: Westminster, 1984.

BARTSCH, H.-W. (ed.). *Kerygma and Myth*. Vol. 1 ET London: SPCK, 1953 (^{2}1964)/New York: Harper, 1961. Vol. 2 ET London: SPCK, 1962. Enlarged one volume edition, London: SPCK, 1972.

BATTLES, F. L. "God Was Accommodating Himself to Human Capacity." *Interpretation* 31 (1977) 19-38.

BAUCKHAM, R. *Jude, 2 Peter*. Waco, TX: Word, 1983/Milton Keynes: Word, 1986.

————. "The Limits of Inerrancy" (unpublished paper).

BAUCKHAM, R., and B. DREWERY (ed.). *Scripture, Tradition and Reason* (R. P. C. Hanson Festschrift). Edinburgh: Clark, 1988.

BAVINCK, H. *Our Reasonable Faith*. ET Grand Rapids: Eerdmans, 1956.

————. *The Philosophy of Revelation*. Grand Rapids: Eerdmans, 1953.

BEARDSLEE, W. A. *Literary Criticism of the New Testament*. Philadelphia: Fortress, 1970.

————. "Narrative form in the New Testament and Process Theology." *Encounter* (Indianapolis) 36 (1975) 301-15.

BECKWITH, R. T. "The Inspiration of Holy Scripture." In W. R. F. Browning (ed.), *The Anglican Synthesis* 29-48. Derby: Peter Smith, 1964.

————. *The Old Testament Canon of the New Testament Church and its Back-*

ground in Early Judaism. London: SPCK, 1985/Grand Rapids: Eerdmans, 1986.

BEECHER, W. J. "The Alleged Triple Canon of the Old Testament." *JBL* 15 (1896) 118-28.

BEEGLE, D. M. *The Inspiration of Scripture.* Philadelphia: Westminster, 1963. Rev. ed., *Scripture, Tradition, and Infallibility.* Grand Rapids: Eerdmans, 1973.

BENOIT, P. *Aspects of Biblical Inspiration.* ET Chicago: Priory, 1965.

────. See also under Synave.

BERGER, P. *A Rumor of Angels.* Garden City, NY: Doubleday, 1969/London: Allen Lane, 1970/Harmondsworth: Penguin, 1971.

BERKOUWER, G. C. *Holy Scripture.* ET Grand Rapids: Eerdmans, 1975.

BEST, E. "Scripture, Tradition, and the Canon of the New Testament." *BJRL* 61 (1979) 258-89.

BLACK, M. *Models and Metaphors.* Ithaca, NY: Cornell UP, 1962.

BLENKINSOPP, J. *Prophecy and Canon.* Notre Dame, IN: U Notre Dame, 1977.

────. "Prophecy and Priesthood in Josephus." *JJS* 25 (1974) 239-62.

BLOESCH, D. G. *Essentials of Evangelical Theology.* 2 vols. San Franciso: Harper, 1978 and 1979.

────. *The Ground of Certainty: Toward an Evangelical Theology of Revelation.* Grand Rapids: Eerdmans, 1971.

────. "The Sword of the Spirit." *Themelios* 5/3 (May, 1980) 14-18.

BOCKMUEHL, M. N. A. *Revelation and Mystery in Ancient Judaism and Pauline Christianity.* Tübingen: Mohr, 1990.

BOER, H. R. *Above the Battle?* Grand Rapids: Eerdmans, 1975.

BOETTNER, L. *The Inspiration of the Scriptures.* Grand Rapids: Eerdmans, 1940.

BOICE, J. M. (ed.). *The Foundation of Biblical Authority.* Grand Rapids: Zondervan, 1978/Glasgow: Pickering, 1979.

BONHOEFFER, D. "The Interpretation of the New Testament." In *No Rusty Swords* (ET London: Collins/New York: Harper, 1965) 308-25. Rev. ed., "The Presentation of New Testament Texts." In *No Rusty Swords* (ET London: Collins Fontana, 1970) 302-20.

────. *The Psalms.* ET Minneapolis: Augsburg, 1974. Different ET Oxford: SLG, 1982.

BONINO, J. M. See under Miguez Bonino.

BOONE, K. C. *The Bible Tells Them So.* Albany, NY: SUNY/London: SCM, 1989.

BORGEN, P. See under Lindars.

BORNKAMM, G. *Early Christian Experience.* ET London: SCM, 1969/New York: Harper, 1970.

BORNKAMM, G., G. BARTH, and H. J. HELD. *Tradition and Interpretation in Matthew.* ET Philadelphia: Westminster/London: SCM, 1963.

BORNKAMM, H. *Luther and the Old Testament.* ET Philadelphia: Fortress, 1969.

BRAATEN, C. E. *History and Hermeneutics.* Philadelphia: Westminster, 1966/London: Lutterworth, 1968.

BRAY, G. L. *Holiness and the Will of God.* London: Marshall/Atlanta: Knox, 1979.

BRETT, M. *Biblical Criticism in Crisis?* Cambridge/New York: CUP, 1991.

BRIGHT, J. *The Authority of the Old Testament.* Nashville: Abingdon/London: SCM, 1967.

———. *A History of Israel.* Philadelphia: Westminster, 1959/London: SCM, 1960; [2]1972; [3]1981.

———. *Early Israel in Recent History Writing.* London: SCM/Naperville, IL: Allenson, 1956.

BROOKS, P. *Lectures on Preaching.* New York: Dutton, 1877/London: Dickenson, 1881; reprinted London: SPCK, 1959.

BROWN, D. "Struggle till Daybreak: On the Nature of Authority in Theology." *JR* 65 (1985) 15-32.

BROWN, R. E. *The Birth of the Messiah.* Garden City, NY: Doubleday, 1977/London: Chapman, 1978.

———. *The Critical Meaning of the Bible.* Ramsey, NJ: Paulist, 1981.

BROWN, R. E., et al. (ed.). *The Jerome Biblical Commentary.* London: Chapman/Englewood Cliffs, NJ: Prentice-Hall, 1968; new ed., 1989/1990.

BRUCE, F. F. *The Canon of Scripture.* Glasgow: Chapter House/Downers Grove, IL: IVP, 1988.

———. *1 and 2 Corinthians.* London: Marshall/Grand Rapids: Eerdmans, 1971.

———. *Tradition Old and New.* Exeter: Paternoster/Grand Rapids: Zondervan, 1970.

BRUEGGEMANN, W. *Abiding Astonishment: Psalms, Modernity, and the Making of History.* Louisville: WJK, 1991.

———. "Bounded by Obedience and Praise." *JSOT* 50 (1991) 63-92.

———. *The Creative Word.* Philadelphia: Fortress, 1982.

———. *Finally Comes the Poet.* Minneapolis: Fortress, 1989.

———. *The Message of the Psalms.* Minneapolis: Augsburg, 1984.

———. *Praying the Psalms.* Winona, MN: St Mary's Press, 1982.

BRUNNER, E. *Revelation and Reason.* ET Philadelphia: Westminster, 1946/London: SCM, 1947.

BRUNS, G. L. "Canon and Power in the Hebrew Scriptures." *CI* 10 (1983-84) 462-80.

BUBER, M. *Moses.* ET Oxford: Phaidon, 1946/New York: Harper, 1958.

———. *Tales of the Hasidim: The Early Masters.* ET New York: Schocken, 1947.

BUCKLEY, J. J. "The Hermeneutical Deadlock between Revelationists, Textualists, and Functionalists." *ModT* 6 (1990) 325-39.

BULTMANN, R. *Faith and Understanding.* Vol. 1. ET London: SCM/New York: Harper, 1969.

———. "History and Eschatology in the New Testament." *NTS* 1 (1954-55) 5-16.

———. *Jesus and the Word.* ET New York: Scribner/London: Collins Fontana, 1958.

BURGON, J. W. *"Inspiration and Interpretation," Seven Sermons.* Oxford: Parker, 1861; reprinted London: Marshall, 1905.

BURNABY, J. *Is the Bible Inspired?* London: Duckworth, 1949.

BURTCHAELL, J. T. *Catholic Theories of Biblical Inspiration since 1810.* Cambridge/New York: CUP, 1969.

BUTTRICK, D. *Homiletic.* Philadelphia: Fortress/London: SCM, 1987.

CAIRD, G. B. *The Gospel of St Luke.* Harmondsworth/Baltimore: Penguin, 1963.

———. *The Language and Imagery of the Bible.* London: Duckworth/Philadelphia: Westminster, 1980.

CALVIN, J. *The Acts of the Apostles 1-13.* ET Edinburgh: Oliver and Boyd/Grand Rapids: Eerdmans, 1965.

———. *Commentaries on the Four Last Books of Moses.* Vol. 4. ET Edinburgh: CTS, 1855.

———. *Commentaries on the Book of Genesis.* Vol. 1. Edinburgh: CTS, 1847.

———. *Commentaries on the Book of Psalms.* Vol. 3. ET Edinburgh: CTS, 1847.

———. *Commentaries on the Book of the Prophet Jeremiah and the Lamentations.* Vol. 4. ET Edinburgh: CTS, 1854.

———. *The Epistle of Paul the Apostle to the Hebrews. . . .* ET Edinburgh: Oliver and Boyd/Grand Rapids: Eerdmans, 1963.

CAMERON, N. M. DE S. *Biblical Higher Criticism and the Defense of Infallibilism in 19th Century Britain.* Lewiston, NY: Edwin Mellen, 1987.

———. "Biblical Interpretation in Some Recent Evangelical Thought" (with a reply by I. H. Marshall). *Scottish Tyndale Bulletin* 1979 42-53.

———. "Dean Burgon and the Bible." *Themelios* 7/2 (1981-82) 16-20.

———. "Inspiration and Criticism." *TynB* 35 (1984) 129-59.

CAMPENHAUSEN, H. F. VON. *The Formation of the Christian Bible.* ET Philadelphia: Fortress/London: Black, 1972.

———. "Marcion et les origines du Canon Néotestamentaire." *Revue d'histoire et de philosophie religieuses* (1966) 213-26.

CANNON, K. G., and E. SCHÜSSLER FIORENZA (ed.). *Interpretation for Liberation. Semeia* 47 (1989).

CARNLEY, P. *The Structure of Resurrection Belief.* Oxford/New York: OUP, 1987.

CARROLL, R. P. *Wolf in the Sheepfold: The Bible as a Problem for Christianity.* London: SPCK, 1991. = *The Bible as a Problem for Christianity.* Philadelphia: TPI, 1991.

CARSON, D. A. (ed.). *Biblical Interpretation and the Church.* Exeter: Paternoster, 1984.

CARSON, D. A., and H. G. M. WILLIAMSON (ed.). *It is Written: Scripture Citing Scripture* (B. Lindars Festschrift). Cambridge/New York: CUP, 1988.

CARSON, D. A., and J. D. WOODBRIDGE (ed.). *Scripture and Truth.* Grand Rapids: Zondervan/Leicester: IVP, 1983.

———— (ed.). *Hermeneutics, Authority and Canon.* Grand Rapids: Zondervan/Leicester: IVP, 1986.

CHATMAN, S. *Story and Discourse.* Ithaca, NY: Cornell UP, 1978.

CHILDS, B. S. *Biblical Theology in Crisis.* Philadelphia: Westminster, 1970.

————. *Biblical Theology of the Old and New Testaments.* London: SCM/Minneapolis: Fortress, 1992.

————. *The Book of Exodus.* Philadelphia: Westminster, 1974. = *Exodus.* London: SCM, 1974.

————. "Critical Reflections on James Barr's Understanding of the Literal and the Allegorical." *JSOT* 46 (1990) 3-9.

————. *Introduction to the Old Testament as Scripture.* Philadelphia: Fortress/London: SCM, 1979.

————. *Myth and Reality in the Old Testament.* London: SCM/Naperville, IL: Allenson, 1960, ²1962.

————. *The New Testament as Canon.* London: SCM, 1984/Philadelphia: Fortress, 1985.

————. *Old Testament Theology in a Canonical Context.* London: SCM/Philadelphia: Fortress, 1985.

CHRIST, C. P. "The New Feminist Theology." *Religious Studies Review* 3 (1977) 203-12.

CHRIST, C. P., and J. PLASKOW (ed.). *Womanspirit Rising.* San Francisco: Harper, 1979.

CLEMENTS, R. E. "History and Theology in Biblical Narrative." *HBT* 4/2 (1982) 45-60.

————. *Old Testament Theology.* London: Marshall/Atlanta: Knox, 1978.

————. *Prophecy and Tradition.* Oxford: Blackwell/Atlanta: Knox, 1975.

CLÉVENOT, M. *Materalist Approaches to the Bible.* ET Maryknoll, NY: Orbis, 1985.

CLINES, D. J. A. *I, He, We, and They.* Sheffield: JSOT, 1976.

————. "Notes for an Old Testament Hermeneutic." *Theology, News and Notes* 21 (1975) 8-10.

————. "Story and Poem." *Interpretation* 34 (1980) 115-27.

————. *What Does Eve Do to Help? and Other Readerly Questions to the Old Testament.* Sheffield: SAP, 1990.

CLINES, D. J. A., et al. (ed.). *The Bible in Three Dimensions.* Sheffield: SAP, 1990.

COAKLEY, S. "Theology and Cultural Relativism." *Neue Zeitschrift für systematische Theologie und Religionsphilosophie* 21 (1979) 223-43.

COATS, G. W., and B. O. LONG (ed.). *Canon and Authority*. Philadelphia: Fortress, 1977.

COHEN, S. J. D. *From the Maccabees to the Mishnah*. Philadelphia: Westminster, 1987.

COLERIDGE, S. T. *Confessions of an Inquiring Spirit*. London: Pickering, 1840/Boston: Munroe, 1841; London: Moxon, [3]1853; reprinted Philadelphia: Fortress, 1988.

COLLINS, J. J. "Apocalyptic Eschatology as the Transcendence of Death." *CBQ* 36 (1974) 21-43. = P. D. Hanson (ed.), *Visionaries and Their Apocalypses* 61-84. Philadelphia: Fortress/London: SPCK, 1983.

―――. "Inspiration or Illusion." *Ex auditu* 6 (1990) 29-38.

―――. "The Symbolism of Transcendence in Jewish Apocalyptic." *Biblical Research* 19 (1974) 5-22.

COLLINS, R. F. *Introduction to the New Testament*. Garden City, NY: Doubleday/London: SCM, 1983.

COMSTOCK, G. L. " 'Everything Depends on the *Type* of the Concepts that the Interpretation is Made to Convey.' " *ModT* 5 (1989) 215-37.

CONN, H. M. (ed.). *Inerrancy and Hermeneutic*. Grand Rapids: Baker, 1988.

CONE, J. H. *God of the Oppressed*. New York: Seabury, 1975/London: SPCK, 1977.

CORNER, M. See under Rowland.

COTTERELL, P., and M. TURNER, *Linguistics and Biblical Interpretation*. Leicester/Downers Grove: IVP, 1989.

COUNTRYMAN, L. W. *Biblical Authority or Biblical Tyranny?* Philadelphia: Fortress, 1981.

COWARD, H. *Sacred Word and Sacred Text*. Maryknoll, NY: Orbis, 1988.

CRADDOCK, F. B. "Preaching the Book of Revelation." *Interpretation* 40 (1986) 270-82.

CRAGG, K. "How Not Islam." *RelS* 13 (1977) 387-94.

CRITES, S. "The Narrative Quality of Experience." *Journal of the American Academy of Religion* 39 (1971) 291-311.

CROATTO, J. S. *Biblical Hermeneutics*. ET Maryknoll, NY: Orbis, 1987.

―――. *Exodus*. ET Maryknoll, NY: Orbis, 1981.

CROSS, F. M., and S. TALMON (ed.). *Qumran and the History of the Biblical Text*. Cambridge, MA/London: Harvard UP, 1975.

CULLER, J. *The Pursuit of Signs*. Ithaca, NY: Cornell UP/London: Routledge, 1981.

CULLMANN, O. *Christ and Time*. ET London: SCM, 1951; [2]1962/Philadelphia: Westminster, 1950; [2]1964.

————. *The Early Church.* ET London: SCM/Philadelphia: Westminster, 1956.

CUNLIFFE-JONES, H. *The Authority of the Biblical Revelation.* London: Clarke, 1945/Boston: Pilgrim, 1948.

CUPITT, D. *Explorations in Theology* 6. London: SCM, 1979.

CUSTER, S. *Does Inspiration Demand Inerrancy?* Nutley, NJ: Craig, 1968.

DAHL, N. A. "Anamnesis." ET *Jesus in the Memory of the Early Church* 11-29. Minneapolis: Augsburg, 1976.

DALY, R. J. (ed.). *Christian Biblical Ethics.* Ramsey, NJ: Paulist, 1984.

DANTO, A. C. *Analytical Philosophy of History.* Cambridge/New York: CUP, 1965.

DAVIES, G. I. "Apocalyptic and Historiography." *JSOT* 5 (1978) 15-28.

DAVIES, W. D. *Jewish and Pauline Studies.* Philadelphia: Fortress/London: SPCK, 1984.

DAVIS, S. T. *The Debate about the Bible.* Philadelphia: Westminster, 1977.

DEMAREST, B. See under Lewis, G. R.

DETWEILER, R. (ed.). *Reader Response Approaches to Biblical and Secular Texts. Semeia* 31 (1985).

DOCTRINE COMMISSION OF THE CHURCH OF ENGLAND. *Believing in the Church.* London: SPCK, 1981.

————. *Christian Believing.* London: SPCK, 1976.

DODD, C. H. *The Authority of the Bible.* London: Nisbet, 1928/New York: Harper, 1929. Rev. ed., London: Collins Fontana, 1960/New York: Harper, 1962.

DONNER, T. "Some Thoughts on the History of the New Testament Canon." *Themelios* 7/3 (1982) 23-27.

DOUGLAS, J. D. (ed.). *Let the Earth Hear His Voice.* Minneapolis: World Wide, 1975.

DOWNING, F. G. *Has Christianity a Revelation?* London: SCM/Philadelphia: Westminster, 1964.

————. "*Models of Revelation* by Avery Dulles. . . ." *Theology* 87 (1984) 295-97.

DULLES, A. *Models of Revelation.* Garden City, NY: Doubleday/Dublin: Gill and Macmillan, 1983.

————. *Models of the Church.* Garden City, NY: Doubleday, 1974/Dublin: Gill and Macmillan, 1976; [2]1988.

————. *Revelation Theology: A History.* New York: Herder, 1969.

————. "Scripture: Recent Protestant and Catholic Views." *ThT* 37 (1980-81) 7-26.

————. "The Theology of Revelation." *TS* 25 (1964) 43-58.

DUNGAN, D. L. "The New Testament Canon in Recent Study." *Interpretation* 29 (1975) 339-51.

DUNN, J. D. G. *The Living Word.* London: SCM, 1987/Philadelphia: Fortress, 1988.

EBELING, G. *The Study of Theology.* ET Philadelphia: Fortress, 1978/London: Collins, 1979.

————. *Theology and Proclamation.* ET London: SCM/Philadelphia: Fortress, 1966.

————. *Word and Faith.* ET London: SCM/Philadelphia: Fortress, 1963.

EDWARDS, D. L., and J. R. W. STOTT. *Essentials.* London: Hodder, 1980.

EDWARDS, O. C. "Historical-critical Method's Failure of Nerve and a Prescription for a Tonic." *ATR* 59 (1977) 115-34. = *Ex auditu* 1 (1985) 92-105.

EISSFELDT, O. *The Old Testament: An Introduction.* ET Oxford: Blackwell/New York: Harper, 1965.

ELLIOTT, J. H. *A Home for the Homeless.* Philadelphia: Fortress, 1981/London: SCM, 1982.

———— (ed.). *Social Scientific Criticism of the New Testament and its Social World. Semeia* 35 (1986).

ELLIS, E. E. *The Old Testament in Early Christianity.* Tübingen: Mohr, 1991/Grand Rapids: Baker, 1992.

ELLIS, J. M. *The Theory of Literary Criticism.* Berkeley/London: U California, 1974.

ESLINGER, L., and G. TAYLOR (ed.). *Ascribe to the Lord* (P. C. Craigie Memorial). Sheffield: JSOT, 1988.

EVANS, C. F. *Explorations in Theology* 2. London: SCM, 1977.

————. "The Inspiration of the Bible." *Theology* 59 (1956) 11-17. = Hodgson and others, *On the Authority of the Bible* (see below) 25-32.

————. *Is "Holy Scripture" Christian?* London: SCM, 1971.

EVANS, D. D. *The Logic of Self-Involvement.* London: SCM/New York: Herder, 1963.

EVANS, G. R. *Authority in the Church.* Norwich: Canterbury, 1990.

———— (ed.). *Christian Authority* (H. Chadwick Festschrift). Oxford/New York: OUP, 1988.

FACKENHEIM, E. L. *The Jewish Bible after the Holocaust.* Manchester: Manchester UP, 1990.

FACKRE, G. *Authority.* The Christian Story vol. 2. Grand Rapids: Eerdmans, 1987.

FARKASFALVY, D. "The Ecclesial Setting of Pseudepigraphy in Second Peter." *TSC* 5 (1985-86) 3-29.

————. See also under Farmer.

FARLEY, E. *Ecclesial Reflection: An Anatomy of Theological Method.* Philadelphia: Fortress, 1982.

————. "Some Critical Reflections on Second Peter." *TSC* 5 (1985-86) 30-46.

FARMER, W. R., and D. M. FARKASFALVY. *The Formation of the New Testament Canon*. Ramsey, NJ: Paulist, 1983.

FARRER, A. M. *The Glass of Vision*. London: Dacre, 1948.

———. *The Revelation of St. John the Divine*. Oxford/New York: OUP, 1964.

FARROW, D. *The Word of Truth and Disputes about Words*. Winona Lake, IN: Eisenbrauns, 1987.

FELDMAN, L. II. "Prophets and Prophecy in Josephus." *JTS* n.s 41 (1990) 386-422.

FERGUSON, E. "Canon Muratori." *Studia patristica* 18 (1982) 677-83.

FEWELL, D. N. See Nolan Fewell.

FIDDES, P. *Past Event and Present Salvation*. London: DLT/Philadelphia: Westminster, 1989.

FIERRO, A. *The Militant Gospel*. ET Maryknoll, NY: Orbis/London: SCM, 1977.

FIORENZA, F. S. "The Crisis of Scriptural Authority." *Interpretation* 44 (1990) 353-68.

FISCH, H. *Poetry with a Purpose*. Bloomington: Indiana UP, 1988.

FISH, S. E. *Self-Consuming Artifacts*. Berkeley: U California, 1972.

FISHBANE, M. *Biblical Interpretation in Ancient Israel*. Oxford/New York: OUP, 1985.

———. *The Garments of Torah*. Bloomington: Indiana UP, 1989.

FLESSEMAN-VAN LEER, E. *Tradition and Scripture in the Early Church*. Assen: Van Gorcum, 1953.

——— (ed.). *The Bible: Its Authority and Interpretation in the Ecumenical Movement*. Geneva: WCC, 1980.

FORD, D. F. *Barth and God's Story*. Frankfurt: Lang, 1981, [2]1985.

———. "Barth's Interpretation of the Bible." In S. W. Sykes (ed.), *Karl Barth — Studies of His Theological Method* 55-87. Oxford/New York: OUP, 1979.

———. See also under Young.

FORSTMAN, H. J. *Word and Spirit: Calvin's Doctrine of Biblical Authority*. Stanford, CA: Stanford UP, 1962.

FOSKETT, J., and D. LYALL. *Helping the Helpers*. London: SPCK, 1988.

FRANCE, R. T. "Evangelical Disagreements about the Bible." *Churchman* 96 (1982) 226-40.

FRANKLIN, E. *How the Critics Can Help*. London: SCM, 1982.

FREI, H. *The Eclipse of Biblical Narrative*. New Haven/London: Yale UP, 1974.

———. *The Identity of Jesus Christ*. Philadelphia: Fortress, 1975.

FRYE, N. *Anatomy of Criticism*. Princeton: Princeton UP/London: OUP, 1957.

———. *The Educated Imagination*. Bloomington: Indiana UP, 1964.

———. *The Secular Scripture*. Cambridge, MA/London: Harvard UP, 1976.

FRYE, R. M. *Language for God and Feminist Language*. Edinburgh: Handsel, 1987. = *SJT* 41 (1988) 441-69. Shortened version in *Interpretation* 43 (1989) 45-57.

FUCHS, E. *Studies of the Historical Jesus*. ET London: SCM/Naperville, IL: Allenson, 1964.

FULLER, D. P. "The Nature of Biblical Inerrancy." *Journal of the American Scientific Affiliation* 24 (1972) 47-51.

FULLER, D. P., and C. PINNOCK. "On Revelation and Biblical Authority." *JETS* 16 (1973) 67-72.

FULLER, R. See under Hanson, R. P. C.

FUNK, R. W. *Language, Hermeneutic, and Word of God*. New York: Harper, 1966.

————. *Parables and Presence*. Philadelphia: Fortress, 1982.

GADAMER, H.-G. *Truth and Method*. ET New York: Seabury/London: Sheed and Ward, 1975; rev. ed., New York: Crossroad, 1989.

GALLIE, W. B. *Philosophy and Historical Understanding*. London: Chatto/New York: Schocken, 1964.

GAMBLE, H. Y. *The New Testament Canon*. Philadelphia: Fortress, 1985.

GARRETT, D. A., and R. R. MELICK (ed.). *Authority and Interpretation*. Grand Rapids: Baker, 1987.

GAUSSEN, S. R. L. *Theopneustia*. ET London: Bagster, 1841/New York: Taylor, 1842. Rev. ed., London: Passmore, 1888/Chicago: Bible Institute, 1915.

GEISLER, N. L. "The Concept of Truth in the Inerrancy Debate." *BSac* 137 (1980) 327-39.

———— (ed.). *Biblical Errancy*. Grand Rapids: Zondervan, 1981.

———— (ed.). *Inerrancy*. Grand Rapids: Zondervan, 1979.

GERHART, M., and J. G. WILLIAMS (ed.). *Genre, Narrativity, and Theology*. *Semeia* 43 (1988).

GILL, R. *Prophecy and Praxis*. London: Marshall, 1981.

GLASER, I. "Towards a Mutual Understanding of Christian and Islamic Concepts of Revelation." *Themelios* 7/3 (1982) 16-22.

GLOEGE, G. "Offenbarung und Überlieferung." *Theologische Literaturzeitung* 79 (1954) 213-36.

GNUSE, R. *The Authority of the Bible*. Ramsey, NJ: Paulist, 1985.

GOETZ, S. C., and C. L. BLOMBERG. "The Burden of Proof." *Journal for the Study of the New Testament* 11 (1981) 39-63.

GOLDINGAY, J. *Approaches to Old Testament Interpretation*. Leicester/Downers Grove, IL: IVP, 1981; [2]1990.

————. "The Bible in the City." *Theology* 92 (1989) 5-15.

————. "Current Issues in Evangelical Interpretation of Scripture." In C. M. Day (ed.), *Anglican Evangelical Assembly Proceedings* 4 (1986) 19-29.

————. *Daniel*. Dallas: Word, 1989/Milton Keynes: Word, 1991.

————. "The Dynamic Cycle of Praise and Prayer in the Psalms." *JSOT* 20 (1981) 85-90.

————. "The Hermeneutics of Liberation Theology." *HBT* 4/2 (1982) 133-61.

————. "Inspiration, Infallibility, and Criticism." *The Churchman* 90 (1976) 6-23.

————. "James Barr on Fundamentalism." *Churchman* 91 (1977) 295-308.

————. "Luther and the Bible." *SJT* 35 (1982) 33-58.

————. "Models for Scripture." *SJT* 44 (1991) 19-37.

————. "Modes of Theological Reflection in the Bible." *Theology* 94 (1991) 181-88.

————. "The Old Testament and Christian Faith." *Themelios* 8/1 (1982) 4-10; 8/2 (1983) 5-12.

————. " 'That You May Know That Yahweh is God': A Study in the Relationship between Theology and Historical Truth in the Old Testament." *TynB* 23 (1972) 58-93.

————. *Theological Diversity and the Authority of the Old Testament*. Grand Rapids: Eerdmans, 1987.

GOODMAN, M. "Sacred Scriptures and 'Defiling the Hands.' " *JTS* n.s. 41 (1990) 99-107.

GOODRICK, E. W. "Let's Put 2 Timothy 3:16 Back in the Bible." *JETS* 25 (1982) 479-87.

GORE, C. "The Holy Spirit and Inspiration." In Gore (ed.), *Lux Mundi* 230-66. London: Murray/New York: Lovell, 1889; 12th ed., 1891.

GOTTWALD, N. K. "Social Matrix and Canonical Shape." *ThT* 42 (1985-86) 307-21.

————. *The Tribes of Yahweh*. Maryknoll, NY: Orbis, 1979/London: SCM, 1980.

GOULDER, M. *Midrash and Lection in Matthew*. London: SPCK, 1974.

GREEN, G. *Imagining God*. San Francisco: Harper, 1989.

———— (ed.). *Scriptural Authority and Narrative Interpretation* (Hans Frei Festschrift). Philadelphia: Fortress, 1987.

GREENSLADE, S. L., and others (ed.). *The Cambridge History of the Bible*. 3 vols. Cambridge/New York: CUP, 1970, 1969, 1963.

GREENWOOD, D. S. "Poststructuralism and Biblical Studies." In R. T. France and D. Wenham (ed.), *Gospel Perspectives* 3:263-88. Sheffield: JSOT, 1983.

GREER, R. A. See under Kugel.

GRIFFIN, D. "Is Revelation Coherent?" *ThT* 28 (1971-72) 278-94.

GRUENWALD, I. *Apocalyptic and Merkavah Mysticism*. Leiden: Brill, 1980.

GUNDRY, R. H. *Matthew: A Commentary on His Literary and Theological Art*. Grand Rapids: Eerdmans, 1982.

GUNTON, C. E. *Enlightenment and Alienation*. Basingstoke: Marshall, 1985.

GUTIÉRREZ, G. *A Theology of Liberation*. ET Maryknoll: Orbis, 1973/London: SCM, 1974.

HALL, R. G. *Revealed Histories*. Sheffield: SAP, 1991.

HANSON, A. T. *The New Testament Interpretation of Scripture*. London: SPCK, 1980.

———. *Studies in the Pastoral Epistles*. London: SPCK, 1968.

HANSON, A. T., and R. P. C. HANSON. *The Bible without Illusions*. London: SCM/Philadelphia: TPI, 1989.

HANSON, P. D. "Jewish Apocalyptic against Its Near Eastern Environment." *Revue Biblique* 78 (1971) 31-58.

———. "Masculine Metaphors for God and Sex-discrimination in the Old Testament." *Ecumenical Review* 27 (1975) 316-24.

HANSON, R. P. C. *The Attractiveness of God*. London: SPCK/Richmond: Knox, 1973.

———. "The Authority of the Bible." In W. R. F. Browning (ed.), *The Anglican Synthesis* 19-26. Derby: Peter Smith, 1964.

———. "The Inspiration of Holy Scripture." *ATR* 43 (1961) 145-52.

———. *Tradition in the Early Church*. London: SCM, 1962/Philadelphia: Westminster, 1963.

———. See also under Hanson, A. T.

HANSON, R. P. C., and R. FULLER. *The Church of Rome: A Dissuasive*. London: SCM, 1950; ²1960/Greenwich, CN: Seabury, ²1960.

HARRIS, R. L. *Inspiration and Canonicity of the Bible*. Grand Rapids: Zondervan, 1957; rev. ed., 1969.

HARRISON, R. K. *Introduction to the Old Testament*. Grand Rapids: Eerdmans, 1969/London: Tyndale, 1970.

HART, R. L. *Unfinished Man and the Imagination*. New York: Herder, 1968.

HARVEY, A. E. *Jesus on Trial*. London: SPCK, 1976.

———. *Strenuous Commands*. London: SCM/Philadelphia: TPI, 1990.

HARVEY, V. A. *The Historian and the Believer*. New York: Macmillan, 1966/London: Macmillan, 1967.

HAWKES, T. *Metaphor*. London: Methuen/New York: Harper, 1972.

HAYS, R. B. *Echoes of Scripture in the Letters of Paul*. New Haven/London: Yale UP, 1989.

———. "Scripture-shaped Community." *Interpretation* 44 (1990) 42-55.

HEBBLETHWAITE, B. L. "The Appeal to Experience in Christology." In S. W. Sykes and J. P. Clayton (ed.), *Christ, Faith and History: Cambridge Studies in Christology* 263-78. London: CUP, 1972.

HEBERT, G. *Fundamentalism and the Church of God*. London: SCM, 1957. = *Fundamentalism and the Church*. Philadelphia: Westminster, 1957.

HEIDEGGER, M. *Being and Time*. ET London: SCM/New York: Harper, 1962.

HELM, P. "*The Bible in the Modern World* by James Barr." *TSF Bulletin* (UK) 69 (1974) 23.

————. *The Divine Revelation.* London: Marshall/Westchester, IL: Crossway, 1982.

————. "Revealed Propositions and Timeless Truths." *RelS* 8 (1972) 127-36.

HENRY, C. F. H. *God, Revelation and Authority.* 6 vols. Waco, TX: Word, 1976-83.

————. *Jesus of Nazareth.* Grand Rapids: Eerdmans/London: Tyndale, 1966.

———— (ed.). *Revelation and the Bible.* Grand Rapids: Baker, 1958/London: Tyndale, 1959.

HERDER, J. G. *The Spirit of Hebrew Poetry.* ET Burlington: Smith, 1833.

HESCHEL, A. J. *The Prophets.* New York: Harper, 1962. Reprinted New York: Harper (Torchbook edition, 2 vols.), 1969 and 1971.

HICK, J. (ed.). *Faith and the Philosophers.* London: Macmillan/New York: St Martin's, 1964.

HICKLING, C. See under Hooker.

HILL, R. "On Looking Again at *sunkatabasis.*" *Prudentia* 13 (1981) 3-11.

————. "St John Chrysostom's Teaching on Inspiration in 'Six Homilies on Isaiah.'" *Vigiliae Christianae* 22 (1968) 19-37.

HODGE, A. A., and B. B. WARFIELD. "Inspiration." *Presbyterian Review* 2 (1881) 225-60.

HODGE, C. "Inspiration." *Biblical Repertory and Princeton Review* 29 (1857) 660-98.

————. *Systematic Theology.* 3 vols. New York: Scribner's, 1871/London: Nelson, 1873.

HODGSON, L. *For Faith and Freedom.* 2 vols. Oxford: Blackwell, 1956 and 1957.

HODGSON, L., and others. *On the Authority of the Bible.* London: SPCK, 1960.

HOFFMAN, T. A. "Inspiration, Normativeness, Canonicity, and the Unique Sacred Character of the Bible." *CBQ* 44 (1982) 447-69.

HOLLENWEGER, W. "Intercultural Theology." *Theological Renewal* 10 (1978) 2-14.

HOOKER, M. and C. HICKLING (ed.). *What about the New Testament?* (C. F. Evans Festschrift). London: SCM, 1975.

HOULDEN, J. L. *Connections.* London: SCM, 1986/Philadelphia: Fortress, 1988.

HUNSINGER, G. H. "Beyond Literalism and Expressivism." *ModT* 3 (1987) 209-23.

HURST, L. D., and N. T. WRIGHT (ed.). *The Glory of Christ in the New Testament* (G. B. Caird Festschrift). Oxford/New York: OUP, 1987.

HUSSERL, E. *The Crisis of European Sciences and Transcendental Phenomenology.* ET Evanston: Northwestern UP, 1970.

HUXTABLE, J. *The Bible Says.* London: SCM/Richmond: Knox, 1962.

JACKSON, B. S. "Legalism." *JJS* 30 (1979) 1-22.

JANSEN, J. F. "Tertullian and the New Testament." *TSC* 2 (1982) 191-207.

JEANROND, W. G. *Text and Interpretation.* ET Dublin: Gill and Macmillan, 1988/New York: Crossroad, 1991.

JEREMIAS, J. *New Testament Theology.* Vol. 1. ET London: SCM/New York: Scribner, 1971.

JOHNSON, M. D. *The Purpose of the Biblical Genealogies.* Cambridge/New York: CUP, 1969.

JONES, H., and others. *The Bible under Attack.* Welwyn: Evangelical, 1978.

JOSIPOVICI, G. *The Book of God.* New Haven/London: Yale UP, 1988.

JOSSUA, J.-P. See under Metz.

JOWETT, B. "On the Interpretation of Scripture." *Essays and Reviews* (by F. Temple and others) 399-527. London: Longman, 1860; 10th ed., 1862.

JÜNGEL, E., G. KRODEL, R. MARLÉ, and J. D. ZIZIOULAS. "Four Preliminary Considerations on the Concept of Authority." *Ecumenical Review* 21 (1969) 150-66.

KAESTLI, J.-D., and O. WERMELINGER (ed.). *Le canon de l'Ancien Testament.* Geneva: Labor et Fides, 1984.

KÄHLER, M. *The So-called Historical Jesus and the Historic, Biblical Christ.* ET Philadelphia: Fortress, 1964.

KÄSEMANN, E. "The Canon of the New Testament and the Unity of the Church." In *Essays on New Testament Themes* 95-107. ET London: SCM/Naperville, IL: Allenson, 1964.

KAISER, W. C. "A Neglected Text in Bibliology Discussions: 1 Corinthians 2:6-16." *WTJ* 43 (1980-81) 301-19.

KALIN, E. "The Inspired Community." *Concordia Theological Monthly* 42 (1971) 541-49.

KAUFMAN, G. D. "What Shall We Do with the Bible?" *Interpretation* 25 (1971) 95-112.

KECK, L. E. "Is the New Testament a Field of Study?" *TSC* 1 (1981) 19-35.

KEE, A. *The Scope of Political Theology.* London: SCM, 1978.

KEEGAN, T. J. *Interpreting the Bible.* Mahwah, NJ: Paulist, 1985.

KELLY, J. F. (ed.) *Perspectives on Scripture and Tradition.* Notre Dame, IN: Fides, 1976.

KELSEY, D. H. "Appeals to Scripture in Theology." *JR* 48 (1968) 1-21.

———. "The Bible and Christian Theology." *Journal of the American Academy of Religion* 48 (1980) 385-402.

———. *The Uses of Scripture in Recent Theology.* Philadelphia: Fortress/London: SCM, 1975.

KERMODE, F. *The Genesis of Secrecy.* Cambridge, MA/London: Harvard UP, 1979.

———. See also under Alter.

KIDNER, D. *Genesis*. London: Tyndale/Downers Grove, IL: IVP, 1967.

KIRK, J. A. *Liberation Theology*. London: Marshall/Atlanta: Knox, 1979.

KLINE, M. G. *The Structure of Biblical Authority*. Grand Rapids: Eerdmans, 1972.

KLOOSTER, F. H. "Karl Barth's Doctrine of the Resurrection of Jesus Christ." *WTJ* 24 (1962) 137-72.

KNIGHT, D. A. (ed.). *Tradition and Theology in the Old Testament*. Philadelphia: Fortress/London: SPCK, 1977.

KNIGHT, H. *The Hebrew Prophetic Consciousness*. London: Lutterworth/Chicago: Allenson, 1947.

KOCH, K. *The Growth of the Biblical Tradition*. ET London: Black/New York: Scribner, 1969.

KOESTER, H. *Ancient Christian Gospels*. London: SCM/Philadelphia: TPI, 1990.

KORT, W. *Story, Text, and Scripture*. University Park/London: Pennsylvania State UP, 1988.

KRODEL, G. See under Jüngel.

KÜMMEL, W. G. *Introduction to the New Testament*. ET London: SCM/Nashville: Abingdon, rev. ed., 1975.

KÜNG, H., and J. MOLTMANN (ed.). *Conflicting Ways of Interpreting the Bible. Concilium* 138 (1980).

KUGEL, J. L., and R. A. GREER. *Early Biblical Interpretation*. Philadelphia: Westminster, 1986.

LAMPE, G. W. H. "Inspiration and Revelation." In G. A. Buttrick (ed.), *The Interpreter's Dictionary of the Bible* 2:713-18. Nashville: Abingdon, 1962.

LANE, A. N. S. "B. B. Warfield on the Humanity of Scripture." *VE* 16 (1986) 77-94.

————. "Scripture, Tradition and Church." *VE* 9 (1975) 37-55.

LASH, N. *Theology on the Way to Emmaus*. London: SCM, 1986.

LATEGAN, B. C., AND W. C. VORSTER, *Text and Reality*. Atlanta: Scholars, 1985.

LATOURELLE, R. *Theology of Revelation*. Staten Island: Alba House, 1966.

LAYTON, B. (ed.). *The Gnostic Scriptures*. Garden City, New York: Doubleday/London: SCM, 1987.

LEE, W. *The Inspiration of Holy Scripture*. New York: Whittaker, 1854.

LEIMAN, S. Z. *The Canonization of Hebrew Scripture*. Hamden, CT: Archon, 1976.

———— (ed.). *The Canon and Masorah of the Hebrew Bible*. New York: KTAV, 1974.

LEMCIO, E. E. "Ephesus and the New Testament Canon." *BJRL* 69 (1986) 210-34.

LENTRICCHIA, F. *After the New Criticism*. Chicago: U Chicago/London: Athlone, 1980.

LETIS, T. P. "The Protestant Dogmaticians and the Late Princeton School on the Status of the Sacred Apographa." *Scottish Bulletin of Evangelical Theology* 8 (1990) 16-42.

LEVENSON, J. D. "The Sources of Torah." In P. D. Miller and others (ed.), *Ancient Israelite Religion* (F. M. Cross Festschrift) 559-74. Philadelphia: Fortress, 1987.

LEWIS, C. S. *Christian Reflections.* London: Bles/Grand Rapids: Eerdmans, 1967.

———. *Miracles.* London: Bles/New York: Macmillan, 1947; reprinted London: Collins Fontana, 1960.

LEWIS, G. R., and B. DEMAREST (ed.). *Challenges to Inerrancy.* Chicago: Moody, 1984.

LEWIS, J. P. "What Do We Mean by Jabneh?" *Journal of Bible and Religion* 32 (1964) 125-32. = Leiman (ed.), *Canon and Masorah* 254-61.

LINDARS, B., and P. BORGEN. "The Place of the Old Testament in the Formation of New Testament Theology." *NTS* 23 (1976) 59-75.

LINDBECK, G. A. *The Nature of Doctrine.* Philadelphia: Westminster/London: SPCK, 1984.

———. "Scripture, Consensus, and Community." *This World* 23 (1988) 5-24. = R. J. Neuhaus (ed.), *Biblical Interpretation in Crisis* 74-101. Grand Rapids: Eerdmans, 1989.

LINDBLOM, J. *Prophecy in Ancient Israel.* Oxford: Blackwell/Philadelphia: Fortress, 1962; rev. ed., 1963.

LINDSAY, T. M. "The Doctrine of Scripture: The Reformers and the Princeton School." *The Expositor* V/1 (1895) 278-93.

———. "Professor W. Robertson Smith's Doctrine of Scripture." *The Expositor* IV/10 (1894) 241-64.

LINDSELL, H. *The Battle for the Bible.* Grand Rapids: Zondervan, 1976.

———. *The Bible in the Balance.* Grand Rapids: Zondervan, 1979.

LISCHER, R. "The Limits of Story." *Interpretation* 38 (1984) 26-38.

———. "Luther and Contemporary Preaching." *SJT* 36 (1983) 487-504.

LÖNNING, I. *"Kanon im Kanon."* Oslo: Universitets Forlaget, 1972.

LOHFINK, N. *The Christian Meaning of the Old Testament.* ET Milwaukee: Bruce, 1968/London: Burns and Oates, 1969.

LORETZ, O. *The Truth of the Bible.* ET London: Burns and Oates/New York: Herder, 1968.

LOWENTHAL, D. *The Past Is a Foreign Country.* Cambridge/New York: CUP, 1985.

LUNDIN, R., A. C. THISELTON, and C. WALHOUT. *The Responsibility of Hermeneutics.* Grand Rapids: Eerdmans/Exeter: Paternoster, 1985.

LYALL, D. See under Foskett.

MAARTEN VAN BEMMELEN, P. *Issues in Biblical Inspiration.* Berrien Springs, MI: Andrews UP, 1988.

McCARTHY, D. J. "Personality, Society, and Inspiration." *TS* 24 (1963) 553-76.

MacDONALD, D. R. *The Legend and the Apostle.* Philadelphia: Westminster, 1983.

McDonald, H. D. *I Want to Know What the Bible Says about the Bible.* Eastbourne: Kingsway, 1979.

———. *Ideas of Revelation: An Historical Study* A.D. *1700 to* A.D. *1860.* London: Macmillan/New York: St Martin's, 1959.

———. *Theories of Revelation: An Historical Study 1860-1960.* London: Allen and Unwin, 1963.

McDonald, L. M. *The Formation of the Christian Biblical Canon.* Nashville: Abingdon, 1988.

McEvenue, S. E. "The Old Testament, Scripture or Theology?" *Interpretation* 35 (1981) 229-42. = *Ex auditu* 1 (1985) 115-24.

McFague, S. *Metaphorical Theology.* Philadelphia: Fortress, 1982/London: SCM, 1983.

———. *Models of God.* Philadelphia: Fortress/London: SCM, 1987.

McFague Teselle, S. *Speaking in Parables.* Philadelphia: Fortress/London: SCM, 1975.

McKenzie, J. L. "The Social Character of Inspiration." *CBQ* 24 (1962) 115-24. = *Myths and Realities* 59-69. Milwaukee: Bruce, 1963.

McKim, D. K. (ed.). *The Authoritative Word.* Grand Rapids: Eerdmans, 1983.

———. *A Guide to Contemporary Hermeneutics.* Grand Rapids: Eerdmans, 1986.

———. See also under Rogers.

McKnight, E. V. *Post-modern Use of the Bible.* Nashville: Abingdon, 1988.

——— (ed.). *Reader Perspectives on the New Testament. Semeia* 48 (1989).

Macquarrie, J. *God-Talk.* London: SCM/New York: Harper, 1967.

Marcus, J. "Mark 4:10-12 and Marcan Epistemology." *JBL* 103 (1984) 557-74.

Marlé, R. See under Jüngel.

Marsden, G. "Fundamentalism as an American Phenomenon." *Church History* 46 (1977) 215-32.

Marshall, I. H. *Biblical Inspiration.* London: Hodder, 1982/Grand Rapids: Eerdmans, 1983.

——— (ed.). *New Testament Interpretation.* Exeter: Paternoster/Grand Rapids: Eerdmans, 1977.

———. See also under Cameron.

Martin, J. "Metaphor Amongst Tropes." *RelS* 17 (1981) 55-66. Cf. *Metaphor and Religious Language* (see under Martin Soskice) 54-66.

Martin Soskice, J. *Metaphor and Religious Language.* Oxford/New York: OUP, 1985.

Marxsen, W. *The New Testament as the Church's Book.* ET Philadelphia: Fortress, 1972.

———. "Das Problem des neutestamentlichen Kanons aus der Sicht des Exegeten." In E. Käsemann (ed.), *Das Neue Testament als Kanon* 233-46.

Göttingen: Vandenhoeck und Ruprecht, 1970. Partial ET in Marxsen, *The NT as the Church's Book* (see above) 49-63.

MATEJKA, L., and K. POMORSKA (ed.). *Readings in Russian Poetics.* Cambridge, MA/London: MIT, 1971.

MENDENHALL, G. E. "Covenant Forms in Israelite Tradition." *Biblical Archaeologist* 17 (1954) 50-76. = *Biblical Archaeologist Reader* 3:25-53. Garden City, NY: Doubleday, 1970.

———. "The Monarchy." *Interpretation* 29 (1975) 15-70.

———. *The Tenth Generation.* Baltimore: Johns Hopkins, 1973.

METZ, J. B., and J.-P. JOSSUA (ed.). *The Crisis in the Language of Faith.* ET *Concilium* (UK) 5.9 (1973) = *Concilium* (USA) 85 (1973).

METZGER, B. M. *The Canon of the New Testament.* Oxford/New York: OUP, 1987.

MIEGGE, R. *Gospel and Myth in the Thought of Rudolf Bultmann.* ET London: Lutterworth/Richmond: Knox, 1960.

MIGUEZ BONINO, J. *Revolutionary Theology Comes of Age.* London: SPCK, 1975. = *Doing Theology in a Revolutionary Situation.* Philadelphia: Fortress, 1975.

MILAVEC, D. A. "The Bible, the Holy Spirit, and Human Powers." *SJT* 29 (1976) 215-35.

MILDENBERGER, F. "The Unity, Truth, and Validity of the Bible." *Interpretation* 29 (1975) 391-405.

MILLER, D. G. *The Authority of the Bible.* Grand Rapids: Eerdmans, 1972.

MIRANDA, J. P. *Being and the Messiah.* ET Maryknoll, NY: Orbis, 1977.

MITCHELL, B. *The Justification of Religious Belief.* London: Macmillan, 1973.

MITCHELL, B., and M. WILES. "Does Christianity Need a Revelation?" *Theology* 83 (1980) 103-14.

MOLTMANN, J. *The Trinity and the Kingdom of God.* ET San Francisco: Harper/London: SCM, 1981.

———. *The Way of Jesus Christ.* ET San Francisco: Harper/London: SCM, 1990.

———. See also under Küng.

MONTGOMERY, J. W. (ed.). *God's Inerrant Word.* Minneapolis: Bethany, 1974.

MOORE, G. F. *Judaism.* 3 vols. Cambridge, MA: Harvard UP, 1927, 1927, 1930.

MORAN, G. *Theology of Revelation.* New York: Herder, 1966.

———. "What Is Revelation?" *TS* 25 (1964) 217-31.

MORGAN, R. See under Pye.

MORRIS, L. "Biblical Authority and the Concept of Inerrancy." *Churchman* 81 (1967) 22-38.

———. *I Believe in Revelation.* London: Hodder/Grand Rapids: Eerdmans, 1976.

MOSALA, I. J. *Biblical Hermeneutics and Black Theology in South Africa.* Grand Rapids: Eerdmans, 1989.

MOULE, C. F. D. *"Is 'Holy Scripture' Christian? and Other Questions* by C. F. Evans. . . ." *Theology* 74 (1971) 418-21.

MOWINCKEL, S. *The Psalms in Israel's Worship.* ET Oxford: Blackwell/Nashville: Abingdon, 1962.

MUDDIMAN, J. *The Bible: Fountain and Well of Truth.* Oxford: Blackwell, 1983.

———. "The Holy Spirit and Inspiration." In R. Morgan (ed.), *The Religion of the Incarnation* 119-35. Bristol: Bristol Classical Press, 1989.

MURRAY, J. *Calvin on Scripture and Divine Sovereignty.* Grand Rapids: Baker, 1960.

NEWMAN, J. H. *The Theological Papers of John Henry Newman on Biblical Inspiration and on Infallibility* (ed. J. D. Holmes). Oxford/New York: OUP, 1979.

NEWSOM, C. A. "The Past as Revelation." *Quarterly Review* 1984, 4:40-53.

NICOLE, R. R. "The Inspiration and Authority of Scripture." *Churchman* 97 (1983) 198-215; 98 (1983-84) 7-27, 198-216.

NICOLE, R. R., and J. R. MICHAELS (ed.). *Inerrancy and Common Sense.* Grand Rapids: Baker, 1980.

NIEBUHR, H. R. *The Meaning of Revelation.* New York: Macmillan, 1946.

NIELSEN, K. "The Primacy of Philosophical Theology." *ThT* 27 (1970-71) 155-69.

NINEHAM, D. E. *Explorations in Theology* 1. London: SCM, 1977.

———. *The Use and Abuse of the Bible.* London: Macmillan/New York: Barnes, 1976.

NOLAN FEWELL, D. *Circle of Sovereignty: A Story of Stories in Daniel 1–6.* Sheffield: SAP, 1988. 2nd ed., *Circle of Sovereignty: Plotting Politics in the Book of Daniel.* Nashville: Abingdon, 1991.

NOTH, M. *The Laws in the Pentateuch and Other Studies.* ET Edinburgh: Oliver and Boyd/Philadelphia: Fortress, 1966.

O'COLLINS, G. *Fundamental Theology.* Ramsey, NJ: Paulist/London: DLT, 1981.

O'DONOVAN, O. M. T. *On the Thirty Nine Articles.* Exeter: Paternoster, 1986.

OEMING, M. "Bedeutung und Funktionen von 'Fiktionen' in der alttestamentlichen Geschichtsschreibung." *Evangelische Theologie* 44 (1984) 254-66.

ÖSTBORN, G. *Cult and Canon.* Uppsala: Lundequistska, 1950.

OGDEN, S. M. "The Authority of Scripture for Theology." *Interpretation* 30 (1976) 242-61.

———. *Christ without Myth.* New York: Harper, 1961/London: Collins, 1962.

OGLETREE, T. W. *Christian Faith and History.* Nashville: Abingdon, 1965.

O'NEILL, J. C. *The Bible's Authority.* Edinburgh: Clark, 1991.

ORR, J. *Revelation and Inspiration.* London: Duckworth, 1909/London: Scribner, 1910.

OWEN, J. *Three Treatises concerning the Scriptures.* Oxford, 1659. = *The Works of John Owen* 16:281-476. Edinburgh: Clark, 1862.

PACHE, R. *The Inspiration and Authority of Scripture.* ET Chicago: Moody, 1969.

PACKER, J. I. *Beyond the Battle for the Bible.* Westchester, IL: Cornerstone, 1980.

―――. "An Evangelical View of Progressive Revelation." In K. S. Kantzer (ed.), *Evangelical Roots* 143-58. Nashville: Nelson, 1978.

―――. *Freedom and Authority.* Chicago: ICBI, 1981. = *Freedom, Authority and Scripture.* Leicester: IVP, 1982.

―――. *"Fundamentalism" and the Word of God.* London: IVF/Grand Rapids: Eerdmans, 1958.

―――. *God Has Spoken.* London: Hodder, 1965; reprinted Downers Grove, IL: IVP, 1979. = *God Speaks to Man.* Philadelphia: Westminster, 1965.

―――. *Keep Yourself from Idols.* London: Church Book Room Press, 1963.

―――. *Our Lord's Understanding of the Law of God.* London: Westminster Chapel, 1962.

PAGELS, E. *The Gnostic Gospels.* New York: Random House, 1979/London: Weidenfeld, 1980.

PANNENBERG, W. *Basic Questions in Theology.* 2 vols. ET London: SCM/Philadelphia: Westminster, 1970, 1971.

―――(ed.). *Revelation as History.* ET New York: Macmillan/London: Collier-Macmillan, 1968; London: Sheed and Ward, 1969.

PARSONS, M. "Warfield and Scripture." *Churchman* 91 (1977) 198-220.

PATRICK, D. *The Rendering of God in the Old Testament.* Philadelphia: Fortress, 1981.

PERRIN, N. "Wisdom and Apocalyptic in the Message of Jesus." In L. C. McGaughy (ed.), *The Society of Biblical Literature One Hundred Eighth Annual Meeting: Book of Seminar Papers* 2:543-72. Missoula, MT: SBL, 1972.

PERSSON, P. E. *Sacra Doctrina: Reason and Revelation in Aquinas.* ET Philadelphia: Fortress/London: Black, 1970.

PHILLIPS, G. A. (ed.). *Poststructural Criticism and the Bible. Semeia* 51 (1990).

PINNOCK, C. H. *Biblical Revelation.* Chicago: Moody, 1971.

―――. *A Defense of Biblical Infallibility.* Philadelphia: Presbyterian and Reformed, 1967.

―――. *The Scripture Principle.* San Francisco: Harper, 1984.

―――. See also under Fuller, D. P.

PLASKOW, J. See under Christ.

POLMAN, A. D. R. *The Word of God according to St. Augustine.* ET Grand Rapids: Eerdmans, 1961/London: Hodder, 1962.

POMORSKA, K. See under Matejka.

POPPER, K. *The Poverty of Historicism.* London: Routledge, 1957; [2]1960; corrected ed., 1961/Boston: Beacon, 1957; New York: Basic, 1960; New York: Harper, 1961.

The Proceedings of the Conference on Biblical Inerrancy 1987. Nashville: Broadman, 1987.

Pui-Lan, K. "Discovering the Bible in the Non-biblical World." In Cannon and Schüssler Fiorenza (ed.), *Interpretation for Liberation* 25-42. = R. S. Sugirtharajah (ed.), *Voices from the Margin: Interpreting the Bible in the Third World* 299-315. Maryknoll: Orbis, 1991.

Pye, M., and R. Morgan (ed.). *The Cardinal Meaning.* The Hague: Mouton, 1973.

Rad, G. von. *Old Testament Theology.* 2 vols. ET Edinburgh: Oliver and Boyd/New York: Harper, 1962 and 1965.

————. *Wisdom in Israel.* ET London: SCM/Nashville: Abingdon, 1972.

Rahner, K. "The Hermeneutics of Eschatological Assertions." *Theological Investigations* 4:323-46. ET Baltimore: Helicon/London: DLT, 1966.

————. *Inspiration in the Bible.* ET New York: Herder, 1961.

Ramsey, A. M. "The Authority of the Bible." In M. Black and H. H. Rowley (ed.), *Peake's Commentary on the Bible* 1-7. London/New York: Nelson, 1962.

Ramsey, G. W. *The Quest for the Historical Israel.* Atlanta: Knox, 1981/London: SCM, 1982.

Reed, W. L. "A Poetics of the Bible." *Literature and Theology* 1 (1987) 154-66.

Reid, J. K. S. *The Authority of Scripture.* London: Methuen/New York: Harper, 1957.

Reventlow, H. Graf. *The Authority of the Bible and the Rise of the Modern World.* ET London: SCM, 1984/Philadelphia: Fortress, 1985.

Richardson, A. "Gnosis and Revelation in the Bible and in Contemporary Thought." *SJT* 9 (1956) 31-45.

Richardson, A., and W. Schweizer (ed.). *Biblical Authority for Today.* London: SCM/Philadelphia: Westminster, 1951.

Richardson, P. " 'I Say, Not the Lord': Personal Opinion, Apostolic Authority and the Development of Early Christian Halakah." *TynB* 31 (1980) 65-86.

Ricoeur, P. "Biblical Hermeneutics." In J. D. Crossan (ed.), *Paul Ricoeur on Biblical Hermeneutics* 29-148. *Semeia* 4 (1975).

————. *The Conflict of Interpretations.* ET Evanston: Northwestern UP, 1974.

————. *Essays on Biblical Interpretation.* ET Philadelphia: Fortress, 1980/London: SPCK, 1981.

————. "The Hermeneutical Function of Distanciation." *Philosophy Today* 17 (1973) 129-41. = *Hermeneutics and the Human Sciences* (see below) 131-44.

————. *Hermeneutics and the Human Sciences.* ET Cambridge/New York: CUP, 1981.

————. "The Hermeneutics of Testimony." ET *ATR* 61 (1979) 435-61. = *Essays on Biblical Interpretation* (see above) 119-54.

————. *Interpretation Theory.* Fort Worth: Texas Christian UP, 1976.

————. "The Narrative Function." In W. A. Beardslee (ed.), *The Poetics of Faith* (A. N. Wilder Festschrift) 2:177-202. *Semeia* 13 (1978). = *Hermeneutics and the Human Sciences* (see above) 274-96.

————. "A Response" (to essays by J. D. Crossan and others). *Biblical Research* 24-25 (1979-80) 70-80.

————. *The Rule of Metaphor.* ET Toronto: U Toronto, 1977/London: Routledge, 1978.

————. *The Symbolism of Evil.* ET New York: Harper, 1967; reprinted Boston: Beacon, 1969.

————. *Time and Narrative.* 3 vols. ET Chicago/London: U Chicago, 1984, 1985, 1988.

————. "Toward a Hermeneutic of the Idea of Revelation." ET *HTR* 70 (1977) 1-37. = *Essays on Biblical Interpretation* (see above) 73-118.

RIDDERBOS, H. N. *The Authority of the New Testament Scriptures.* ET Philadelphia: Presbyterian and Reformed, 1963. 2nd ed., *Redemptive History and the New Testament Scriptures.* Phillipsburg, NJ: Presbyterian and Reformed, 1988.

————. *Studies in Scripture and Its Authority.* Grand Rapids: Eerdmans, 1978.

RITSCHL, D. "A Plea for the Maxim: Scripture and Tradition." *Interpretation* 25 (1971) 113-28.

RITSCHL, D., and H. JONES. *"Story" als Rohmaterial der Theologie.* Munich: Kaiser, 1976.

ROBINSON, H. W. *Inspiration and Revelation in the Old Testament.* Oxford/New York: OUP, 1946.

ROBINSON, J. M. (ed.). *The Beginnings of Dialectic Theology.* Vol. 1. Richmond: Knox, 1968.

ROBINSON, J. M., and J. B. COBB (ed.). *The New Hermeneutic.* New York/London: Harper, 1964.

RODGER, P. C., and L. VISCHER (ed.). *The Fourth World Conference on Faith and Order: Montreal 1963.* Faith and Order Papers 42. London: SCM, 1964.

ROGERS, J. B. (ed.). *Biblical Authority.* Waco, TX: Word, 1977.

ROGERS, J. B., and D. K. MCKIM. *The Authority and Interpretation of the Bible.* San Francisco: Harper, 1979.

ROGERSON, J. W. "Can a Doctrine of Providence Be Based on the Old Testament?" In Eslinger and Taylor (ed.), *Ascribe to the Lord* 529-43.

————. "Progressive Revelation." *Epworth Review* 9/2 (1982) 73-86.

ROWLAND, C. *The Open Heaven.* London: SPCK/New York: Crossroad, 1982.

ROWLAND, C., and M. CORNER. *Liberating Exegesis.* London: SPCK/Louisville: WJK, 1990.

RUNIA, K. "The Authority of Scripture." *Calvin Theological Journal* 4 (1969) 165-94.

————. *Karl Barth's Doctrine of Holy Scripture.* Grand Rapids: Eerdmans, 1962.

RUSSELL, D. S. *The Method and Message of Jewish Apocalyptic.* London: SCM/Philadelphia: Westminster, 1964.

RUSSELL, L. M. (ed.). *Feminist Interpretation of the Bible.* Philadelphia: Westminster/Oxford: Blackwell, 1985.

RYKEN, L. *Triumphs of the Imagination.* Downers Grove, IL/Leicester: IVP, 1979.

RYLE, H. E. *The Canon of the Old Testament.* London/New York: Macmillan, 1892, [2]1895.

RYRIE, C. C. "The Importance of Inerrancy." *BSac* 120 (1963) 137-44.

SAKENFELD, K. D. "Feminist Perspectives on Bible and Theology." *Interpretation* 42 (1988) 5-14.

SANDAY, W. *Inspiration.* London/New York: Longmans, 1893, [3]1896.

————. *The Oracles of God.* London/New York: Longmans. 1891.

SANDERS, E. P. *Jewish Law from Jesus to the Mishnah.* London: SCM/Philadelphia: TPI, 1990.

SANDERS, E. P., et al. (ed.). *Jewish and Christian Self-Definition.* 3 vols. London: SCM/Philadelphia: Fortress, 1980, 1981, 1982.

SANDERS, J. A. *Canon and Community.* Philadelphia: Fortress, 1984.

————. "First Testament and Second." *Biblical Theology Bulletin* 17 (1987) 47-49.

————. *From Sacred Story to Sacred Text.* Philadelphia: Fortress, 1987.

SCHAEFFER, F. A. "*It Is Essential for the Truth of Christianity That the Bible Relates Truth about History and the Cosmos, As Well As about Spiritual Matters.*" Greatham: L'Abri Fellowship, 1981(?).

————. *No Final Conflict.* London: Hodder, 1975.

————. "Race and Reason." *The Other Side* 10/3 (1974) 12-16, 57-61.

SCHILLEBEECKX, E. *Christ: The Christian Experience in the Modern World.* ET London: SCM/New York: Crossroad, 1980.

————. *Revelation and Theology.* ET London/New York: Sheed and Ward, 1967.

SCHLATTER, A. *Die christliche Dogma.* Calw: Vereinsbuchhandlung, 1911; [2]1923.

SCHOFIELD, J. N. *Introducing Old Testament Theology.* London: SCM/Philadelphia: Westminster, 1964.

SCHOLEM, G. *Major Trends in Jewish Mysticism.* Jerusalem: Schocken, 1941; 3rd ed. reprinted New York: Schocken, 1961.

————. "Revelation and Tradition as Religious Categories in Judaism." In *The Messianic Idea in Judaism* 282-303, 363. ET New York: Schocken, 1971.

SCHOLES, R. E., and R. KELLOGG. *The Nature of Narrative.* London/New York: OUP, 1966.

SCHÜRER, E. *The History of the Jewish People in the Age of Jesus Christ.* Vol. 2. Edinburgh: Clark, rev. ed. 1979.

SCHÜSSLER FIORENZA, E. *Bread Not Stone: The Challenge of Feminist Biblical Interpretation.* Boston: Beacon, 1984/Edinburgh: Clark, 1990.

————. *In Memory of Her.* New York: Crossroad/London: SCM, 1983.

————. See also under Cannon.

SCHÜTZ, J. H. *Paul and the Anatomy of Apostolic Authority.* Cambridge/New York: CUP, 1975.

SCHWEIZER, E. *Jesus.* ET London: SCM/Richmond: Knox, 1971.

SCHWEIZER, W. See under Richardson, A.

SCULLION, J. *The Theology of Inspiration.* Notre Dame, IN: Fides/Cork: Mercier, 1970.

SEARLE, J. R. *Expression and Meaning.* Cambridge/New York: CUP, 1979.

————. "The Logical Status of Fictional Discourse." *NLH* 6 (1974-75) 319-32.

————. *Speech Acts.* Cambridge/New York: CUP, 1969.

SEELY, P. H. *Inerrant Wisdom.* Portland, OR: Evangelical Reform, 1989.

SEGUNDO, J. L. *Liberation of Theology.* Maryknoll, NY: Orbis, 1976/Dublin: Gill and Macmillan, 1977.

————. "The Shift within Latin American Theology." *Journal of Theology for Southern Africa* 52 (1985) 17-29.

SHAW, G. *The Cost of Authority.* London: SCM/Philadelphia: Fortress, 1983.

SILVA, M. *Has the Church Misread the Bible?* Grand Rapids: Zondervan/Leicester: IVP, 1987.

SMART, J. D. *The Strange Silence of the Bible in the Church.* Philadelphia: Fortress/London: SCM, 1970.

————. "The Treacherousness of Tradition." *Interpretation* 30 (1976) 18-25.

SMITH, M. *Palestinian Parties and Politics That Shaped the Old Testament.* New York/London: Columbia UP, 1971. Rev. ed., London: SCM, 1987.

SOSKICE, J. M. See under Martin and Martin Soskice.

STANTON, G. N. *Jesus of Nazareth in New Testament Preaching.* Cambridge/New York: CUP, 1974.

STEINER, G. " 'Critic'/'Reader.' " *NLH* 10 (1978-79) 423-52.

————. *On Difficulty and Other Essays.* Oxford/New York: OUP, 1978.

————. *Real Presences: Is There Anything* in *What We Say?* London/Boston: Faber, 1989.

STEMBERGER, G. "Die sogenannte 'Synod von Jabne' und das frühe Christentum." *Kairos* 19 (1977) 14-21.

STERNBERG, M. *The Poetics of Biblical Narrative.* Bloomington: Indiana UP, 1985.

STONEHOUSE, N., and P. WOOLLEY (ed.). *The Infallible Word.* Philadelphia: Presbyterian Guardian, 1946.

STOTT, J. R. W. *The Authority and Relevance of the Bible in the Modern World.* Canberra: Bible Society in Australia, 1979.

————. See also under Edwards.

STOUT, J. *The Flight from Authority.* Notre Dame, IN: U Notre Dame, 1981.

SUNDBERG, A. C. "The Bible Canon and the Christian Doctrine of Inspiration." *Interpretation* 29 (1975) 352-71.

————. "Canon Muratori." *HTR* 66 (1973) 1-41.

————. "The Old Testament of the Early Church." *HTR* 51 (1958) 205-26.

————. *The Old Testament of the Early Church.* Cambridge, MA: Harvard UP/London: OUP, 1964.

————. "The Protestant Old Testament Canon: Should It Be Reconsidered?" *CBQ* 28 (1966) 194-203.

SWINBURNE, R. *Responsibility and Atonement.* Oxford/New York: OUP, 1989.

————. *Revelation.* Oxford/New York: OUP, 1991.

SYNAVE, P., and P. BENOIT. *Prophecy and Inspiration.* ET New York: Desclee, 1961.

TALMON, S. "The 'Comparative Method' in Biblical Interpretation." *Congress Volume: Göttingen 1977* 320-56. *Vetus Testamentum* Supplements 29. Leiden: Brill, 1978.

————. See also under Cross.

TERRIEN, S. *Till the Heart Sings.* Philadelphia: Fortress, 1985.

TESELLE, S. See under McFague TeSelle.

THIEMANN, R. F. "Revelation and Imaginative Construction." *JR* 61 (1981) 242-63.

————. *Revelation and Theology.* Notre Dame, IN: U Notre Dame, 1985.

THISELTON, A. C. *New Horizons in Hermeneutics.* London: HarperCollins/Grand Rapids: Zondervan, 1992.

————. "The Parables as Language-event." *SJT* 23 (1970) 437-68.

————. "The Supposed Power of Words in the Biblical Writings." *JTS* n.s. 25 (1974) 283-99.

————. *The Two Horizons.* Exeter: Paternoster/Grand Rapids: Eerdmans, 1980.

————. See also under Lundin.

THOMAS, O. C. "Theology and Experience." *HTR* 78 (1985) 179-201.

TOLBERT, M. A. (ed.). *The Bible and Feminist Hermeneutics. Semeia* 28 (1983).

TRACY, D. *The Analogical Imagination.* New York: Crossroad/London: SCM, 1981.

————. "Metaphor and Religion." *CI* 5 (1978-79) 91-106.

TREMBATH, K. R. "Biblical Inspiration and the Believing Community." *EvQ* 58 (1986) 245-56. = *Evangelical Review of Theology* 12 (1988) 29-40.

————. *Evangelical Theories of Biblical Inspiration.* Oxford/New York: OUP, 1987.

TRIBLE, P. (ed.). "The Effects of Women's Studies on Biblical Studies." *JSOT* 22 (1982) 3-71.

TRITES, A. A. *The New Testament Concept of Witness.* Cambridge/New York: CUP, 1977.

TROELTSCH, E. "Historiography." In J. Hastings (ed.), *Encyclopaedia of Religion and Ethics* 6:716-23. Edinburgh: Clark, 1914.

TURNER, G. "Biblical Inspiration and the Paraclete." *New Blackfriars* 65 (1984) 420-28.

TURNER, M. See under Cotterell.

TURRETIN, F. *The Doctrine of Scripture* (ed. J. W. Beardslee). Grand Rapids: Baker, 1981.

UNNIK, W. C. VAN. "Ἡ καινὴ διαθήκη." *Studia patristica* 4 (1961) 212-27.

VAIHINGER, H. *The Philosophy of "As If."* ET New York: Harcourt/London: Routledge, 1924; ²1935.

VAN BUREN, P. M. *A Theology of the Jewish-Christian Reality.* 3 vols. San Francisco: Harper, 1980, 1983, 1988/Edinburgh: Clark, 1991.

VAN DIJK-HEMMES, F. "The Imagination of Power and the Power of Imagination." *JSOT* 44 (1989) 75-88.

VANHOOZER, K. J. *Biblical Narrative in the Philosophy of Paul Ricoeur.* Cambridge/New York: CUP, 1990.

VAN TIL, C. *The Protestant Doctrine of Scripture.* Ripon, CA: Den Dijk Christian Foundation, 1967.

VAUX, R. DE. *Ancient Israel.* ET London: DLT/New York: McGraw Hill, 1961.

VAWTER, B. *Biblical Inspiration.* Philadelphia: Westminster/London: Hutchinson, 1972.

VIDALES, R. "Methodological Issues in Liberation Theology." In R. Gibellini (ed.), *Frontiers of Theology in Latin America.* ET Maryknoll, NY: Orbis, 1979/London: SCM, 1980.

VISCHER, L. See under Rodger.

WADSWORTH, M. (ed.). *Ways of Reading the Bible.* Brighton: Harvester/Totowa, NJ: Barnes, 1981.

WAINWRIGHT, G. *Doxology.* London: Epworth/New York: OUP, 1980.

———. "The New Testament as Canon." *SJT* 28 (1975) 551-71.

WALHOUT, C. See under Lundin.

WARFIELD, B. B. *Biblical Foundations.* London: Tyndale, 1958.

———. "Calvin's Doctrine of the Knowledge of God." In *Calvin and Augustine* 29-130. Philadelphia: Presbyterian and Reformed, 1956.

———. *The Inspiration and Authority of the Bible.* Philadelphia: Presbyterian and Reformed, 1948/London: Marshall, 1951.

———. *Limited Inspiration.* Philadelphia: Presbyterian and Reformed, 1962.

———. *Revelation and Inspiration.* New York: OUP, 1927.

———. See also under Hodge, A. A.

WARNER, M. (ed.). *The Bible as Rhetoric.* London/New York: Routledge, 1990.

WCELA, E. A. "Who Do You Say That They Are?" *CBQ* 53 (1991) 1-17.

WEBER, H.-R. "The Promise of the Land." *Study Encounter* 7/4 (1971).

WEISER, A. *Introduction to the Old Testament.* ET London: DLT, 1961. = *The Old Testament: Its Formation and Development.* New York: Association, 1961.

————. *The Psalms.* ET London: SCM/Philadelphia: Westminster, 1962.

WELLS, P. R. *James Barr and the Bible.* Phillipsburg, NJ: Presbyterian and Reformed, 1980.

WENHAM, J. W. *Christ and the Bible.* London: Tyndale/Downers Grove, IL: IVP, 1972.

WESLEY, J. *Explanatory Notes upon the New Testament.* London: Bagster, 1754; reprinted London: Epworth, 1929.

————. *The Journal of the Rev. John Wesley.* Standard Edition (ed. N. Curnock). 8 vols. London: Kelly, 1909-16.

WEST, G. *Biblical Hermeneutics of Liberation.* Pietermaritzburg: Cluster, 1991.

WESTCOTT, B. F. *The Epistle to the Hebrews.* London/New York: Macmillan, 1889, ^{2}1892.

WESTERMANN, C. *The Old Testament and Jesus Christ.* Minneapolis: Augsburg, 1970.

WHITE, H. "The Historical Text as Literary Object." *Clio* 3 (1974) 277-303.

————. "Interpretation in History." *NLH* 4 (1972-73) 281-314.

————. *Metahistory.* Baltimore/London: Johns Hopkins UP, 1973.

————. "The Question of Narrative in Contemporary Historical Theory." *History and Theory* 23 (1984) 1-33.

————. "The Value of Narrativity in the Representation of Reality." *CI* 7 (1980-81) 5-27.

WHITE, H. C. (ed.). *Speech Act Theory and Biblical Criticism. Semeia* 41 (1988).

WICKER, B. *The Story-Shaped World.* Notre Dame, IN: U Notre Dame/London: Athlone, 1975.

WILDER, A. N. *The Language of the Gospel.* New York: Harper, 1964. = *Early Christian Rhetoric.* London: SCM, 1964.

————. *The New Voice.* New York: Herder, 1966.

WILES, M. *Explorations in Theology 4.* London: SCM, 1979.

————. *The Remaking of Christian Doctrine.* London: SCM, 1974.

————. See also under Mitchell.

WILKEN, R. T. "Diversity and Unity in Early Christianity." *TSC* 1 (1981) 101-10.

WILLIAMS, J. G. See under Gerhart.

WILLIAMSON, H. G. M. See under Carson.

WINK, W. *Transforming Bible Study.* Nashville: Abingdon, 1980/London: SCM, 1981; second ed., Nashville: Abingdon/London: Mowbray, ^{2}1990.

————. *Unmasking the Powers.* Philadelphia: Fortress, 1986.

WINTER, D. *But This I Can Believe.* London: Hodder, 1980. = *Believing the Bible.* Wilton, CT: Morehouse-Barlow, 1983.

WITTGENSTEIN, L. *Philosophical Investigations.* Oxford: Blackwell/New York: Macmillan, 1953.

WITVLIET, T. *The Way of the Black Messiah.* ET London: SCM/New York: Meyer Stone, 1987.

WOLSTERSTORFF, N. *Works and Worlds of Art.* Oxford/New York: OUP, 1980.

WOOD, C. M. *The Formation of Christian Understanding.* Philadelphia: Westminster, 1981.

WOODBRIDGE, J. D. *Biblical Authority.* Grand Rapids: Zondervan, 1982.

———. See also under Carson.

WREN, B. *What Language Shall I Borrow?* London: SCM/New York: Crossroad, 1989.

WRIGHT, D. F. "Soundings in the Doctrine of Scripture in British Evangelicalism in the First Half of the Twentieth Century." *TynB* 31 (1980) 87-106.

WRIGHT, N. T. "How Can the Bible Be Authoritative?" *VE* 21 (1991) 7-32.

———. See also under Hurst.

YOUNG, E. J. *Genesis 3.* London: Banner of Truth, 1966.

———. *Thy Word Is Truth.* Grand Rapids: Eerdmans, 1957/London: Banner of Truth, 1963.

YOUNG, F. *The Art of Performance: Towards a Theology of Holy Scripture.* London: DLT, 1990.

YOUNG, F., and D. F. FORD. *Meaning and Truth in 2 Corinthians.* London: SPCK, 1987/Grand Rapids: Eerdmans, 1988.

YOUNG, P. D. *Feminist Theology/Christian Theology.* Minneapolis: Fortress, 1990.

ZAEHNER, R. C. "Why Not Islam." *RelS* 11 (1975) 167-79.

ZAHAROPOULOS, D. Z. *Theodore of Mopsuestia on the Bible.* Mahwah, NJ: Paulist, 1989.

ZIZIOULAS, J. D. See under Jüngel.

Index of Authors

Abraham, W. J., 1, 12, 36, 37, 38, 184, 206, 209, 219, 223, 227, 229, 233, 234, 245, 264, 269, 273, 275, 302, 330
Achtemeier, P. J., 12, 27, 55, 124, 171, 206, 362
Ackroyd, P. R., 106, 169
Aland, K., 148, 149
Alexander, L., 112
Allchin, A. M., 185
Alonso Schökel, L., 10, 218, 224, 229, 230, 231, 241, 247, 249, 259, 308, 349
Alter, R., 30, 56, 58, 68, 74, 257
Althaus, P., 113, 167, 345
Amihai, M., 112
Anderson, B. W., 240
Arendt, H., 6
Aristotle, 72, 73, 188
Assmann, H., 110, 194
Athenagoras, 224
Athanasius of Alexandria, 148, 149, 166
Audet, J. P., 148
Augustine of Hippo, 91, 120, 126, 148, 166, 177, 224, 227, 262, 263, 268, 321, 343, 344
Auld, A. G., 363
Aune, D. E., 175
Austin, J. L., 211

Bacon, F., 274
Baker, T. G. A., 253

Balmer, R. H., 266
Barbour, I. G., 7
Barclay, O. R., 273
Barr, D. L., 313
Barr, J., 1, 2, 6, 12, 33, 52, 57, 65, 66, 71, 91, 93, 98, 111, 114, 116, 123, 127, 128, 129, 131, 137, 144, 168, 170, 187, 189, 201, 218, 241, 243, 248, 249, 250, 270, 278, 291, 292, 302, 304, 309, 332, 335, 339, 350, 360, 362
Barrett, C. K., 94, 218
Barth, K., i, 15, 25, 27, 31, 32, 33, 37, 44, 58, 59, 60, 66, 68, 70, 82, 105, 106, 114, 126, 178, 219, 221, 238, 259, 274, 309, 319, 321, 322, 341
Barthélemy, D., 149
Barthes, R., 66
Bartlett, D. L., 9, 33, 59, 65, 82, 235, 349, 363
Barton, J., 2, 28, 33, 102, 103, 104, 143, 144, 145, 146, 147, 175, 271, 291, 309, 362, 369
Bartsch, H.-W., 31, 38, 307, 321, 322
Battles, F. L., 344
Bauckham, R., 113, 119, 187, 232, 254, 278, 288
Bavinck, H., 123, 245, 249, 308, 330
Baxter, R., 180
Beardslee, W. A., 56, 65, 75, 315

Beckwith, R. T., 9, 116, 140, 141, 142, 143, 144
Beecher, 142
Beegle, W. J., 272
Bellah, R., 190
Benn, S. I., 85
Berg, T. F., 290
Berger, P., 120
Berkouwer, G. C., 28, 55, 113, 123, 131, 171, 180, 182, 213, 235, 236, 239, 245, 249, 250, 253, 272, 278, 280, 344, 346, 347
Best, E., 185
Black, M., 7
Blenkinsopp, J., 88, 101; 104, 107, 139, 175
Bloesch, D., 190, 246, 327
Blomberg, C. L., 36
Bockmuehl, M. N. A., 175, 295, 307
Boer, H. R., 277
Boff, L., 344
Boice, J. M., 267, 277
Bonhoeffer, D., 77, 354
Bonino, J. M. *See under* Miguez Bonino
Boone, K. C., 120
Bornkamm, G., 51, 236
Bornkamm, H., 113, 149
Braaten, C. E., 32
Bray, G., 121, 160
Brett, M., 107, 119, 171, 288
Briggs, S., 344
Bright, J., 29, 47, 127
Bring, R., 246
Brooks, P., 248
Brown, D., 6
Brown, R. E., 70, 230, 240, 259, 269, 281, 341
Bruce, F. F., 27, 94, 113, 149, 150, 162, 166, 173, 176, 177, 186
Brueggemann, W., 22, 32, 53, 57, 64, 87, 194, 211, 256, 287, 336, 350, 371
Brunner, E., 124, 178, 287, 308, 311
Bruns, G. L., 101, 106, 107
Buber, M., 53, 64
Buckley, J. J., 17
Bühler, K., 10

Bultmann, R., 30, 31, 32, 34, 92, 246, 255, 291, 306, 309, 321, 341
Buren, P. M. van, 24, 88, 187, 188, 301, 303, 305, 310, 345
Burgon, J. W., 253, 254
Burnaby, J., 265
Burtchaell, 212, 213, 231, 237, 240, 267, 274, 278, 281
Buttrick, D., 9

Caird, G. B., 54, 92, 211
Calvin, J., 118, 179, 180, 224, 227, 230, 247, 258, 263, 268, 270, 271, 343
Campbell, A. F., 112
Campenhausen, H. F. von, 132, 135, 152, 154, 155, 159, 161, 174, 177
Cannon, K. G., 344
Cano, M., 228
Carnley, P., 32, 33, 34, 38, 54, 59, 69
Carson, D. A., 94, 266, 282, 300, 356
Chadwick, H., 187
Charles, R. H., 143
Chatman, S., 49
Childs, B. S., 95, 106, 130, 164, 170, 277, 326, 337
Christ, C., 190, 191
Chrysostom, 227, 228, 263, 342, 343
Clement of Alexandria, 165, 216, 220, 342
Clement of Rome, 153, 154, 165, 174, 176, 177, 242, 252
Clements, R., 273
Clements, R. E., 43, 141
Clines, D. J. A., 9, 112, 121, 214, 307
Cobb, J. B., 360
Coleridge, S. T., 181, 280
Collingwood, R. G., 73
Collins, J. J., 73, 297, 313, 326
Collins, R. F., 250, 275
Comstock, G. L., 361
Cone, J. H., 109, 110, 129
Corner, M., 191
Countryman, L. W., 188
Coward, H., 112
Cowper, W., 278
Craddock, F. B., 287

Cragg, K., 207
Cremer, H., 217
Crites, S., 17
Croatto, J. S., 53, 79, 214, 249, 310
Cross, F. M., 144
Crossan, J. D., 256
Culler, J., 331
Cullmann, O., 27, 53, 131, 174, 184, 309
Cupitt, D., 193
Cyprian, 165, 166

Dahl, N. A., 26, 165
Daly, R. J., 99
Danto, A. C., 61
Davies, G. I., 294
Davies, W. D., 109, 220
Davis, S., 273
Detweiler, R., 5, 106, 108
Dickey Young, P., 111, 129, 130, 190
Doctrine Commission of the Church of
    England, 126, 239
Dodd, C. H., 9
Douglas, J. D., 270
Downing, F. G., 1, 6, 291
Drewery, B., 113, 119, 187, 288
Dulles, A., 6, 7, 8, 119, 238, 288, 291
Dummett, M., 271
Dungan, D. L., 168
Dunn, J. D. G., 321, 322

Eagleton, T., 107, 108
Ebeling, G., 31, 66, 113, 136, 318, 346,
    350
Edwards, P., 85
Eissfeldt, O., 146
Ejxenbaum, B. M., 334
Elliott, J. H., 8, 316
Ellis, E. E., 142, 145
Ellis, J. M., 105
Eslinger, L., 363
Eusebius of Caesarea, 148, 154, 161,
    165, 166, 173, 177, 220
Evans, C. F., 3, 32, 113, 114, 126, 136,
    174, 304
Evans, D. D., 33, 211
Evans, G. R., 187, 291

Ewald, H., 217

Fackenheim, E. L., 3
Fackre, G., 109, 185
Farkasfalvy, D., 154, 157
Farley, E., 1, 12, 15, 98, 103, 104, 113,
    119, 121, 125, 128, 242
Farmer, H., 154, 156
Farrer, A. M., 38, 301, 321, 327
Feinberg, J. S., 270
Feldman, L. H., 175, 220
Ferguson, E., 165
Fewell, D. N. See under Nolan Fewell
Fiddes, P., 47
Fierro, A., 110
Finlayson, R. A., 282, 341
Fiorenza, E. S. See under Schüssler
    Fiorenza
Fiorenza, F. S., 2, 129
Fisch, H., 316
Fish, S. E., 112
Fishbane, M., 4, 87, 88, 302, 303
Flessemann-van Leer, E., 15, 160, 184
Ford, D. F., 66, 67, 70, 95
Foskett, J., 364, 365, 366
Franklin, E., 60
Freedman, D. N., 104, 139, 141
Frei, H., 45, 65, 69
Freud, S., 311
Friedrich, C. J., 6
Frye, N., 62, 72, 316
Frye, R. M., 66, 326, 327
Fuchs, E., 64, 360
Fuller, D., 270
Fuller, R., 120
Funk, R. W., 54, 64, 86, 113, 162, 177

Gadamer, H.-G., 191, 192, 333
Gallie, W. B., 73
Gaussen, S. R. L., 13
Geisler, N. L., 27, 235, 250, 270, 273,
    274, 280, 340
Gerhart, M., 290
Gibbon, E., 71
Gill, R., 89
Glaser, I., 9, 98

Gloege, G., 307
Goetz, S. C., 36
Goldingay, J., 44, 114, 292, 334, 341, 370
Gore, C., 241
Gottwald, N. K., 47, 106
Goulder, M. 362
Graetz, H., 145
Grant, R. M., 161
Green, G., 17, 58, 67, 72, 103, 118, 122,
    123, 129, 172, 182, 191, 192, 195,
    221, 256, 315, 319, 336, 359, 361
Greenfield, J. C., 104
Greenwood, D. S., 256
Greer, R. A., 159, 163
Gregory of Nazianzus, 262
Gregory the Great, 224, 349
Griffin, D., 269
Grudem, W. A., 94, 282
Gruenwald, I., 300
Gundry, R. H., 276
Gunn, D. M., 307
Gunton, C. E., 35, 96, 244, 290, 335
Gutiérrez, G., 99, 195, 364, 365

Hall, R. A., 293, 294, 298, 307
Hanson, A. T., 28, 30, 77, 132, 218, 226,
    269, 270, 280
Hanson, P. D., 323, 327
Hanson, R. P. C., 1, 28, 30, 77, 120,
    154, 269, 270, 280
Harnack, A., 157, 163
Harrelson, W., 27
Harrison, R. K., 51
Hart, R. L., 128
Hartlich, C., 37
Harvey, A. E., 26, 94, 239
Harvey, V. A., 33, 35, 37, 38, 42, 44, 119
Hauerwas, S., 361
Hawkes, T., 317
Hays, R. B., 112, 194
Hebblethwaite, B. L., 193
Hebert, G., 240, 244
Hegel, G. W. F., 235
Helm, P., 189, 302
Henry, C. F. H., 120, 180, 267, 282, 288,
    308, 341

Henry, M., 264, 268, 280
Heracleon, 156
Heschel, A., 87, 235
Hick, J., 330
Hickling, C., 91, 136, 180
Hill, D., 352
Hill, R. C., 342
Hippolytus, 141, 165, 224
Hobbes, T., 235
Hodge, A. A., 266
Hodge, C., 264, 266, 268, 273
Hodgson, L., 94, 130
Hoffman, T. A., 217
Hollenweger, W., 82
Hooker, M., 91, 136, 150, 180, 186, 188
Houlden, J. L., 78, 111, 122
Houston, W. J., 211
Hull, J., 344
Hume, D., 35, 235, 288
Hunsinger, G. H., 67, 319
Hurst, L. D., 33, 109, 211
Husserl, E., 62
Huxtable, J., 137, 253

Ignatius of Antioch, 148, 153, 154, 161,
    174, 176, 242
Irenaeus of Lyons, 25, 120, 131, 148,
    149, 157, 158, 159, 160, 162, 163,
    165, 174, 215, 242, 243, 252, 288

Jackman, D., 273
Jackson, B. S., 98
Jahn, J., 267
James, J., 334
Jansen, J. F., 120
Jeanrond, W. G., 129, 318, 336
Jeremias, J., 362
Jerome, 149, 150, 166, 170, 177, 227,
    228
Jobling, D., 111
Johnson, M. D., 70
Jones, H. (i), 277
Jones, H. (ii), 361
Josephus, 143, 205, 216, 225, 226, 361
Josipovici, G., 93, 107, 121, 290, 307
Jossua, J.-P., 361

Jowett, B., 205
Justin Martyr, 155, 156, 159, 232, 242

Kähler, M., 32, 77, 129
Käsemann, E., 164, 173
Kaestli, J.-D., 149
Kaiser, W. C., 13
Kalin, E., 179
Kant, I., 195, 315
Kantzer, K. S., 308
Kaufman, G. D., 127
Keck, L. E., 103, 173
Kee, A., 110
Keegan, T. J., 105, 315
Kelber, W. H., 290
Kellogg, R., 72
Kelly, J. F., 161
Kelsey, D. H., 104, 117, 336
Kermode, F., 62, 74, 290
Kidner, D., 40, 270, 277
Kirk, J. A., 195
Kittel, G., 362
Kline, M. G., 115, 139
Klooster, F. H., 31
Knight, D. A., 27, 79
Knight, H., 226, 227
Koch, K., 53, 57
Koester, H., 154, 155
Kort, W., 17
Kümmel, W. G., 174
Küng, H., 37
Kugel, J. L., 303

Lampe, G. W. H., 217
Lanser, S. S., 65
Lash, N., 38, 62, 119, 191
Lategan, B. C., 75
Latourelle, R., 288
Leiman, S. Z., 139, 141, 144, 146, 218
Lemcio, E. E., 161
Lentricchia, F., 256
Leo XIII, 267
Letis, T. P., 272
Lewis, C. S., 75, 248, 307
Leonard, R. C., 9
Levenson, J. D., 88

Lewis, J. P., 146
Lightfoot, R. H., 113
Lindars, B., 134, 356
Lindbeck, G. A., 6, 17, 109, 192
Lindblom, J., 226, 249, 300
Lindsay, T. M., 272
Lindsell, H., 30, 51, 180, 263, 277, 278
Lischer, R., 17, 109, 256, 361
Lohfink, N., 271, 340
Loretz, O., 212, 240
Lowenthal, D., 67
Lundin, R., 67, 73
Luther, M., 17, 48, 112, 113, 149, 150,
    166, 172, 173, 180, 183, 186, 246,
    263, 268, 321, 345, 346, 347
Lyall, D., 364, 365, 366

Maarten van Bemmelen, P., 265
McDonald, H. D., 6, 137, 267, 278
McDonald, L. M., 86, 164
McFague (TeSelle), S., 7, 11, 16, 128,
    191, 318
McKenzie, J. L., 219
McKim, D. K., 228, 263, 266, 272
McKnight, E. V., 256, 290
Mafeje, A., 195
Marcus, J., 290
Markus, R. A., 164
Marsden, G., 266
Marshall, I. H., 272, 322, 356
Martin Soskice, J., 7, 317, 318
Marx, K., 195, 311
Marxsen, W., 69, 130
Matejka, L., 334
Melito, 148
Mendenhall, G. E., 48
Metz, J. B., 361
Metzger, B. M., 86, 102, 153, 157, 161,
    163, 164, 166, 177, 179, 182
Miegge, R., 321
Miguez Bonino, J., 129
Milavec, A. A., 238
Mildenberger, F., 136, 178
Miller, A., 33
Miller, D. G., 193
Miranda, J. P., 195

Mitchell, B., 31, 38, 234, 302
Mofekeng, I. T., 91
Moltmann, J., 37, 58, 195, 290
Montgomery, J. W., 262, 270, 271
Moore, G. F., 146
Morgan, R., 119
Morris, L., 291
Mosala, I. J., 195
Motyer, J. A., 273
Moule, C. F. D., 32, 176, 193
Mowinckel, S., 260
Muddiman, J., 184, 237
Murdoch, I., 96
Murray, J., 271

Neusner, J., 294
Newman, J. H., 217, 234, 247, 261
Newsom, C. A., 305
Nicole, R. R., 266
Nielsen, K., 269
Nietzsche, F., 235, 311
Nineham, D. E., 26, 52, 68, 70, 94, 111,
    113, 119, 126, 130, 180, 333
Nolan Fewell, D., 74
Noth, M., 87, 306
Novatian, 121, 339, 340

O'Collins, G., 24, 191, 308
O'Donovan, O. M. T., 118, 185, 333, 335
Oeming, M., 67, 72
Ogden, S. M., 37, 113, 129, 130, 136,
    178
Ogletree, T. W., 33
Origen, 141, 148, 165, 215, 228, 246,
    262, 263, 283, 342, 343
Orr, J., 180, 246, 264, 266, 272
Ostborn, G., 139
Overbeck, F., 157
Owen, J., 179, 272

Pache, R., 238
Packer, J. I., 68, 120, 122, 123, 131, 137,
    223, 226, 228, 232, 240, 245, 248, 250,
    253, 263, 266, 271, 272, 276, 277, 332
Pagels, E., 176
Pailin, D. A., 119, 288

Pannenberg, W., 32, 33, 38, 43, 48, 66,
    110, 124, 291, 304, 308
Papias, 154, 174, 176
Pascal, B., 122
Patrick, D., 68
Perrin, N., 317
Persson, P. E., 288
Peterson, W. L., 155
Philo of Alexandria, 216, 220, 223, 224,
    227, 231, 245, 342
Pinnock, C., 69, 262, 264, 270, 308
Pitts, E., 367
Plaskow, J., 190
Plato, 188
Platzer, F., 308
Plutarch, 36, 280
Polanyi, M., 118, 237, 238
Polman, A. D. R., 263
Polzin, R., 112
Polycarp of Smyrna, 153, 154
Pomorska, K., 334
Popper, K., 307
Price, H., 330
Prosch, M., 118
Pseudo-Clement, 158
Pseudo-Justin, 224
Pui-Lan, K., 106, 111, 124, 189
Pye, M., 119

Rad, G. von, 56, 79, 81, 87, 209, 230,
    350
Rahner, K., 239, 290, 297
Ramsay, I. T., 16
Ramsey, A. M., 222, 342
Ramsey, G. W., 42
Reed, W. L., 334
Reid, J. K. S., 170, 241, 281, 362
Reventlow, H. Graf, 97, 98
Richardson, A., 97, 253, 290
Richardson, P., 94
Ricoeur, P., 13, 15, 45, 53, 61, 73, 82,
    254, 256, 315, 317, 318, 328
Ridderbos, H. N., 180, 344
Ritschl, D., 17, 361, 364, 368
Robinson, H. W., 234
Robinson, J. M., 360

Rodger, P. C., 15
Rogers, C., 190, 191
Rogers, J. B., 228, 263, 266, 272
Rogerson, J. W., 307, 308, 341
Rossouw, H. W., 347
Rowland, C., 191, 292, 300, 301
Ruether, R. R., 128, 190
Rufinus, 166
Runia, K., 15, 28
Russell, D. S., 300
Russell, L., 9, 128, 190
Ryken, L., 62, 314
Ryle, H. C., 145

Saiving Goldstein, V., 190
Sakenfeld, K. D., 190
Sanday, W., 206, 215, 222, 234, 260, 262, 265
Sanders, E. P., 88, 92, 104, 139, 164
Sanders, J. A., 2, 104, 144, 334
Sartre, J.-P., 194
Schaeffer, F. A., 188, 273, 276, 280
Schillebeeckx, E., 105, 113, 190, 191, 192, 193, 290
Schlatter, A., 68
Schleiermacher, F. D. E., 288
Schniewind, J., 321
Schofield, J. N., 292
Scholem, G., 65, 303
Scholes, R. E., 72
Schürer, E., 142
Schüssler Fiorenza, E., 47, 111, 128, 163, 194, 344
Schütz, J. H., 95
Schultz, A., 316
Schumann, F. K., 321
Schweizer, E., 97
Searle, J. R., 75
Segundo, J. L., 129, 195, 338, 344
Shakespeare, W., 249
Shaw, G., 95, 112, 135
Silva, M., 2
Skorupski, J., 123
Smart, J. D., 114, 186
Smend, R., 79
Smith, M., 140

Spinoza, B., 235
Springsteen, B., 315
Spurgeon, C. H., 266
Stanton, G. N., 36, 68
Steiner, G., 105, 169
Sternberg, M., 256
Stott, J. R. W., 240, 273
Stout, J., 36, 121, 122, 123, 183
Sundberg, A. C., 145, 149, 164, 169, 170, 179, 243, 258
Sutherland, S., 71
Swinburne, R., 269

Talmon, S., 30, 74, 104, 144
Tatian, 155, 162, 165, 173
Taylor, G., 363
Taylor, M. C., 93
Terrien, S., 327
Tertullian, 87, 120, 131, 158, 160, 163, 215
Theodore of Mopsuestia, 166, 259
Thielicke, H., 322
Theophilus of Antioch, 220
Thiemann, R. F., 12, 288
Thiselton, A. C., 7, 64, 65, 75, 109, 114, 124, 127, 136, 157, 209, 320, 327, 350, 356
Thomas, O. C., 190, 191, 193
Thomas Aquinas, 183, 250
Thucydides, 280, 361
Tillich, P., 31
Tolbert, M. A., 193
Tracy, D., 66, 72, 119, 129, 181, 315
Trembath, K. R., 12, 13, 217, 234
Trible, P., 128
Trigg, R., 35, 72, 271
Troeltsch, E., 38
Turner, G., 242
Turretin, F., 266

Vaihinger, H., 72
van Dijk-Hemmes, F., 344
Vanhoozer, K., 45
van Unnik, W., 164
Vawter, B., 215, 228, 232, 241, 246, 259, 267, 333, 342, 343, 360
Vidales, R., 110

Vischer, L., 15

Wadsworth, M., 207
Wainwright, G., 173, 371
Walhout, C., 65
Warfield, B. B., 6, 13, 100, 120, 180,
    216, 217, 219, 220, 222, 229, 232,
    240, 247, 248, 250, 252, 253, 264,
    265, 266, 267, 268, 269, 270, 272,
    273, 274, 275, 278, 330
Warner, M., 26, 35, 71, 72, 271, 362, 369
Weber, H.-R., 273
Weems, R. J., 344
Weinrich, H., 361
Weiser, A., 87, 170
Wenham, G. J., 60
Wenham, J., 136, 273
Wermelinger, O., 149
Wesley, J., 227, 264, 266, 268
West, G., 91, 337
Westcott, B. F., 220, 260
Westermann, C., 132, 352
White, H., 61, 66, 73, 307
White, H. C., 65
Whitehead, A. N., 191, 315
Wicker, B., 318

Wilckens, U., 291
Wilder, A. N., 65, 75
Wiles, M., 17, 24, 91, 180, 193
Wilken, R. T., 156
Williams, J. G., 290
Wiliamson, H. G. M., 300, 356
Wink, W., 302, 324
Winter, D., 276
Wittgenstein, L., 7
Witvliet, T., 63, 109
Wolterstorff, N., 75
Wood, C. M., 103, 221, 255, 334
Woodbridge, J. D., 94, 266, 282
Wren, B., 317, 319, 327, 328, 344
Wright, D. F., 240, 265, 266, 341
Wright, N. T., 33, 93, 109, 211
Wyclif, J., 272

Young, E. J., 277
Young, F., 95, 238, 246
Young, P. D. *See under* Dickey Young

Zaehner, R. C., 207
Zaharopoulos, D. Z., 259
Zimmerli, W., 79, 80
Zizioulas, J. D., 6

Index of Scriptural and Other Ancient Jewish and Christian Writings

FIRST TESTAMENT

Genesis–Esther	18

Genesis–Kings   22, 23, 39, 40, 56-57, 140, 141, 210, 348, 366

Genesis–Joshua   22, 115, 141, 210

Genesis–Deuteronomy
14, 18, 39, 54, 77, 78, 81, 95, 101, 104, 115, 121, 132, 138, 139, 140, 141, 147, 331, 349, 351

Genesis	57, 307, 336
1–3	168, 270
1–2	56, 115
1	40, 42, 70, 188, 209, 210, 263, 271, 280, 310, 344
1:4, 16	343
2–3	65
2	40, 70
2:8	344
2:21	343
3–6	210
3	40, 277
3:8	343
5:1-2	228
6:13	357
8–9; 11; 12	210
14	263
14:18-24	367
15:1, 4	206
15:16	229
16	100
21	100
22	68
22:2	68, 355
22:3	304
22:12	68
27	209
35:7	289
Exodus	249, 337, 338, 370
4:15-16	228
6:2-3	289
6:7	26
7:1	228
9:20-21	206
13	328
14:13-14	223
14:13	220
17:14	101
19–24	210, 370
20–24	139
20	230
20:1	206
20:2-3	115
20:18	239
24:1-8	139, 142
24:3-8	140
14:3	206
32:16	101
Leviticus	253, 370
18	289
Numbers	51
11:23-24, 25-29	206

12:6	206	*Ruth*	23, 134, 143,	2:4	211, 213
22:31	303		245, 367-68	2:27	206, 211, 213
23:4-6	224			3:5	289
23:19	282	*Samuel–Kings*	55, 334	6:11	206
24	295			6:12	211, 213
24:2	206	*1 Samuel*		8:12-13	321
27:20	85	1:19	304	8:15, 20	211, 213
36:13	223	1:23	213	8:24-26	211
		2:27	289	8:24, 26	213
		3:1	206	8:27-30	321
Deuteronomy	139, 210,	3:7	206, 289	8:27	320
	370	3:21	291, 329	8:56	212
2:29	289	9:15	289	11:41	100
4:9	26	9:27	206	12:15	211, 213
4:10, 36	206	10:6	225	12:22	206, 211
5–11	90	10:10	206	12:24	206
5	230	10:25	139	16:23-28	58
6:13, 16	90	14:8, 11	289	17:24	213
6:20-23	26	15:1, 10	206	18:12	207
7:9	213	15:11	206, 282	22:16	213
8:3	90	15:13, 23, 26	206	22:19-22	228
9:5	213	15:29	282		
17:18-19	139	17	268	*2 Kings*	56, 57
29:20-21	101	19:20	206	2:16	206
30:19	214	20:2, 12, 13	289	5:18-19	367
31	139			8:8	303
31:9-13, 22, 24-26	101	*2 Samuel*		10:10	212
		1:18	101	14:25	73
Joshua–Kings	15, 41,	6:20	289	17:25	273
	139, 211, 298	7:4	206	18:19-25	230
		7:25	211, 213	21:13	86
Joshua	41, 57, 75,	7:27	289	22	203, 204
	367	7:28	211, 213	22:8	139, 303
4	26	11	40	23:1-3	139, 140
6	41, 42	12:1-6	40	25	39-40, 42, 69
6:12	304	14:3, 19	228		
8:8, 27	206	16:23	206	*Chronicles–Nehemiah*	
8:31	90	21:19	268		23, 140, 348
10:13-14	100	23:2	206		
10:13	100	24:1	333	*1 and 2 Chronicles*	
11	41	24:11	206		51, 55, 63, 132, 134,
13:1	41				143, 210, 298, 334,
21:45; 23:14	212	*1 and 2 Kings*	58, 63,		342, 366
24:25-26	139		69, 360		
				1 Chronicles	
Judges	75	*1 Kings*		8:1-32	264
1	41	2:3	90		

12:18	206		331, 337, 340, 350,	75	206
17	211		360	77:8	212
17:3	206	3–37	331	78	259
17:23	213	4:12-21	331	81	206
17:25	289	4:13	229	81:5	260
21:1	333	33:14-18	331	82:6	100
28:8	303	33:15	229	85:8	260
29:29	100	38–41	331	85:9	228
		38:17	298	88	224, 352
				91	90, 91-92
2 Chronicles				93:5	213
1:9	211, 213	*Psalms*	78, 81, 100, 101,	95	206
6	211		140, 141, 143, 259,	95:7-11	219
6:17	213		260, 298, 331-32,	97	81
12:5-8	211		334, 336, 348, 349,	98:2	289
13:4-12	211		350, 351, 352, 353,	98:3	213
20:14-17	211		354, 371	100:5	213
21:12-15	211	1	336, 351	105	21-22, 96
23:18	90	2	81, 259, 355	106	22, 81
29:20	304	2:2	355	107	22, 81
30:5	90	2:7	355	107:20	209
34:27	100	8:1	254	107:43	22
35:25	101	12	206, 332	109:8	260
		12:6	213, 282	110	260
Ezra-Nehemiah	143	18:25	352	111:7	213
		18:30	213, 282	119	87-89, 96, 211-12,
Ezra	134, 148, 367	19:7	212		349
3:2, 4	90	19:9	345	119:18	303
7:10	303	22	133, 227, 352	119:40	213
		24:3-5	352	119:45	303
Nehemiah	148	29:4-5	239	119:89	282
7:5	100	31	133	119:94	303
8–10	139	33:4, 6, 9	209	119:105	86
8:15	90	35:19	100	119:130	345
9:38	101	37:11	351-52	119:155	303
12:23	100	39:3	244	126	351
		42	133	128	351
Esther	23, 73, 140,	45:1	244, 259	132:11	213
	143, 148, 149,	46	206	137	78, 354
	172, 173, 179,	49:3-4	244, 259	143:1	213
	253	49:4	228	147:12-20	210
3:14	289	50	206, 259	148:5-8	209
8:13	289	59:5	254	148:6	212
9:29	85	60	332	150	336
		62:11	228		
Job	10, 73, 74, 75, 81,	69:25	260	*Proverbs*	141, 143, 172,
	143, 245, 253, 307,	73	332		

	175, 245, 259, 332,	42:1-9	355	17:9	234
	336, 337, 362, 363	42:1	355	20	234
1–9	363	43:8-13	80	20:1	225
1:1-7	336	43:9-10	26	22:13-19	204
20:19	289	43:18	79	23:15-32	312
22:20	101	44:6-8	80	23:18, 22	228
30:5-6	282	44:8	26	23:29	210
30:5	213	49:7	213	23:31	228
		49:9	289	25:11-12	303
Ecclesiastes	10, 81, 141,	51:1-3; 52:11-12	80	28:16-17	211
	143, 146, 175, 179,	52:13–53:12	213, 297	30:2	101
	245, 253, 259, 332,	52:13	325	31:31-34	80
	334, 340, 362	53:1	289	31:34	112
1:16; 2:1	259	53:7	133	31:39	86
8:8	85	53:11	325	33:6	306
		53:12	133	36	101, 201-4, 234
Song of Songs	141, 143,	54:1-3	80	36:4-6	227
	146, 179, 180, 245,	54:17–55:2	352	38:21-23	329
	337, 344, 349	55:3-5	80	45	202
		55:10-11	210	51:60-64	101
Isaiah	100, 249, 250,	56:1	306		
	253, 298, 330,	59:21	228	*Lamentations*	141, 143,
	352	61	351		148
1:1	330, 368	61:1-2	351		
5:1-7	10, 79, 231,	61:1	369	*Ezekiel*	146, 147, 248,
	235	61:7	351-52		249
5:9	228	65:6	101	1–3	300, 329
6	211, 227, 300	66:24	325	1	301
8	295			1:3, 22	225
8:1	101	*Jeremiah*	148, 208, 250,	2:8	230
8:11	225		253	3:12, 14	207, 225
8:19	303	1:1-2	207	3:22, 24	225
9:1-7	297	1:9-10	211	7	295
10	295	1:9	228	7:4, 27	80
12:4-5	289	2:2, 4, 5	207	8:1	225
14	298	5:14	210	8:3	207, 225
22:14	228, 291, 329	7:1-2	228	9–10	293, 300
28:17	86	8:18–9:6	349	9:1, 5	228
29:9-12	228	9:2-3	234	11:1, 5, 24	225
29:11-12	100	11:21	230	16; 20	79, 330
30:8	101	12; 14	234	21:24	289
34:16	303	14:1-10	362	23	79, 330
40–55	355	15	234	31	298
40:5	306	15:10	220	36:11	228
40:8	210, 254	15:15-21	208	37	211
40:13	345	15:16	230	37:1-2	225

37:6	80	*Hosea–Malachi*	23, 148	*Zechariah*	
37:13	26, 80			1:16	86
37:29	228	*Hosea*	208, 344	7:7	223
40:1	225	1:1	207		
40:3-8	86	1:4	79	*Malachi*	132
43:5	225	2	344	2:7	227
		4:2	207		
		5	207		
Daniel	3, 14, 22, 23,	6:5	210, 211	**SECOND TESTAMENT**	
	69, 73, 74, 134, 142,	7:1	289		
	143, 148, 292, 305,	8:13	79	*Matthew*	34, 49, 70,
	306, 307, 316, 323,	11:1-9	349		155, 158, 161,
	326, 332, 347	12:3	79		162
2–7	300	13:8	317	1:1-17	43, 50, 70,
2:19, 22, 28, 29,	292				238, 264
30, 47		*Joel*		1:18–2:23	50, 215, 276,
4:31	239	2:28-29	242		295
7–8	323			1:19	50
7	358	*Amos*	63	1:22	214, 223
8:8	229	1:2	211	2:1-23	359
8:9-12	293	2:9-11	79	2:15, 23	214, 223
9	211, 300, 301,	3:2	79	3	355-58
	303	3:7	289, 329	3:7-10	354
10–12	292-313,	4:1	317	3:9, 10	60
	322-26	5:1-2	231, 317	3:11	262
10	292-93,	5:6-15	231	3:17	355-58
	299-301, 302,	5:18-20	80	4:1-11	89-92, 101, 278
	324	5:25	79	4:4, 7, 10	4
10:9	229	7:10	210	4:23	351
10:21	296, 323	7:14-15	225	5–7	14
11:2-39	293, 294-96,	7:16	231	5	189
	299, 305-6, 323	8:2	357	5:1-12	351-52
11:21-39	324	9:7	79	5:17-18	214
11:29	295			5:20-32	354
11:32-35	312	*Jonah*	23, 73, 74, 75,	6:24-34	363
11:33	302		119, 210, 307	7:15-19	354
11:36-39	296			7:21	97
11:36	293, 296	*Micah*		7:24-27	363
11:40–12:13	296-98, 299	1:2-5, 8-12	231	7:29	85
11:40–12:3	313	2:1-2, 6-11	231	8:8	215
12:1	293, 298	6:5	289	8:9	85, 86
12:2-3	326			8:12	354
12:2	298, 324, 337	*Habakkuk*		8:16	215
12:5-8	293	2	295	8:17	214
12:6	303			8:18-27	50
12:10	312	*Haggai*		11:2-6	132, 351
		1:1	223		

11:25-27	290	*Luke*	34, 49, 155,	7:39	353
11:25	289		157, 161, 162,	9:32	35
11:28-30	363		172, 174, 280	10:34	99
13:35	214	1–2	238	12:38	214
13:52	362	1:1-4	5, 16, 25, 26,	13:18	214
16:17	289, 290		40, 49, 361	14–16	242
19:5	252	1:2	174	14:6	366
19:17	51, 343	1:4	3	14:24	255
20:29-34	262	2:26, 32, 35	289	14:26	227
21:4	214	4:16-30	49	15:1	320
24	34	4:16-21	351	15:25	100
27:3-10	70, 276	6:46	97	16:4	342
27:9-10	269	7:13	257	16:25	314
27:9	262	9:28	280	17:12	214
27:46	352	10:16	236	17:14, 17	255
28:18	94	11:2-6	351	19:35	26
		16:17	214	19:36	214
Mark	34, 49, 155,	17:30	306	20:30-31	26
	162, 172, 174,	18:1-8	354	20:31	66
	290, 337, 360	18:35-43	262	21:1	289
1:1-8	238	21	34	21:11	279
1:11	132	20:20	85	21:25	46
1:27	85	20:27	333		
2–3	94	22:37	214	*Acts (see also under*	
2:10	85	23:46	133	*Luke-Acts)*	18, 23, 27,
2:23-28	92	24:27	113, 346		70, 130, 162,
4:35-41	50	24:44	101, 214		164, 165, 255,
7:1-13	27, 184	24:46	101		366
8:31; 9:30-31	133	24:48	26	1:7	345
10:2-9	92, 115			1:8	26
10:5	281, 342	*John*	25-26, 51, 155,	1:16	214, 219, 223,
10:18	51		158, 161, 162,		260
10:46-52	262		337	1:18-19	70, 276
11:27-33	93	1	156	1:20	260
12:18-27	142	1:1-18	215, 239	1:22	26
12:36	219, 225	1:4, 9, 14	289	2	118, 242
13	34	1:18	343	2:23	248
13:11	242	1:27	262	2:24	249
13:32	239, 345	2:12-25	262	2:32	26
14:1-12	10	2:22	113	3:15	26
14:34	133	5:39	78, 189, 247	4:4	280
14:49	214	6	246	4:12	366
15	59	6:19	280	4:25	219, 223
15:34	133	6:31	100	4:31	255
		6:35	51	5:3-5	215
Luke-Acts	307, 348	7:17	194	5:30-32	113

6:5	282
6:7	255
6:10	282
6:14	27
6:15	282
7:14	264, 271
7:38	214, 252
7:55	282
8:31	346
8:35	113
10:10	229
10:42-43	78
11:1	255
11:5	229
12:24	255
17:11	346
19:20	255
20:24	80, 330
20:32	255
20:35	152
22:15	82, 330
22:17	229
23:11	80
26:16	82, 330
26:22	330
27:15	219
28:23	330
28:25	223

Romans	135, 152, 162,
	227, 365
1:2	4
1:16-17	290
1:16	256
1:17	100, 289
1:18–3:20	306
1:18	215, 289
1:19-20	289
1:25	215
2:5	306
3–8	353
3	357
3:2	242, 252
3:4	100, 213, 272
3:10, 19	100
3:21-26	357

3:21	77
4	338, 357
5:5	242
6:17	27
7	93, 349
7:12	4
8:11, 14, 15, 16	242
8:18, 19	306
8:32	356
9–11	307, 357, 365
9:4	170
9:6	214
10:8	236
11	81
11:25	289
11:33	345
12–15	152
12:1-2	194
12:1	327
15:4	221
15:24	280
15:26	101
16:25-26	289, 290
16:25	289

1 and 2 Corinthians	
	120, 152, 337
1 Corinthians	82, 365
1:14-16	279
1:16	254
1:17	4
1:19	100
2:9-13	205
2:10	289
2:13	236, 242, 255
4:14-15	95
7:10	152, 260
7:12	94, 260
7:25	4, 94, 260
7:40	94
9:14	152
10:7	100
11	94, 152
11:2	27
11:8	280

11:14	192
11:23	16, 26, 152
11:29	247
12:3	242
12:11	242
13:12	111
14	163, 243
14:6	289
14:21	100
14:26, 30	289
14:37	94
15	82, 152
15:1-11	349
15:1-3	26
15:3	16, 54
15:45	100

2 Corinthians	349
3:6	93
3:15	346
4	95
4:3-4	346
5:16	58
5:19	255, 256
8:15	100
9:9	100
12	4, 293
12:2	280
12:11	254
13:10	4

Galatians	120, 162, 349
1:1	95
1:14	27
1:16	289
3:1	81
3:2	189
3:10	101
3:10, 13	100
3:23-25	342
4:21-22	100
4:22	100
6:16	3, 86

Ephesians	
1:17	290

3:1-11	307	*Titus*	157, 165, 342	*2 Peter*	154, 164, 165,
3:3, 5	289				173, 179
3:14-15	319	*Hebrews*	135, 154, 158,	1:16-21	218
5:26	246		162, 163, 164,	1:19	232, 346
			165, 166, 172,	1:20	217
Philippians	82, 136, 162		173, 175, 177,	1:21	219, 220, 225,
2	93		179, 215, 356		232
3	189, 349	1:1	201, 222, 358	1:23-25	254
3:15	289	1:3	214	2:21	27
		1:5, 7, 8-9, 10-12, 13	260	3:5, 7	214
Colossians	156, 162	2:6	78	3:15-16	154
1:17	359	2:12	352	3:16	345, 346
2:8	27, 156	3:7	215, 220		
2:18	156	4:7	220	*1 John*	136, 154, 162,
4:16	152	4:12	214		164, 165, 166,
		5:11-14	342		173
1 and 2 Thessalonians		5:12	252	1:2; 4:14	80
	162	7:3	263		
		9:8	220	*2 John*	162, 164, 165,
1 Thessalonians		10:15-17	220		173, 180
1:10	81	11:1	81		
2:13	26, 236, 255	11:3	214	*3 John*	164, 165, 173,
2:15-16	162	11:21	264, 271		180
4:13	255	12:5	215		
4:15	152	13:7	255	*Jude*	164, 165, 166,
					172, 173, 179,
2 Thessalonians		*James*	147, 163, 164,		253
2:3	306		165, 166, 172,	3	27
2:15	27		173, 179, 180	9	298
3:6	27	1:18, 21	255	14-15	103, 145
		4:5	145		
1 Timothy	157, 165, 342			*Revelation*	3, 5, 14, 40,
3:2	215				75, 135, 158,
		1 Peter	154, 162, 164,		162, 163, 164,
2 Timothy	157, 163, 165,		165, 166, 173,		165, 166, 172,
	342		315-16		173, 179, 253,
2:18	213, 272	1:1	315		287, 292, 301,
3:15-17	216-18, 272	1:5, 7	289, 306		306
3:15	4	1:10-12	227, 297	1:1-2	292
3:16-17	116	1:11-12	242	1:3	113, 220
3:16	3, 5, 13, 15,	1:13	289, 306	1:9	80
	116, 205, 222,	1:17	315	1:10-12	292
	252, 268, 272,	1:18-21	255	1:10	220
	274	2:11	315	2:7, 11	220
3:17	197	3:19	325	4	301
4:7, 13	254	4:11	242	4:2	220

6:9-11   354
7   369
10:11   220
14:13   220
15:4   289
17:3   220
21:10   220
22:6, 7, 18, 19   220

**DEUTEROCANONICAL
AND LATER JEWISH
WRITINGS**

Wisdom of Solomon
        103, 138, 145, 148,
        149, 150, 154, 164,
                166, 180

Ecclesiasticus (Sirach)
        143, 145, 146, 148,
            166, 170, 175
Prologue   142, 143
39:1-8   303

1 Esdras   148, 150

2 Esdras   148, 150
4–5   148
14:45   143

Judith   150, 154

Tobit   143, 148, 154

Maccabees 138, 148, 172

2 Maccabees
2:14-15   142
12:43-45   149

Additions to Daniel   149

Daniel 13   148

Susanna   148

Letter of Jeremiah   148

Baruch   148

Prayer of Manasseh   150

Jubilees
2:23   143

1 Enoch   103, 165, 172,
                    305
1:9   145
89   148

Mishnah
'Abot 1:2; 3:15   89
Ḥagigah 2:1   292

Babylonian Talmud
Yoma 9b   220
Ṣota 48b   220
Sanhedrin 11b   220

Tosefta
Yadayim 2:13   175

**EXTRACANONICAL
CHRISTIAN
WRITINGS**

(Ignatius, Clement, and
later writers are in-
cluded in the index of
authors.)

Gospel of Peter
        155, 165, 172

Gospel of Thomas
                155, 165

Acts of John   165

Gospel of the Hebrews
                    165

Acts of Peter   161, 172

Apocalypse of Peter
        163, 164, 165, 172

Acts of Paul and Thecla
                    163

3 Corinthians   165

Laodiceans   165, 180

Acts of Paul   165

Didache   165, 166, 175

Judgment of Peter
                166, 172

Preaching of Peter
                165, 172

Shepherd of Hermas
        148, 158, 162, 163,
        164, 165, 166, 174,
                176, 177

Barnabas   148, 165